African-Atlantic Cultures and the South Carolina Lowcountry

African-Atlantic Cultures and the South Carolina Lowcountry examines perceptions of the natural world revealed by the religious ideas and practices of African-descended communities in South Carolina from the colonial period into the twentieth century. Focusing on Kongo nature spirits known as the *simbi*, Ras Michael Brown describes the essential role religion played in key historical processes, such as establishing new communities and incorporating American forms of Christianity into an African-based spirituality. This book illuminates how people of African descent engaged the spiritual landscape of the Lowcountry through their subsistence practices, religious experiences, and political discourse.

Ras Michael Brown is assistant professor of History and Africana Studies at Southern Illinois University, Carbondale.

Cambridge Studies on the American South

Series Editors:

Mark M. Smith, University of South Carolina, Columbia
David Moltke-Hansen, Center for the Study of the American South, University of North Carolina at Chapel Hill

Interdisciplinary in its scope and intent, this series builds upon and extends Cambridge University Press's longstanding commitment to studies on the American South. The series not only will offer the best new work on the South's distinctive institutional, social, economic, and cultural history but will also feature works in national, comparative, and transnational perspectives.

Titles in the Series

Robert E. Bonner, *Mastering America: Southern Slaveholders and the Crisis of American Nationhood*

Christopher Michael Curtis, *Jefferson's Freeholders and the Politics of Ownership in the Old Dominion*

Peter McCandless, *Slavery, Disease, and Suffering in the Southern Lowcountry*

Jonathan Daniel Wells, *Women Writers and Journalists in the Nineteenth-Century South*

Ras Michael Brown, *African-Atlantic Cultures and the South Carolina Lowcountry*

African-Atlantic Cultures and the South Carolina Lowcountry

Southern Illinois University, Carbondale

CAMBRIDGE
UNIVERSITY PRESS

32 Avenue of the Americas, New York NY 10013-2473, USA

Cambridge University Press is part of the University of Cambridge.

It furthers the University's mission by disseminating knowledge in the pursuit of education, learning and research at the highest international levels of excellence.

www.cambridge.org
Information on this title: www.cambridge.org/9781107668829

© Ras Michael Brown 2012

First published 2012
First paperback edition 2013

A catalogue record for this publication is available from the British Library

Library of Congress Cataloguing in Publication data
Brown, Ras Michael, 1970–
African-Atlantic cultures and the South Carolina lowcountry / Ras Michael Brown, Southern Illinois University, Carbondale.
pages cm. – (Cambridge studies on the American South)
Includes bibliographical references and index.
ISBN 978-1-107-02409-0 (hardback)
1. African Americans – Religion.   2. Africans – South Carolina – Religion.
3. Congo (Democratic Republic) – Religion.   4. South Carolina –
Religion.   5. Christianity and other religions – Congo (Democratic Republic)
6. South Carolina – Social life and customs.   I. Title.
BL2525.B76   2013
200.89´9607307576–dc23   2012013665

ISBN 978-1-107-02409-0 Hardback
ISBN 978-1-107-66882-9 Paperback

Contents

Tables

Figures

Maps

Prologue

Apparently, in places that became part of the United States, "the gods of Africa died."[1] Scholars and other interested observers have often commented on the striking contrast between the religious cultures of African America and those of the larger African Diaspora, especially Cuba, Haiti, and Brazil. Explanations for the differences have focused on the relative influences of European-derived religious institutions or on the population characteristics of the trans-Atlantic trade in captives and plantation communities. An extraordinary range of factors external to the actual relationships people had with potent spirits has been entertained and examined to account for the death of African gods in North America, in part because it appeared that little or no evidence existed of these relationships. Yet, one variety of an African god arrived on these shores and made an enduring abode of the freshwater springs of the South Carolina Lowcountry. This kind of god was seen as a category of nature spirits known in Kongo as the *simbi* (*basimbi* or *bisimbi* in Kongo speech). People in the Kongo communities of West-Central Africa knew and relied on these powerful spirits to address all of the most critical aspects of daily life. They were so important to Kongo people that they also made the journey across *Kalunga* (the Atlantic Ocean) to Cuba, Haiti, Brazil, and as it turns out, the South Carolina Lowcountry. The simbi in the Lowcountry did indeed die, but they did so only after many generations of African-descended people passed into the land of the dead after becoming part of Lowcountry Protestant Christianity and twentieth-century political and

---

[1] Albert J. Raboteau, *Slave Religion: The "Invisible Institution" in the Antebellum South*, updated edition (New York: Oxford University Press, 2004), 86.

xiii

economic agendas destroyed their natural abodes. The story of the simbi in the Lowcountry reminds us that African-American religious cultures are very much a part of the spiritual world of the African Diaspora, and that the appearances of the cultural present do not always reveal the complexities of the cultural past.

Exploring the story of the simbi requires first being able to see them. This book begins that endeavor by placing the simbi in the Lowcountry and engaging ideas about how to interpret their presence and transformations over time. As expressions of the spiritual cultures of African-descended people, the simbi reflected the ways that Africans and their diaspora-born progeny managed cultural dialogues between the diverse peoples dispersed throughout the Atlantic world. Further, the simbi become most visible when we view them in those contexts where perceptions about the natural environment intersected with ideas and practices conventionally associated with religion. Doing so opens vantage points on African-inspired spiritual cultures often obscured by limited visions of religious experience that overlook the enduring significance of nature spirits.

Following the first chapter, the next three chapters examine the historical and cultural ties of the people and spirits shared by the Lowcountry and West-Central Africa during the era of enslavement. Chapter 2 assesses the transport and settlement of captive Africans in the Lowcountry from the 1670s through the 1740s, and the meanings of this process to Africans new to these lands. At the same time that they built the plantation landscape and created communities in the original settlement zone along the Ashley, Cooper, and Stono Rivers, captive Africans introduced the foundational elements of their notions about the physical and spiritual landscapes that linked the Lowcountry to Africa. One of the concepts that informed the perceptions of Africans concerning their place on South Carolina's physical landscape was an ancient "frontier ideology," through which West-Central Africans and West Africans understood the spiritual and social meanings of inhabiting new lands. Nature spirits such as the simbi that were central to this ideology comprise the focus of Chapter 3. This chapter outlines the contours of the Kongo spiritual landscape in which people conceived of the "land of the living" (the visible, physical world) and the "land of dead" (the invisible, spirit world) as embedded in the features of the natural environment. We proceed to a detailed appraisal of characteristics and functions of Kongo nature spirits, particularly the simbi, with special attention given to changes in the relationships between communities of the living and nature spirits stimulated by the detrimental effects of Atlantic trade on West-Central Africa. This wealth of knowledge about the enduring meanings and evolving characteristics of the simbi accompanied captive Kongo people into the diaspora, where these spirits became part of the physical and spiritual landscapes of the Lowcountry. Chapter 4 examines the ways that African-descended people engaged the physical and spiritual dimensions of the Lowcountry's natural environment. They not only toiled in the fields of the plantations but also cultivated their own gardens, which they filled with African plants known by African names. They also ventured beyond the confines of the plantation to hunt and fish, using terms and techniques that Africans brought to South Carolina. The ideas and methods employed in these endeavors included objects and observances that acknowledged the spiritual aspects of farming, hunting, and fishing. The fourth chapter concludes by explaining the historical processes through which African newcomers placed the simbi in the freshwater springs of the Lowcountry and contemplating the meanings these nature spirits held for Africans and indigenous people enslaved in early Carolina.

The remainder of the book extends the connections revealed in the first four chapters to analyze the remarkable transformations of the simbi in the nineteenth and early twentieth centuries. Chapter 5 identifies the simbi in the process known as "seeking," through which young people experienced spiritual transformation and earned acceptance into local Christian communities. During the period when African-descended communities in the Lowcountry began elaborating their own understanding of Protestant Christianity, the simbi made the transition, too, by becoming white beings, white bundles, and white babies encountered in the visions of seekers. The move into the imagined spiritual landscape of Christian novices, however, signaled a slow death for the simbi in this realm of religious experience. By the time that Protestant Christianity gained ascendancy, the white beings, bundles, and babies had lost relevance to Christian forms of spiritual change, and the simbi disappeared altogether from the process of seeking. Looking outside of the context of Christianity, we find another transformation of the simbi, in which these nature spirits took on the identity of mermaids in stories told by African-descended people about episodes of turmoil in the nineteenth century. Chapter 6 analyzes Lowcountry narratives that presented mermaids as agents of destruction who unleashed the power of nature through the rain and sea to punish people who held the mermaids captive. This innovation in the way people talked about the simbi appeared in similar expressions in other parts of the African-Atlantic world, including West-Central

Africa, Brazil, Cuba, and Haiti, where people also associated African water spirits with mermaids. In all of these cases, African-Atlantic mermaids possessed great authority and embodied qualities associated with motherhood and feminine power directed toward helping their spiritual children. By emphasizing the same characteristics, narratives about Lowcountry mermaids served as critiques of enslavement and oppression that allowed African Americans to express such subversive notions under the cover of "folklore" and fanciful tales. The book concludes by describing the destruction of the place where the simbi and African-descended people had coexisted for more than two and a half centuries following the completion of a hydroelectric project during the late 1930s and early 1940s. The inundation of the simbi abodes, displacement of the communities near them, and devastation of the natural environment that had been home to the simbi and their people marked the end of the story of the simbi in the Lowcountry.

Constructing a history that connects people, places, and spirits over vast distances and extended periods of time requires an equally broad range of sources. Discussions of society and culture in the Lowcountry from the late seventeenth century into the mid-nineteenth century rely on land warrants, probate inventories of estates, plantation records, newspaper advertisements, data on trans-Atlantic voyages, missionary reports, memoirs, and personal diaries. For the same period in West-Central Africa, writings by European missionaries, merchants, colonial agents, and other travelers provide information in Portuguese, French, Italian, and English. We must keep in mind, however, that the voices of African-descended people were often muffled, if not silenced, by the European and Euro-American authors of these documents. This changed, however, when Africans and African Americans had greater opportunities to contribute their own explanations of their cultures. They did so in the early decades of the twentieth century through ethnographic essays in Kongo and through recorded and transcribed interviews about folklore and spiritual culture in the Lowcountry. Balancing the strengths and limitations of all of these sources – whether written or oral, endogenous or exogenous – remains the challenge for any scholar of the past and especially for those attempting to research the elusive cultural histories of African-descended people in the diaspora. I have chosen to be as inclusive as possible with sources and to combine the array of materials in ways that amplify their explanatory power. In the end, my guiding principle has been to find and use evidence that allows this story of the simbi and their people to be seen and heard once more.

Acknowledgements

I begin by giving thanks to my ancestors. They opened paths in the wilderness in their lifetimes and continue to do so now.

I would like to thank several institutions for providing funds, facilities, and other forms of assistance during the past two decades in support of the research that informs this book. The Department of History at the University of Georgia provided travel funds that allowed me to begin archival work. I received generous support for research and project development through two endeavors sponsored by the United Negro College Fund/Andrew W. Mellon Foundation Programs, particularly the UNCF/ Mellon Faculty International Summer Seminar in 2002 and a UNCF/ Mellon Faculty Doctoral Fellowship in 2003. The Office of Academic Affairs and the Department of Philosophy and Religion at Dillard University awarded grants in 2003 that extended my access to materials on African-Atlantic spiritual cultures. When I was at Northwestern University as a Katrina Fellow in 2005, the Alice Kaplan Institute for the Humanities supplied housing, office space, and access to the holdings of the Northwestern University Library, most notably the materials housed in the Melville J. Herskovits Library of African Studies. The College of Liberal Arts and the Department of History at Southern Illinois University, Carbondale, provided support for travel on several occasions since 2007 and course release in 2011. Finally, I offer thanks to the archivists and other staff members for expert and friendly assistance at the South Carolina Historical Society, the South Caroliniana Library at the University of South Carolina, the South Carolina Department of Archives and History, the Southern Historical Collection and the Southern Folklore Collection at the University of North Carolina, the Will W. Alexander Library at

Dillard University, the Melville J. Herskovits Library of African Studies at Northwestern University, the Indiana University Archives of Traditional Music, the Howard-Tilton Memorial Library at Tulane University, the J. Edgar and Louise S. Monroe Library at Loyola University New Orleans, and the Morris Library at Southern Illinois University, Carbondale.

This book draws from many relationships cultivated over many years in many places. I will not presume to reveal the nature of all those relationships here. I hope that the people named below will readily recall our connections and enjoy knowing that they helped make this book real. My early years in the academic world at South Carolina State College/University allowed me to get to know Alex Azad, Winston Denmark, Dawn Evans, Stanley Harrold, Ricky Hill, William Hine, Cornelius St. Mark, and all the other Bulldogs that made State my home. The churches and people of the 7th District of the African Methodist Episcopal Church provided a nurturing context to explore spiritual matters, and I grew a great deal from observing and talking with the Reverend Allen W. Parrott and the Reverend John H. Gillison. The community I belonged to at Bowling Green State University was built around Lillian Ashcraft-Eason, Djisovi Eason, Lawrence Friedman, and Tom Klein, who were much needed during that transition. The University of Georgia presented me with the opportunity to work with exceptional scholars and colleagues including Steve Estes, Michael Gomez, Peter C. Hoffer, Mark Huddle, John Inscoe, Sonja Lanehart, William McFeely, Diane Batts Morrow, John Morrow, Eve Troutt Powell, Robert Pratt, David Schoenbrun, and Michael Winship. Many people at Dillard University in New Orleans provided encouragement and friendship, especially Reverend Gail Bowman, Sylvia Carey, Al Colon, Isabel Cristina Ferreira dos Reis, Dan Frost, Henry Lacey, Donna Patterson, Darryl Peterkin, Rhetta Seymour, Dorothy Smith, Marshall Stevenson, Barbara Thompson, Chiquita Webb, and Kerrie Cotten Williams. My affiliation with Dillard led to ties with Cynthia Neal Spence and Gabrielle Samuel-O'Brien at the United Negro College Fund/Andrew W. Mellon Foundation Programs office at Spelman College. Through my participation in the UNCF/Mellon Faculty International Summer Seminar in 2002, I had the chance to work with Wole Soyinka, Arturo Lindsay, Kokahvah Zauditu-Selassie, and Opal Moore.

The fall of 2005 marked a fundamental break in my life, as the failure of the levees in New Orleans after Hurricane Katrina changed everything. In addition to being fortunate enough to carry relationships from life before Katrina into life after Katrina, I have had the pleasure of creating new ties in difficult circumstances. Elzbieta Foeller-Pituch and Darlene Clark Hine made Northwestern University a comforting and productive academic home during my first exile from New Orleans in 2005. My second exile took me to Southern Illinois University in Carbondale, where I have come to rely on a number of people including Michael Batinski, Father Joseph Brown, Randy Burnside, Andrew Bynom, Kay Carr, Mariola Espinosa, Holly Hurlburt, Robbie Lieberman, Rhetta Seymour, Alan Vaux, Jonathan Wiesen, and Natasha Zaretsky.

Over the many years that I have been an educator at Dillard and SIUC, my relationships with students have been intellectually and emotionally sustaining. Further, the process of teaching and learning has been essential to generating and refining a number of the ideas that drive this book. For their dedication and acumen, I would like to thank Joe Abney, Cyrelene Amoah-Boampong, Raven Bailey, Nathan Brouwer, Barrye Brown, Art Fitz-Gerald, Fatuma Guyo, Raquel Janeau, Ersheka Joseph, Cristina Lopes, Dennis McDonald, S. Kristopher Morella, Kristin Nevels, Sultan Shahid, Maria Stuart, Donovan Weight, and Deb Wilson.

The conversations, seminar papers, conference presentations, article drafts, and manuscripts that contributed to the making of this book were shaped by people mentioned already (whom I will acknowledge once again in this context) and others. For their ideas and attention to my work, I would like to thank Rick Abbott, Michael Batinski, Father Joseph Brown, Kay Carr, Douglas Chambers, T. J. Desch-Obi, Dianne Diakité, Mariola Espinosa, Chris Fernandez del Riego, Michael Gomez, Linda Hewett, Linda Heywood, Holly Hurlburt, John Inscoe, John Janzen, Cris Lopes, Joseph Miller, Donna Patterson, Robert Pratt, David Schoenbrun, John Thornton, Jonathan Wiesen, and Natasha Zaretsky. I want to make special mention of two others. Kairn Klieman committed much time and effort to early versions of the book that gave me necessary direction in enhancing strengths and redressing weaknesses. Tiffany Player has been the one person most engaged with the swirl of ideas and countless drafts generated as I worked on this project. Her sharp insights and keen editing have made every piece I have written far better than anything I could produce on my own. Once the book manuscript reached a mature stage, I had the good fortune to connect with Eric Crahan at Cambridge University Press. The expert editors of the Cambridge Studies on the American South series, David Moltke-Hansen and Mark M. Smith, and two anonymous readers provided criticism and guidance crucial to developing arguments and correcting oversights. In its many forms, the material that has become this book has been in the hands of many intelligent and insightful people. I hope that the final version of the work truly represents their invaluable contributions. Any errors that remain despite their dedicated interventions are solely my responsibility.

Finally, I want to express my gratitude to my families. The Browns, Blickenstaffs, Players, and many allied families have provided an unfailing web of support. My mother Susan and my father Theron introduced to me to a life of cultivating the mind. My grandparents have nurtured my awareness of the power of knowledge and my connections to my ancestors. My first priority has always been Tiffany, Dawn, Josie, and Orlando. Their love has sustained me and reminds me every day of the most important things in life.

Abbreviations Used in Notes

LDTC	Lorenzo Dow Turner Collection, Georgia and South Carolina, Sea Islands, 1931–33, Indiana University Archives of Traditional Music (Bloomington)
LDTP	Lorenzo Dow Turner Papers, Melville J. Herskovits Library, Northwestern University (Evanston, Illinois)
RASP	*Records of Ante-Bellum Southern Plantations from the Revolution through the Civil War* (microfilm), edited by Kenneth M. Stampp (Frederick, MD: University Publications of America, 1985)
RSP-SCDAH	Inventories of Estates and Miscellaneous Records, Records of the Secretary of the Province, South Carolina Department of Archives and History (Columbia)
SCG	*South Carolina Gazette*
SCHS	South Carolina Historical Society (Charleston)
SCL	South Caroliniana Library, University of South Carolina (Columbia)
SFC	Southern Folklore Collection, University of North Carolina (Chapel Hill)
SHC	Southern Historical Collection, University of North Carolina (Chapel Hill)
Voyages Database	Voyages Database, 2009. *Voyages: The Trans-Atlantic Slave Trade Database*. http://www.slavevoyages.org
WPA-SCL	Works Progress Administration, Federal Writers' Project, Manuscript Collection, South Caroliniana Library, University of South Carolina (Columbia)

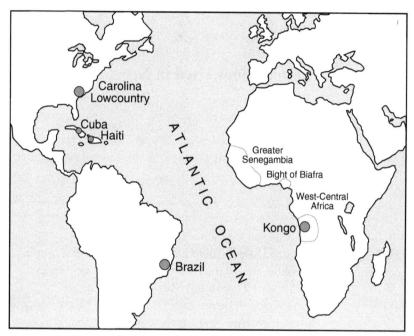

MAP 1. The Simbi in the African-Atlantic World. Prepared by Kay J. Carr.

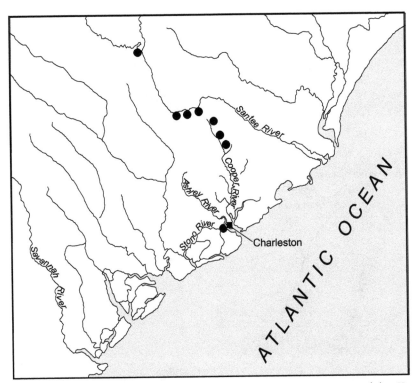

MAP 2. South Carolina Lowcountry and Simbi Locations. Prepared by Kay
J. Carr.

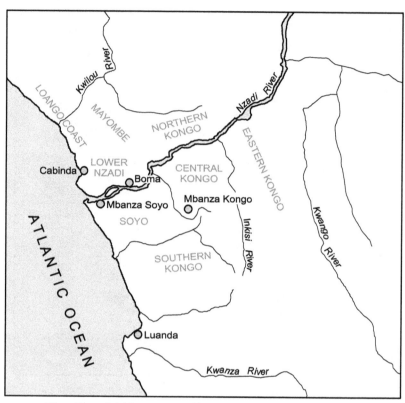

MAP 3. West-Central Africa. Prepared by Kay J. Carr.

I

Place, Culture, and Power

As part of an effort to revitalize the Pooshee plantation in St. John's Berkeley parish during the early decades of the nineteenth century, Dr. Henry Ravenel endeavored to have a wall built to enclose and raise the water around a limestone spring. This spring was no ordinary pool of water, however. Like many other limestone springs in the area, it had a deep opening and on occasion expelled considerable amounts of water. Because of this, people had taken to calling it a fountain following the terminology of the time. Within and around this fountain resided a water spirit known as a "cymbee." The presence of the cymbee prompted a local elder of African and Native descent to confront Ravenel about the construction of the wall, which the elder contended would offend the spirit, thus causing the cymbee to leave and the spring to disappear. Despite the elder's protestations, Ravenel built his wall, and the fountain and its cymbee remained features of the plantation for a few more generations. The elder's warning, however, came true almost a century later as the springs, Pooshee, and many other plantations vanished under the floodwaters created by the damming of the Cooper River.[1]

The Pooshee cymbee survived the Ravenel crisis, which came as no surprise, as it had already endured droughts, wars, and the endemic violence of enslavement experienced by the sons and daughters of Africa who knew and venerated the spirit. The Pooshee cymbee was not alone;

---

[1] Edmund Ruffin, *Agriculture, Geology, and Society in Antebellum South Carolina: The Private Diary of Edmund Ruffin, 1843*, ed. William M. Mathew (Athens: University of Georgia Press, 1992), 164–7; and Walter B. Edgar, *History of the Santee Cooper, 1934–1984* (Columbia, SC: R. L. Bryan Co., 1984), 164–7.

throughout the parishes of upper St. John's Berkeley and St. Stephen's, the waters of several limestone springs on plantations housed cymbees. These cymbees, too, had remained in their abodes and in the lives of African-descended people well into the twentieth century. These remarkable residents of the springs were the Lowcountry manifestations of Kongo nature spirits known as the simbi, entities once central to Kongo perceptions of the spiritual landscape. The simbi served as guardians of the natural environment and of the people who lived in their domains and functioned as the chief intermediaries between the physical "land of the living" and the spiritual "land of the dead."[2]

The simbi represented much more, as well. They were markers of beginnings and of the deep past. They exemplified the original inhabitants of a territory, and the relationships these spirits had with people imparted a status of primacy to anchor communities of the living in a country. Where people recognized the existence of the simbi, they were simultaneously making certain claims about their own relationship to their surroundings.[3] In short, the living declared that they belonged to the land and that the land belonged to them. For captive Africans displaced from their home societies and familiar environments, such a statement served to ground them in novel settings in ways absolutely necessary to reestablishing connections between the land of the living and the land of the dead, bring children into this new world, grow food for their families, resist the ravages of disease, struggle with the countless assaults on their humanity inherent in the experiences of captivity and enslavement, contest the claims to power by oppressors, live, and die.

In fortifying the bonds between people and the land in both its physical and spiritual aspects, the simbi played an essential role in the

---

[2] Bound Volume of Research Notes (pp. 62B, 112B), John Bennett Papers, SCHS. For an introduction to the simbi in Kongo, see Wyatt MacGaffey, *Religion and Society: The BaKongo of Lower Zaire* (Chicago: University of Chicago Press, 1986), 63–5, 74–82, 85–8, 99–102; and Luc de Heusch, *Le Roi de Kongo et les Monstres Sacrés, Mythes et Rites Bantous. III* (Paris: Gallimard, 2000), 161–4, 191–7, 214–22.

[3] This interpretation of the simbi derives from the analysis of nature spirits in Bantu-speaking societies in J. M. Schoffeleers, "Introduction," in *Guardians of the Land: Essays on Central African Territorial Cults*, ed. J. M. Schoffeleers (Gwelo, Zimbabwe: Mambo Press, 1978), 1–46; Jan Vansina, *Paths in the Rainforests: Toward a History of Political Tradition in Equatorial Africa* (Madison: University of Wisconsin Press, 1990), 56, 95, 98, 146, 148–9; David Lee Schoenbrun, *A Green Place, A Good Place: Agrarian Change, Gender, and Social Identity in the Great Lakes Region to the 15th Century* (Portsmouth, NH: Heinemann, 1998), 199–206; and Kairn A. Klieman, *"The Pygmies Were Our Compass": Bantu and Batwa in the History of West Central Africa, Early Times to c. 1900 C.E.* (Portsmouth, NH: Heinemann, 2003), 74–89, 145–7, 149–53.

formation and maintenance of communities of the living. Although it may seem that the simbi as nature spirits belonged to a realm removed from the activities and concerns of human society, they were always profoundly interested in those who inhabited their domains. They often initiated relationships with the living by communicating through dreams or by "seizing" those who ventured near their abodes. They commanded storms, floods, and droughts to remind people of their obligations to the simbi and bestowed blessings for proper veneration. Additionally, the simbi punished or rewarded based on adherence to their codes for behavior. Those who violated these laws typically instigated familial discord and social disorder, which elicited additional trouble from the simbi. In all of these ways, the simbi could help build communities of the living or take away the support needed to preserve them.

The simbi, then, tell us about the people who knew them and interacted with them as indispensible aspects of daily life. As such, the simbi are fundamental to the story of how African newcomers and their Lowcountry-born descendants conceived of their relationships with the natural environment and the meanings they attached to the spiritual landscape. This story about the formation and elaboration of the environmental and spiritual cultures of African-descended people in the South Carolina Lowcountry includes many other elements that on the surface do not appear related to the affinities between the simbi and communities of the living. Yet even the most mundane pursuits, such as planting, fishing, and hunting, entailed engagement with the spiritual forces inherent in the natural world. African newcomers from diverse backgrounds understood this, and those from Kongo knew this required contact with the simbi. People of African descent also accepted that the physical landscape had sacred dimensions that had to be engaged for both the spiritual development of individuals and the well-being of communities. This notion, too, was embraced by many of the African societies from which the captives who landed in the Lowcountry originated. People from Kongo and West-Central Africa in general expected that this process involved the simbi or similar nature spirits known by different names. It was for these reasons that people remembered and respected the Lowcountry simbi long after the African newcomers arrived on the shores of South Carolina and became part of the soil in this new land. It is for these reasons, too, that the simbi remain essential to any reconstruction of the histories of the environmental and spiritual cultures of African-descended communities in the Lowcountry.

Indeed, the simbi comprised a vital component of the cultural dialogue in the long transition from the polycultural world formed by diverse Africans and their descendants during the height of the Atlantic trade to a single community largely unified in terms of culture and identity in the nineteenth century. This process transpired over several generations, and the simbi remained relevant and acquired new meanings during this shift, so that they transformed from a specific legacy of Kongo people to become a shared element of Black Lowcountry culture into the twentieth century. Similar to other aspects of Black Lowcountry culture that grew from older African contexts, the simbi represented both a link to the ancestral cultures of African-descended people and a means to bring people together to forge new communities of the living. Further, the simbi ensured that these new communities would be nourished through strong roots in the landscape of the Lowcountry.[4]

THE SIMBI AND THE LOWCOUNTRY AS A CULTURAL PLACE

The simbi in their various manifestations played evolving roles in the spiritual culture of African-descended people throughout the Lowcountry, yet their stronghold remained the springs found near the headwaters of the western branch of the Cooper River in upper St. John's Berkeley parish and into adjacent areas of St. Stephen's parish, a section known as the limestone region.[5] No absolute rule or overriding principle in the Kongo background of the simbi dictated that they had to inhabit these springs, although simbi in many parts of Kongo appeared frequently in pools as well as in rivers, waterfalls, stones, forests, and mountains. The

---

[4] The sense of cultural dialogue referenced here derives from J. Lorand Matory, "The 'New World' Surrounds an Ocean: Theorizing the Live Dialogue between African and African American Cultures," in *Afro-Atlantic Dialogues: Anthropology in the Diaspora*, ed. Kevin A. Yelvington (Santa Fe, NM: School of American Research, 2006), 151–92. Connections between African cultural antecedents and community formation in the U.S. South and the Lowcountry are explored in Sterling Stuckey, *Slave Culture: Nationalist Theory and the Foundations of Black America* (New York: Oxford University Press, 1987); Margaret Washington Creel, *"A Peculiar People": Slave Religion and Community-Culture among the Gullahs* (New York: New York University Press, 1988); and Michael A. Gomez, *Exchanging Our Country Marks: The Transformations of African Identities in the Colonial and Antebellum South* (Chapel Hill: University of North Carolina Press, 1998).

[5] Henry William Ravenel, "Limestone Fountains of Berkeley District," undated essay, Henry William Ravenel Papers, SCL; and Edmund Ravenel, "The Limestone Springs of St. John's, Berkeley, and their probable Availability for increasing the quantity of Fresh Water in Cooper River," *Proceedings of the Elliott Society of Science and Art, or Charleston, South Carolina* 2 (October 1860): 28–31.

features and spaces that could be occupied by the simbi were many. The springs of the limestone region, however, were special as natural landmarks and spiritual sites. The confluence of both meant that the springs served as the home of the simbi from some time early in the settlement of the Lowcountry to well into the twentieth century. For this reason alone, the limestone region was a place like no other in the Lowcountry and, indeed, in mainland North America.[6]

At the same time that the presence of the simbi made this small part of the Lowcountry unique, it revealed the Lowcountry to be an extension of the far-flung Bantu-Atlantic spiritual landscape rooted in West-Central Africa with branches that extended throughout the diaspora, including Brazil, Cuba, Dutch Guiana (Suriname), and Saint-Domingue (Haiti). This historical geography illustrates that each simbi represented a specific manifestation of an individual spirit in a particular place, while the simbi as a kind of spirit existed everywhere. Moreover, the ubiquity of the simbi indicates that captive West-Central Africans expected to find these spirits on the western shores of the Atlantic, and they did. The fact that Kongo captives taken to the Lowcountry, like their compatriots in other lands, found the simbi there lends credence to the understanding that the shared spiritual cultures of Africans from particular regions could find meaningful expression in different locations despite divergences in the unique combinations of economic, political, and demographic variables that shaped the histories of various American societies.[7]

---

[6] Notions of place and environment in this book derive much from Yi-Fu Tuan, *Topophilia: A Study of Environmental Perception, Attitudes and Values* (Englewood Cliffs, NJ: Prentice Hall, 1974); Yi-Fu Tuan, *Space and Place: The Perspective of Experience* (Minneapolis: University of Minnesota Press, 1977); Mart A. Stewart, *"What Nature Suffers to Groe": Life, Labor, and Landscape on the Georgia Coast, 1680–1920* (Athens: University of Georgia Press, 1996), 5–12; Ute Luig and Achim von Oppen, "Landscape in Africa: Process and Vision," *Paideuma* 43 (1997): 7–45; Sandra E. Greene, *Sacred Sites and the Colonial Encounter: A History of Meaning and Memory in Ghana* (Bloomington: Indiana University Press, 2002); Charles Mather, "Shrines and the Domestication of Landscape," *Journal of Anthropological Research* 59, 1 (2003): 23–45; and Tim Cresswell, *Place: A Short Introduction* (Malden, MA: Blackwell Publishing, 2004).

[7] For the simbi in the diaspora, see (Brazil) John M. Janzen, *Lemba, 1650–1930: A Drum of Affliction in Africa and the New World* (New York: Garland Publishing, 1982), 273–7; Ornato J. Sil, *Introdução de Muzenza nos Cultos Bantos* (Rio de Janeiro: Pallas Editora, 1998), 110; and Nei Lopes, *Novo Dicionário Banto do Brasil* (Rio de Janeiro: Pallas, 2003), 505, 553; (Cuba) Lydia Cabrera, *Reglas de Congo: Palo Monte Mayombe* (Miami: Peninsular Print, 1979), 128; Jorge Castellanos and Isabel Castellanos, *Cultura Afrocubana 3: Las Religiones y las Lenguas* (Miami: Ediciones Universal, 1992), 137; (Haiti) Melville J. Herskovits, *Life in a Haitian Valley* (New York: Knopf, 1937), 151–2; Alfred Metraux, *Voodoo in Haiti*, trans. Hugo Charteris (New York: Schocken Books, 1972 [1959]), 267, 310–12; and Wyatt MacGaffey, "Twins, Simbi Spirits, and Lwas in

The recognition of the presence of the simbi in South Carolina locates the Lowcountry as a cultural place firmly within the African-Atlantic world and not an anomaly (as has been the case in North American–centered scholarship). Further, this reinforces the understanding that the fundamental character of African-based culture in the Lowcountry derived from the same sources as other African-Atlantic cultures; the minds and actions of African-descended people. While this does not constitute a particularly innovative observation, the centrality of the cultural knowledge and choices of people of African descent has often been treated as a factor secondary to a kind of geographical or environmental determinism in cultural processes. For many, including scholars, the Lowcountry and its sea islands have long represented a cultural preserve in which the customs of many generations past have been sustained without change, at least until the intrusion of the modern world and land developers began an unrelenting surge of personal dislocation and cultural destruction. Whereas the rest of African America increasingly assimilated into the larger American cultural setting during slavery and especially after emancipation, the land and water of the coastal plain created a barrier of islands, waterways, and swamps that separated the inhabitants from the same social and cultural forces that reshaped the lives of African-descended people everywhere else. The fidelity of an original cultural heritage derived from this isolation and made the sea islands a place where a "whole body of traditions, superstitions, language and mental background were [sic] handed down practically unchanged" among a people "untouched by a changing world."[8]

Kongo and Haiti," in *Central Africans and Cultural Transformations in the American Diaspora*, ed. Linda M. Heywood (New York: Cambridge University Press, 2002), 211–26. Demographic and cultural aspects of the Bantu (West-Central African) diaspora in the Atlantic world and the Lowcountry are addressed in Robert Farris Thompson, *Flash of the Spirit: African and Afro-American Art and Philosophy* (New York: Vintage, 1984), 101–59; Joseph E. Holloway and Winifred K. Vass, *The African Heritage of American English* (Bloomington: Indiana University Press, 1993); Heywood, *Central Africans and Cultural Transformations*; Maureen Warner-Lewis, *Central Africa in the Caribbean: Transcending Time, Transforming Cultures* (Kingston, Jamaica: University of West Indies Press, 2003); Betty Kuyk, *African Voices in the African American Heritage* (Bloomington: Indiana University Press, 2003); and Jason R. Young, *Rituals of Resistance: African Atlantic Religion in Kongo and the Lowcountry South in the Era of Slavery* (Baton Rouge: Louisiana State University Press, 2007). The significance of historical variables in explaining differences in the cultures of various African-descended populations has its origins in the work of Melville J. Herskovits, most notably his *Myth of the Negro Past* (Boston: Beacon Press, 1990 [1941]), 33–53, 111–42.

[8] Cassles R. Tiedeman, "Low Country Gullah," WPA-SCL. On the ubiquity of the term "isolation" in explanations of the sea islands culture, see Mason Crum, *Gullah: Negro*

This characterization, as pervasive as it remains, misrepresents the cultural history of the Lowcountry and African America. Its greatest weakness derives from its reliance on a form of geographical or environmental determinism that ignores the ability of African-descended people to actively form and transmit their own cultures. We will return to this concern shortly. Most significant at this point is that the imagined geographical isolation of the South Carolina Lowcountry does not have a firm basis in the historical geography of the region. For people attuned to traveling over land in cars that need roads and bridges, the water presents barriers. The multitude of waterways and wetlands would appear as inhibitors to effective movement and interaction. People who have lived with and on the water have seen it differently, however. Many rivers and channels dissected the seaboard and made overland travel difficult, but in no way isolated Lowcountry communities. In assessing the economic value of this trait of the region one eighteenth-century commentator related, "The coast is also chequered with a variety of fine islands, around which the sea flows, and opens excellent channels, for the easy conveyance of produce to the market."[9] Another keen observer from the early eighteenth century remarking on the coastal plain's hydrography said that, "These inland Passages are of great Use to the Inhabitants, who without being exposed to the open Sea, travel with Safety in Boats and *Peeriagua's*."[10] The interlocking system of navigable waterways that connected barrier islands to marshlands and penetrated the mainland at numerous points along the

Life in the Carolina Sea Islands (Durham: Duke University Press, 1940), ix, 116, 226; Lorenzo Dow Turner, *Africanisms in the Gullah Dialect* (Chicago: University of Chicago Press, 1949), 5; Patricia Jones-Jackson, *When Roots Die: Endangered Traditions on the Sea Islands* (Athens: University of Georgia Press, 1987), xix, 133, 137, 147; Michael Montgomery, "Introduction," in *The Crucible of Carolina: Essays in the Development of Gullah Language and Culture*, ed. Michael Montgomery (Athens: University of Georgia Press, 1994), 4, 6; Joseph E. Holloway, "The Sacred World of the Gullahs," in *Africanisms in American Culture*, ed. Joseph E. Holloway (Bloomington: Indiana University Press, 2005), 187; William S. Pollitzer, *The Gullah People and Their African Heritage* (Athens: University of Georgia Press, 2005), 7, 34, 53, 62, 189; Margaret Washington, "Gullah Attitudes Toward Life and Death," in Holloway, *Africanisms in American Culture*, 152; and J. Lorand Matory, "The Illusion of Isolation: The Gullah/Geechees and the Political Economy of African Culture in the Americas," *Comparative Studies in Society and History* 50, 4 (2008): 956–77.

9 Alexander Hewatt, *An Historical Account of the Rise and Progress of the Colonies of South Carolina and Georgia* (London: Alexander Donaldson, 1779) 1: 80.

10 Mark Catesby, *The Natural History of Carolina, Florida and the Bahama Islands* (London: Mark Catesby, 1743) 2: iii.

coast provided one of the distinct features of the coastal plain's geography that facilitated rather than hindered the cohesion of Lowcountry society.[11]

Waterways provided the most efficient means of transporting people and goods, encouraging early European colonizers to build plantations on accessible locations by rivers. If anything, reliance on water transport united the entire seaboard into a single, cohesive realm. From the late seventeenth century through the mid-nineteenth century when the work of enslaved people in the forests and fields served the interests of enslavers, commerce, travel, and communication relied on the waterways that ran toward the sea and linked every manor to the busy Atlantic port of Charleston. No plantation could afford to be isolated since access to markets was of the utmost economic importance.[12]

Establishing plantations in this way eased movement and communication for enslaved people, as well. Plantation boatmen spent days on the water, various plantations, and in Charleston delivering messages and commodities to planters and markets while associating and trading with other enslaved people along the way. Enslaved people throughout the Lowcountry made or had access to boats for hunting and fishing or even to sell to plantation owners. This extensive mobility allowed enslaved people to maintain familial, ethnic, and commercial connections throughout the Lowcountry. These ties not only kept people on various plantations in contact but also linked Charleston to the countryside, particularly through market activities. This business carried on to the extent that white residents of the Lowcountry routinely grumbled about enslaved people's capacity to "keep canoes, and to breed and raise horses, neat cattle and hogs, and to traffic and barter in several parts of

---

[11] Charles F. Kovacik and John J. Winberry, *South Carolina: A Geography* (Boulder, CO: Westview, 1987), 7–9, 18–29, 65–85, 87–91, 99–103.

[12] Rusty Fleetwood, *Tidecraft: The Boats of South Carolina, Georgia, and Northeastern Florida, 1550–1950* (Tybee Island, GA: WBG Marine Press, 1995); David Beard, "'Good Wharves and Other Conveniences': An Archaeological Study of Riverine Adaptation in the South Carolina Lowcountry," in *Carolina's Historical Landscapes: Archaeological Perspectives*, ed. Linda F. Stine, Martha Zierden, Lesley M. Drucker, and Christopher Judge (Knoxville: University of Tennessee Press, 1997), 61–70; Jim Errante, "Waterscape Archaeology: Recognizing the Archaeological Significance of the Plantation Waterscape," in Stine, Zierden, Drucker, and Judge, *Carolina's Historical Landscapes*, 205–10; and Ras Michael Brown, "'Walk in the Feenda': West-Central Africans and the Forest in the South Carolina–Georgia Lowcountry," in Heywood, *Central Africans and Cultural Transformations*, 292–3. Colonists initially referred to their premier settlement as Charles Town and only later refined the name to Charleston. For the sake of consistency, I employ the later, enduring moniker Charleston.

the Province, for the particular and peculiar benefit of such slaves."[13] Further, enslaved people also traversed dense woods between the water and roads with such confidence that they often served as guides for less capable travelers.[14] These early endeavors to ply the waters and cross the land to maintain personal bonds and gain some wealth remained the norm after emancipation. Even for those on small and remote islands, the coastal routes of local steamships ensured regular connections between Charleston and Savannah, and from these ports links to the larger world beyond.[15]

The illusion of isolation has had the effect of rendering the relationship between African-descended people and their natural surroundings as passive, a claim that remains fundamentally contradictory to their history.[16] The engagement of Africans and their Carolina-born descendants with the landscape of the Lowcountry has been profound and continuous, changing as the world around them has changed. African-descended people during the days of slavery mastered the cultivation of rice, indigo, and long-staple cotton as each of these in turn emerged as the predominant means for enslavers to amass wealth. Later, becoming free people and landowners imbued the landscape with other dimensions of power. In the first half of the twentieth century, however, the boll weevil's decimation of cotton, abuse of oyster beds by overharvesting and pollution, and flooding of homes and fields for a massive electrification project sent people in various directions, whether into neighboring communities, growing cities of the South, or up North in search of jobs and other opportunities. Unfortunately for many, as the twentieth century entered its second half, the loss of ownership and access to the land denied African-descended

---

[13] David J. McCord, ed., *The Statutes at Large of South Carolina* (Columbia: A. S. Johnston, 1840), 7: 409.

[14] Peter H. Wood, *Black Majority: Negroes in Colonial South Carolina from 1670 through the Stono Rebellion* (New York: Norton, 1974), 117–19, 256–7; Philip D. Morgan and George D. Terry, "Slavery in Microcosm: A Conspiracy Scare in Colonial South Carolina," *Southern Studies* 21, 2 (1982): 130–4; and Philip D. Morgan, *Slave Counterpoint: Black Culture in the Eighteenth-Century Chesapeake and Lowcountry* (Chapel Hill: University of North Carolina Press, 1998), 236–44.

[15] On the movement of islanders and other Lowcountry people in the late nineteenth century and afterward, see Clyde Kiser, *Sea Island to City: A Study of St. Helena Islanders in Harlem and Other Urban Centers* (New York: Columbia University Press, 1932); Sam Gadsden, *An Oral History of Edisto Island: Sam Gadsden Tells the Story* (Goshen, IN: Pinchpenny Press, 1975); and William Brown, *An Oral History of Edito Island: The Life and Times of Bubberson Brown* (Goshen, IN: Pinchpenny Press, 1977).

[16] The phrase "illusion of isolation" and its application to cultural processes come from Matory, "Illusion of Isolation."

people economic choices and divorced communities from a fundamental element of their cultural grounding.[17] Each of these shifts entailed
the challenges of reconsidering livelihoods, relocating the places called
home, and redefining how people lived with the land. Clearly, the role
of the landscape in influencing the cultures of the islands and the rural
mainland was not in isolating people from the outside world. Rather, the
long, sustained relationship with the land and water of the Lowcountry
provided a context in which knowledge imparted by African ancestors
remained most relevant as successive generations recalled and reworked
this knowledge to inform their understandings of the physical and spiritual meanings of the natural environment.

One of the best-known expressions of this relationship has been the
burial of the dead with personal and symbolic items placed on graves.
These sacred sites were found throughout South Carolina, not just the
Lowcountry, and in other places in the American South.[18] For example,
two key sources that documented grave decoration in the nineteenth

[17] For the era of enslavement, see Daniel C. Littlefield, *Rice and Slaves: Ethnicity and the Slave Trade in Colonial South Carolina* (Baton Rouge: Louisiana State University Press, 1981); Mart A. Stewart, "Rice, Water, and Power: Landscapes of Domination and Resistance in the Lowcountry, 1790–1880," *Environmental History Review* 15, 3 (1991): 47–64; Joyce E. Chaplin, *An Anxious Pursuit: Agricultural Innovation & Modernity in the Lower South, 1730–1815* (Chapel Hill: University of North Carolina Press, 1993); Judith A. Carney, *Black Rice: The African Origins of Rice Cultivation in the Americas* (Cambridge, MA: Harvard University Press, 2001); and S. Max Edelson, *Plantation Enterprise in Colonial South Carolina* (Cambridge, MA: Harvard University Press, 2006). For the era after emancipation and into the twentieth century, see Guion Griffis Johnson, *A Social History of the Sea Islands, with Special Reference to St. Helena Island, South Carolina* (Chapel Hill: University of North Carolina Press, 1930); T. J. Woofter, *Black Yeomanry: Life on St. Helena Island* (New York: Henry Holt and Co., 1930); Kiser, *Sea Island to City*; Paul Sanford Salter, "Changing Agricultural Patterns on South Carolina Sea Islands," *Journal of Geography* 67 (1968): 223–8; June Manning Thomas, "The Impact of Corporate Tourism on Gullah Blacks: Notes on Issues of Employment," *Phylon* 41, 1 (1980): 1–11; Lisa V. Faulkenberry, John H. Coggeshall, Kenneth Backman, and Sheila Backman, "A Culture of Servitude: The Impact of Tourism and Development on South Carolina's Coast," *Human Organization* 59, 1 (2000): 86–95; and National Park Service, *Low Country Gullah Culture: Special Resource Study and Final Environmental Impact Statement* (Atlanta, GA: National Park Service Southeast Regional Office, 2005), 81–93.

[18] Thompson, *Flash of the Spirit*, 132–42; Mechal Sobel, *The World They Made Together: Black and White Values in Eighteenth-Century Virginia* (Princeton, NJ: Princeton University Press, 1987), 218–21; Robert Farris Thompson, *Face of the Gods: Art and Altars of the Africa and the African Americas* (New York: The Museum of African Art, 1993), 76–84; Gray Gundaker, "Introduction: Home Ground," in *Keep Your Head to the Sky: Interpreting African American Home Ground*, ed. Gray Gundaker (Charlottesville: University Press of Virginia, 1998), 15–21; and Young, *Rituals of Resistance*, 162–6.

century derived from observations of the practice in the cemeteries of the "poorer negroes" in Columbia. Instead of invoking geographical or environmental isolation to explain the continuation of the observance in the growing capital of the state, the authors of these accounts attributed the "savage or childlike" practice to a supposed intellectual isolation of African-descended people. According to this view, the "negroes of South Carolina are simply following the customs of their savage ancestors, and are unwittingly perpetuating the fetishism so deeply impressed."[19] Such a sentiment reveals most plainly its racist and ethnocentric essence, though we must note that its explanatory premise does not depart significantly from the same basis for the appeal to geographical or environmental isolation, in that both ideas deny the cultural agency of African-descended people. Yet, neither topography nor a savage mentality prompted African-descended people to decorate graves; they chose to do this. They chose to make graves places of connection between the land of the living and the land of the dead in a variety of settings and locations because they understood the relationship of physical and spiritual landscapes in ways shaped by the knowledge of their ancestors. They chose to maintain the old practice because it embodied meanings that the living still valued in both familiar and novel settings.

This brings us back to the simbi. The presence of the simbi in St. John's Berkeley parish provides a deeper, historical context for understanding the spiritual connections between people and the landscape from which sprang the practice of grave decoration. Indeed, the foundations of the relationship between African-descended people and the land had been pioneered by the original communities of enslaved Africans concentrated along the densely settled courses of the Ashley, Cooper, and Stono Rivers. While this historical hearth of people and culture has not always been linked adequately to the communities and cultures that later developed on the sea islands, now celebrated as the core of African-based lifestyles in the Lowcountry, the earliest polycultural communities were established in this old plantation core. It is there, then, that we should look to find the complex root architecture of the Black Lowcountry culture that began to take its more familiar form in the nineteenth century.

This book will explore the place of the simbi in the landscape and culture created by African-descended people by first examining the forced

---

[19] H. Carrington Bolton, "Decoration of Graves of Negroes in South Carolina," *Journal of American Folklore* 4, 14 (1891): 214; and Ernest Ingersoll, "Decoration of Negro Graves," *Journal of American Folklore* 5, 6 (1892): 68–9.

relocation and settlement of captive Africans during the formative period for enslaved communities from the late seventeenth century through the mid-eighteenth century. After making a detailed appraisal of the simbi and similar entities in West-Central African and West African spiritual cultures, the focus returns to South Carolina to assess the ways these cultural foundations shaped perceptions of the physical and spiritual landscapes of the Lowcountry, including locating the simbi in the limestone springs of St. John's Berkeley parish. The book culminates with an assessment of the changes wrought during the course of the nineteenth century, especially the spread and further development of Protestant Christianity and the coming of emancipation, that precipitated reworkings of the simbi in which they transformed into key figures in conversion experiences and coded critiques of slavery. The early twentieth century, however, witnessed the fading of the simbi and ultimately the destruction of their stronghold.

INTERPRETING CULTURES

African-Atlantic Cultures and the South Carolina Lowcountry enters into a long-standing, vibrant discussion about the cultural history of people of African descent in North America. The effort to define the relationship between the peoples and cultures of Africa with those of African America has been central to this discussion since the early explorations of pan-African connections in the nineteenth century.[20] Works based in the discipline of history appeared in the early decades of the twentieth century

---

[20] While it is not usual practice to link early "pan-Africanist" literature to the later academic study of the African-Atlantic/Black Atlantic world, it is clear that the earlier writings provide the intellectual foundations and rationale for the profoundly political enterprise that this kind of work represents. For context, see Sterling Stuckey, "Black Americans and African Consciousness: DuBois, Woodson, and the Spell of Africa," *Negro Digest* 16, 4 (1967): 20–4, 60–74; Tiffany Ruby Patterson and Robin D. G. Kelley, "Unfinished Migrations: Reflections on the African Diaspora and the Making of the Modern World," *African Studies Review* 43, 1 (2000): 11–45; Brent Hayes Edwards, "The Uses of Diaspora," *Social Text* 19, 1 (2001): 45–73; James Sidbury, *Becoming African in America: Race and Nation in the Early Black Atlantic* (New York: Oxford University Press, 2007); Douglas B. Chambers, "The Black Atlantic: Theory, Method, and Practice," in *The Atlantic World, 1450–2000*, ed. Toyin Falola and Kevin D. Roberts (Bloomington: Indiana University Press, 2008), 151–73; Stephen G. Hall, *A Faithful Account of the Race: African American Historical Writing in Nineteenth-Century America* (Chapel Hill: University of North Carolina Press, 2009); and Kim D. Butler, "Clio and the Griot: The African Diaspora in the Discipline of History," in *The African Diaspora and the Disciplines*, ed. Tejumola Olaniyan and James H. Sweet (Bloomington: Indiana University Press, 2010), 21–52.

by leading African-American scholars including Carter G. Woodson, W.
E. B. DuBois, and others.[21] Soon after these innovators legitimated the
study of these historical ties as a basis for further analysis of shared identities and cultures, investigators extended research into other disciplines.
For example, the linguist Lorenzo Dow Turner conducted a pioneering
study of African-American speech in the coastal communities of South
Carolina and Georgia.[22] Further, the work of Melville J. Herskovits, an
anthropologist, proved especially effective in stimulating a contentious
dispute over the presence and nature of cultural practices that originated
in Africa ("Africanisms") and were retained in North America. While
the majority of his research in the Americas applied to Caribbean basin
societies and Brazil, he also integrated observations on North America in
his analyses.[23] The most basic assertion of the scholarship produced by
this cohort was that historical and cultural connections between Africa
and North America existed, and these connections mattered for people of
African descent in the present. Not everyone agreed, however. A contrary
perspective had been posited by the sociologist E. Franklin Frazier, who
indicated that African cultural influences in North America remained
only "Forgotten Memories" as "never before in history has a people been
so nearly completely stripped of its social heritage as were the Negroes
who were brought to America."[24]

Herskovits's attack of Frazier's position sparked what was sub-
sequently dubbed the Frazier-Herskovits debate. While this debate

---

[21] W. E. B. DuBois, *The Negro* (New York: Henry Holt and Company, 1915); Carter G.
Woodson, *The Negro in Our History*, 2d ed. (Washington, DC: Associated Publishers,
1922); Carter G. Woodson, *The African Background Outlined; or, Handbook for the
Study of the Negro* (Washington, DC: The Association for the Study of Negro Life and
History, 1936); and W. E. B. DuBois, *Black Folk, Then and Now: An Essay in the History
and Sociology of the Black Race* (New York: Henry Holt and Company, 1939). For
the political, intellectual, and institutional context that supported this work, see Robin
D.G. Kelley, "'But a Local Phase of a World Problem': Black History's Global Vision,
1883–1950," *Journal of American History* 86, 3 (1999): 1045–77; and Jason C. Parker,
"'Made-in-America Revolutions'? The 'Black University' and the American Role in
the Decolonization of the Black Atlantic," *Journal of American History* 96, 3 (2009):
727–50.
[22] Turner, *Africanisms*. The role of Turner in advancing the study of African linguistic and cultural influences during this early phase has been seriously underestimated.
See Margaret Wade-Lewis, *Lorenzo Dow Turner: Father of Gullah Studies* (Columbia:
University of South Carolina Press, 2007).
[23] Herskovits, *Myth of the Negro Past*.
[24] E. Franklin Frazier, *The Negro Family in the United States* (Chicago: University of
Chicago Press, 1939), 21. "Forgotten Memories" is the title of Chapter 1 in Frazier's
book.

ostensibly revolved around clashes in methodologies and research agendas, its heat derived from the contemporary political meanings associated with the assertion of the cultural independence of African-descended people. Frazier and others feared that the enemies of legal equality and social justice for African-Americans could take the work of Herskovits and claim the fundamental cultural difference of African-Americans as justification for continued separation, marginalization, and exclusion. Woodson, DuBois, Turner, and Herskovits in their own ways asserted that the recognition of a unique, vital history rooted in African civilizations and cultures could allow African-Americans to develop greater confidence and undermine claims of racial inferiority. This political context may be the most significant aspect of the debate, yet it has often been muted or even overlooked in the many recountings that have appeared in later scholarship, typically in passages that purport to discuss culture theory. The Frazier-Herskovits debate was not about contrasting theories of culture change, however. It was a debate about the politics of scholarship, and the "Negro Past" has long served as an intellectual battleground for larger political conflicts.[25]

While the Frazier-Herskovits debate does not always come up by name anymore, its residue remains in fundamental disagreements over the essential character of African-American cultures in the diaspora. As with the original debate, the divergence becomes a matter of emphasizing either the African or American more. This oversimplifies specific concerns with theory, method, and evidence, of course, but it captures the tone of the enduring quarrel. The terms of the discussion, however, have changed somewhat since the 1940s, following the emergence of a new concept in the late 1960s and 1970s to replace Frazier's position in the artificial dualism assigned to the dispute. The new concept came to be identified as "creolization." Creolization did not emerge from Frazier's argument, although both perspectives stressed the American over the African. While Frazier based his position on the supposed absence of any African cultural inheritance in North America, proponents of creolization have acknowledged African cultural input, yet subordinate it to the American component of African-American as evidence of the "miraculous" cultural

[25] Jonathan Scott Holloway, *Confronting the Veil: Abram Harris Jr., E. Franklin Frazier, and Ralph Bunche, 1919–1941* (Chapel Hill: University of North Carolina Press, 2002), 123–56; Jerry Gershenhorn, *Melville J. Herskovits and the Racial Politics of Knowledge* (Lincoln: University of Nebraska Press, 2004), 93–121; and Kevin A. Yelvington, "The Invention of Africa in Latin America and the Caribbean: Political Discourse and Anthropological Praxis, 1920–1940," in Yelvington, *Afro-Atlantic Dialogues*, 3–82.

past of African-descended people.[26] This generated the new terms of the argument, which pitted Africanisms and continuity against creolization and creativity. The irony inherent in this version of the debate is that both positions derived from the work of Herskovits.

The idea of creolization developed from an interesting mixture of scholarship produced by historians, linguists, and anthropologists who devised innovative ways to explain the unique cultural pasts of Caribbean societies. Edward Kamau Brathwaite articulated a process through which Africans, Europeans, and New World–born people participated in cultural reformation within the setting of plantation slavery in Jamaica. For Brathwaite, creolization entailed "a cultural action – material, psychological and spiritual – based upon the stimulus/response of individuals within the society to their environment and – as white/black, culturally discrete groups – to each other."[27] A similar vision of cultural interchange (not destruction or replacement, as portrayed by Frazier and others) informed the most influential text on creolization to date, an essay by Sidney W. Mintz and Richard Price that became the book *The Birth of African-American Culture*.[28] These anthropologists revisited the insights of Herskovits to emphasize local historical and social contexts in explaining the kinds of interactions that produced culture change. They departed from Herskovits, however, in diminishing the possibility that African newcomers retained an abiding attachment to their pre-captivity cultural lives and transmitted this commitment in some meaningful way to subsequent generations. Instead, the cultures of captive Africans "would have been a limited but crucial resource" and "could have served as a catalyst in the processes by which individuals from diverse societies forged new institutions, and could have provided certain frameworks within which new forms could have developed."[29]

Charles Joyner, an assertive supporter of creolization, applied the concept to frame his masterpiece *Down by the Riverside*, which remains one of the most imaginative and thorough treatments of African-American culture in South Carolina during the era of enslavement. Joyner's advocacy of creolization as an explanatory paradigm appears most clearly in

---

[26] For thoughts on the meanings and uses of creolization, see Richard Price, "On the Miracle of Creolization," in Yelvington, *Afro-Atlantic Dialogues: Anthropology in the Diaspora*, 115–47; and Charles Joyner, "Response," *Historically Speaking* 11, 3 (2010): 29–31.

[27] Edward Kamau Brathwaite, *The Development of Creole Society in Jamaica, 1770–1820* (Oxford: Clarendon Press, 1971), 296.

[28] Sidney W. Mintz and Richard Price, *The Birth of African-American Culture: An Anthropological Perspective* (Boston, MA: Beacon Press, 1992).

[29] Mintz and Price, *Birth of African-American Culture*, 14.

his charge, "To underestimate the Africanity of African-American culture is to rob the slaves of their heritage. But to overestimate the Africanity of that culture is to deny the slaves their creativity."[30] In his formulation, creativity deserves greater attention, as enslaved Africans were "[h]erded together with others with whom they shared only a common condition of servitude and some degree of cultural overlap...[and] were compelled to create a new language, a new religion, and a precarious new lifestyle."[31] Philip D. Morgan has gone beyond this position to assert that any emphasis on "Africanity" makes "excessive claims for the autonomy of slaves and the primacy of their African background. Ultimately, such an argument belittles the slaves' achievements by minimizing the staggering obstacles they faced in forging a culture."[32]

As with the earlier iterations of the Frazier-Herskovits debate, these sincere statements by creolizationists say far less about methodology than they reveal about the sentiments behind them. Above all, these scholars have valued the cultural agency of African-descended people. The proper way to highlight this, they contend, has been to stress creativity on the western side of the Atlantic where the circumstances of enslavement aligned against such a possibility. Michel-Rolph Trouillot penned the clearest expressions of this outlook when he wrote, "Creolization is a miracle begging for analysis."[33] With these few words, Trouillot articulated both the most powerful aspect of creolization and the greatest limitation of creolization theory. In the end, he cannot describe creolization as a method to explain the cultural past but only as an object of that cultural past that must be analyzed by other means.[34]

---

[30] Charles Joyner, "'Let Us Break Bread Together': Cultural Interaction in the Old South," in Charles Joyner, *Shared Traditions: Southern History and Folk Culture* (Urbana: University of Illinois Pres, 1999), 35.

[31] Charles Joyner, *Down by the Riverside: A South Carolina Slave Community* (Urbana: University of Illinois Press, 1984), xxi.

[32] Morgan, *Slave Counterpoint*, 657. For a more complex rendering of creolization, see Ira Berlin, *Many Thousands Gone: The First Two Centuries of Slavery in North America* (Cambridge, MA: Harvard University Press, 1998). See also, Philip D. Morgan, "The Cultural Implications of the Atlantic Slave Trade: African Regional Origins, American Destinations and New World Developments," *Slavery & Abolition* 18, 1 (1997): 122–45.

[33] Michel-Rolph Trouillot, "Culture on the Edges: Creolization in the Plantation Context," *Plantation Society in the Americas* 1, 1 (1998): 8.

[34] For provocative thoughts on the objectification of the cultural past, see David Scott, "That Event, This Memory: Notes on the Anthropology of African Diasporas in the New World," *Diaspora* 1, 3 (1991): 261–84; and David Scott, *Refashioning Futures: Criticism After Postcoloniality* (Princeton, NJ: Princeton University Press, 1999), 106–27.

The proponents of this vision of creolization have been in contentious dialogue with the other heirs of Herskovits, who have maintained the focus on African societies and cultures to explain cultural processes in the diaspora. Among those interested in early African-American communities in continental North America such as Sterling Stuckey, Gwendolyn Midlo Hall, Michael A. Gomez, John K. Thornton, Linda M. Heywood, Douglas B. Chambers, Walter C. Rucker, and Jason R. Young the unifying emphasis has been that "the knowledge and culture of Africans from particular coasts and ethnicities were not erased by the trans-Atlantic crossing."[35] From that starting point, each of these scholars has explored diverse facets of the ways the backgrounds of captive Africans provided fundamental resources for the recreation and elaboration of cultures and identities among those dispersed throughout the Atlantic world. In other words, the emphasis remains on the African in investigating African-American cultural histories.[36]

Lost in strident advocacy for either position, however, is the realization that both continuity and creativity entail cultural agency and represent normal interdependent processes. Nevertheless, the old quandary of highlighting either the African or American continues to color the debate over the making of African-American cultures in the same way that it influenced the original Frazier-Herskovits debate. At stake, it seems, is the identity of the African-American cultural past rather than the actual processes that produced African-American cultures. Indeed, recurring conflagrations over an essential African or American identity testify to

---

[35] Quote from Gwendolyn Midlo Hall, "Africa and Africans in the African Diaspora: The Uses of Relational Databases," *American Historical Review* 115, 1 (2010): 138. The works of the scholars cited include Sterling Stuckey, *Slave Culture*; Gwendolyn Midlo Hall, *Africans in Colonial Louisiana: The Development of Afro-Creole Culture in the Eighteenth Century* (Baton Rouge: Louisiana State University Press, 1992); John K. Thornton, *Africa and Africans in the Making of the Atlantic World, 1400–1800*, 2nd ed. (New York: Cambridge University Press, 1998); Gomez, *Exchanging Our Country Marks*; Douglas B. Chambers, *Murder at Montpelier: Igbo Africans in Virginia* (Jackson: University Press of Mississippi, 2005); Gwendolyn Midlo Hall, *Slavery and African Ethnicities in the Americas: Restoring the Links* (Chapel Hill: University of North Carolina Press, 2005); Walter C. Rucker, *The River Flows On: Black Resistance, Culture, and Identity Formation in Early America* (Baton Rouge: Louisiana State University Press, 2006); Linda M. Heywood and John K. Thornton, *Central Africans, Atlantic Creoles, and the Foundations of the Americas, 1585–1660* (New York: Cambridge University Press, 2007); and Young, *Rituals of Resistance*.

[36] Paul E. Lovejoy, "The African Diaspora: Revisionist Interpretation of Ethnicity, Culture and Religion under Slavery," *Studies in the World History of Slavery, Abolition and Emancipation* 2, 1 (1997) (http://www.yorku.ca/nhp/publications/Lovejoy_Studies%20in%20the%20World%20History%20of%20Slavery.pdf).

the powerful meanings attached to interpreting the cultural histories of African-descended people.[37]

This book relies on the productive tension produced by interpretations of the processes of continuity and creativity in both the African and American aspects of early African-American culture in South Carolina. The Lowcountry simbi embodied this tension, as they originated in West-Central Africa, arrived in the minds of the Kongo captives, and then became a variety of spirits and beings rooted firmly in the landscape of the Lowcountry. As we will see throughout this book, a deep excavation of the intellectual and cultural material that people of African descent have relied upon in forming their understandings of the spiritual meanings of the landscape provides an ideal context for exploring cultural processes that have intricately bound the African and American together.

The simbi entered this complex cultural history of the Lowcountry during a long polycultural period that extended from the original settlement of Europeans and captive Africans in the late seventeenth century into the early decades of the nineteenth century. During the initial stage of this period, newcomers from diverse African, European, and Atlantic societies formed both contentious and cooperative relationships with local indigenous peoples and Native captives taken to Carolina from various inland areas of North America. As the colonization of the coastal plain expanded, captives from West-Central Africa and West Africa predominated among all newcomers, thus reinforcing a degree of cultural heterogeneity built largely from African antecedents. Through this period, varied forms of contact between people of such diverse backgrounds ensured that the early Lowcountry was a polycultural society for several generations. Following the insights of Michael A. Gomez on colonial-era cultural processes, the polyculturalism of the early Lowcountry functioned on at least two levels for African-descended people. At one level, they had to engage the cultural realm of the politically dominant enslavers. On a second level, they lived within another dimension of diversity comprised of African-descended people from various African societies

[37] For those who assume that this matter is (or should be) tired, stale, or dead, see the insightful observations of Kenneth Bilby, "African American Memory at the Crossroads: Grounding the Miraculous with Tooy," *Small Axe* 13, 2 (2009): 185–99. See also, Joseph C. Miller, "Retention, Reinvention, and Remembering: Restoring Identities Through Enslavement in Africa and Under Slavery in Brazil," in *Enslaving Connections: Changing Cultures of Africa and Brazil during the Era of Slavery*, ed. José C. Curto and Paul E. Lovejoy (Amherst, NY: Prometheus/Humanity Press, 2004), 81–121; and Stephan Palmié, "Creolization and Its Discontents," *Annual Review of Anthropology* 35 (2006): 433–56.

and those born in the Lowcountry. The first level engendered a "culture of coercion" that reflected the power disparities inherent in enslavement and appeared in contexts visible to enslavers and others of European descent. The latter level, however, entailed much greater cultural agency within African-descended communities and resulted in "cultures of volition" that remained invisible to outsiders.[38] As long as African newcomers continued to disembark the "floating tombs" that carried them across the Atlantic to South Carolina, this second domain of polyculturalism among African-descended people would persist as an especially vibrant and at times contentious setting for cultural dialogues.[39]

In addition to the coexistence, interaction, and transformation of groups from varied cultural backgrounds and places of power in Lowcountry society, we find many individuals who led polycultural lives as they communicated between and across cultures without necessarily attempting to reinterpret these influences into the formation of a single, "new" culture. This polycultural orientation derived from the dynamics of contact seen in Africa during the era of the trans-Atlantic trade in captives, particularly in West-Central Africa. Linda M. Heywood and John K. Thornton have characterized the interactions of West-Central Africans and Europeans as a kind of creolization that affected broad areas and many communities on the eastern side of the Atlantic world before many of the people of that region entered the Atlantic realm as captives.[40] Certainly, a number of individuals in West-Central Africa formulated and embraced thorough mixtures of diverse cultural influences in ways that could be identified as creolization, especially in those populations that embodied the physical coexistence and convergence of Africans and Europeans. Yet, we may more productively see the larger West-Central African context examined by Heywood and Thornton as having been polycultural rather than syncretic. A recurring pattern in African-Atlantic societies has been the creation of space in their cultures for new ideas and practices that accommodated differences and preserved access to a larger range of cultural options. This has resulted in the elaboration of parallel

---

[38] Gomez, *Exchanging Our Country Marks*, 9–10.

[39] "Floating tombs" comes from Joseph C. Miller, *Way of Death: Merchant Capitalism and the Angolan Slave Trade, 1730–1830* (Madison: University of Wisconsin Press, 1988), 314.

[40] Linda M. Heywood, "Portuguese into African: The Eighteenth-Century Central African Background to Atlantic Creole Cultures," in Heywood, *Central Africans and Cultural Transformations*, 91–113; and Heywood and Thornton, *Central Africans, Atlantic Creoles*, graphically represented in maps on pp. 227–35.

cultural "arenas," in which "participants come and go."[41] While in some instances this polycultural dynamic may have stimulated the phenomon we call creolization, people in Africa and the diaspora did not necessarily attempt to resolve cultural differences through monocultural processes, as has been assumed in some prominent models of cultural change.[42]

Striking examples of the polycultural dynamic in West-Central Africa appear in the responses to missionary Catholicism during the late seventeenth century and early eighteenth century.[43] In the state of Soyo, located along the lower course of the Nzadi River, the monocultural perspective of European missionaries clashed with West-Central African notions of the interaction of spiritual cultures. As a reaction to the detection of the operations and sacred sites of male and female "fetishers" (*banganga*, or spiritual experts), missionaries under the authority of the Prince of Soyo offered a sort of spiritual amnesty to those who revealed themselves as worshipers of "idols" and presented their consecrated objects for public burning. After destroying these "idols and other instruments," the missionaries convened an assembly of those who submitted to this offer of pardon to determine the state of their conviction to Roman Catholic doctrine and authority. The missionaries asked if the people wished "either to observe the laws of God or to observe their superstitious ceremonies." The group expressed their strong devotion to the Christian god and the teachings of the missionaries, yet stated that they continued to

---

[41] Sandra T. Barnes, "The Many Faces of Ogun: Introduction to the First Edition," in *Africa's Ogun: Old World and New*, 2nd edition, ed. Sandra T. Barnes (Bloomington: Indiana University Press, 1997), 10–11. See also, James H. Sweet, *Recreating Africa: Culture, Kinship, and Religion in the African-Portuguese World, 1441–1770* (Chapel Hill: University of North Carolina Press, 2003), 113–15.

[42] For indications of this in the diaspora, see Leslie G. Desmangles, *The Faces of the Gods: Vodou and Roman Catholicism in Haiti* (Chapel Hill: University of North Carolina Press, 1992), 8–11; David H. Brown, *Santería Enthroned: Art, Ritual, and Innovation in an Afro-Cuban Religion* (Chicago: University of Chicago Press, 2003), 71; and Stefania Capone, *Searching for Africa in Brazil: Power and Tradition in Candomblé*, trans. Lucy Lyall Grant (Durham, NC: Duke University Press, 2010), 7–9.

[43] For the larger context of Christianity in West-Central Africa during this era, see John K. Thornton, "The Development of an African Catholic Church in the Kingdom of Kongo, 1491–1750," *Journal of African History* 25, 2 (1984): 147–67; Anne Hilton, *The Kingdom of Kongo* (Oxford: Clarendon Press, 1985), 51–3, 60–5, 90–103, 136–41, 154–61, 179–98, 202–8, 216–20; Richard Gray, *Black Christians, White Missionaries* (New Haven, CT: Yale University Press, 1990); John K. Thornton, "Religious and Ceremonial Life in the Kongo and Mbundu Areas, 1500–1700," in Heywood, *Central Africans and Cultural Transformations*, 83–91; Kabolo Iko Kwabita, *Le royaume Kongo et la mission catholique, 1750–1838: Du déclin à l'extinction* (Paris: Éditions Karthala, 2004); and Heywood and Thornton, *Central Africans*, 49–108, 169–235.

value "their ceremonies and vain observances."[44] While the missionaries demanded a choice of one or the other, this group expressed the preference for one and the other. This represented neither the replacement of the old spiritual culture with a new spiritual culture nor the development of a novel synthesis of both to create a creolized religion. Instead, it revealed a polycultural approach to cultivating a growing religious field that could readily accommodate local spiritual cultures and those brought from other contexts.

The notion of a polycultural orientation should not be perceived as a denial of the transformative power of cultural interaction and change. To the contrary, the continuous dialogue among African and European spiritual cultures produced the early eighteenth-century movement of Dona Beatriz Kimpa Vita that very much represented an innovative synthesis of traditional Kongo and Roman Catholic religion as chronicled in the elegant volume *The Kongolese Saint Anthony* by Thornton.[45] Its meanings, however, grew from its place in the larger Kongo spiritual context, in which the Antonian movement could be seen by Roman Catholic missionaries as a heresy (thus, a Christian, though unorthodox, movement) and at the same time be understood by people in many parts of Kongo through familiar traditional ideas and practices. In this case, creolization occurred within a polycultural setting, though not as an entirely separate process and certainly not as the only outcome of cultural interaction.

West-Central Africans taken to the Lowcountry came from this polycultural setting with its long engagement with Atlantic influences, and other captives had experienced similar circumstances in various parts of West Africa. We must assume that they brought this approach to dealing with intercultural communication with them in addition to the ideas and practices that developed in their home societies as a result of this same dynamic. While the many cultures present in the Lowcountry did not always contribute to new cultural forms, did not always merge with other cultures to form syncretic expressions, and in many cases did not even experience transmission to subsequent generations, the dynamic of communication among cultures established during this polycultural period provided the foundation for a subsequent transitional era that

---

[44] Andrea da Pavia, "Rapport circonstancié d'Andrea da Pavia aux cardinaux de la Propagande à son retour du Congo," in "Andrea da Pavia au Congo, à Lisbonne, à Madère. Journal d'un Missionaire Capucin, 1685–1702," ed. and trans. Louis Jadin, *Bulletin de l'Institute Historique Belge de Rome* 41 (1970): 551–2.

[45] John K. Thornton, *The Kongolese Saint Anthony: Dona Beatriz Kimpa Vita and the Antonian Movement, 1684–1706* (New York: Cambridge University Press, 1998).

corresponded with two major demographic trends. As Lowcountry-born people continued to grow into a larger majority of the African-descended population and African newcomers ceased to arrive in large numbers, the polycultural society gave way to a more unified culture during the first few decades of the nineteenth century. Further, as some aspects of the earlier era faded, others converged into more focused or narrow expressions in what scholars now often recognize as a creolized Black Lowcountry culture.

In St. John's Berkeley parish, the simbi emerged from the polycultural period intact and in manifestations consonant with earlier Kongo forms of nature spirits. Even after this section of the Lowcountry had experienced the influx of diverse Africans and large increase of Carolina-born people over several generations, the African-descended communities of the parish continued to accept the simbi as the most prominent way to talk about nature spirits. They did so in part because the Kongo people who first identified the simbi in the Lowcountry were involved in the earliest dialogue about nature spirits that established an influential precedent, but also because Kongo people continued to have a prominent voice in that ongoing dialogue with the continuing arrival of West-Central Africans in South Carolina throughout the eighteenth century and early nineteenth century. Just as important as these factors, though, was the interest in nature spirits shared by most of the West-Central Africans and West Africans who found themselves thrust together in a strange, new land. While these people had notions about the characteristics and roles of nature spirits specific to their home cultures, they also held in common key ideas about the centrality of nature spirits to daily existence. Nature spirits, then, represented not only a high priority in the reconstitution of spiritual cultures, but also a common topic on which diverse Africans could communicate with each other in the formation of their communities and the elaboration of their early polycultural society. We find reflections of this polycultural past in the continuing significance of the simbi in St. John's Berkeley parish, the presence of the Mende *ngafa* spirits and Igbo *juju* spirits in coastal communities, and the vast array of powerful spirits of undetermined origins that populated the Lowcountry landscape well into the twentieth century.[46]

---

[46] The presence of ngafa and juju spirits is documented in Turner, *Africanisms*, 193, 195. For others spirits associated with the natural environment, see Writers' Program of the Work Projects Administration in the State of South Carolina, *South Carolina Folk Tales: Stories of Animals and Supernatural Beings* (Columbia: University of South Carolina, 1941).

These indications of a polycultural dialogue about nature spirits and the enduring resonance of the meanings of the *simbi* in nineteenth-century Black Lowcountry culture testify to the varied ways that people of African descent have engaged the land and waters of the Lowcountry. The historical relationship between African-descended communities and the natural environment and reformed landscapes of the Lowcountry has long been a focus of research. Almost all of the people made captive and carried from Africa came from societies that relied on planting or herding, which ensured that their understandings of farming would have remained essential in their adaptations to the work regimes and living conditions in enslavement. Several innovative projects have put the agricultural knowledge and work of enslaved people at the center of analysis providing insight into the technology, labor conditions, and social and cultural practices associated with the functioning of plantation agriculture. Those dealing with rice cultivation, such as Peter H. Wood, Daniel C. Littlefield, Judith A. Carney, S. Max Edelson, David Eltis, Philip Morgan, and David Richardson have explored and argued about the development of this core feature of Lowcountry slavery and its possible connections to the expertise introduced and disseminated by African-descended people. Frederick C. Knight has extended the position of Wood, Littlefield, and Carney to argue that this kind of influence by African-descended people applied to other key crops throughout the Anglo-Atlantic world.[47]

Just as the emphasis on planting has reflected an enduring theme in the agricultural history of the South Carolina Lowcountry (and the South generally), it has also served as a core component of both Southern environmental history and the emerging area of African-American environmental

---

[47] Wood, *Black Majority*; Littlefield, *Rice and Slaves*; Carney, *Black Rice*; Edelson, *Plantation Enterprise*; David Eltis, Philip Morgan, and David Richardson, "Agency and Diaspora in Atlantic History: Reassessing the African Contribution to Rice Cultivation in the Americas," *American Historical Review* 112, 5 (2007): 1329–58; and Frederick C. Knight, *Working the Diaspora: The Impact of African Labor on the Anglo-American World, 1650–1850* (New York: New York University Press, 2010). See also the series of essays on Judith A. Carney's "black rice" argument, including David Eltis, Philip Morgan, and David Richardson, "Black, Brown, or White? Color-Coding American Commercial Rice Cultivation with Slave Labor," *American Historical Review* 115, 1 (2010): 164–71; S. Max Edelson, "Beyond 'Black Rice': Reconstructing Material and Cultural Contexts for Early Plantation Agriculture," *American Historical Review* 115, 1 (2010): 125–35; Hall, "Africa and Africans," 136–50; and Walter Hawthorne, "From 'Black Rice' to 'Brown': Rethinking the History of Risiculture in the Seventeenth- and Eighteenth-Century Atlantic," *American Historical Review* 115, 1 (2010): 151–63.

history.[48] A few scholars whose work embraces the particular interests of African-American environmental history have looked beyond agriculture and the work of slavery to explore perceptions of the natural environment as part of the contested terrain of power struggles between the enslaved and enslavers.[49] Others have plumbed the literary and political thought of influential African-American voices to find additional meanings attached to the landscape.[50] The vast majority of this work pertains to the nineteenth century and afterward given the limited store of revealing written sources. This leaves incomplete the effort to recover older fundamental meanings attached to the relationship between people and the natural world within the African-Atlantic cultures that informed later concepts and actions. As it turns out, much of what is commonly restricted to the topic of "religion" encompasses this rich cultural background, an insight that only a small number of prescient scholars of early African America have developed to any appreciable degree.[51]

---

[48] Albert Cowdrey, *This Land, This South: An Environmental History* (Lexington: University of Kentucky Press, 1983); Timothy Silver, *A New Face on the Countryside: Indians, Colonists, and Slaves in the South Atlantic Forests, 1500–1800* (New York: Cambridge University Press, 1990); Mart A. Stewart, "Southern Environmental History," in *A Companion to the American South*, ed. John B. Boles (Malden, MA: Blackwell, 2002), 409–23; Timothy Silver, "Learning to Live with Nature: Colonial Historians and the Southern Environment," *Journal of Southern History* 73, 3 (2007): 539–52; and Christopher Morris, "A More Southern Environmental History." *Journal of Southern History* 75, 3 (2009): 581–98.

[49] For historical studies of the meanings of "space," see Joyner, *Down by the Riverside*, 117–26; Mechal Sobel in *World They Made Together*, 71–126; John Michael Vlach, *Back of the Big House: The Architecture of Plantation Slavery* (Chapel Hill: University of North Carolina Press, 1993); Stewart, *What Nature Suffers to Groe*; Morgan, *Slave Counterpoint*, 475–76, 519–30; Elizabeth Blum, "Power, Danger, Control: Slave Women's Perceptions of Wilderness in the Nineteenth Century," *Women's Studies* 31, 2 (2002): 247–65; Anthony E. Kaye, *Joining Places: Slave Neighborhoods in the Old South* (Chapel Hill: University of North Carolina Press, 2007), and Scott E. Giltner, *Hunting and Fishing in the New South: Black Labor and White Leisure after the Civil War* (Baltimore: Johns Hopkins University Press, 2008).

[50] Kimberly K. Smith, *African American Environmental Thought: Foundations* (Lawrence: University Press of Kansas, 2007); and Dianne D. Glave, *Rooted in the Earth: Reclaiming the African American Environmental Heritage* (Chicago: Chicago Review Press, 2010).

[51] Most notably Sobel's *The World They Made Together*, 71–126; Dianne D. Glave, "African Diaspora Studies," *Environmental History* 10, 4 (2005): 692–4; Mark Stoll, "Religion and African American Environmental Activism," in *"To Love the Wind and the Rain": African Americans and Environmental History*, ed. Dianne D. Glave and Mark Stoll (Pittsburgh, PA: University of Pittsburgh Press, 2006), 150–63; Dianne D. Glave, "Black Environmental Liberation Theology," in Glave and Stoll, *To Love the Wind*, 189–99; Jason Taylor Carson, *Making An Atlantic World: Circles, Paths, and Stories from the Colonial South* (Knoxville: University of Tennessee Press, 2007), 34–44; and Knight, *Working the Diaspora*, 131–53. Explorations of this for other parts of the diaspora

INTERPRETING SPIRITS

Studies of the formative era of African-American spiritual cultures in the eighteenth and early nineteenth centuries have gained greater sophistication, especially as scholars have pursued detailed explorations of the specific cultures of founding generations of African newcomers that shaped early expressions of spirituality in the Lowcountry.[52] The notable influence of West-Central Africans, particularly people from Kongo, has featured centrally in these works. Conspicuously absent or largely overlooked, however, are the *simbi*.[53] This neglect results in large part from an elementary misunderstanding of the significance of nature spirits in West-Central African (and West African, for that matter) religious thought and

include Lydia Cabrera, *El Monte (Igbo – Finda, Ewe Orisha, Vititi Nfinda)* (Miami, FL: Ediciones Universal, 1975); John Rashford, "Plants, Spirits and the Meaning of 'John' in Jamaica," *Jamaica Journal* 17, 2 (1984): 62–70; John Rashford, "The Cotton Tree and the Spiritual Realm in Jamaica," *Jamaica Journal* 18, 1 (1985): 49–57; George Brandon, "The Uses of Plants in Healing in an Afro-Cuba Religion, Santería," *Journal of Black Studies* 22, 1 (1991): 55–76; Robert A. Voeks, *Sacred Leaves of Candomblé: African Magic, Medicine, and Religion in Brazil* (Austin: University of Texas Press, 1997); and Arvilla Payne-Jackson and Mervyn C. Alleyne, *Jamaican Folk Medicine: A Source of Healing* (Kingston, JA: University of the West Indies Press, 2004).

[52] Joyner, *Down by the Riverside*; Stuckey, *Slave Culture*; Creel, *Peculiar People*; Mechal Sobel, *Trabelin' On: The Slave Journey to an Afro-Baptist Faith* (Princeton, NJ: Princeton University Press, 1988); Charles Joyner, "'Believer I Know': The Emergence of African-American Christianity," in *African-American Christianity: Essays in History*, ed. Paul E. Johnson (Berkeley: University of California Press, 1994), 18–46; Sylvia R. Frey and Betty Wood, *Come Shouting to Zion: African American Protestantism in the American South and British Caribbean to 1830* (Chapel Hill: University of North Carolina Press, 1998); Gomez, *Exchanging Our Country Marks*; Morgan, *Slave Counterpoint*, 610–58; Raboteau, *Slave Religion*; Michael A. Gomez, *Black Crescent: The Experience and Legacy of African Muslims in the Americas* (New York: Cambridge University Press, 2005), 143–84; and Young, *Rituals of Resistance*. For those works that give particular attention to Anglican relations with enslaved people in South Carolina and the British Atlantic during the eighteenth century, see Creel, *Peculiar People*, 67–76; Frey and Wood, *Come Shouting to Zion*, 63–79; Robert Olwell, *Masters, Slaves, and Subjects: The Culture of Power in the South Carolina Low Country, 1740–1790* (Ithaca, NY: Cornell University Press, 1998), 103–39; and Annette Laing, "'Heathens and Infidels'? African Christianization and Anglicanism in the South Carolina Low Country, 1700–1750," *Religion and American Culture* 12, 2 (2002): 197–228. For context, see Jon F. Sensbach, "Religion and the Early South in an Age of Atlantic Empire," *Journal of Southern History* 73, 3 (2007): 631–42.

[53] Sparse references to the Lowcountry *simbi* in secondary sources appear in John W. Blassingame, *The Slave Community: Plantation Life in the Antebellum South*, 2d ed. (New York: Oxford University Press, 1979), 40; Robert Farris Thompson, "Bighearted Power: Kongo Presence in the Landscape and Art of Black America," in Gundaker, *Keep Your Head to the Sky*, 61; Brown, "Walk in the Feenda," 312–13; and Young, *Rituals of Resistance*, 83–4.

practice. The problem may be explained by three factors, which include the misidentification of nature spirits as merely subordinate or intermediary entities, the inability to locate nature spirits in the dialogue between African and European spiritual cultures, and the dismissal of nature spirits as an important aspect of African-Atlantic religious history.

The inattentiveness to the core meanings of the *simbi* becomes most clear in the common phrasing among scholars of referring to nature spirits or local spirits as "lesser deities" or "lesser spirits" and so on. The "lesser" designation comes from the supposed subordination of these spirits to a high, creator god that corresponds in key ways to Christian and Islamic perceptions of a monotheistic god.[54] The implication of a hierarchy of spirits likely derives from the initial attempts of European missionaries to comprehend local African spiritual cultures. Certainly, West-Central Africans at home and in diaspora held ideas about the great spirit Nzambi Mpungo, who exists everywhere and ultimately animates everything. These ideas allowed Africans to engage in "god talk" with missionaries.[55] We should hesitate, however, to presume certain relationships of this spirit to other spirits simply because the translation "god" appealed to the sensibilities and agendas of missionaries. The body of assumptions about monotheistic divinity inherent in Abrahamic theologies did not matter in West-Central African spiritual cultures. Nzambi Mpungo did not exist in the same hierarchy-based universe as the omniscient, omnipotent god of Judaism, Christianity, and Islam. A hierarchy may be intellectualized in some effort to impose "order" on spirits, but this does not correspond with the ways that people in West-Central Africa have lived their spiritual cultures. Little in the practices of people paying respect and making offerings to nature or territorial spirits indicates that

---

[54] Thornton, *Africa and Africans*, 251–2; Frey and Wood, *Come Shouting to Zion*, 11, 32; Morgan, *Slave Counterpoint*, 610, 612, 630, 657; Thornton, "Religious and Ceremonial Life," 75; Sweet, *Recreating Africa*, 107; and Raboteau, *Slave Religion*, 8–9, 17. The popularity of this characterization may be attributed to the influential work of Robin Horton best represented in the collection of his essays in *Patterns of Thought in Africa and the West: Essays on Magic, Religion and Science* (Cambridge: Cambridge University Press, 1993), 166–84.

[55] Christian Georg Andreas Oldendorp, *Historie der caribischen Inseln Sanct Thomas, Sanct Crux und Sanct Jan, insbesondere der dasigen Neger und der Mission der ecangelischen Brüder unter denselben*, ed. Gudrun Meier, Stephan Palmié, Peter Stein, and Horst Ulbricht (Berlin: Verlag für Wissenschaft und Bildung, 2000), 1: 438, 443, 446, 448, 462; and Hilton, *Kingdom of Kongo*, 91–2. See additional commentaries in MacGaffey, *Religion and Society*, 78–9; and Todd Ramón Ocha, *Society of the Dead: Quita Manaquita and Palo Praise in Cuba* (Berkeley: University of California Press, 2010), 267n.25.

they considered these entities subordinate to any other power. Moreover, the complex and changing perceptions of these entities over time suggest that people have not found much value in defining rigid hierarchies and classifications for "gods," "spirits," and "deities" outside of individual initiation societies and local political institutions.[56]

Complicating the matter further have been the preconceptions of many scholars about what constitutes "religion." The basic problem with "religion" remains that the word and its extensive web of assumptions and connotations derive from the particular historical experiences connected to the "encounter between Westerners and peoples who apparently had *different* religions."[57] As a product of difference-making constructed from these culturally and historically specific contexts, "religion" cannot serve as an unproblematic term or concept or as a generic category for understanding experience. Further, the use of "religion" usually introduces a "general template of Judeo-Christian forms and evaluations" as the basis for a supposedly neutral framework of analysis, even in cases when scholars intend to avoid such a bias.[58]

Intentional or not, this template has had its effect as the simbi have become marginalized as "lesser spirits" and effectively silenced as essential agents in the spiritual cultures of African-descended people in the Americas, at least in the work of scholars. This tendency becomes more pronounced as researchers have often tried to explain the transition from

[56] Louis Brenner, "'Religious' Discourses in and about Africa," in *Discourse and Its Disguises: The Interpretation of African Oral Texts*, ed. Karin Barber and P.F. de Moraes Farias (Birmingham: Centre of West African Studies, Birmingham University, 1989), 91–5; Rosalind Shaw, "The Invention of 'African Traditional Religion'," *Religion* 20, 4 (1990): 347–9; and Dunja Hersak, "There Are Many Kongo Worlds: Particularities of Magico-Religious Beliefs Among The Vili and Yombe of Congo-Brazzaville," *Africa* 71, 4 (2001): 614–40.

[57] Paul Landau, "'Religion' and Christian Conversion in African History: A New Model," *Journal of Religious History* 23, 1 (1999): 13. Other scholars have drawn attention to "religion" as a construct including Brenner, "Religious Discourses," 87–99; and Talal Asad, *Genealogies of Religion: Discipline and Reasons of Power in Christianity and Islam* (Baltimore, MD: Johns Hopkins University Press, 1993), 27–54. Although "religion" is a problematic term, I follow the scholars cited here in continuing to employ the word once the concerns with its use have been acknowledged.

[58] Shaw, "Invention of African Traditional Religion," 344; Aisha Khan, "Isms and Schisms: Interpreting Religion in the Americas," *Anthropological Quarterly* 76, 4 (2003): 768–70; and Nile Green and Mary Searle-Chatterjee, "Religion, Language, and Power: An Introductory Essay," in *Religion, Language, and Power*, ed. Nile Green and Mary Searle-Chatterjee (New York: Routledge, 2008), 1–23. For historians interested in early written sources on West-Central African spiritual cultures, see the insightful observations in Anne Hilton, "European Sources for the Study of Religious Change in Sixteenth and Seventeenth Century Kongo," *Paideuma* 33 (1987): 289–312.

"traditional" religion to Christianity in North America by finding points of correspondence between African and Christian cosmologies.[59] While the simbi may resemble the saints in Roman Catholicism, they correspond with nothing in Protestant Christianity, especially the evangelical forms that gained large numbers of African-descended followers in the nineteenth century. As we will see in Chapter 5, the simbi were indeed part of this transition in the Lowcountry, but did not survive for more than a couple of generations. The inability to see the simbi as essential to the spiritual dialogue, however, precludes any consideration of this process altogether. Further, this blind spot in the vision of scholars implies that the simbi did not matter in the cultures of captives and their descendants.

How could such a significant aspect of Kongo culture simply cease to matter in the diaspora? Rather than either presume that a "spiritual holocaust" answers the question or simply avoid the issue, we must begin with the understanding that the simbi did continue to matter and that the meanings and forms attached to the simbi changed in ways not readily apparent to those disinclined to see the simbi in the first place. The fact that the simbi remained key entities in the cultures of African-descended people in geographically and linguistically diverse places throughout the African-Atlantic diaspora suggests that we must be prepared to see the simbi and then make the effort to explain how they transformed into ambiguous forms or failed to take root at all in some locations.[60]

---

[59] On this transition and the expanding influence of Protestant Christianity in the Lowcountry, see Creel, *Peculiar People*; Joyner, "Believer I Know," 18–46; Frey and Wood, *Come Shouting to Zion*, 63–79, 89–92, 112–16, 156–61; and Young, *Rituals of Resistance*, 67–103. Others have focused on interactions between African and Roman Catholic ideas and practices in Africa. See John K. Thornton, "On the Trail of Voodoo: African Christianity in Africa and the Americas," *The Americas* 44, 3 (1988): 261–78; Mark M. Smith, "Remembering Mary, Shaping Revolt: Reconsidering the Stono Rebellion," *Journal of Southern History* 67, 3 (2001): 513–34; John K. Thornton, "Religious and Ceremonial Life," 83–90; Heywood, "Portuguese into African," 91–113; and Young, *Rituals of Resistance*, 46–66. The correlation of the saints and nature spirits appears in the works of Heywood and Thornton, though the implications of this association for diaspora religions are not explored.

[60] "Spiritual holocaust" comes from Jon Butler, *Awash in a Sea of Faith: Christianizing the American People* (Cambridge, MA: Harvard University Press, 1990), 129–63. For a more productive perspective, see Jon F. Sensbach, "Before the Bible Belt: Indians, Africans, and the New Synthesis of Eighteenth-Century Southern Religious History," in *Religion in the American South: Protestants and Others in History and Culture*, ed. Beth Barton Schweiger and Donald G. Mathews (Chapel Hill: University of North Carolina Press, 2004), 13–15.

Additionally, the simbi and similar beings have not registered in studies of the culture of African-descended people in Protestant Atlantic societies. This is not only because they have been misperceived as "lesser deities," but also because they can be dismissed as mere "nature spirits." The category of "nature spirits" just does not seem to register as significant or serious enough for many scholars of African-Atlantic spiritual cultures to examine fully. The fact remains that the ubiquitous shrines and beings that early European visitors to West Africa and West-Central Africa described as "idols," "fetishes," and "demons" represented what can be characterized generally as nature spirits – that is, beings who emanated from and influenced the workings of the natural environment.[61] The designation "nature spirits" may not be entirely unproblematic, however. As one expert on the simbi has argued, terms such as "local" or "territorial" spirits to identify these beings function as more accurate descriptors than does "nature" as a modifier for the spirits.[62] This certainly holds true for the shrine-based spirits in the Lower Nzadi region, along the Loango Coast, and in parts of Angola described in historical sources where the physical sites dedicated to certain entities consisted of built or modified structures. Spirits like these, including the *nkisi si* ("nkisi of the land") and some *kilundu* discussed in Chapter 3, influenced the peoples and environments of their localities or territories based on their interactions with the living at their shrines. But the simbi of Kongo have deviated from many of their spirit kin and neighbors on this matter. As mentioned above, the simbi have usually occupied features of the natural environment, particularly pools (of springs and waterfalls), rivers, streams, rocks, stones, forests, and mountains. It was in these locations that people encountered the simbi, whether the living sought out the simbi intentionally or stumbled upon them accidentally. But like the shrine-based spirits of West-Central Africa, the simbi also affected the weather and the condition of the flora and fauna, thus controlling to a certain extent the natural environment. For the simbi, then, the designation of nature spirits is most appropriate as their abodes and domains of power were indeed found in "nature."

---

[61] Thornton, *Africa and Africans*, 252–3; Rosalind Shaw, *Memories of the Slave Trade: Ritual and the Historical Imagination in Sierra Leone* (Chicago, IL: University of Chicago Press, 2002), 52–4, 72, 79, 211, 213; Thornton, "Religious and Ceremonial Life," 77–8; Robin Law, *Ouidah: The Social History of a West African Slaving "Port," 1727–1892* (Athens: Ohio University Press, 2004), 88; Heywood and Thornton, *Central Africans*, 59, 62–3, 79, 100; and Carson, *Making an Atlantic World*, 34–7.

[62] MacGaffey, "Twins, Simbi Spirits, and Lwas," 212.

This should not mislead us, however, to presume that the simbi remained detached from the realm of people and sheltered in the pristine wilderness, a notion often evoked by the use of the terms "nature" and "natural." The connections between the simbi and the living remained an essential feature of the existence of the simbi and represented the very complicated relationship between the living and the natural environment as experienced in both physical and spiritual ways. Above all, regardless of the distinctions between the labels "nature spirit," "local spirit," and "territorial spirit," these terms still indicate that the simbi, the nkisi, the kilundu, and all the other similar entities in West-Central Africa and West Africa are spirits of place and that the places attached to these spirits, whether built shrines or natural landmarks, are places of power for the living.[63]

This identification of the simbi as nature spirits introduces another dimension of Kongo culture that cannot be fully apprehended through the analytical prism of "religion" favored by most scholars. A Western, Christian conception of "religion" as essentially metaphysical and separate from other core spheres of experience assigns the beings and forces of the land of the dead to the realm of the "supernatural." In this conception, the idea of the supernatural does more than provide a cognate for the "spiritual"; it poses a fundamental divide between the physical, natural and the invisible, spiritual domains.[64] Kongo cultures, however, acknowledge no such duality. Instead, the world consists of the visible and the invisible intertwined in the same space. The land of the living and the land of the dead do not represent two separate worlds. They coexist as two places within one space. This one space, the natural world, encompasses both the visible and invisible, the physical and the spiritual. In essence, when entering the land of the dead, a person does not go somewhere else, but instead experiences the same space in a new, comprehensive way as the visible and invisible both become apparent. Following this understanding, it becomes possible to see a river as a natural physical body of water that does what all rivers do and to perceive that same river as a "supernatural" path to the land of the dead where the normal dimensions of the visible realm give way to other understandings of time, space, and power. But experiencing the river as a portal to the land of the dead

---

[63] The phrase "places of power" comes from Elizabeth Colson, "Places of Power and Shrines of the Land," *Paideuma* 43 (1997): 48–53, although I employ it in a sense different from that advocated by Colson.

[64] Aisha Khan, *Callaloo Nation: Metaphors of Race and Religious Identity among South Asians in Trinidad* (Durham, NC: Duke University Press, 2004), 22–3.

is hardly "supernatural" as this is to be expected of almost any body of water, and thus it is essentially natural. It is the normal state of bodies of water to allow for the flow of people and power between the land of the dead and the land of the living. The supposed divide of the natural from the supernatural does not exist as all that is natural is at once physical *and* spiritual. The simbi embody the fundamental meaning of this idea. The simbi are no less natural to the landscape than rivers, rocks, trees, plants, animals, the earth, the sky, and the rain. And they remind and reassure the living that the natural environment encompassing all human experience represents a place that can sustain them materially and a place that can empower them spiritually.

Understanding the fundamental significance of the simbi and other nature spirits to West-Central African and West African religious expressions requires scholars of African diaspora spiritual cultures to do far more than mention nature spirits and then set them aside. The essential roles attributed to the nature spirits demand that any examination of the interactions of African-descended people with their natural surroundings must be grounded in a substantial knowledge of spiritual thought and practice. Thus, in order to fully explore African-inspired religions in the diaspora we must also examine the environmental cultures of people of African descent. And at the same time that we study the early forms of their interactions with their natural surroundings, we have to consider the spiritual dimensions of physical engagement with the land. The simbi and their fellow nature spirits of other backgrounds link these two domains.

While we will appraise the simbi primarily in their manifestations as nature spirits, we must remain prepared to see them in their many guises. The simbi have served as a means for the living to engage all kinds of spiritual issues, to talk about the past in spiritual terms, and to bring spiritual solutions to common problems encountered in the present. This wide range of roles has allowed people to perceive and portray the simbi as nature spirits as well as local shrine spirits, ancestral spirits, non-lineal spirits of the dead, living people (especially children born with unusual characteristics and the extremely elderly), animals, natural objects (most notably stones), and forms of energy. The simbi thus resist easy and exclusive categorization as beings in both the visible and invisible realms. This frustrates our attempts to formulate uncomplicated definitions of their attributes and duties, but it faithfully reflects the ingenuity of Africans and their diaspora-born descendants to address the many facets of their lives through the simbi.

Connecting and extending the insights produced in the rich scholarship on early cultural processes in the African diaspora in North America, the evolving relationship of African-descended people to the landscape, and the development of African-American spiritual cultures allows this book to reimagine the roles of captive West-Central Africans and their spiritual knowledge in shaping community and culture formation in the South Carolina Lowcountry. While this knowledge about interacting with the physical landscape and its spiritual inhabitants came from the particular context of Kongo in West-Central Africa, it also resonated with ideas that informed the religions and ways of life found in many West African societies. As such, Kongo spiritual culture came to feature prominently in the long process of forging cohesion out of difference, especially as African-descended communities increasingly consisted of Lowcountry-born people. Though rooted deeply in the land of the Lowcountry, an emerging African-American people nurtured a continuing relationship with the simbi that connected them across time and space with people, spirits, and knowledge spread throughout the African-Atlantic world.

Overall, *African-Atlantic Cultures and the South Carolina Lowcountry* presents a history of the meanings of the simbi for particular communities of African-descended people that maintained relationships with them. The simbi are evidence of dialogues among the living about place, culture, and power that came from a specific Kongo, African context and that helped to shape African-descended communities and their culture in South Carolina. The existence of the simbi in the Lowcountry represented a stage in continuing discourses that began with Niger-Congo ancestors thousands of years before, continued within West-Central African societies, and extended into communities formed in the Americas through the Bantu diaspora in the Atlantic world. The appearance of the cymbee in the written record of Pooshee plantation in 1843 captured a moment in the long transition of the simbi from familiar guardians of freshwater springs into the new forms (white guardians, white babies, and avenging mermaids) that African-descended people employed in striving to define the meanings of place, culture, and power in the Lowcountry from the earliest days of enslavement through the formation of Black Lowcountry culture in the nineteenth century.

2

Land of the Living

God done make the world and it been all cover over with water and it been
dark, and God ain't love the dark so He turn around and make the sun,
and the moon, and put the star in the heaven, and He thinks it looks more
better. Then He study about all the water what the cover the earth and He
dig canal and ditch and quarter drain for drain the water off and make the
land get dry.

               – A Lowcountry Creation Story

Africans carried to the Lowcountry arrived as captives condemned to
work in the slave labor camps of planters to produce profitable export
crops including rice, indigo, and cotton from the 1670s to the end of
the legal trade in the first decade of the nineteenth century.[1] For those
who endured it, this terrible experience had to be understood in spiritual
terms. In the above account of the creation of the world, the Creator
formed land from the water "what cover the earth" with the same techniques that African-descended people used to create the hydraulic system
of rice plantations in the Carolina Lowcountry.[2] Certainly, every person
descended from those enslaved on the plantations knew who had the
knowledge and did the work needed to claim land from the swamps,
cultivate rice, and make rich men of enslavers. As Gabe Lance of Sandy

---

[1] The phrase "slave labor camps" comes from Peter H. Wood, "Slave Labor Camps in Early
America: Overcoming Denial and Discovering the Gulag," in *Inequality in America*, ed.
Carla Gardina Pestana and Sharon V. Salinger (Hanover, NH: University Press of New
England, 1999), 222–38.

[2] Albert H. Stoddard, "Origin, Dialect, Beliefs and Characteristics of the Negroes of
the South Carolina and Georgia Coasts," *Georgia Historical Quarterly* 28, 3 (1944):
186–95.

Island, South Carolina, stated proudly, "All them rice field been nothing but swamp. Slavery people cut canal and dig ditch and cut down the wood....All been clear up for plant rice by slavery people."[3] This vision of creation interlaced the power of the spiritual realm with the backbreaking work of cutting canals and digging ditches into a single story of the origins of the land.

What kind of spiritual culture produced an origin story that had the Creator fashion the world through the kind of work done by enslaved people or implied enslaved people mastered the same kind of work the Creator used to shape all Creation? It had to be a spiritual culture that regarded the natural environment and spiritual landscape as realms interconnected in the most fundamental ways. Indeed, African-descended people in the Lowcountry lived a heritage gained from the cultures of their African ancestors centered on the intimate interactions of people with their surroundings and molded by the desire to comprehend the spiritual meanings manifested in the natural environment.

The foundation of this perspective derived from the meanings that African-descended people attached to their presence on the land and relationships with the spirits that governed the domains they occupied. The first portion of this formula, the presence of African-descended people on the land, can be reconstructed through an examination of the historical settlement geography of the Lowcountry. The patterns discerned in such an inquiry allow us to interpret the relocation and placement of captive Africans as a process with inherent cultural meanings for these newcomers to early Carolina. The period from the founding of the Carolina colony in the 1670s through the 1720s has been considered by scholars a "frontier" phase, a condition that supposedly had a marked influence on the character of the society created by European colonizers. This period, however, was not experienced in the same way for African-descended people, as the earliest captive Africans brought their own cultural understandings of what it meant to live in what was to them a new land. This older cultural framework coupled with the context of enslavement in Carolina meant that life on the Lowcountry's early frontiers had distinct connotations for African-descended people.

The overlapping phases of the importation of captive Africans and the expansion of the plantation complex in the Lowcountry involved people of African descent in the continuous shifting of frontiers, the

---

[3] George P. Rawick, ed., *The American Slave: A Composite Autobiography* (Westport, CT: Greenwood Press, 1972), vol. 3, pt. 3: 92.

boundaries of which were for the most part delineated by the presence and work of enslaved men, women, and children. Creating, maintaining, and traversing these evolving frontiers entailed a remarkable level of physical effort through the movement of people and the transformation of landscapes for agricultural production. The physical aspects of these processes included the agonizing experience of captivity and transport into enslavement in the Americas as well as the hard labor needed to manipulate the landscape for material purposes. These same experiences also involved the intellectual processes of defining the meanings attached to being the people in the vanguard of the evolving Lowcountry frontiers and learning how to live in this new land. For most Africans this usually meant, among other things, aligning their understandings of the physical dimensions of their surroundings with the spiritual dimensions of their environment. This chapter focuses on the physical presence of African-descended people on the land and introduces the cultural framework within which African newcomers came to define their place on the landscape in spiritual terms. It begins by taking stock of the patterns of settlement and plantation development in the early Lowcountry and then correlates these patterns to trends in the importation of captive Africans to South Carolina. The chapter concludes by considering the role of an "African frontier ideology" as the foundation for community formation among African-descended people in the Lowcountry.

AFRICAN PEOPLE ON THE LAND

In eighty years, Carolina grew from a small, struggling settlement of a few hundred newcomers sequestered near the confluence of the Ashley and Cooper Rivers into a prosperous colony fueled primarily by the export of rice and inhabited by more than 60,000 people, the vast majority of whom lived near the rivers of the coastal plain. Such is one of the stories about the land and people of early Carolina and the Lowcountry region. The subsequent history of South Carolina has validated this version as the story of the land and people. Not surprisingly, this interpretation frames both the land and the people in concepts derived from the views of European colonizers who came to dominate the natural environment and human communities of South Carolina. We cannot ignore the significance of the fact that the key labels for the landscape in this short description – Carolina, Ashley, Cooper, Lowcountry – emerged from the physical and intellectual colonization of the region by Europeans and their Carolina-born descendants and indicates that the "standard" narrative of settlement and expansion rests on certain presumptions that overlook alternative realities during this early era that faded as Carolina secured its dominion.

Yet this is not the only story of the land and the people. The land that increasingly came to be claimed by the polity of South Carolina already supported numerous communities long before the arrival of English colonizers in 1670. Old and well-worn paths established many generations before the founding of Carolina cut through the Lowcountry to connect piedmont villages and chiefdoms with coastal enclaves. People came and went on these paths to take advantage of seasonal variations in food sources as well as trade, visit, and make war. The presence of the paramount chiefdom of Cofitachequi that extended south to the confluence of the Wateree, Congaree, and Santee rivers in the transition zone between the Lowcountry and the piedmont testified to the activity of the people in the region.[4]

The demise of Cofitachequi around 1680 evidenced another dynamic that forever altered indigenous communities in the southeast. The rise of the trade in Native captives through Virginia made the hunting of men, women, and children the primary means of commerce to acquire European firearms and other manufactured items. The intensity and violence of this new stimulus dismantled the few remnant chiefdoms from the old political order that had appeared throughout the southeast in the previous several centuries and forced a dramatic alteration of the human geography throughout much of North America east of the Mississippi River. The English colonizers of the Lowcountry arrived in the midst of this tumult and soon became dominant agents in the amplification of the reverberations felt through the "shatter zone" that reshaped every indigenous community in the southeast.[5] As such, the story of the land and people of the Lowcountry extended deeper into the past than the founding

---

[4] Chester B. DePratter, "The Chiefdom of Cofitachequi," in *The Forgotten Centuries: Indians and Europeans in the American South, 1521–1704*, ed. Charles Hudson and Carmen Chaves Tesser (Athens: University of Georgia Press, 1994), 197–226; and Charles Hudson, Robin A. Beck, Jr., Chester B. DePratter, Robbie Ethridge, and John E. Worth, "On Interpreting Cofitachequi," *Ethnohistory* 55, 3 (2008): 465–90.

[5] Robbie Ethridge, "Creating the Shatter Zone: Indian Slave Traders and the Collapse of the Southeastern Chiefdoms," in *Light on the Path: The Anthropology and History of the Southeastern Indians*, ed. Thomas J. Pluckhahn and Robbie Ethridge (Tuscaloosa: University of Alabama Press, 2006), 207–18; Robbie Ethridge, "Introduction: Mapping the Mississippian Shatter Zone," in *Mapping the Mississippian Shatter Zone: The Colonial Indian Slave Trade and Regional Instability in the American South*, ed. Robbie Ethridge and Sheri M. Shuck-Hall (Lincoln: University of Nebraska Press, 2009), 1–62.

of the Carolina colony, and the trajectory of later transformations of the land and people had been set well before 1670.[6]

By the third decade of the eighteenth century, the trade in Native captives had given way to new economic and political relationships with new Native groups formed from the coalescence of fractured segments from older communities. While these emergent societies may have preferred the "white path" of peaceful trade with the English, French, and Spanish colonizers, the story of the land and the people of the Lowcountry remained saturated with the violence of captivity.[7] The English had established firm control of the central colonized zone along the banks of the Ashley and Cooper Rivers early in their encounters with small coastal communities, and required these vulnerable groups to capture enslaved people who attempted to escape into the wilderness of the Lowcountry. According to Edmond Atkin in the mid-eighteenth century, the "Ancient Natives" who remained in "Settlements among the plantations" proved their value to Carolina enslavers by "hunting Game, destroying Vermin, and Beasts of Prey, and in catching Runaway Slaves."[8] Instead of bringing indigenous captives from the interior to Carolinian trading posts, the Catawba, Creek, and Cherokee supported their connections to Europeans by hunting Africans who sought freedom outside of the borders of South Carolina. In time, Creek and Cherokee communities enslaved African-descended people within their own nations and maintained the institution after removal from the southeast in the nineteenth century. In the same context, however, many from Lowcountry plantations found refuge in southeastern Native nations during the eighteenth century. This reveals the complicated relationships that African-descended people had

---

[6] For the emphasis on competing narratives, see Alan Gallay, *The Indian Slave Trade: The Rise of the English Empire in the American South, 1670–1717* (New Haven: Yale University Press, 2002), 1–19; Charles Hudson, "Introduction," in *The Transformation of the Southeastern Indians, 1540–1760*, ed. Robbie Ethridge and Charles Hudson (Jackson: University Press of Mississippi, 2002), xxxviii-xxxix; and Carson, *Making An Atlantic World*, xviii-xix.

[7] The development of "coalescent societies" in North America is examined in Robbie Ethridge and Charles Hudson, "The Early Historic Transformation of the Southeastern Indians," in *Cultural Diversity in the U.S. South: Anthropological Contributions to a Region in Transition*, ed. Carole E. Hill and Patricia D. Beaver (Athens: University of Georgia Press, 1998), 34–50; Stephen A. Kowalewski, "Coalescent Societies," in *Light on the Path: The Anthropology and History of the Southeastern Indians* (Tuscaloosa: University of Alabama Press, 2006), 94–122; and Ethridge, "Introduction," 36–42.

[8] William R. Jacobs, ed., *The Appalachian Indian Frontier: The Edmond Atkins Report and Plan of 1755* (Lincoln: University of Nebraska Press, 1967), 44–5. See also, Morgan, *Slave Counterpoint*, 482–3.

with Native societies, although it does not negate the key role that indigenous nations played in maintaining the social order of enslaving Africans
in both English and Native domains.[9] The position of the Catawba,
Creek, and Cherokee as pursuers of self-emancipated people or potential
enslavers ensured that as individuals and groups, maroons faced highly
uncertain prospects in taking to the wilderness. This rendered much of
the southeast a landscape of violence and captivity for its inhabitants of
African descent.[10]

This version of the story of the land and people in the Lowcountry and
greater southeast points to the interwoven histories of Native societies,
European colonizers, and African newcomers neglected by the dominant
narrative that has portrayed Native people as indigenous interlopers destined to disappear or inevitably succumb to "the new order of things"
established by English and Anglo-American polities.[11] The story of
Africans and their Carolina-born descendants in reconfiguring the landscape and its human geography has become appended to the dominant
narrative, as increasing numbers of enslaved people were essential at every
stage of early South Carolina's expanding claims to the Lowcountry. This
story is more than a mere appendage, however. African-descended people
were more than slaves, more than human tools laboring according to the
commands of enslavers. Arriving in Charleston in the holds of ships was
more than the last stop of a sea voyage; making a life in the forests of a
strange land was more than building a shed for shelter; clearing land to
then dig canals for rice fields was more than cutting trees and shoveling
dirt; and planting provision crops was more than growing food to eat or
sell. Their story certainly paralleled the histories of Native societies and

---

[9] Daniel F. Littlefield, *Africans and Creeks: From the Colonial Period to the Civil War*
(Westport, CT: Greenwood Press, 1979); Theda Perdue, *Slavery and the Evolution of
Cherokee Society, 1540–1866* (Knoxville: University of Tennessee Press, 1979); Morgan,
Slave Counterpoint, 482–5; Claudio Saunt, *A New Order of Things: Property, Power, and
the Transformation of the Creek Indians, 1733–1816* (New York: Cambridge University
Press, 1999), 50–4, 111–35; Gary Zellar, *African Creeks: Estelvste and the Creek Nation*
(Norman: University of Oklahoma Press, 2007); and Celia E. Naylor, *African Cherokees
in Indian Territory: From Chattel to Citizens* (Chapel Hill: University of North Carolina
Press, 2008).

[10] Timothy James Lockley, *Maroon Communities in South Carolina: A Documentary
Record* (Columbia: University of South Carolina Press, 2009), 11–12, 23–33, 53–4,
58, 69.

[11] The phrase "the new order of things" comes from a letter written by Benjamin Hawkins,
an Indian agent for the United States, in 1801. See, Benjamin Hawkins to Henry
Dearborn, 1 June 1801, in *Letters, Journals, and Writings of Benjamin Hawkins*, ed.
C.L. Grant (Savannah, GA: Beehive Press, 1980), 1: 359, quoted in Saunt, *New Order
of Things*, 1.

European newcomers, but it had its own dynamic sensitive to the geography of settlement, the timing of the importation of captive Africans, and the cultural outcomes of these processes.

This section of the chapter addresses the first two matters of settlement and importation, focusing on the era between 1670 and 1750 when, I contend, African-descended people established the foundations of the spiritual and environmental cultures that would endure for many generations after. While the workings of settlement and importation followed the dictates of the Carolina's European-descended inhabitants, it is clear that people of African descent chose to live and understand their circumstances in ways that their enslavers never intended or even imagined. We will begin to address this third concern, the cultural outcomes of the processes of settlement and importation, in the concluding section of this chapter and remaining chapters of the book.

Very early in the colonization of the Lowcountry, enslavers perceived it as a land to be forcibly settled and reformed by African-descended people bound to life-long servitude in the interests of European colonization. This was all part of the Divine Will of God, as some enslavers would have it. John Archdale opined in his 1707 tract on "that Fertile and Pleasant Province of Carolina" that the "Hand of God was eminently seen in thining [sic] the Indians, to make room for the English."[12] This "Hand of God" included warfare among Westo and Savannah communities that lessened their numbers considerably as well the "unusual Sicknesses," which "it at other times pleased Almighty God to send" to the remaining Native communities.[13] With the landscape fortuitously denuded of non-English inhabitants, the "industrious Planter" of Carolina could prosper in "a most Fertile and flourishing Region, every thing generally growing there, that will grow in any Parts of Europe" and that "produces also Rice the best of the known World."[14] The "Hand of Providence" and "industrious Planter" thus transformed the Lowcountry into "the American Canaan, a Land that flows with Milk and Honey."[15] Absent

---

[12] John Archdale, "A New Description of That Fertile and Pleasant Province of Carolina," in Alexander S. Salley, Jr., ed., *Narratives of Early Carolina, 1650–1708* (New York: Charles Scribner's Sons, 1911), 285. For an analysis of early promotional writings, see Edelson, *Plantation Enterprise*, 15–24.

[13] Archdale, "New Description," 285. For a comprehensive assessment of the role of disease in shaping the Lowcountry, see Peter McCandless, *Slavery, Disease, and Suffering in the Southern Lowcountry* (New York: Cambridge University Press, 2011).

[14] Archdale, "New Description," 305 ("industrious Planter"), 288 ("Fertile and flourishing Region"), 289 ("Rice").

[15] Archdale, "New Description," 308.

from Archdales's rapturous account were mentions of enslaved people of both African and Native origins, even though he arrived to govern Carolina at the very time that men, women, and children of African descent first reached a numerical majority in the colony.

Later observers such as Charles Pinckney perpetuated this oversight while celebrating the innovative Planter as the moving, and apparently only, force behind the reformation of the Lowcountry landscape:

> Our Fathers avoided the running out those rich and deep Swamps, so proper and necessary for the Cultivation of RICE…had they not…*ventured* upon the *new* laborious and dangerous Experiment of entering into thick and deep Swamps, and there cultivating RICE, how many fine Estates would to this Day have remained ungotten; and how many valuable Tracts of Land would now have remain'd in the very Heart of our Settlements wast[e] and uncultivated, and Harbours only for Beasts and Tygers and other Beasts of Prey?[16]

In his appraisal of the development of South Carolina, Governor James Glen stated, "The Country abound every where with large Swamps, which, when cleared, opened, and sweetened by Culture, yield plentiful Crops of *Rice*." To this familiar tale, which overlooked the majority of the human actors, Glen added a mere glimmer of recognition of the centrality of enslaved people to this enterprise in his short "Account of what the Labour of one *Negro* employed on our best Lands will annually produce in *Rice*, *Corn*, and *Indigo*."[17] The subsequent account then described the hard work of enslaved people in a passive voice, so that rice "is threshed with a Flail" or "is beat with a Pestle…to free the *Rice* from a thick Skin," which "is the most laborious Part of the Work."[18] Like others before him, Glen essentially rendered African-descended people invisible as mere appendages of the larger endeavor of "Culture."[19]

Some white observers saw less in the workings of the "Hand of Providence" or even in the glorious commission of the "industrious Planter" than in the hardships of nature, which according to this view

---

[16] Letter of Agricola, *SCG*, 8 October 1744, quoted in Edelson, *Plantation Enterprise*, 57.

[17] James Glen, *A Description of South Carolina* (1761), in Chapman J. Milling, ed., *Colonial South Carolina: Two Contemporary Descriptions* (Columbia: University of South Carolina Press, 1951), 14.

[18] Glen, *Description*, 7.

[19] S. Max Edelson, "The Nature of Slavery: Environmental Disorder and Slave Agency in Colonial South Carolina," in *Cultures and Identities in Colonial British America*, ed. Robert Olwell and Alan Tulley (Baltimore, MD: The Johns Hopkins University Press, 2006), 21–44.

fated African-descended people to labor in the swamps, forests, and fields of the Lowcountry.[20] A Charleston merchant in 1735 commented:

> I observed, whilst at Georgia great Quantity's of Choice good Land for Rice, And am positive that that Commodity can't (in any great quantity's) be produced by white people. Because the Work is too laborious, the heat very intent, and the Whites can't work in the wett at that Season of the year as Neg^{rs} do to weed the Rice.[21]

Another commentator remarked during the late 1770s that, "The low lands of Carolina, which are unquestionably the richest grounds in the country, must long have remained a wilderness had not Africans, whose natural constitutions were suited to the clime and work, been employed in cultivating this useful article of food and commerce."[22] As exports of naval stores and the cultivation of rice, indigo, and sea island cotton expanded from the seventeenth century into the early nineteenth century, whites imported larger numbers of enslaved people, producing a captive labor force and general population composed largely of Africans and their descendents in the Lowcountry.

Regardless of the ideological foundations for justifications of colonization and captivity, these perspectives revealed that whites interpreted the Lowcountry as a land of plantations and thus as a landscape of enslavement for African-descended people. As early as 1711, this understanding had taken firm root, as one colonist wrote to a family member in England that "there is no living here without slaves."[23] The earliest phases of permanent settlement by newcomers in the Lowcountry included African-descended people, who contributed essential skills and labor to the growth and defense of Carolina. When considering the demography of the early Lowcountry, the emergence of the black majority stands out as the most significant trend. As the colony matured in the eighteenth century, South Carolina figured as the only British North American society to have the numerically dominant portion of its people enslaved and of African origin.

---

[20] Wood, *Black Majority*, 63–91; H. Roy Merrens and George D. Terry, "Dying in Paradise: Malaria, Mortality, and the Perceptual Environment in Colonial South Carolina," *Journal of Southern History* 50, 4 (1984): 533–50; Mart A. Stewart, "'Let Us Begin with the Weather': Climate, Race and Cultural Distinctiveness in the American South," in *Nature and Society in Historical Context*, ed. Mikuláš Teich, Roy Porter, and Bo Gustafsson (New York: Cambridge University Press, 1997), 240–56; and McCandless, *Slavery, Disease, and Suffering*, 18–38, 130–147.

[21] Quoted in Wood, *Black Majority*, 84.

[22] Hewatt, *Historical Account*, 1: 120.

[23] Mary Stafford, "A Letter Written in 1711 by Mary Stafford to her Kinswoman in England," ed. St. Julien R. Childs, *South Carolina Historical Magazine* 81, 1 (1980): 4.

In this manner, the Lowcountry appeared more akin to the societies of the Caribbean than those of its mainland neighbors. This development, which occurred no later than the first decade of the eighteenth century, was the product of a very radical population shift that began about twenty years earlier in a period that has been neglected as a foundational era in the formation of community and culture for people of African descent.

The African-descended population started small. From 30 people who arrived in 1670 to the 4,100 who constituted a slight majority of the overall population by 1708, enslaved people did not crowd the countryside in numbers that matched the large enslaved populations of other colonies in the English Atlantic realm. Further, this early phase did not necessarily presage the plantation society that took firm root in the Lowcountry during the eighteenth century. The key transition came in the 1680s, as the rise in the number of African-descended people expanded at a greater rate than the number of whites. While both populations grew at a similar pace in the first decade of settlement, the divergence of the 1680s set the trajectory for the demographic disparities that created a black majority by the early eighteenth century.

In addition to reaching a numerical majority, we must note that the period between 1670 and 1740 marked an exceptionally intense era of Africanization of the Lowcountry population. The expansion of African-descended communities in this early stage proceeded at a pace far beyond the rate of growth during the most active periods of the documented importation of Africans in mid- and late eighteenth century. In four of the first five decades, the size of the African-descended population more than doubled, with the greatest expansions coming in the first two decades. Even the relative lull in the 1690s, in which the African-descended population rose by 60 percent, marked a higher rate of growth than three of the five decades from 1730–1770, which included the 1750s and 1760s, during which the Lowcountry-born population had achieved reliable levels of reproduction and at least 2,000 new Africans arrived each year (Table 1).[24] The fact that the absolute numbers of people in the early decades did not match the large figures for growth (through both importation and reproduction) in the eighteenth century should not lead us to dismiss the importance of

---

[24] Russell R. Menard, "The Africanization of the Lowcountry Labor Force, 1670–1730," in *Race and Family in the Colonial South*, ed. Winthrop D. Jordan and S.L. Skemp (Jackson: University Press of Mississippi, 1987), 104; and Morgan, *Slave Counterpoint*, 61. For annual figures for the importation of captive Africans, see Voyages Database – *http://slavevoyages.org/tast/database/search.faces?yearFrom=1754&yearTo=1775&mjslptim p=21300.*

TABLE 1. *Estimated Enslaved Population of the South Carolina Lowcountry, 1670–1750*

	Enslaved People of African Descent	Enslaved Native People	Anglos & Other Europeans	Total	Percentage Enslaved People
1670	30		170	200	15%
1680	200		1,000	1,200	17%
1690	1,500	100	2,400	3,900	41%
1700	2,400	200	3,300	5,900	44%
1710	5,000	1,500	4,200	10,700	61%
1720	12,000	2,000	6,500	20,500	68%
1730	22,700	500	10,000	33,200	70%
1740	39,000		15,000	54,000	72%
1750	40,000		18,200	58,200	69%

Sources: Russell R. Menard, "The Africanization of the Lowcountry Labor Force, 1670–1730," in Winthrop D. Jordan and S.L. Skemp, eds., *Race and Family in the Colonial South* (Jackson: University of Mississippi Press, 1987), 104; Morgan, *Slave Counterpoint*, 61.

these early stages. As we might imagine, such a significant demographic trend entailed profound social and cultural changes for African-descended inhabitants of Carolina as well as for the larger colonial society.

The presence of people of African descent in Carolina began with the remarkable example of John Sr., Elizabeth, and John Jr., who arrived in 1670. They came from Bermuda and comprised part of the first wave of African-descended people to settle in the colony.[25] A common pattern in the 1670s was for only one or two enslaved people to land in the Lowcountry under the sponsorship of English settlers, who in these early stages received land for importing both indentured and enslaved servants. Individuals such as Crow, Grace, Yackae, Tony, and Peter reached the Lowcountry separately with their enslavers during the first two years of settlement.[26] Others arrived in pairs, such as Andrew and Jone or Richard and Salisbury during the same period.[27]

[25] Nathaniel Sayle and James Sayle, 28 November 1672, in Alexander S. Salley, Jr., ed., *Warrants for Lands in South Carolina, 1672–1711* (Columbia: Published for the South Carolina Department of Archives and History by the University of South Carolina, 1973), 52.

[26] John Culpepper, 2 December 1672; Jane Robinson, 2 December 1672; John Robinson, 2 December 1672; Joane Carner, 18 April 1674; and Robert Browne, 10 December 1675, in Salley, *Warrants*, 53, 54, 72, and 110.

[27] Dorcas Smith, 26 April 1673; and William Thomas, [no day] March 1675, in Salley, *Warrants*, 60 and 113.

As important as their presence was in marking the earliest phase of the development of the African-descended community of Carolina, the family of John Sr., Elizabeth, and John Jr. represented an exceptional case in the larger process of populating the Carolina Lowcountry, in part because they came to serve the first governor of Carolina, William Sayle. Very few of the later arrivals came as parents with children, and we could assume reasonably that this family likely performed domestic duties. Five men named Rentee, Gilbert, Resom, Josse, and Simon more accurately resembled the growing African-descended population of the Lowcountry. It appears that most people of African descent brought during the first few years of settlement held the legal status of enslaved laborers without the benefit of kinship ties. Further, most came as men destined to undertake the hard work of turning the Carolina wilderness into a productive colony. An exception included an enslaved mother, Hannah, and two of her three children, Jupiter and Jone. Still, this small family accompanied the group of men that included Rentee, Gilbert, Resom, Jossee, and Simon from Barbados in 1672 to work for Margaret Yeamans. Overall, the majority of those brought through the Yeamans connection consisted of males. This tie to Barbados had already resulted in the arrival of enslaved people, as Governor John Yeamans, the husband of Lady Yeamans, initiated work on his extensive holdings outside of Charleston.[28] This earlier group certainly consisted largely of men, as they had been armed and left to defend Yeaman's plantation during hostilities with local Native groups.[29] Over all, nearly four-fifths of the newcomers among the enslaved individuals who appear in the historical record for the early 1670s consisted of males (all but two of them adults).[30]

From the 30 African-descended people present during the first year of the colony, the enslaved population of Carolina reached 200 people

---

[28] On the larger significance of the Barbados connection to the Lowcountry, see Russell R. Menard, *Sweet Negotiations: Sugar, Slavery, and Plantation Agriculture in Early Barbados* (Charlottesville: University Press of Virginia, 2006), 106–21.

[29] For Hannah and her children and Rentee, Gilbert, Resom, Josse, and Simon, see warrant for Margarett Yeamans, 5 September 1674 in Salley, *Warrants*, 82, 112. For John Yeamans and the people he enslaved, see *Collections of the South Carolina Historical Society* (Charleston: South Carolina Historical Society, 1897), 5: 337; Edward McCrady, *The History of South Carolina under the Proprietary Government, 1670–1719* (New York: Macmillan, 1897), 151, 345; and Wood, *Black Majority*, 23, 25–6.

[30] William Sayle (1672), Joh Culpeper (1672), Jane Robinson (1672), Dorcas Smith (1673), Nathaniel Sayle and James Sayle (1672), William Thomas (1673), Joane Carner (1674), Margarrett Yeamans (1674), Simon Berringer (1674), Dorcas Smith (1674), Richard Conant (1674), Robert Browne (1675), William Thomas (1675), Ffrancis [sic] Boult Gent (1678) in Salley, *Warrants*, 52, 53, 54, 60, 61, 72, 81, 84, 87, 89, 110, 112, 113, 114, 190.

by 1680, mostly through importation sponsored by "soe many con-siderable men from Barbadoes" who had the resources to "make the Plantation which will stock the country with Negroes, Cattle and other Necessarys."[31] Similar to the Yeamans family, another settler from a prom-inent Barbados family, Simon Berringer, received 3,000 acres for bring-ing "soe many Servts and Negroes" in 1671 and 1672.[32] The Barbados connection ensured that the still relatively small but growing enslaved population added individuals such as Crow, Grace, Yackae, Tony, Peter, Andrew, Jone, Richard, and Salisbury.[33] Even at the earliest stage of set-tlement, it became readily apparent that English colonizers of sufficient means intended to transport significant numbers of enslaved people to build and maintain their Carolina plantation enterprises.

The remarkable expansion of the enslaved population had to await the stabilization of the colony surrounding Charleston, achieved in the late 1670s. The free and enslaved inhabitants directed much of their work of the first decade toward creating a self-sustaining colony, a tactic that did not promote the importation of a substantial number of enslaved people. The end of that first decade, however, marked a significant tran-sition in the overall development of the colony and the dramatic rise in the presence of enslaved people. While it may seem logical to correlate this growth with the development of rice as the first plantation crop, the demographic turn occurred well before rice cultivation became a key export and stemmed from the growth of other aspects of Carolina's econ-omy. For example, the keeping of hogs provided the means to accumulate wealth and import enslaved people for other endeavors. John Colleton, one of the colony's founders, expected that settlers would be to be able to produce "a quantity of Hoggs flesh wch will soonest come to bare to send to Barbados wch will pduce us Neagroes & Sarvts: to rayse a plan-tacon."[34] By the early 1680s, Samuel Wilson reported that this design worked well for the colonizers:

[31] Anthony Ashley to John Yeamans, 15 December 1671, and Ashley to Mathias Halsted, 16 December 1671 in McCrady *Collections*, 5: 361 and 364.

[32] Simon Berringer (1674) in Salley, *Warrants*, 84.

[33] For Crow, Grace, Yackae, Tony, and Peter, see warrants for John Culpepper, 2 December 1672; Jane Robinson, 2 December 1672; John Robinson, 2 December 1672; Joane Carner, 18 April 1674; and Robert Browne, 10 December 1675, in Salley, *Warrants*, 53, 54, 72, and 110. For Andrew, Jone, Richard, and Salisbury, see warrants for Dorcas Smith, 26 April 1673; and William Thomas, [no day] March 1675, in Salley, *Warrants*, 60 and 113.

[34] William S. Powell, ed., *Ye Countie of Albemarle in Carolina: A Collection of Documents, 1664–1675* (Raleigh: North Carolina Office of Archives and History, 1958), 7.

Hogs increase in Carolina abundantly, and in a manner without any charge or trouble to the Planter...there are many Planters that are single and have never a Servant, that have two or three hundred Hogs, of which they make great profit: Barbados, Jamaica, and New-England, affording a constant good price for their Pork; by which means they get wherewithal to build them more convenient Houses and to purchase Servants, and Negro slaves.[35]

Early planters reaped considerable earnings from exports of meat (hogs and cattle) and forest products (lumber, tar, and turpentine) used to support shipping. Certainly, profits provided a strong incentive for generating these exports, but the prime motivation always remained the acquisition of a large number of enslaved people given the abundance of other resources, including land. As one promoter of the colony stated quite clearly:

But a rational man will certainly inquire, When I have Land, what shall I doe with it? What Comoditys shall I be able to produce that will yield me mony in other Countrys, that I may be inabled to buy Negro slaves (without which a Planter can never do any great matter) and purchase other things for my pleasure and convenience, that Carolina doth not produce?[36]

These early planters did not intend to remain small planters, and they began to fulfill their aspirations in earnest during the 1680s.

While no warrants for land included enslaved people between 1673 and 1678, subsequent records reveal a renewed vigor in the English effort to increase landholdings and the enslaved population. It was during the 1680s that we can say that Carolinian enslavers began to import enslaved men, women, and children. This represented a fundamental break with the prevailing practice of individual English settlers relocating only one or a few bonded servants with them in their move to Carolina. Stephen Fox acquired 1,350 acres for the 12 enslaved men, women, and children he brought in 1679. Elinor Willkins received 800 acres for bringing 8 enslaved people in 1681. The 10 enslaved people carried by John Lawson netted him 980 acres in 1682, as well.[37] Barbadians and others with ties to the eastern Caribbean led the expansion. Arthur Middleton and Robert Gibbes each received multiple parcels of land for the "severall servants and slaves arriveing in this Country" under their

[35] Samuel Wilson, "An Account of the Province of Carolina," in Salley, *Narratives of Early Carolina*, 172.
[36] Wilson, "Account," 174.
[37] Stephen Ffox [sic], 10 March 1681/2; Elinor Willkins, 7 June 1682; John Lawson, 2 March 1682/3 in Salley, *Warrants*, 270, 275, 315–16.

sponsorship.[38] The term "severall" in the land warrant for Middleton referred to the ten enslaved people who occupied his plantation near Goose Creek. This group included seven men (Samson, Will, Prince, Quaminy, Hanson, Guy, and Santoe) and Cassander with her daughter Dyana and son Pompy.[39] Gibbes proved to be an ambitious enslaver, as he arranged for a considerable, although ultimately undetermined, number of African-descended people to arrive in Carolina in the early 1680s in addition to at least another sixteen enslaved people in 1694.[40]

The most prolific colonizer during the 1680s was Nathaniel Johnson, who imported more than 100 enslaved people including 2 groups that arrived in 1688, the first of which came in January with 12 enslaved people and the second in September with 10 enslaved people.[41] By 1691, Johnson received 2,300 acres for these people and the "arivall of Ninety five Servants & Negroes at Sundry times on his account in this part of the province."[42] The Anglican reverend Samuel Thomas later remarked that Johnson's Silk Hope plantation on the Cooper River included "many servants and slaves."[43] The scope of Johnson's demand for enslaved people was such that he commanded an estate by the early 1690s that would have placed him in the upper echelon of planters in Jamaica and Barbados at that time in terms of the numbers of people enslaved on his land.[44]

This development corresponded with the emergence of an economic identity for Carolina within the larger Anglo-Atlantic commercial world. As many historians have noted, the economic surge that transformed South Carolina into a profitable exporting colony derived from provisions and naval stores, not the crops more often regarded as the typical exports of plantation-based trade such as sugar in the Caribbean or

---

[38] Salley, *Warrants*, 290, 333. On the backgrounds of Middleton and Gibbs, see McCrady, *History of South Carolina*, 238, 327.

[39] The African-descended people are identified in a marriage contract recorded the same month as his land warrant. See Wood, *Black Majority*, 332 (Appendix B); and G. Winston Lane, Jr., "Economic Power among Eighteenth-Century Women of the Carolina Lowcountry," in *Money, Trade, and Power: The Evolution of South Carolina's Plantation Society*, ed. Jack P. Greene, Rosemary Brana-Shute, and Randy J. Sparks (Columbia: University of South Carolina Press, 2001), 324.

[40] Salley, *Warrants*, 333, 484, 487.

[41] Nathaniell Johnson, 12 October 1689, 27 April 1691, 28 August 1694, in Salley, *Warrants*, 426, 429, and 476.

[42] Nathaniell Johnson in Salley, *Warrants*, 426, 429, 476.

[43] Samuel Thomas to the Rev. Dr. Woodward, 29 January 1702, in Samuel Thomas, "Letters of Rev. Samuel Thomas, 1702–1710," *South Carolina Historical and Genealogical Magazine*, 4, 3 (1903): 226; and Wood, *Black Majority*, 47.

[44] Richard S. Dunn, *Sugar and Slaves: The Rise of the Planter Class in the English West Indies, 1624–1713* (New York: Norton, 1972), 91, 171.

the rice, indigo, and cotton that would later generate grand profits for Lowcountry planters. Nevertheless, the early effort to transform earnings (from whatever source) into more laborers and expand the production of export-oriented plantations created the conditions that allowed rice to eventually become the premier crop of the colony.[45]

It is no coincidence, then, that the emergence of Carolina as a significant source of provisions and naval stores occurred at the same time that the colony took its first big step into the greater importation of enslaved people in the 1680s. The second decade of the Carolina colony witnessed the most rapid expansion of the enslaved population in the entire history of the Lowcountry, as the number of enslaved people rose from 200 in 1680 to 1,500 in 1690. This boosted the proportion of African-descended people in the overall population from 17 percent to 39 percent. This last figure coupled with the growing number of Native captives swelled the proportion of enslaved people to 41 percent of Carolina's population. The turn toward the plantation model reliant on chattel slavery had been achieved in the 1680s, even before the adoption of a "classic" plantation crop such as rice, by a marked and disproportionate influx of African-descended people promoted by the immigrant planter class.

The demographic profile of the African-descended population during the first two decades supports the interpretation of early Carolina as a society structured on the plantation model, particularly in regard to the proportion of males to females. As mentioned earlier, males predominated among enslaved people identified in land warrants during the 1670s, and this trend continued through the 1680s. For those whose genders were specified or could be surmised from their names, 72 percent were males. Further, more than two-thirds of the enslaved people brought to Carolina during 1680s arrived in groups of seven or more, and more than one-half came within cohorts of ten or more people. The sex imbalance and sizes of the groups of new arrivals suggest that the enslaved people carried to Carolina during this decade came as captives reexported from the Caribbean, not acculturated or "seasoned" Africans or even so-called Creoles. In essence, the Africanization of the Lowcountry was the last leg of an intercolonial trade that began on the coasts of West and Central

---

[45] Converse D. Clowse, *Economic Beginnings in Colonial South Carolina, 1670–1730* (Columbia: University of South Carolina Press, 1971); Peter A. Coclanis, *The Shadow of a Dream: Economic Life and Death in the South Carolina Low Country, 1670–1920* (New York: Oxford University Press, 1989), 80–3, 115, 117–8, 135–8; and Edelson, *Plantation Enterprise*, 53–91.

Africa, went through the Caribbean, and terminated on the shores of Carolina.

Other evidence that has not thus far been considered by scholars supports this interpretation. The land warrants that included the names of servants contained fifty-six names for African-descended people brought to the Lowcountry during the 1680s.[46] A significant proportion of these names suggest that their bearers came from Africa, not Anglo-Atlantic societies. Not surprisingly, many of the names derived from names or words commonly employed in English-speaking societies, including "plantation" names (i.e., "classical" names such as Hercules, often assigned to enslaved people). Thirty-four (61 percent) fell into this category, with multiple Toms, Jacks, and Hannahs, along with the less common Worm, Bolognia, and Somersey.[47] Three other names (Preste, Ragon, Corosoe) may fit in this category as well, although they do not readily conform to known English names for enslaved people. Further, it is possible that Ragon and Corosoe may be African in origin given their apparent phonetics, although no parallels have been identified at this point.

The remaining nineteen people (39 percent) had names that indicate an African provenience. Aphee, Affia, Conny, Sambo, Togo, and Warree had names that paralleled words used in West African and West-Central African societies that spoke the Twi, Ewe, Fon, Hausa, Yoruba, Mende, Vai, or Kongo languages. While these individuals certainly did not come from all of these societies, the words used to form these names have appeared in these languages. Further, the African names in this set remained in use in the Lowcountry well into the twentieth century.[48] The name Semudo may prove to have been of African origin, although such an origin could not be found. The other twelve identified people did not have names that originated in African languages, but they bore Iberian names commonly employed in West-Central Africa, particularly in Kongo. As Linda M. Heywood and John K. Thornton have shown, many West-Central Africans entered the Atlantic diaspora with names derived from their exposure to Luso-Atlantic culture in Kongo and Angola. We may suppose that the same process played out in the Lowcountry as it

---

[46] For warrants for the 1680s that included names, Salley, *Warrants*, 312, 379, 382, 390, 396, 399, 400, 401–402, 419, 426, 476.

[47] Three names (Preste, Ragon, Corosoe) may fit in this category as well, although they do not readily conform to known Anglo names for enslaved people. It is possible that Ragon and Corosoe may even be African in origin given their apparent phonetics, but I have not been able to determine as much at this point.

[48] Turner, *Africanisms*, 45, 113, 115, 155, 172, 178.

did in other parts of the English and Dutch Atlantic.[49] In the records for Carolina, we find two men had the name Mingoe (Mingo, shortened form of Domingo) and two women were called Maria. Five men named Antonio, Francisco, Salvidore, Emanuel, Mattheias (Mateus) and a woman called Isabel appeared in the records, as well. The other two people, a male named StMayo and another person Osepha (Josefa?) possessed what were likely Iberian names, although these examples were not as clear as the previous examples.

When considering the significance of these names, we must keep a few key points in mind. We should not expect that enslavers in the Caribbean gave African or Iberian names to enslaved people. As such, the captives bearing African or Iberian names likely arrived in the Americas with the names they acquired in their home societies in Africa. Additionally, we cannot assume that the enslaved people who had English or plantation names were not Africans, even if they had arrived in the Americas fairly recently. English-speaking enslavers had no inhibitions about imposing English or plantation names on African-born people, and enslaved Africans often chose to take or give English names to themselves and their children when afforded the opportunity to do so. Overall, then, we can take the incidence of African and Iberian names as a strong indicator of the presence of African-born people, while the presence of English names may or may not denote origins in the English-speaking parts of the Americas.[50] The significance of the English names becomes more complicated when we reflect upon the common practice in those times of transliterating Iberian names that had ready English equivalents, such as Peter for Pedro, John for João, Simon for Simão, or even Hannah for Anna.[51] If this occurred in the several cases in which enslaved people had these English names, the number of Iberian names would increase to seventeen and raise the proportion of non-English and non-plantation names to 43 percent. Even without doing so, the high proportion of definitively

---

[49] Heywood and Thornton, *Central Africans, Atlantic Creoles*, 275–81.

[50] Insight into naming practices can be found in Wood, *Black Majority*, 181–6; John C. Inscoe, "Carolina Slave Names: An Index to Acculturation," *Journal of Southern History* 49, 4 (1983): 527–54; Cheryll Ann Cody, "There Was No 'Absalom' on the Ball Plantations: Slave-Naming Practices in the South Carolina Low Country," *American Historical Review* 92, 3 (1987): 563–96; Jerome S. Handler and JoAnn Jacoby, "Slave Names and Naming in Barbados, 1650–1830," *William and Mary Quarterly*, 3d Series, 53, 4 (1996): 685–728; and Heywood and Thornton, *Central Africans, Atlantic Creoles*, 275.

[51] John K. Thornton, "Central African Names and African-American Naming Patterns," *William and Mary Quarterly*, 3d Series, 50, 4 (1993): 730.

African and Iberian names points to a greater presence of African-born people in the early Lowcountry than scholars have supposed.

A similar trend appears in the set of seventy-five names for the enslaved people recorded in land warrants for the 1690s.[52] Of these, twelve people had names with African origins and fifteen had Iberian-derived names. Together, the twenty-seven instances of African and Iberian names comprised 36 percent of the names for enslaved people in land warrants. The people with African names included five men called Sambo (including Old Sambo and New Sambo in one group imported in 1695), two men named Cuffy, and three other men called Mackaya, Tobe, and Sandy. Additionally, two people of undetermined sex named Gasy and Tackoo arrived in 1694 and 1695, respectively. These names could have originated with speakers of Twi, Ewe, Fon, Ga, Hausa, Yoruba, Bambara, Wolof, Vai, Mende, or Kongo languages, although it remains unlikely that we will be able to determine precise sources from this broad range.[53] Among the people with Iberian names, we find six men called Mingo and three women called Maria. The others included two men known as Cesar (or Sesar, as written for one), one man called Hector, and three fellows identified as Tony. Heywood and Thornton assert that Tony represented a contracted form of Antonio, similar to the example of Mingo for Domingo. We should also consider the possibility that the form of the name as Tony entered the nomenclature as Ntoni, the common Kongo rendering of the Portuguese Antonio.[54] With this name, we see another dimension of the interaction of Kongo and Portuguese cultures exported into the English domains of the Atlantic world.

A significant implication that we can draw from the array of English, plantation, African, and Iberian names is that West-Central Africans comprised a conspicuous proportion of newcomers to the Lowcountry. Assuming that only those people who had Iberian names came from Kongo, West-Central Africans would have represented at least 21 percent of captives transported to the Lowcountry in the 1680s and 20 percent of those who arrived in the 1690s. The probability that many African-born people taken to Carolina had acquired English names suggests that we can assume a higher although undeterminable proportion for West-Central

---

[52] For warrants for the 1690s that included names, see Salley, *Warrants*, 433, 442, 456, 474, 486, 487, 489, 490, 491, 492, 493, 497, 500, 506, 507, 508, 509, 510, 513.

[53] Turner, *Africanism*, 71, 90, 114, 117, 127, 156, 165, 171, 172.

[54] Turner, *Africanism*, 171; and Manuel Alfredo de Morais Martins, "Contribução para o Estudo da Influçência do Português na Língua Quicongo," *Garcia de Orta* 6, 1 (1958): 7.

Africans as well as for people from other regions of Africa in relation to those who may have been born in or long-term residents of the English Caribbean. Certainly, the enslaved people carried to Carolina in this early stage originated in different places in Africa and the Americas. Still, the Iberian/Kongo names indicate the largest group with identifiable origins. This point takes on additional significance, as this sizeable minority came from late seventeenth-century Kongo, a society for which we have exceptional written documentation of ways of life including spiritual culture. This fortuitous coincidence allows us to establish a historical connection between West-Central Africa and the Lowcountry in the early formation of the local spiritual and environmental cultures, which will be taken up in the following chapters.

The landscape in which African-descended newcomers settled consisted largely of the lands along the main waterways of the coastal plain, including the Ashley, Cooper, and Stono Rivers. The growth of plantations followed the course of these rivers near Charleston (both the old town on the Ashley River and the new town on the peninsula). This was a natural extension of settlement, as the rivers and connected waterways provided the most efficient means for transporting people and goods. An early settler of Carolina commented that with "all Plantations being seated on the Rivers, they can go to and fro by Canoo or Boat as well and as soon as they can ride [horses]."[55] Certainly, early planters could not afford to have their lands far from navigable watercourses, as access to Charleston, with its links to Atlantic markets, fulfilled the fundamental economic purpose of the plantations. As Governor James Glen observed of one of the key arteries in this transportation system in 1751, the "Cooper River appears sometimes a kind of Floating Market, and we have numbers of Canoes, Boats, and Pettyaguas that ply incessantly, bringing down the Country Produce to Town, and returning with such Necessarys as are wanted by the Planters."[56]

From the earliest period of settlement, the apportionment of landholdings focused on proximity and access to rivers. The basic formula for granting tracts of land included detailed instructions regarding the amount of land that could abut a waterway.[57] The typical warrant

[55] Quote from "Letters of Thomas Newe (1682)," in Salley, *Narratives of Early Carolina*, 184.

[56] Quoted in Fleetwood, *Tidecraft*, 41.

[57] Great Britain, Public Records Office, *Records in the British Public Record Office Relating to South Carolina, 1663–1782* (Columbia, SC: Printed for the Historical Commission of South Carolina, 1928), 1: passim.

advised every landholder that, "if ye same happen upon any Navigable river or river capable to made Navigable you are to allow only the fifth part of the depth thereof by the water side."[58] Following this legal dictate, the geography of river plantations developed such that estates had narrow river boundaries relative to longer lateral boundaries that extended away from the river toward higher ground. This scheme ensured not only river berths, but also inclusion of multiple kinds of soils and vegetation. Functional plantations typically included some lowlands for rice and hardwoods and an expanse of higher ground for provisions and pines, which afforded naval stores. For example, the land surveyed for Samuell Wilson in the mid-1680s was bounded on the north by the eastern branch of the Cooper River, a cedar swamp, and on the south (away from the river) by poplar, pine, white oak, gum, and hickory trees.[59]

The key word in the phrasing of the warrants, "navigable," highlighted the necessity of water access. Edward McCrady, a venerable historian of colonial South Carolina, stated clearly the necessity of this early plantation geography: "The oldest plantations were all upon the rivers; indeed a water front and landing was an essential to such an establishment, for it must have the perriauguer for plantation purposes, and the trim sloop and large cypress canoe for the master's use."[60] For the duration of the plantation system in the Lowcountry, water-based transportation provided the most efficient means of moving people and goods.[61]

The clustering of plantations along key rivers did not conform to the frontier image of isolated plantations in a sparsely populated region. The main channels of travel and commerce featured concentrations of plantation along their banks as well as on the many smaller waterways that fed them. While the colony's population was small, the largest proportion of its members lived and worked on properties in Charleston or within several miles of Charleston. This allowed for the formation of social networks between plantations along stretches of the waterways as well as with the nearby settlement at Charleston.

Enslaved people in the maturing plantation zone engaged in a number of economic pursuits for their enslavers. Many scattered thinly throughout the countryside to tend livestock. These individuals have been identified

---

[58] Salley, *Warrants*, passim.
[59] The plat is reproduced in Salley, *Warrants*, 422.
[60] McCrady, *History of South Carolina*, 516.
[61] For more on significance of water access and transportation in the early Lowcountry, see Fleetwood, *Tidecraft*; Beard, "Good Wharves," 61–70; and Errante, "Waterscape Archaeology," 205–10.

and celebrated by scholars as early "cowboys," a number of whom likely came from societies in the Western Sahel that kept herds of cattle and brought their knowledge of husbandry with them. As the earliest lucrative enterprise that involved enslaved people, full-time livestock tending engaged a significant number of enslaved people in early Carolina.[62] No evidence exists, however, that establishes the proportion of enslaved people that worked in the cowpens during the first few decades of the colony. An estimate may be garnered from an early eighteenth-century authority who wrote about preparations for hostilities with the French and Spanish: "We are making all necessary preparations of Fortifying and Entrenching, to give the Enemy a warm reception; we shall have 1500 white men well arm'd, 1000 good Negroes that knows the Swamps and Woods, most of them Cattle-hunters."[63] Given the correlation between "Cattle-hunters" and military capabilities (useful against indigenous and European enemies), we may assume that the figure of 1,000 represents the maximum extent of full-time livestock tenders in the enslaved population. This figure would put the proportion of enslaved people engaged as cattle-hunters at less than one-fifth using the population estimates for 1710. As such, the remainder of the African-descended population lived either in Charleston (likely a few hundred at most) or along the banks of the Ashley, Cooper, and Stono Rivers, creating the plantations that came to dominate the inhabited portions of the countryside even when livestock and naval stores comprised the most lucrative exports.[64]

According to the prevailing portrayal of the early Lowcountry as a frontier with fluid social boundaries, it was only with the advent of rice cultivation that the Lowcountry left the frontier stage and entered into the plantation stage.[65] This perspective ignores the fundamental interdependence of livestock, naval stores production, and planting that defined Carolina plantations from the second decade of settlement. As one observer in Charleston noted of this relationship in 1682, "They do send a great deal of Pork, Corn and Cedar to Barbados, besides the

---

[62] Wood, *Black Majority*, 30–1; Clarence L. Ver Steeg, *Origins of a Southern Mosaic: Studies of Early Carolina and Georgia* (Athens: University of Georgia Press, 1975), 107–14; John S. Otto, "Livestock Raising in Early South Carolina, 1670–1700: Prelude to the Rice Plantation Economy," *Agricultural History* 61, 4 (1987): 13–24.

[63] *The Boston News-Letter*, 17–24 May 1708, quoted in Ver Steeg, *Origins of a Southern Mosaic*, 105–6.

[64] Wood, *Black Majority*, 20–8; Coclanis, *Shadow of a Dream*, 4–5; and Philip D. Morgan, "Black Life in Eighteenth-Century Charleston," *Perspectives in American History* 1 (1984): 188.

[65] Berlin, *Many Thousands Gone*, 142–76.

victualling of servall Vessels that come in here."[66] By the close of the following decade, Edward Randolph understood the solidity of the connection in his remarks to the Board of Trade in 1699 that, "They are set upon making Pitch Tarr and Turpentine and planting Rice and can send over great quantities yearly if they had encouragement from England to make it having about 5000 slaves to be employed in that service upon occasion [sic]."[67] Further, the interplay of Carolina's economic endeavors in stimulating the rise of the enslaved population through importation was acknowledged toward the end of the 1710s by the governor of Carolina, who noted that the growing trade in naval stores "encouraged merchants abroad to import into the province great numbers of Negro slaves from Africa and brought a great concourse of ships into this port."[68] While the tending of animals and production of sellable goods from the forest remained profitable aspects of the plantation enterprise in the seventeenth century through much of the eighteenth century, the largest proportion of the growing numbers of enslaved people spent most of their working hours on the various exhausting aspects of planting in the fields that yielded crops for provisions and export.[69] Thus, the plantation landscape and its social circumstances took shape in the seventeenth century well before rice cultivation commanded the Lowcountry economy. The rise of rice merely hardened the existing plantation regime that was already well established by the 1690s.

While the 1690s did not match the 1680s in terms of the numbers of African-descended people taken to the Lowcountry, the last decade of the seventeenth century continued the process of expanding the plantation enterprise in Carolina and increasing the proportion of enslaved people from 41 percent to 44 percent by 1700. In 1710, African-descended people made up 47 percent of the Carolina's population, a demographic

---

[66] "Letters of Thomas Newe," in Salley, *Narratives of Early Carolina*, 184.

[67] "Letter of Edward Randolph to the Board of Trade, 1699," in Salley, *Narratives of Early Carolina*, 207.

[68] "A Governor Answers a Questionnaire, 1719/1720," in H. Roy Merrens, ed., *The Colonial South Carolina Scene: Contemporary Views, 1697–1774* (Columbia: University of South Carolina Press, 1977), 64; Converse D. Clowse, *Measuring Charleston's Overseas Commerce, 1717–1767: Statistics from the Port's Naval Lists* (Washington, DC: University Press of America, 1981), 31; and Daniel C. Littlefield, "The Slave Trade to Colonial South Carolina: A Profile," *South Carolina Historical Magazine* 91, 1 (1990): 71–2.

[69] S. Max. Edelson, "Clearing Swamps, Harvesting Forests: Trees and the Making of a Plantation Landscape in the Colonial South," *Agricultural History* 81, 3 (2007): 381–406.

dominance that increased to 72 percent by 1740. Explanations for the growth of the African-descended population have had to rely on indirect evidence, as reliable records of the importation of captive Africans do not exist for the decades before the 1730s. Nevertheless, we must suppose a fairly vigorous trade in captives to Carolina given the steep increase in the numbers of African-descended people from 2,400 in 1700 to 5,000 in 1710, a rise of 108 percent. Extant records of importation for the first decade of the eighteenth century report only 337 captives arriving in Carolina from 1706 through 1710. We could hardly expect that the increase occurred through reproduction given the extraordinary fertility required to achieve such growth and relatively low proportion of children (the best indicator of fertility, of course) in census and probate records from the two decades leading up to 1710.[70] The only way to account for the difference is to suppose that the importation of enslaved people was drastically underreported, as indicated in the governor's report that remarked on "great numbers of Negro slaves from Africa." Further evidence of this trend appears in the dramatic growth of 140 percent from 1710 to 1720, with 7,000 additional people of African descent in the Lowcountry, who comprised 59 percent of the total population.

The culmination of fifty years of importation and plantation expansion produced an African-descended population of nearly 12,000 people in 1720. The early pattern of river settlement established in the 1680s resulted in the concentration of enslaved people in the parishes that encompassed lands along the Ashley, Cooper, and Stono Rivers as well as the Goose Creek tributary of the Cooper River. The most intensely settled portion of these parishes (St. Andrew's, St. James Goose Creek, St. Paul's, St. John's Berkeley, and St. Thomas & St. Dennis) together contained almost three-fourths (72 percent) of the total enslaved population.[71]

This plantation core zone received a significant share of new captives from Africa during this early eighteenth-century influx. The enslaved inhabitants of St. John's Berkeley parish numbered about 180 in 1705 and grew to 1,439 by 1720, as plantations expanded along the eastern and western branches of the Cooper River.[72] The trend continued

[70] Russell R. Menard, "Slave Demography in the Lowcountry, 1670–1740: From Frontier Society to Plantation Regime," *South Carolina Historical Magazine* 96, 3 (1995): 286–9.

[71] This figure excludes St. Philip's parish, which includes Charleston.

[72] George David Terry, "'Champaign Country': A Social History of an Eighteenth Century Lowcountry Parish in South Carolina, St. John's Berkeley County" (PhD Dissertation, University of South Carolina, 1981), 116.

in other long-settled portions of the Lowcountry such as St. George's parish. Located inland along the upper stretches of the Ashley River, St. George's parish had 536 enslaved people and 340 free people in 1720. Six years later, the enslaved population increased to 1,300 and the free population to 536. The demography of the parish also reveals the development of larger plantations featuring concentrations of enslaved people on a scale that had not existed before. The plantations of John Williams, Walter Izard, and Alex Skeene, for example, had ninety-four, ninety-one, and seventy-seven enslaved inhabitants, respectively. Overall, 18 of 108 properties in the parish had 25 or more enslaved residents.[73] The 1720s witnessed an unprecedented intensification of the importation of captive Africans. Early summaries of importation numbers indicate 1721 as the first year that more than 1,000 arrived in South Carolina during a single year.[74] From 1721 through 1729, more than 10,000 captives reached Charleston, a pattern that maintained momentum through the 1730s, with Carolinians importing 1,000–3,000 captives every year from 1731 to 1739.[75]

The arrival of large numbers of Africans fed the intensification and spread of the plantation complex as rice cultivation reached peak levels during the 1730s with the settlement of new lands. Further, the expansion north and south of Charleston accompanied the reformation of land policies.[76] By the end of the decade, planters in Prince George Winyah parish commanded plantations with hundreds of cleared acres, several buildings, and full complements of skilled and field laborers.[77] One plantation advertised for sale included 1,000 acres (200 cleared), cattle, and

---

[73] The 1726 census of St. George's parish appears in Frank J. Klingberg, *An Appraisal of the Negro in Colonial South Carolina: A Study in Americanization* (Washington, DC: Associated Publishers, 1941), 58–60. For analysis, see Wood, *Black Majority*, 156–65.

[74] Keep in mind, however, that it is certain that estimates for the first two decades of the eighteenth century undercount the number of Africans imported. See Menard, "Slave Demography," 300. The numbers reported in this paragraph far exceed those provided in the Voyages Database because the database derives information from records that tracked voyages from Africa to other Atlantic ports without consideration of the reexport trade from the Caribbean. See also W. Robert Higgins, "The Geographical Origins of Negro Slaves in Colonial South Carolina," *South Atlantic Quarterly* 70 (1971): 34–47; Littlefield, "Slave Trade," 68–99; and David Richardson, "The British Slave Trade to Colonial South Carolina," *Slavery and Abolition* 12, 3 (1991): 125–71.

[75] Wood, *Black Majority*, 151; and United States Department of Commerce, Bureau of the Census, *Historical Statistics of the United States, Colonial Times to the 1970* (Washington, DC: U.S. Government Printing Office, 1975), 2: 1173.

[76] On land reform, see Coclanis, *Shadow of a Dream*, 102–3.

[77] George C. Rogers, Jr., *The History of Georgetown County, South Carolina* (Columbia: University of South Carolina Press, 1970), 16–29.

enslaved coopers, sawyers, smiths, and sailors.[78] Through the 1730s and 1740s, established planters from lands upriver from Charleston extended their operations to the southern reaches of the province, as well. St. Bartholomew's parish, which included lands between the Edisto and Combahee Rivers, had only 144 enslaved people in 1720. By 1736, the number reached 1,200. Within several years the enslaved population there included 3,000–4,000 people.[79] Plantations along the south bank of the Combahee as well as those on the Pocotaglio and Coosawhatchie Rivers became home to communities of enslaved people that consisted mostly of recently imported Africans in addition to some enslaved people who had relocated from older plantations.[80] The movement of African-descended people from established plantations to new settlements corresponded with the expansion of multiple properties under the ownership of individual planters. For example, George Smith's vast estate included an Ashley River plantation with sixty-three enslaved people and three other properties outside of the old plantation core, including a Black River plantation with twenty enslaved people, a plantation in the interior with twenty-eight enslaved people, and Ferry Place near Georgetown with seven enslaved people. All told, Smith's estate included 118 enslaved people.[81] This signaled the early stages of a new form of colonization in South Carolina where the old core served as the hearth for an expansion of the plantation complex from the Ashley-Cooper-Stono River network to the rivers and swamps located to the north and south, ultimately including the major waterways on the Georgia coast.[82]

In addition to the settlement of new lands, the areas in the old plantation core zone experienced significant growth. The African-descended population of the parish of St. James Goose Creek expanded from 1,500 in 1727 to 2,752 in 1742.[83] The number of enslaved people in St. George's parish increased from 1,300 in 1726 to 3,347 in 1741.[84] Similarly, African-descended people in St. John's parish numbered 1,500

---

[78] *SCG*, 12 May 1739.

[79] Florence Gambrill Geiger, ed., "St. Bartholomew's Parish as Seen by its Rectors," *South Carolina Genealogical and Historical Magazine* 50, 4 (1949): 175, 178, 182–3.

[80] Lawrence S. Rowland, Alexander Moore, and George C. Rogers, *The History of Beaufort County, South Carolina: Volume 1, 1514–1861* (Columbia: University of South Carolina Press, 1996), 111–16.

[81] George Smith, 21 February 1734 and 19 May 1735, Vol. CC, 1732–1736, RSP-SCDAH.

[82] Edelson, *Plantation Enterprise*, 126–65.

[83] Klingberg, *Appraisal of the Negro*, 50, 93.

[84] Klingberg, *Appraisal of the Negro*, 58–60, 87.

in 1728 and doubled to 3,000 by 1746. In that same period, the proportion of African-descended people in St. John's parish increased from 75 to 85 percent.[85] The enslaved population of the whole region increased to such a degree that one European observer of the Lowcountry in 1737 stated, "Carolina looks more like a negro country than like a country settled by white people."[86]

Estimates for the enslaved population reflected this appraisal. By 1730, the number of people of African descent increased to a total of 22,700 people, who represented 70 percent of all inhabitants of South Carolina. Ten years later, another 16,300 African-descended people lived in the Lowcountry, lifting this segment to 39,000 people and 72 percent of the overall population of the colony. The 1740s, however, marked the end of the rapid growth of the African-descended population during the first several generations of settlement in the Lowcountry. The importation of captive Africans resumed in earnest in 1749, but this initiated a new era quite distinct from the eight decades that preceded it.

From the mid-eighteenth century onward, the plantation complex extended into new territories of the Lowcountry including the sea islands of the parishes of St. Helena and St. Luke's (in present day Beaufort County, South Carolina), where planters relied on the cultivation of indigo. This also reached the major waterways of coastal Georgia, where slavery had recently become legal for planters with the will and resources to establish rice plantations in fresh soils. Just as the spread of rice cultivation north into Prince George Winyah parish and south into Prince William parish in the 1730s entailed the resettlement of African-descended people from the old plantation core, the population of the indigo plantations on South Carolina's sea islands drew from the early hearth for enslaved people in addition to the renewed trade from Africa.[87] Similarly, the African-descended population of Georgia originated largely with the resettlement of people from South Carolina. William De Brahm remarked that upon his arrival in Georgia in 1751, he "scarce met three dozen African Servants, and they had not been above ten months introduced in the Province."[88] The following year marked the first large influx

---

[85] Terry, "Champaign Country," 116.

[86] R.W. Kelsey, "Swiss Settlers in South Carolina," *South Carolina Historical and Genealogical Magazine* 23, 3 (1922): 90.

[87] Rowland et al., *History of Beaufort County*, 111–18, and 161–2.

[88] John Gerar William De Brahm, *Report of the General Survey in the Southern District of North America*, ed. Louis De Vorsey, Jr. (Columbia: University of South Carolina Press, 1971), 162.

of enslaved people. De Brahm recounted that, "Many rich Carolina Planters...came with all their Families and Negroes to settle in Georgia; the Spirit of Emigration out of South Carolina into Georgia became so universal that year, that this and the following year near one thousand Negroes were brought in Georgia."[89] Another observer noted in 1760, "There are already about five thousand Negroes or Moorish slaves in this colony; and, because the people are beginning to become wealthy because of the good harvest of rice, indigo, boards, barrel staves, roof shingles, lumber, etc., such black slaves are brought here for sale from Carolina or the West Indies."[90]

Planters such as Jonathan Bryan best represented this trend as Bryan extended his family's Carolina holdings to Georgia's coastal rivers from Savannah to the Altamaha during the 1750s. He first acquired a grant for 500 acres near Savannah in 1750 and soon thereafter settled 40–50 enslaved people on that tract. Within 2 years, he received another 500 acres along the Little Ogeechee River. By 1755, Bryan's holdings expanded to include land on the Great Ogeechee and Sapelo rivers. Although Bryan ultimately concentrated his interests on his Savannah River lands, this pattern of expansion along coastal rivers had succeeded to the extent that Governor James Wright acknowledged that within one decade of legal slavery all the lands suitable for rice cultivation had been granted between the Savannah and Altamaha Rivers.[91] When the merchant Henry Laurens ventured into the business of planting in the 1760s, he acquired a base at Mepkin plantation on the Cooper River, from which he directed enslaved people and resources to support his rice cultivation ventures in the late 1760s on the far southern frontier along the Altamaha River in Georgia as well as on another rice plantation near Savannah. For his Broughton Island plantation on the Altamaha, Laurens sent fifty enslaved people in 1766 "to attempt a settlement on that island."[92]

[89] De Brahm, *Report of the General Survey*, 142.

[90] Samuel Urlsperger, ed., *Detailed Reports of the Salzburger Emigrants Who Settled in America* (Athens: University of Georgia Press, 1992), 17: 265.

[91] Savannah Unit, Federal Writers' Project, "Plantation Development in Chatham County," *Georgia Historical Quarterly* 22 (1938): 305–30; and Alan Gallay, *The Formation of a Planter Elite: Jonathan Bryan and the Southern Colonial Frontier* (Athens: University of Georgia Press, 1989), 85–6.

[92] Henry Laurens to James Grant, 2 April 1766, in Philip M. Hamer, George C. Rogers, Jr., and Peggy J. Wehage, eds., *The Papers of Henry Laurens* (Columbia: University of South Carolina Press, 1968–1985), 5: 107–8. See also David R. Chesnutt, "South Carolina's Penetration of Georgia in the 1760's: Henry Laurens as a Case Study," *South Carolina Historical Magazine* 73, 4 (1972): 194–208; and Edelson, *Plantation Enterprise*, 200–54.

The 1790s marked the beginning of another significant era for the incorporation of new lands into the realm of plantation agriculture. Planters sought new areas for cultivation of long-staple cotton, particularly the variety known as sea island cotton, primarily on the Georgia coast south of the old rice-growing areas during the 1790s and in Beaufort County, South Carolina, during the first decade of the nineteenth century.[93] Expansion along the Georgia coast led to the creation of large plantations on the sea islands and adjacent mainland in Liberty, McIntosh, Glynn, and Camden counties. A prime example of this movement was undertaken by Pierce Butler, who followed the practice of earlier planters of relocating enslaved people from South Carolina to new Georgia plantations. Beginning in the early 1790s, Butler stated, "My sincere wish is to move 15 or 20 of my Negroes at Captain Saunders, to my place Hampton Point on Great St. Simons Island, in order to prepare for planting about 130 acres of Cotton."[94] Butler's operations grew from this start to include 441 enslaved people by 1793, all of whom came from South Carolina plantations. This process of relocation fueled the swelling of the enslaved population of Glynn County, in which Hampton Point was located, from 215 in 1790 to 1,092 in 1800.[95]

The intensive development of the Georgia sea islands beginning in the last decade of the eighteenth century brought to a close the major phases of expansion of the Lowcountry plantation complex into new lands. Following this period, existing plantations grew larger and some areas already long settled experienced filling in with new farms and plantations. Until 1808 when the trade in captives ceased to be legal and the decades afterward when ships brought captives illegally, Africans who landed in Charleston, Savannah, and secretive coastal locations joined Lowcountry-born people throughout the coastal plain of South Carolina and Georgia (Table 2). A large proportion of these Africans were also sent

---

[93] Rowland et al., *History of Beaufort County*, 277–83.

[94] Pierce Butler to Mr. James LaMotte, 30 October 1791, quoted in Malcolm Bell, *Major Butler's Legacy: Five Generations of a Slaveholding Family* (Athens: University of Georgia Press, 1987), 58.

[95] United States Census Office, *Return of the Whole Number of Persons within the Several Districts of the United States, According to "An Act Providing for the Enumeration of the Inhabitants of the United States."* (Philadelphia: Childs and Swaine, 1791); and United States Census Office, *Return of the Whole Number of Persons within the Several Districts of the United States: According to An Act Providing for the Second Census or Enumeration of the Inhabitants of the United States, Passed February the Twenty Eighth, One Thousand Eight Hundred* (Washington: Printed by order of the House of Representatives, 1801).

TABLE 2. *Captive Africans Imported Directly to South Carolina,*
1749–1808

Region of Embarkation	Number (1749–1775)	Percentage (1749–1775)	Number (1783–1808)	Percentage (1783–1808)
Greater Senegambia				
Senegambia	15,637	27.1%	5,033	9.8%
Sierra Leone	8,888	15.4%	8,931	17.4%
Windward Coast	7,141	12.4%	2,424	4.7%
Lower Guinea West				
Gold Coast	7,667	13.3%	7,772	15.1%
Bight of Benin	1,941	3.4%	647	1.3%
Lower Guinea East				
Bight of Biafra	5,876	10.2%	3,408	6.6%
West-Central Africa	9,879	17.2%	20,687	40.2%
Southeastern Africa	288	0.5%	562	1.0%
Unidentified Africa	300	0.5%	2,024	3.9%
Total	57,617	100.0%	51,488	100.0%

Source: Voyages Database.

into the interior or reexported to other North American markets such as New Orleans.[96] Additionally, the older plantation sectors underwent various transformations as new crops, evolving methods, and changing markets reshaped the experience of enslavement for African-descended people until emancipation in the 1860s.[97]

In every instance when new portions in the Lowcountry were to be cleared, planted, and ultimately settled, African-descended people led the way. In this manner, they not only worked and lived on the Lowcountry's evolving frontiers, they made them. The long, hard process of redefining the Lowcountry's boundaries and reshaping its landscape from the late seventeenth century to the end of the eighteenth century relied on the ingenuity and toil of the many waves of African newcomers carried across the Atlantic and several generations of those born to the land and waters of the Lowcountry. The formative period for this engagement, an era which defined the fundamental contours of the physical, intellectual, and spiritual interaction of African-descended people with natural environment,

[96] James A. McMillin, *The Final Victims: Foreign Slave Trade to North America, 1783–1810* (Columbia: University of South Carolina Press, 2004), 98–100; and Adam Rothman, *Slave Country: American Expansion and the Origins of the Deep South* (Cambridge, MA: Harvard University Press, 2005), 85–6.

[97] Coclanis, *Shadow of a Dream*, 111–58; and Chaplin, *Anxious Pursuit*, 330–68.

occurred in the original plantation core built along the Ashley, Cooper, and Stono Rivers from the earliest time of settlement to the middle of the eighteenth century. As African-descended pioneers stretched the plantation complex in new directions in later periods, they took the spiritual and environmental cultures developed in the old plantation hearth with them to these new lands.

AFRICAN NEWCOMERS: 1670–1750

In order to assess the ways that people of African descent perceived and interacted with the natural environment, we must have an adequate sense of the origins of the African newcomers who became the fathers and mothers of the African-descended communities of the Lowcountry. This informs speculation on the societies and cultures from which captive Africans derived before they arrived in South Carolina. It is not a simple task, however, as the workings of captivity and commerce in West-Central Africa and West Africa varied over time and space. Additionally, the groups of these vast regions did not remain static in their locations and cultures, as the flows of people stimulated by the Atlantic trade and the more or less normal processes of interaction and exchange among communities promoted demographic and cultural changes. Nevertheless, the combination of evidence from West-Central Africa, West Africa, and the Americas can provide much more than a vague sense of the peoples and their cultures carried to the Lowcountry. The written record and inferences made from it indicate that the broad regions from which most of the captive Africans brought to the Lowcountry originated included Greater Senegambia, the Bight of Biafra, and West-Central Africa, although the proportions of people from these regions shifted throughout the duration of the trade to South Carolina.[98]

Greater Senegambia included numerous groups that spoke languages from two language families, Mande and West Atlantic. Mande-speaking people shared a great deal linguistically and culturally, as they represented successive waves of relatively recent migrations and conquests from the Mande homeland in the interior of West Africa's Sahel region. In addition to dominating and displacing the original West Atlantic-speaking inhabitants in some cases, Mande-speaking groups entered into the sustained interaction of the peoples of Greater Senegambia. One of the results

---

[98] For an overview of the peoples of these regions in the Atlantic trade, see Hall, *Slavery and African Ethnicities*, 80–100, 126–64.

of this engagement was the interlacing of Mande- and West Atlantic-speaking communities into a linguistic and cultural mosaic throughout Greater Senegambia.[99]

By the time Europeans ventured to the coast of Greater Senegambia in the fifteenth century, they encountered groups with diverse names that reflected this complex history. An English observer recorded the peoples who lived along the Gambia River as the "Mundingoes, Jolloifs [Wolofs], Pholeys [Fulas, or the Fulbe], Floops [Jolas], and Portuguese [people of mixed European and African ancestry]."[100] Contact between the various groups of the region did not preclude warfare and other forms of conflict, particularly recurring clashes between Muslims and non-Muslims, that rendered many people captives for the Atlantic trade. For the European merchants who transported Africans to the English colonies of the Americas, including South Carolina, in the seventeenth and eighteenth centuries, the trading networks of the Gambia River channeled captives to the factories on the coast. These networks drew people from throughout Greater Senegambia, while other webs in these networks directed captives toward other trading factories farther south along the coast in Sierra Leone. Among the Mande-speaking captives sent to the Lowcountry were many from Mandinka ("Mandingo"), Bamana ("Bambara"), and Mende communities, while West Atlantic-speaking captives often included those from Fulbe/Fula ("Foulah") communities.

The exile of people from the Bight of Biafra centered on the ports where the Niger and Cross Rivers emptied into the Gulf of Guinea. While the communities of this region did not experience a succession of centralized, competing states as seen in much of Greater Senegambia, affiliations based on political, commercial, and spiritual affinities linked Biafran societies in ways that promoted cultural interaction and ultimately facilitated the movement of captives into the Atlantic trade. While this region included a number of distinct language groups and well-defined local identities, the dominant commercial and cultural collective included those people known as Igbo (or "Ebo" in the Atlantic diaspora). One set of the larger Igbo realm, the Aro, played a particularly prominent role in

[99] Boubacar Barry, *Senegambia and the Atlantic Slave Trade*, trans. Ayi Kwei Armah (New York: Cambridge University Press, 1998), 35. For more on ethnicity and identity, see Paul Nugent, "Putting the History Back into Ethnicity: Enslavement, Religion, and Cultural Brokerage in the Construction of Mandinka/Jola and Ewe/Agotime Identities in West Africa, c. 1650–1930," *Comparative Studies in Society and History* 50, 4 (2008): 920–48.

[100] Francis Moore, *Travels into the Inland Parts of Africa* (London: E. Cave, 1738), 29.

the flow of captives to the coastal trading settlements. Their reputation as possessors of exceptional spiritual potency enhanced the abilities of the Aro to acquire and move captives for the trade. Under the direction of the Aro, people culled from societies in the core region of Igbo communities traveled through the lower Niger River network to reach the ports of Elem Kalabari and Bonny or through another network that terminated in the trading settlements know as Old Calabar on the Cross River estuary.[101]

According to historian K. Onwuka Dike, the effect of the social and economic forces unleashed by the rise of the Atlantic trade's influence on the region produced in the nineteenth century a "population, which evolved out of this mingling of peoples, [that] was neither Benin, nor Efik, Ibo nor Ibibio. They were a people apart, the product of the clashing cultures of the tribal hinterland and of the Atlantic community to both of which they belonged."[102] Dike's description of nineteenth-century identities in societies of the Bight of Biafra reveals the complicated interactions of the peoples in the region, which has made the scholar's task of defining the backgrounds of those carried from Elem Kalabari, Bonny, and Old Calabar notoriously difficult. Nevertheless, a significant number of these captives self-identified as Igbo (or some equivalent in the orthographies of those who recorded this information), which suggests that the term had greater meaning for enslaved people than as an ethnonym imposed by enslavers or an artifact of the nomenclature of the Atlantic trade in captives.[103]

West-Central Africans caught in the westward flow of captives to the Atlantic entered through three commercial networks that led to the ports of the Loango Coast, Luanda, and Benguela.[104] Almost all West-Central

---

[101] Chambers, *Murder at Montpelier*, 25–30; and G. Ugo Nwokeji, *The Slave Trade and Culture in the Bight of Biafra: An African Society in the Atlantic World* (New York: Cambridge University Press, 2010), 22–81.

[102] K. Onwuka Dike, *Trade and Politics in the Niger Delta, 1830–1885: An Introduction to the Economic and Political History of Nigeria* (Oxford: Clarendon Press, 1956), 30.

[103] Hall, *Slavery and African Ethnicities*, 133–5; and Alexander X. Byrd, *Captives and Voyagers: Black Migrants Across the Eighteenth-Century British Atlantic World* (Baton Rouge: Louisiana State University Press, 2008), 32–56. See also David Northrup, "Igbo and Myth Igbo: Culture and Ethnicity in the Atlantic World, 1600–1850," *Slavery and Abolition* 21, 3 (2001): 1–20; and Douglas B. Chambers, "The Significance of Igbo in the Bight of Biafra Slave-Trade: A Rejoinder to Northrup's 'Myth Igbo,'" *Slavery and Abolition* 23, 1 (2002): 101–20.

[104] Miller, *Way of Death*, 207–44; and Joseph C. Miller, "Central Africa During the Era of the Slave Trade, c. 1490s-1850s," in *Central Africans and Cultural Transformations in the American Diaspora*, ed. Linda M. Heywood (New York: Cambridge University Press, 2002), 21–69.

Africans taken to the Lowcountry began their crossing of the Atlantic at terminals of the northern network, which included the ports of Loango Bay, Malemba, Cabinda, and trading centers such as Boma in the Lower Nzadi region. Trade in Kongo centered on the functions of the regional market system, merchant caravans, and coastal trading centers. Leaders of adjacent towns formed committees to create markets that assembled every four or eight days. Some markets served small areas while others drew people in from greater distances, including overseas merchants.[105] These markets were fed in large part by caravans organized by trading specialists, most notably the groups known as the Vili (Mubiri) of Loango and the Zombo of Mbata.[106]

The availability of captives in Loango coast markets developed as Vili agents expanded contacts throughout the areas south of the Nzadi after about 1630. These trading specialists from the northern coast became widely recognized for their mercantile prowess. The products they traded included copper, ivory, salt, cloth, tobacco, elephant tails, guns, and captives. By the middle of the seventeenth century, Vili traders had established a trading community in the capital of Kongo, Mbanza Kongo, or São Salvador, and extended their operations southward to Matamba. The Vili trading network prospered to such an extent that the Portuguese in Luanda complained that the Vili disrupted their own efforts to acquire captives south of Kongo.[107] The Vili succeeded for several reasons. Above all, they carried desired goods to hungry markets. While the Portuguese prohibited the sale of firearms at Luanda, Vili merchants acquired guns and powder from the French, English, and Dutch on the coast and traded them throughout Kongo and as far south as Matamba and possibly

---

[105] Cherubino de Savona, "Aperçu de la Situation du Congo en 1760 et Rite d'Election des Rois en 1775, d'après le P. Cherubino da Savona, Missionaire au Congo de 1759 à 1774," ed. Louis Jadin. *Bulletin de l'Institute Historique Belge de Rome* 35 (1963): 382–3; J.J. Monteiro, *Angola and the River Congo* (London: Macmillan, 1875), 1: 179, 210; John H. Weeks, *Among the Primitive Bakongo: A Record of Thirty Years' Close Intercourse with the Bakongo and Other Tribes of Equatorial Africa, with a Description of Their Habits, Customs & Religious Beliefs* (London: Seeley, Service and Co., 1914), 199–201; and Susan Herlin Broadhead, "Beyond Decline: The Kingdom of the Kongo in the Eighteenth and Nineteenth Centuries," *International Journal of African Historical Studies* 12, 4 (1979): 637–8.

[106] Jan Vansina, *The Tio Kingdom of the Middle Congo, 1880–1892* (London: Oxford University Press, 1973), 427, 447; and Broadhead, "Beyond Decline," 638.

[107] Phyllis Martin, *The External Trade of the Loango Coast, 1576–1870* (Oxford: Clarendon Press, 1972), 69–70. On Vili competition with the Portuguese, see David Birmingham, *Trade and Conflict in Angola: The Mbundu and Their Neighbours under the Influence of the Portuguese, 1483–1790* (Oxford: Clarendon Press, 1966), 131–3.

Kasanje.[108] Vili merchants also earned a reputation for their trading acumen. As a representative of the Dutch West India Company put it, they "know how to get by in business, and...are not in a foul mood, if only they gain something."[109] Additionally, the Vili became familiar yet distinct members of Kongo communities. As a foreign people they retained a certain measure of independence from the internal issues that plagued Kongo. At the same time, it seems that they adapted to local circumstances through their acceptance of the king of Kongo's authority and their demonstrated respect for the Catholicism of the Kongo elite.[110] Finally, people perceived the Vili as purveyors of spiritual power, which afforded them influence and protection. A Portuguese observer noted, "When one says that something belongs to a Mubiri [Vili], nobody touches it."[111] Their special status may have derived from their direct involvement in Atlantic trade, an endeavor that carried significant spiritual as well as commercial consequences.

Another important group of trading specialists included people from eastern Kongo regions, known as Zombo, who dominated the trafficking of captives from interior sources to Kongo markets. Like the Vili merchants, Zombo traders possessed expert knowledge of commerce and traveled great distances to acquire captives. Their regular routes led them throughout the Inkisi River Valley and to Malebo Pool and extended into the Kwango and Kwilu River Valleys. The road-weary appearance of itinerant Zombo traders throughout these regions inspired the Kongo epithet *zombo kwaku*, which labeled the object of scorn as a "dirty zombo."[112] Together, Vili and Zombo traders facilitated the circulation of captives throughout the northern commercial network that supplied northern coast and lower Nzadi ports.

---

[108] Birmingham, *Trade and Conflict*, 131–2; and Martin, *External Trade*, 70.

[109] F. Cappelle, "Brève description des lieux principaux situés en Angola à savoir Comma, Goeby, Maiomba, Loango, Cacongo, Malemba, Zarry, Sohio, Congo et autres lieux circonvoisins et de leurs mœurs et coutumes," in *Rivalités luso-néerlandaises au Sohio, Congo, 1600–1675*, ed. Louis Jadin (Bruxelles: Institut Historique Belge de Rome, 1966), 230.

[110] Jean Cuvelier, "Contribution à l'histoire du Bas-Congo," *Bulletin des Seances de l'Institut Royal Colonial Belge* 19, 2 (1948): 908; and John K. Thornton, *The Kingdom of Kongo: Civil War and Transition* (Madison: University of Wisconsin Press, 1983), 26.

[111] António de Oliveira de Cadornega, *História Geral das Guerras Angolanas: 1680*, ed. José Matias Delgado and Manuel Alves da Cunha (Lisboa: Agência Geral das Colonias, 1940–1942), 2: 271.

[112] Joseph Van Wing, *Études Bakongo: II, Religion et Magie* (Bruxelles: Académie Royale des Sciences d'Outre-Mer, 1938), 75; and Norm Schrag, "Mboma and the Lower Zaire: A Socioeconomic Study of A Kongo Trading Community, c. 1785–1885" (PhD Dissertation, Indiana University, 1985), 85–6.

Although both the Vili and Zombo fit within the broader Kongo cultural realm, an early eighteenth-century missionary claimed that trade did not engage most Kongo people.[113] The profitability of the Atlantic trade and the decline in centralized government in the eighteenth century, however, inevitably drew an increasing proportion of Kongo into commerce. In the early part of the century the Kongo elite participated in the Atlantic commercial world, but interest in trade spread among the general populace by the middle of the century. By the late nineteenth century, they were described as "born traders" very much concerned with international commerce.[114] Additionally, individuals received protection and financial support for these activities through initiation societies.[115] Overall, the involvement of Kongo peoples in the trade ensured that many captives sent to the Lowcountry had at least minimal contact with the Kongo cultural realm before their departure from West-Central Africa.

By 1680, the area of intensive slaving for the northern network of Atlantic trade in West-Central Africa included the Loango hinterlands, all of Kongo, Matamba and Kasanje lands in the middle Kwango Valley, and to a lesser extent the territories near Luanda up to the middle Kwanza Valley. The last decades of the seventeenth century witnessed the transformation of kingdoms at the eastern edge of the expanding slaving area. The civil war in Matamba during the 1680s marked the transition of that kingdom from a military power that sent its locally acquired war captives to Portuguese traders at Luanda into a broker state that profited from directing captives from the interior to Kongo markets. These changes came as the slaving area spread east with the rapid and violent conquests of Ruund soldiers from the Lunda confederation. By 1720, interior sources included the woodland savannas between the lower Kwango and Kasai rivers. Within three more decades, the slaving area

---

[113] Lorenzo da Lucca, *Relations sur le Congo du Père Laurent de Lucques (1700–1717)*, ed. and trans. Jean Cuvelier (Brussels: Institute Royale Colonial Belge, 1953), 84.

[114] Monteiro, *Angola and the River Congo*, 1: 195; Weeks, *Among the Primitive Bakongo*, 199; and Karl E. Laman, *The Kongo* (Uppsala: Studia Ethnographia Upsaliensa, 1953), 1: 150–1. Broadhead discusses the transition in "Beyond Decline," 639–41; and "Slave Wives, Free Sisters: Bakongo, Women and Slavery, c. 1700–1850," in *Women and Slavery in Africa*, ed. Claire C. Robertson and Martin A. Klein (Madison: University of Wisconsin Press, 1983), 174.

[115] W. Holman Bentley, *Pioneering on the Congo* (London: Religious Tract Society, 1900), 1: 282, 451; John H. Weeks, "Notes on Some Customs of the Lower Congo People," *Folklore* 20, 1 (1909): 189, 198–201; Weeks, *Among the Primitive Bakongo*, 70, 176–7; Laman, *Kongo*, 1: 150–1; Wyatt MacGaffey, *Custom and Government in the Lower Congo* (Berkeley: University of California Press, 1970), 248–50; and Broadhead, "Beyond Decline," 641.

extended further south and east to include lands near the upper Kwango Valley and past the Kasai River. Further expansion resumed in the late eighteenth century, as waters of the central Nzadi basin carried captives from deep within the rainforests and overland routes extended to the center of the southern savannas.[116]

The most important interior source regions in the eighteenth century stretched from the Kwango River Valley in the west to the middle Kasai River Valley in the east.[117] The lower and middle Kwango Valley at the western portion of this range served as a central dispersal point for captives headed toward the coast. Traders assembled captives into groups destined west for Zombo markets in the Inkisi Valley of eastern Kongo or southwest for Ndembu markets.[118] The Zombo markets also received captives from the interior through river traffic that followed the Kasai confluents into the Kwa and Nzadi Rivers. Zombo traders then acquired people at the major Nzadi market near Malebo Pool. Ndembu markets received additional captives from the southeast through the competing Jinga, Kasanje, and Holo kingdoms. The captives sent through these intermediate markets derived ultimately from the same interior region unsettled by the Ruund/Lunda confederacy's expansion that began in the late seventeenth century.[119] The movements of people through the market networks should not mislead us into thinking that all or most of the captives taken to the barracoons of the coast were marched directly from the interior source regions. Instead, we must suppose that the influx of new captives from the interior allowed people with enough wealth in the markets between the sources and the coast to make decisions about their dependents, particularly which ones to keep and which ones to sell into the larger market for captives. In many cases, we may assume that "local" dependants were sold in favor of acquiring new "foreign" captives or that new captives became part of growing communities of dependants from which captives were later sold to the Vili or Zombo during times of famine or economic hardship. The expansion of the "slaving frontier" into the interior river valleys resulted in what we would have to call ripples, rather than true flows, in the affected populations.[120]

---

[116] Birmingham, *Trade and Conflict*, 133–54; Martin, *External Trade*, 117–35; and Miller, *Way of Death*, 140–53.

[117] Miller, *Way of Death*, 209.

[118] Jan Vansina, *The Children of Woot: A History of the Kuba People* (Madison: University of Wisconsin Press, 1978), 186–95; and Miller, *Way of Death*, 209.

[119] Miller, *Way of Death*, 208–17.

[120] Miller, *Way of Death*, 105–69; and Miller, "Central Africa During the Era of the Slave Trade," 50–2, 54–8.

Overall, the interior networks of trading coupled with shifting patterns of captains' activities in various West-Central African ports suggest that captives in the northern commercial network predominated among those carried on British and North American vessels. This meant that people from all regions within the Kongo realm, the Kwango River basin, and to a lesser extent the interior Nzadi basin networks figured heavily among these captives. Most of them likely hailed from the cultural/linguistic groups labeled in recent times as Kongo, Vili, Yombe, Yaka, Pende, and Mbundu.[121] The trend in the late eighteenth and early nineteenth centuries to the Lower Nzadi suggests a greater supply from central and southern Kongo networks, which would have accentuated the representation of people from the central and southern Kongo, Pende, Yaka, Mbundu, and neighboring cultural/linguistic groups.

Knowledge of the dynamics of the regional commerce extending throughout the interior and Atlantic trade based in the ports of West Africa and West-Central Africa provides a necessary framework for assessing the possible backgrounds of captives carried to the Lowcountry. This information, however, does not offer enough detail to determine conclusively the local origins of a large proportion of those people destined to endure the Middle Passage. To enhance our understanding of who arrived on South Carolina's shores, we have to turn to evidence from the Lowcountry that references the backgrounds of African newcomers in a variety of ways. Records of the trans-Atlantic trade indicate that 565 vessels brought at least 52,000 people from Greater Senegambia, 13,000 people from the ports of the Bight of Biafra, and 42,000 people from West-Central Africa to the South Carolina Lowcountry during the legal trade in captive Africans.[122] Taken together, people from these three regions formed more than 82 percent of the captives disembarked in Charleston and the secondary ports of South Carolina. The largest share of these figures comes from the period between the mid-1720s and

---

[121] These names are used for convenience. They are not intended to reflect terms of self-identification among West-Central Africans in the past or present. They represent only the broad and generally accepted understandings of cultural/linguistic groups among Western scholars.

[122] For the figures for Greater Senegambia, see Voyages Database, *http://slavevoyages.org/ tast//database/search.faces?yearFrom=1710&yearTo=1810&mjslptimp=21300&mjby ptimp=60100.60200.60300*. For Bight of Biafra, see Voyages Database, *http://slavevoy- ages.org/tast//database/search.faces?yearFrom=1710&yearTo=1810&mjslptimp=2130 0&mjbyptimp=60600*. For West-Central Africa, see Voyages Database, *http://slavevoy- ages.org/tast//database/search.faces?yearFrom=1710&yearTo=1810&mjslptimp=2130 0&mjbyptimp=60700*.

the end of the legal trade in 1808. Yet as seen earlier in this chapter, African-descended people had been present in the Lowcountry for more than 5 decades before the start of this period, and numbered 12,000 by 1720. While a significant segment of the African-descended population in the 1720s consisted of Carolina-born children, most were adults who had come from somewhere else within the previous two generations. The home societies of these adults were found in the three regions of Greater Senegambia, the Bight of Biafra, and West-Central Africa. The presence of Africans in the Lowcountry before the 1730s has been overlooked or downplayed by most scholars, and few have attempted to link this presence to the development of cultures of African-descended people. As the remainder of this chapter will show, Africans, most notably people from West-Central Africa, arrived in Carolina through multiple routes from the earliest period of plantation-building on the Lowcountry's coastal plain through the mid-eighteenth century. Further, those from West-Central Africa played a leading cultural role in this foundational era, as they helped define the relationship between African newcomers and the land through the transplanting of an African frontier ideology and the location of the simbi in the springs of St. John's Berkeley parish.

Determining the regional origins of Africans brought to the Lowcountry before the early 1720s remains especially problematic, as a large majority of captives came by way of the intercolonial trade from the Caribbean.[123] During the 1680s and 1690s, almost all African newcomers reached Carolina in this manner. In order to assess their regional origins in Africa, we must extrapolate from the composition of the trade to the colonies in the English Caribbean where these Africans stopped in their journeys to the North American mainland. Given the personal and business ties of early Carolina enslavers, Barbados and the Leeward Islands represent the likeliest first American disembarkation points for captive Africans destined for the Lowcountry (Table 3).

English vessels during this first period of the importation of African-descended people to the Lowcountry carried the largest share of captives (40.9 percent) from ports along the Bight of Benin, commonly known as the Slave Coast during the era of the trade. Captives from this region comprised a prominent component in the trade into the eighteenth century, as English enslavers in the Caribbean expressed a marked preference

---

[123] Gregory E. O'Malley, "Beyond the Middle Passage: Slave Migration from the Caribbean to North America, 1619–1807," *William and Mary Quarterly*, 3d Series, 66, 1 (2009): 125–72.

TABLE 3. *Captive Africans Imported to Barbados and Leeward Islands,*
1680–1696

Region of Embarkation	Number	Percentage
Greater Senegambia		
Senegambia	5,284	10.6%
Sierra Leone	1,145	2.3%
Lower Guinea West		
Gold Coast	6,164	12.3%
Bight of Benin	20,498	40.9%
Lower Guinea East		
Bight of Biafra	5,091	10.2%
West-Central Africa	7,925	15.8%
Southeastern Africa	3,958	7.9%
Total	50,065	100.0%

Source: Voyages Database.

for them second only to those Africans shipped from the Gold Coast.[124] During this brief period in the late seventeenth century, however, captives from the Gold Coast did not figure to the same degree among those transported, in this case only 12.3 percent. More significant were people carried from regions considered much less desirable to American enslavers. As operatives in the Royal African Company noted in communicating to one of their factors in the Caribbean, "We observe what you writt that Angola, Gambia & Bite Negroes are not acceptable to our Planters."[125] This attitude rendered captives from West-Central Africa ("Angola"), Senegambia ("Gambia"), and the Bight of Biafra ("Bite") ideal for the intercolonial trade to Spanish colonies and smaller English colonies such as Carolina. If these preferences did indeed influence which Africans were retained in the Caribbean and which traded again, we should assume that a high proportion of those arriving in Carolina came from the 19,445 people (38.9 percent) from West-Central Africa, Greater Senegambia, and the Bight of Biafra sent to the English colonies of the eastern Caribbean between 1680 and 1696.

The African and Iberian names for enslaved people recorded in land warrants discussed earlier suggest that the bearers of those names hailed

[124] David Eltis, *The Rise of African Slavery in the Americas* (Cambridge: Cambridge University Press, 2000), 246–7.
[125] RAC to Chas Chaplin, Jamaica, Feb. 23, 1703, T70/58, f. 28, quoted in Eltis, *Rise of African Slavery*, 252.

from societies within the slaving areas of Lower Guinea West, Greater Senegambia, and West-Central Africa, all regions well represented in importation figures for the eastern Caribbean. Another set of names for four men, a young woman, and a boy, all of whom had been acquired in Barbados and taken to Charleston aboard the *Betty* in 1683, included June, Meningo, Walle, Bache, Cumboe, and Popler.[126] Four of the names (Meningo, Walle, Bache, and Cumboe) indicate possible African origins, and three can be linked to parallels in Bambara, Hausa, Vai, and Vili (Walle = Wali, Wàali), Mende or Kongo (Cumboe = Kombo) as well as Kongo alone (Bache = Baki).[127] Further, the large contingent of people with Iberian names may reveal an especially significant presence of West-Central Africans from Kongo and Angola where Portuguese and Roman Catholic influence was greatest.

Assessing the African backgrounds of newcomers in the early eighteenth century presents more of a challenge, as a large proportion of the voyage records did not include information on the ports where British vessels collected more than 45,000 captives. Nevertheless, we can assess the regional origins of captive Africans taken to the Caribbean on British vessels, including those sent first to Jamaica, which became another reexportation source for South Carolina by the early eighteenth century. According to a 1709 report from the colony's officials to the Board of Trade, "Wee are allso furnished with negroes from the American Islands, chiefly from Barbados and Jamaica."[128] For the 115,884 Africans from identified regions, the representation of those taken from the Gold Coast and the Bight of Benin appears to mirror the preferences of British enslavers in the Caribbean, as 59,673 (51.5 percent) and 32,369 (27.9 percent) boarded ships in ports of the Gold Coast and Bight of Benin, respectively (Table 4). Captive Africans acquired in West-Central Africa, Greater Senegambia, and the Bight of Biafra apparently played a much smaller role in the trade of this era, although a disproportionately high portion of the many people from unidentified ports may have come from these regions. As in the late seventeenth-century intercolonial trade, we

---

[126] Wood, *Black Majority*, 45

[127] Turner, *Africanism*, 58, 115, 177; and Karl E. Laman, *Dictionnaire Kikongo-Français, avec une Étude Phonétique Décrivant les Dialects les Plus Importants de la Langue dite Kikongo* (Bruxelles: Librairie Falk Fils, 1936), 10, 309, 1090.

[128] "Governor and Council of South Carolina to the Board of Trade," 17 September 1709, in Elizabeth Donnan, ed., *Documents Illustrative of the History of the Slave Trade to America* (Washington, DC: Carnegie Institute of Washington, 1930–1935), 4: 256 (document 139).

TABLE 4. *Captive Africans Imported to British Caribbean Colonies,*
1700–1722

Region of Embarkation	Number	Percentage
Greater Senegambia		
Senegambia	5,967	5.2%
Sierra Leone	1,620	1.4%
Lower Guinea West		
Gold Coast	59,673	51.5%
Bight of Benin	32,369	27.9%
Lower Guinea East		
Bight of Biafra	66,54	5.7%
West-Central Africa	7,856	6.8%
Southeastern Africa	1,183	1.1%
Total	115,884	100.0%

Note: This table excludes the 45,524 captives from unidentified regions of Africa.
Source: Voyages Database.

may suppose that a fair number of Africans from the less-favored regions figured prominently in the captives sent to the Lowcountry between 1700 and 1722. Evidence of West-Central Africans among the enslaved population at this time appears in an Anglican missionary's comment in 1710 that, "I have in this parish a few Negroe Slaves...born and baptised among the Portuguese."[129] These Roman Catholic Africans likely represented the continuing presence of people from Kongo in the earliest stages of African settlement in the Lowcountry.[130]

The short period from 1723 to 1729 (Table 5) marked a significant development in the transport of captive Africans to South Carolina. This was the first time that ships arriving directly from Africa landed enslaved people in an uninterrupted span of several consecutive years. These shipments reveal the intent to channel the trade from Greater Senegambia to South Carolina, quite possibly as an attempt to target a portion of the trade not dominated by the wealthier, better-connected factors and planters in the Caribbean. The trend began in the previous decade, although the mid-1720s provides the best evidence of the success of this strategy. From 1723 to 1729, South Carolina developed into the premier destination

---

[129] Francis Le Jau, *The Carolina Chronicle of Dr. Francis Le Jau, 1706–1717*, ed. Frank J. Klingberg (Berkeley: University of California Press, 1956), 69.

[130] John K. Thornton, "African Dimensions of the Stono Rebellion," *American Historical Review* 96, 4 (1991): 1103–5.

TABLE 5. *Captive Africans Imported Directly to South Carolina,*
1723–1729

Region of Embarkation	Number (SC)	Percentage (SC)	Number (Other British)	Percentage (Other British)
Greater Senegambia				
Senegambia	1,339	62.5%	2,242	5.1%
Sierra Leone	348	16.3%	1,071	2.5%
Windward Coast	–	–	737	1.7%
Lower Guinea West				
Gold Coast	236	11.0%	12,430	28.4%
Bight of Benin	–	–	9,982	22.8%
Lower Guinea East				
Bight of Biafra	–	–	6,654	15.2%
West-Central Africa	–	–	10,145	23.2%
Southeastern Africa	–	–	490	1.1%
Unidentified Africa	218	10.2%	–	–
Total	2,141	100.0%	43,751	100.0%

Notes – Columns labeled "SC" included figures for British vessels to South Carolina; Columns labeled "Other British" included figure for British vessels to all other destinations.
Source: Voyages Database.

for British vessels with captives taken from Greater Senegambia.[131] The direct trade to the Lowcountry, however, did not comprise the only flow of captive Africans. The intercolonial trade from the Caribbean reached higher levels as well, which certainly brought sizeable contingents of people from West-Central Africa and the Bight of Biafra. Fragments of indirect evidence suggest that the regional composition of the intercolonial trade followed earlier patterns. Many of the captives from West-Central Africa and the Bight of Biafra landed in Jamaica were considered suitable for secondary markets in the Spanish colonies and smaller English colonies such as South Carolina. One factor in Jamaica noted, "The ships from Angola and Calabar bring in three assortments of negroes. The first for us [traders], the second for the Planters, And the third for the illicit traders....And we did not put by one, that we thought would please the Spaniards."[132] These comments reveal that traders geared toward

[131] Voyages Database, *http://slavevoyages.org/tast/database/search.faces?yearFrom=1723 &yearTo=1729&natinimp=7&mjbyptimp=60100.60200.60300.*
[132] "John Merewether to Peter Burrell," 30 September 1737, in Donnan, *Documents*, 2: 461. See also, *SCG*, 9 March 1738, reprinted in Donnan, *Documents*, 4: 292.

the intercolonial market acquired as many captives as they could from Angola and Calabar even before Jamaican planters had a chance to purchase them.

While importation data indicate the clear presence of Africans from the societies of Greater Senegambia, the same sources do not provide enough information on those from other regions to place African newcomers from West-Central Africa and the Bight of Biafra in the Lowcountry during the 1720s. Nevertheless, another indicator of the origins of Africans in the Lowcountry during the 1720s comes from probate inventories. Although small relative to the overall enslaved population, the examples of enslaved Africans identified by "nation names" yield some insight. Estates inventoried between 1723 and 1725 included eight Africans with names such as Gambo, Gamboa, Carantee Maria, Cormuntee Will, Popow Phillis, Golla, Gola Maria, and Angola Phillis. The first two names, Gambo and Gamboa, may have been renderings of Gambia, thus tagging these individuals as having hailed from the Greater Senegambia region.[133] Carantee Maria may actually have been from the Gold Coast, like Cormuntee Will, while Popow Phillis likely referred to a woman taken from the Bight of Benin.[134] The last three people with nation names, Golla, Gola Maria, and Angola Phillis, came from West-Central Africa.[135] In addition to these men and women, we can add another West-Central African, Angola Amy, who arrived as a young girl on the Comingtee plantation in St. John's Berkeley parish in 1726, and later became the matriarch of an extensive family tree of descendants that spread in subsequent generations among the Ball family plantations on the branches of the Cooper River.[136]

The presence of West-Central Africans became especially significant with the vast expansion of the direct trade from Africa in the 1730s

---

[133] Thomas Stewart, 28 March 1723, Vols. B & C, 1722–1726; and Gesper Baskerfild, 24 August 1725, Vol. D, 1724–1725, RSP-SCDAH.

[134] Phillip Gendroon, 8 May 1724, Vols. B & C, 1722–1726; Elias Hancock, Vol. H, 1729–1731; and John Cawood, 4 January 1725, Vol. E, 1726–1727, RSP-SCDAH.

[135] Francis Courage, 13 August 1725, Vol. D, 1724–1725; Phillip Gendroon, 8 May 1724, Vols. B & C, 1722–1726; and John Cawood, 4 January 1725, Vol. E, 1726–1727, RSP-SCDAH.

[136] Angola Amy's presence and the names and dates recording the lives of her progeny appear at various points in the Plantation Account Book, 1720–1787, in the John Ball Papers, SCHS. Cheryll Ann Cody provides a detailed analysis of the enslaved population at Comingtee in "Slave Demography and Family Formation: A Community Study of the Ball Family Plantations, 1720–1896" (PhD Dissertation, University of Minnesota, 1982); and Cody, "There Was No Absalom," 573–5.

TABLE 6. *Captive Africans Imported to South Carolina, 1730–1744*

Region of Embarkation	Number	Percentage
Greater Senegambia		
Senegambia	2,023	11.3%
Sierra Leone	–	
Lower Guinea West		
Gold Coast	236	1.3%
Bight of Benin	–	
Lower Guinea East		
Bight of Biafra	3,983	22.3%
West-Central Africa	11,615	65.1%
Total	17,857	100.0%

Source: Voyages Database.

(Table 6). From 1730 to 1744, more than 65 percent of captive Africans carried to South Carolina entered the Atlantic world through West-Central African ports. Additionally, captives taken from the Bight of Biafra region constituted the second-largest cohort of African newcomers. The surge of people from West-Central Africa and the Bight of Biafra corresponded with the rise of these regions in the overall British trade, as these two surpassed all other regions in supplying British ships with captive Africans. The 44,492 (34 percent) and 37,397 (29 percent) captives from West-Central Africa and the Bight of Biafra, respectively, taken aboard British vessels to various British, French, Dutch, and Spanish colonies represented a fundamental shift in the British trade toward these regions as the leading sources for captives.[137]

The occurrence of nation names associated with enslaved people in probate inventories in the 1730s and 1740s reveals the effects of the changes in British trading on the enslaved population in the Lowcountry. As those from Greater Senegambia were prominent in the trade during the 1720s, it comes as no surprise to find six men from this region, including Bambro, Bambra, Bambrea, Bambra Jack, Mundingo Jack, and Mundingo Tom.[138] Representing the new developments in the trade to South Carolina, five West-Central Africans included three men named Congo, another man

[137] Voyages Database, *http://slavevoyages.org/tast/database/search.faces?yearFrom=1730 &yearTo=1810&natinimp=7*.

[138] Henry Nicholas, 12 April 1730, Vol. H, 1729–1731; Elias Horry, 3 October 1737, Vol. II, 1736–1739; William Sanders, 22 May 1736; Wilson Sanders, 26 July 1736, Vol. CC; and Levi Guichard, 23 June 1731, Vol. H, 1729–1731, RSP-SCDAH.

named Congoe, and one more named Angola Jack.[139] We also encounter the first nation names linked to the Bight of Biafra attached to five people, including three men named Ebo Jack as well as Ebo Joo and Ebo Peter.[140] The predominance of men among those with nation names reflected the sex ratios of the British trade at the time, in which three of four captives were males.[141] Probate inventories confirm this also, as Charlesworth Glover's estate included twelve men and five women and John Herbert's Goose Creek plantation held ten men, three women, six boys, and one girl. Further, Hugh Hext's Berkeley parish plantation included sixteen men, three women, four boys, and three girls.[142]

Conspicuous within the Lowcountry as a "negro country" were West-Central Africans as seen in a planter's appraisal of the whereabouts of an "Angola" named "Clawss" that, "As there is abundance of Negroes in this Province of that Nation, he may chance be harboured among some of them."[143] The abundance of West-Central Africans in the 1740s appears in the nation names among enslaved people in probate inventories. West-Central Africans accounted for twenty-six of the seventy (37 percent) enslaved people with nation names. All but two bore the label Angola (or a common variant, such as Gola or Gullah), the others identified with the names Congo and Loango. Comparable to the composition of the trade in the previous two decades, people with nation names associated with the Bight of Biafra and Greater Senegambia appeared frequently, as well. The eighteen people with Ebo or Eboe before their names represented the second highest percentage of people with nation names (26 percent). Those from the Greater Senegambia region numbered sixteen people, with half bearing variants of Gambia, while those with variants of Bambora or Mundingo as part of their names together made up the other half.

---

[139] Samuell West, 12 July 1731, Vol. H, 1729–1731; Jonathan Jamer, 2 April 1731; Vol. I, 1731–1733; Joseph Mackey, 9 August 1736, Gilson Clapps, 24 January 1738, Vol. II, 1736–1739; and William Downing, 30 September 1732, Vol. I, 1731–1733, RSP-SCDAH.

[140] George Smith, 3 & 4 December 1730, Vol. H, 1729–1731; William Downing, 30 September 1732, Vol. I, 1731–1733; George Smith, 21 February 1734; Thomas Rose, 12 December 1733, Vol. CC; William Moore, 21 September 1736, Vol. II, 1736–1739, RSP-SCDAH. Another inventory also includes two individuals named Madgascar and Guinee Adam (Andrew Allen, 18 October 1735, Vol. CC).

[141] Voyages Database, *http://slavevoyages.org/tast/database/search.faces?yearFrom=1730 &yearTo=1744&natinimp=7&menrat7From=0&menrat7To=100.*

[142] Charlesworth Glover, 14 February 1732/1733; John Herbert, 15 June 1733; and Hugh Hext, 1 June 1733, Vol. CC, 1732–1736, RSP-SCDAH.

[143] *SCG,* 6 August 1737.

In most cases, individuals with nation names appeared singly in estate records, such as Angola Peggy, Mundingo Samson, and Ebo London.[144] Some of the plantations on which these African lived, however, included several people from different regions. The most diverse plantation community in the probate inventories was Noah Serre's, which included three West-Central Africans (two named Gola Grippa and one Gola Clarinda), three women from the Bight of Biafra (Eboe Pathina, Eboe Venus, and Eboe Lucy), and three others (Echaw Peter, Echaw Jack, and Itchaw Susy).[145] Another varied group of Africans lived on the estate of William Wateis, which included two men and one woman from the Bight of Biafra (Ebo Caesar, Ebo Pompey, and Ebo Phillis), two West-Central African men (Angola Hector and Angola Samson), and one man from the Bight of Benin (Pau Paw Samson).[146] We should note also that ten of eleven instances of multiple nation names on an estate included at least one West-Central African.[147] No other African region was so broadly represented throughout the probate inventories, providing yet another indicator of the ubiquity of West-Central Africans in the Lowcountry at this time.

Another source first available in the 1730s that documents African-descended people comes from newspaper advertisements for enslaved people who ran away. For these two decades, 94 percent of the 112 Africans identified by place of origin came from West-Central Africa, Greater Senegambia, or the Bight of Benin. The origin of the sixty-six West-Central Africans in advertisements was designated by the single term "Angola" with no variation such as "Congo" or "Loango," as seen in the probate inventories. The twenty people from Greater Senegambia included eighteen identified as coming from Gambia, with one each called Mandingo and Bambara. Of those from the Bight of Biafra, seventeen were labeled as Ebo (or some other equivalent of Igbo), while two others were designated as coming from Calabar.[148]

---

[144] Ralph Izard, 25 January 1743/1744, Vol. KK, 1739–1743; Royal Spry, 16 May 1747, Vol. MM, 1741–1748; and William Guy, 29 January 1750; Vol. B, 1748–1751, RSP-SCDAH.

[145] Noah Serre, 11 February 1746, Vol. LL, 1744–1746, RSP-SCDAH.

[146] William Wateis, 30 July 1743, Vol. KK, 1739–1743, RSP-SCDAH.

[147] In addition to the estates mentioned in this paragraph, see Hugh Hext, 25 March 1745, Vol. LL, 1744–1746; Bengamin Donning, 20 October 1741; Alexander Hext, 26 June 1742; Barnebe Reily, 7 April 1747, Vol. MM, 1741–1748; Benjamin Godin, 20 & 21 June 1749, 24 May 1749; Daniel Britton, 19 January 1749; and William Elliot, 25 March 1751, Vol. B, 1748–1751, RSP-SCDAH. The one exception was the estate of Andrew Broughton, 30 July 1743, Vol. KK, 1739–1743.

[148] The numbers for this period and the entire colonial period are presented and analyzed in Littlefield, *Rice and Slaves*, 115–33, 118–22 (Table 3). See also Daniel C. Littlefield,

In addition to confirming the predominance of West-Central Africans during this era, the advertisements reveal aspects of the social lives West-Central African newcomers and their associations in the 1730s and 1740s. Less than half absconded as individuals. Nineteen men, such as Soho, Cudjo, and Kinsale, took off on their own.[149] The women who ran away alone included three named Flora, one Jenny, and an unnamed fourteen year old.[150] More West-Central Africans (twenty-nine) escaped in groups. Typically, two or three West-Central African men left together. In all, eight parties followed this pattern. Hector and his brother Peter joined with Dublin to escape from a Wando Neck plantation in the early 1730s. They had apparently planned this endeavor well, as "they have carried away with them their Axes and Hoes" and were "supposed [to] have carried away Mr. Jeffrie's Canoe, from his landing."[151] In two instances, a West-Central African man and woman ran away together. Pompey and Menda took "two young Childrens" (theirs?) with them in 1740. Manuel and Plaby attempted to flee slavery five years later.[152] Six West-Central African men ran with people from other backgrounds. Dick was accompanied by a white servant boy, Peter, in their flight from Edisto Island.[153] On two separate occasions, West-Central African men teamed up with men from the Bight of Biafra. Levi and an Eboe named Kent fled in 1738. Five years later, Cesar and an Eboe called Cyrus ran from Wadmalaw Island.[154] Another interesting grouping included the West-Central Africans Ben and Symon, a Lowcountry-born man Cyrus, Cain (a Bambra from Senegambia), and a man of unknown origins, Will.[155]

The best-known of the West-Central Africans to resist enslavement during this period were "some Angola Negroes...to the number of Twenty" led by "one who was called Jemmy," who together fought against enslavers and destroyed plantations in September 1739 in what scholars have called the Stono Rebellion. In addition to the physical violence of their struggle, they displayed aspects of their culture at one point during the

---

"'Abundance of Negroes of that Nation': The Significance of African Ethnicity in Colonial South Carolina," in *The Meaning of South Carolina History: Essays in Honor of George C. Rogers, Jr.*, ed. David R. Chesnutt and Clyde N. Wilson (Columbia: University of South Carolina Press, 1991), 19–38.

[149] *SCG*, 9–16 September 1735, 12–19 March 1737, 6 July 1738.
[150] *SCG*, 5–12 June 1736, 1–8 August 1740, 24–31 October 1748 (Floras), 4 June 1744 (Jenny), 21 December 1738 (unnamed girl).
[151] *SCG*, 2–9 February 1733–1734.
[152] *SCG*, 2–16 February 1740, 1 April 1745.
[153] *SCG*, 15–22 May 1736.
[154] *SCG*, 12–19 January 1738, and 4 April 1743.
[155] *SCG*, 22 June 1738.

uprising when "they halted in a field, and set to dancing, Singing and beating Drums."[156] This act, the battle tactics of the participants, and the timing of the event have been interpreted by recent historians as the deeds of Kongo soldiers committed to their liberty and expressions of Roman Catholicism, particularly their veneration of the Virgin Mary. The upris- ing may have represented an attempt by these West-Central Africans to escape to the Spanish (and Roman Catholic) settlement at St. Augustine in eastern Florida, where refugees from enslavement in South Carolina had the opportunity to gain their freedom since the 1680s.[157]

Following the Stono Rebellion and the outbreak of King George's War in 1739, South Carolina's African trade foundered under the weight of prohibitive duties on importation of enslaved people and decreased com- merce generally.[158] People brought during the height of the importation of captives during the 1720s and 1730s thus constituted the last large influx of Africans for another decade. This brief respite coincided with the sta- bilization of self-reproducing communities by the end of the 1740s.[159] Angola Amy of Comingtee plantation, mentioned earlier, represented a generation of African newcomers who launched this expansion. Between 1743 and 1758, she and her husband Windsor had seven children – four daughters named Easter, Dye, Subrina, and Cleopatra and three sons named Christmas, Surry, and Smart. Their daughters gave birth to thirty- one children from the late 1760s through the early 1790s.[160] Over the course of this same half-century, African men and women begat one

[156] The quotes come from "Account of the Negroe Insurrection in South Carolina" likely written in October 1739 and republished along with other relevant primary and second- ary sources in Mark M. Smith, ed., *Stono: Documenting and Interpreting a Southern Slave Revolt* (Columbia: University of South Carolina Press, 2005), 13–15. Key schol- arly appraisals include Wood, *Black Majority*, 308–26; Thornton, "African Dimensions," 1101–13; Edward A. Pearson, "'A Countryside Full of Flames': A Reconsideration of the Stono Rebellion and Slave Rebelliousness in the Early Eighteenth-Century South Carolina Lowcountry," *Slavery and Abolition* 17, 2 (1996): 22–50; and Smith, "Remembering Mary," 513–34.

[157] Jane Landers, "Gracia Real de Santa Teresa de Mose: A Free Black Town in Spanish Colonial Florida," *American Historical Review* 95, 1 (1990): 9–30.

[158] Glen, *Description of South Carolina*, 45. See also, Stuart O. Stumpf, "Implications of King George's War for the Charleston Mercantile Community," *South Carolina Historical Magazine* 77, 3 (1976): 161–88; and Richardson, "British Slave Trade," 131.

[159] Glen, *Description of South Carolina*, 45. For analyses of demography of the enslaved population throughout the eighteenth century, see Peter H. Wood, "'More Like A Negro Country': Demographic Patterns in Colonial South Carolina, 1700–1749," in *Race and Slavery in the Western Hemisphere: Quantitative Studies*, ed. Stanley L. Engerman and Eugene D. Genovese (Princeton: Princeton University Press, 1975), 131–67; Menard, "Slave Demography," 291–302; and Morgan, *Slave Counterpoint*, 79–95.

[160] For Angola Amy's family tree, see Cody, "There Was No Absalom," 574.

generation and helped raise another with such success that the proportion of the Lowcountry-born among the enslaved population grew from 34 percent in 1740 to 77 percent in 1790.[161]

To this point, we have seen that the early enslaved population included a larger proportion of people born in Africa than previously thought. A notable share of these newcomers came from West-Central Africa, a regional cohort that was augmented considerably when the trade in captive Africans accelerated dramatically in the 1730s. Also, while the plantation zone began with a relatively small number of enslaved people, this population grew rapidly beginning in the 1680s and continued to do so through natural increase and the heavy importation of Africans over the next several decades. This created concentrations of African-descended people along the courses of major waterways, particularly the Ashley, Cooper, and Stono Rivers. Demographic factors thus promoted the formation of communities among enslaved people through social and trading networks that connected plantations on these rivers to each other and to the port city of Charleston (Charles Town). As the importation of captive Africans and the expansion of the plantation complex gained momentum during the second half of the eighteenth century and early decades of the nineteenth century, the original hearth of communities of African-descended people served as the primary source for pioneer populations in the newly cultivated areas of the South Carolina and Georgia Lowcountry. With these patterns of importation and settlement in mind, we can begin to imagine how the earliest stages of this long process set the trajectory for the formation and elaboration of culture within African-descended communities in the generations that followed.

AFRICAN FRONTIERS IN THE LOWCOUNTRY

Based on the previous accounting of the origins of captive Africans, we can determine that a large majority of those taken to South Carolina came from communities whose cultural and linguistic roots reached back to their distant Niger-Congo ancestors. All of the people carried from Greater Senegambia, the Bight of Biafra, and West-Central Africa spoke languages from the Niger-Congo family including the Mande, Atlantic, Igboid, and Bantu branches.[162] In addition to speaking the earliest forms

---

[161] Morgan, *Slave Counterpoint*, 61.

[162] Kay Williamson and Roger Blench, "Niger-Congo," in *African Languages: An Introduction*, ed. Bernd Heine and Derek Nurse (New York: Cambridge University Press, 2000), 11–42.

of Niger-Congo languages, the Niger-Congo ancestors devised conceptual frameworks that remained central to the cultures of their descendants as these subsequent generations diverged into distinct and far-flung societies throughout Central, Eastern, and South Africa. Foremost among these were ideas about interacting with the spirits of the land of the dead, which included nature spirits and ancestors, and with the natural environment of the land of the living. Basic to these concepts were assumptions about how people could understand their relationships to each other and to the lands that they inhabited, including lands to which they had arrived as newcomers.[163] For those carried across the Atlantic, ideas of this kind proved invaluable in reconstituting communities and reestablishing connections to the invisible, spiritual domain necessary for daily life.

Whether frontiers were geographical, social, cultural, intellectual, or any combination of these, captive Africans taken to the Lowcountry possessed a conceptual kit that informed their attempts to understand their place on the landscape in addition to grappling with the place ascribed to them by enslavers. Certainly, discrepancies in these understandings generated tension and conflict, as numerous people of African descent rejected Carolina in favor of conditional liberty in Spanish colonial Florida as early as the 1680s.[164] Just as their notions of what it meant to be newcomers to a new land differed from those of whites, the significance of the early Lowcountry as a frontier has varied in the eyes of historians. The initial scholarly expressions of the meanings of the frontier came from the Americanist Frederick Jackson Turner, who envisioned an American society shaped profoundly by the historical "advance" westward in which the frontier was "the outer edge of the wave – the meeting point between savagery and civilization" and where "American social development" underwent "perennial rebirth...with its new opportunities" and "continuous touch with the simplicity of primitive society."[165] The particular historical context of early Carolina supposedly represented a similar phenomenon, as the colonial southeastern frontier constituted a

---

[163] Igor Kopytoff, "The Internal African Frontier: The Making of African Political Culture," in *The African Frontier: The Reproduction of Traditional African Societies*, ed. Igor Kopytoff (Bloomington: Indiana University Press, 1987), 3–84; Jane I. Guyer, "Traditions of Invention in Equatorial Africa," *African Studies Review* 39, 3 (1996): 1–28; Klieman, *Pygmies were Our Compass*, 66–7, 88; and Christopher Ehret, *Civilizations of Africa: A History to 1800* (Charlottesville: University Press of Virginia, 2002), 50.

[164] Landers, "Gracia Real," 9–30; and Jane Landers, *Black Society in Spanish Florida* (Urbana: University of Illinois Press, 1999), 29–60.

[165] Frederick Jackson Turner, *The Frontier in American History* (New York: Henry Holt and Company, 1921), 2–3.

"constantly fluctuating, advancing" realm that "was no line, but rather a zone, indeed a series of zones, merging into the wilderness."[166] In this narrative, African-descended people figured only as the property of enslavers and human tools of white pioneers in their push into the wilderness, an unsurprising oversight given the absence of any significant acknowledgment of Native peoples, as well.

The limits of the early interpretations of the frontier with their "ethnocentrism, triumphalism, gender bias, and linearity" became readily apparent to historians from the mid-twentieth century onward, as the discipline experienced a long-overdue awakening to the fact that Anglo-American males were not the only historical actors worthy of study.[167] Of course, numerous academic historians had known this for some time, but the thrust toward more inclusive and complex narratives established watershed reconfigurations of the frontier that have spawned "New Western" and "New Indian" scholarship and informed the elaboration of alternative frameworks such as "borderlands."[168]

Leading the way in this new direction in African-Americanist scholarship was Peter H. Wood's landmark study *Black Majority*, which presented what has become an enduring characterization of the social milieu for African-descended people in the late seventeenth century. Wood depicted the Lowcountry as a sparsely settled region populated by free and indentured whites who coexisted with a growing set of enslaved Caribbean creoles to form a society that shared "crude and egalitarian intimacies inevitable on a frontier" in this formative period before the emergence of a true plantation slave society in the eighteenth century.[169] Further, the use of the term "black pioneers" to describe "the region's first real 'Afro-Americans'" served to highlight the extent to which this once-excluded group "participated in – and in some ways dominated – the evolution of that social and geographical frontier."[170] This reworking

---

[166] Verner W. Crane, *The Southern Frontier 1670–1732* (Tuscaloosa: University of Alabama Press, 2004 [1928]), vii.

[167] Quote from Andrew R.L. Clayton and Fredrika J. Teute, "On the Connection of Frontiers," in *Contact Points: American Frontiers from the Mohawk Valley to the Mississippi, 1750–1830*, ed. Andrew R.L. Clayton and Fredrika J. Teute (Chapel Hill: University of North Carolina Press, 1998), 3. The tone of the assessment of the discipline is mine.

[168] For the historiographical context, see Clayton and Teute, "On the Connection of Frontiers," 3; and Jeremy Adelman and Stephen Aron, "From Borderlands to Borders: Empires, Nation-States, and the Peoples in between in North American History," *American Historical Review* 104, 3 (1999): 814–41.

[169] Wood, *Black Majority*, 96.

[170] Wood, *Black Majority*, 95.

of the social composition of early Carolina offered a revision not only of the understanding of the frontier but also of the nature of slavery on this frontier. Echoing the sentiment of "perennial rebirth" in the original formulation of Americanist frontier theory, Wood asserted that "common hardships and the continuing shortage of hands put the different races... upon a more equal footing than they would see in subsequent generations." The image of an enslaver, Elias Horry, who "worked many days with a Negro man at the Whip saw," exemplified the "rude practicality which minimized social barriers on the early coastal frontier."[171] Above all, Wood's portrayal of Carolina's frontier in the seventeenth century and early eighteenth century provided a stark contrast to the emergence of the plantation era with its harsh work regime, declining birthrate, and increasing mortality rate in what Wood later called "slave labor camps" to emphasize their oppressive essence.[172]

This revision, while continuing to stand as an inclusive and astute intervention, nevertheless overstated the permeability of the social order and underestimated the heavy imprint of the early plantation complex with its race-based hierarchy on the landscape of the Lowcountry. At no time did English colonizers question the status of African-descended people as property bound to generations of servitude by chattel slavery. The "hardships" of establishing a new colony may have weighed on some European newcomers and tempered their sense of privilege, but the labors of free colonists in no way improved the lot of enslaved African-descended people or ameliorated their hardships. Although necessity may have dictated that European colonists interact more intimately with enslaved people than they wished, this meant only that free whites had greater exposure to a solid, rapidly growing African community that was taking shape with or without the personal intrusions of enslavers and temporarily indentured servants. This chapter has shown that in the first decades of the Carolina colony, steadily increasing numbers of Africans entered the Lowcountry to be settled in the relatively dense, well-connected networks of river plantation neighborhoods along the Ashley, Cooper, and Stono Rivers. For the most part, these neighborhoods were made and inhabited

---

[171] "Whip saw" quote from Peter Horry and Alexander S. Salley, "Journal of General Peter Horry," *South Carolina Historical and Genealogical Magazine* 38, 2 (1937): 51–2. "Rude practicality" quote from Wood, *Black Majority*, 97. Wood's interpretation provided the basis for Ira Berlin's assertion of "sawbuck equality" in early Carolina in *Many Thousands Gone*, 66, 142–61. Although less romanticized, the same idea appears in Edelson, *Plantation Enterprise*, 83.

[172] Wood, *Black Majority*, 165; and Wood, "Slave Labor Camps," 222–38.

by what would soon become the Lowcountry's black majority, composed of men, women, and children forcibly relocated to this wilderness to pass the rest of their lives as perpetual servants to the imperialist ambitions of European settlers. The frontier experience of African-descended people was thus quite different from the frontier experience of those who enslaved them.

As mentioned at the beginning of this section, the cultural groundings of captive Africans ensured that they would perceive their existence in this new land in ways distinct from their enslavers. Key to this process were several central features of sub-Saharan political cultures combined by the Africanist Igor Kopytoff under the rubric of an "African frontier thesis" inspired and informed by the influential Americanist notion of the frontier as an analytical tool.[173] The core concept addressed by Kopytoff and that informs our understanding of the intersection of spiritual and environmental cultures in the following chapters centers on a principle of precedence in which the firstcomers to a territory have a special prestige and legitimacy in later intergroup relations as well as interactions with the spiritual domain accessed in that territory. Further, the firstcomers retain the status of "owners" of the land, which subsequent arrivals to the area, the latecomers (or newcomers), must acknowledge and take into account in defining their status in the hierarchy of precedence. This represents an ideological component of the physical movement of people into new lands (frontiers), with which newcomers, even those who achieve dominance through the conquest of firstcomer peoples, construct their own stories of precedence to legitimate their presence and standing. Peoples in the same territory typically devise competing accounts of precedence, although the various versions may overlap and change over time as power relationships also change. Further and not unexpectedly, the precedence narrative of the dominant group tends to become the story of precedence. The existence of alternative narratives, however, reveals that dominance is not always absolute.[174]

The dominant precedence narrative itself often acknowledges this tension. Only rarely have the standard claims of latecomers that the firstcomers simply dispersed upon the arrival of new settlers, thus leaving an "empty" land, been historically valid, as opposed to politically expedient. More often, a politically and numerically dominant group has had to acknowledge the firstcomers, albeit as marginalized "outcasts," who

---

[173] Kopytoff, "Internal African Frontier," 3–84.
[174] Kopytoff, "Internal African Frontier," 52–8.

continue to exist at the margins in a parallel society. In those cases when the politically dominant group had fewer people than the firstcomer population, the solution might include assigning "ritual power to the old-timers and political power to the newcomers," with the firstcomers (the oldtimers in this case) possessing titles commemorating their spiritual status.[175] This approach more often functioned as an intermediary step, however, as latecomers also attempted to appropriate the ritual status of firstcomers, thus redefining their relationship to the land as the primary spiritual intermediaries between the local spirits and living people rather than as powerful but dependent supplicants.[176]

This principle has formed a key component in interpretations of nature spirits among people in West-Central Africa as long ago as the earliest phases of the historical phenomenon scholars have labeled the Bantu Expansion. In her interpretation of Kopytoff's African frontier thesis, Africanist Kairn Klieman has examined how Bantu spiritual cultures were shaped profoundly by the process in which Niger-Congo-descended people encountered and intermingled with the firstcomers in the equatorial forests. In addition to retaining core aspects of their inherited Niger-Congo tradition, early Bantu-speaking people innovated as they encountered these new lands and peoples. They forged relationships with the firstcomers in the equatorial forests from which unique aspects of the developing Bantu spiritual culture emerged, including the idea that the original forest people and their short-statured descendants (the latter being better known as "pygmies") represented fundamental intermediaries between communities of the living and the land of the dead. Over time and across lands beyond the rainforests, this idea remained essential in Bantu spiritual thought in a modified form that merged notions about these early intercessors and older beliefs about nature spirits in conceptualizations of dwarves and other people born with unusual physical features as manifestations of nature spirits and their powers.[177]

Additionally, descendants of the Bantu newcomers incorporated the outcomes of contacts with firstcomers into their relationships with nature spirits. Kongo oral traditions abound in stories of migration that resulted in the settling of the various clans and founding of various states

175 Kopytoff, "Internal African Frontier," 55.
176 Kopytoff, "Internal African Frontier," 55–6.
177 Klieman, *Pygmies Were Our Compass*, 66–89, 133–63; and Kairn Klieman, "Of Ancestors and Earth Spirits: New Approaches for Interpreting Central African Politics, Religion, and Art," in *Eternal Ancestors: The Art of Central African Reliquary*, ed. Alisa Lagamma (New Haven, CT: Yale University Press, 2007), 43–8.

throughout the larger Lower Nzadi region. While scholars may debate
the extent of the "history" (in the most narrow, academic sense) encoded
in these traditions, the narratives reveal the profound significance that
the theme of distant ancestors arriving as newcomers has had for people within the wider Kongo cultural realm. The theme also appears at
the heart of ideas about nature spirits such as the simbi. The simbi as
they have been understood by Kongo people may owe their existence
to a process of remembering a violent past of conquest and displacement in spiritual terms. The Kongo scholar Buakasa Tulu Kia Mpansu
has suggested that ritualized relations between people founding a village (and by extension a society) and the simbi, who are the original
spiritual proprietors of the land, have signified attempts by the descendants of the early Kongo settlers to perpetually make restitution with the
spiritual representatives of those whom the Kongo ancestors replaced.
According to Buakasa's thought, the Kongo founders, through a combination of extermination, assimilation, and subjugation, dominated the
original inhabitants of the land. This "could have inspired in the Kongo a
sense of remorse, of anguish" eased only through making peace with the
simbi through certain ritual practices and observation of the laws of the
simbi.[178] This accommodation, a consequence of the violence of Kongo
"conquest" of the land, has served as a constant reminder that the essential bond between communities of the living and local nature spirits was
forged at a great cost and thus must be cultivated with care. As long as
people maintained this contract with the simbi, they would be allowed to
live on the land and under the best of circumstances to prosper in spiritual and material ways. The simbi, then, have embodied the continuing
vitality of the principle of precedence for the Kongo descendants of the
distant Niger-Congo ancestors, with whom this concept originated.

Finding the simbi in the Lowcountry indicates powerfully that this
complex of ideas about how African newcomers could relate to a new
land, to which they had no ancestral claim, served as a key element in the
difficult but necessary process of remaking communities and reconnecting with the spiritual realm. It appears that Bantu-Kongo conceptions
of the principle of precedence provided the foundation for African newcomers to reconstruct this view of the relationship between people and
the land not only because the simbi remained relevant as the preeminent
African nature spirits on the Lowcountry's landscape but also because

---

[178] Buakasa Tulu Kia Mpansu, *L'Impense du Discours: "Kindoki" et "Nkisi" en Pays Kongo
du Zaïre* (Kinshasa: Presses Universitaires du Zaïre, 1973), 294–5.

the descendants of African newcomers continued to employ a large repertoire of Kongo terms to name the natural environment, including the plants and animals that African-descended people relied upon to subsist. This comes as little surprise, as we have already seen that West-Central Africans figured prominently among the African newcomers who populated the early phases of expansion of the plantation zone into new lands, the first during the 1680s and 1690s and the second in 1730s and 1740s. Just as the captive Africans did not come from one region, however, the ideas, practices, and words African-descended people used to relate to the natural environment reflected the diverse heritages of African newcomers.

The challenge for Africans and their Lowcountry-born descendants remained bridging differences to form strong communities of the living that could be maintained over many generations while also being capable of incorporating the near-constant influx of newcomers carried across the Atlantic. The creation and efflorescence of African-inspired culture in the Lowcountry attest to the abilities of African-descended people to do this. As the next chapter will show, nature spirits in West-Central Africa have long been instrumental in the same processes of building communities, coping with the most severe crises, and negotiating social and cultural change. The simbi, then, were ideal allies in facing the hardships of enslavement in the Lowcountry and the rest of the Atlantic diaspora.

Chapters 3 and 4 will examine further the ways in which the simbi and the Kongo people, who first acknowledged and named these nature spirits, played especially significant roles in shaping the material and spiritual meanings of the land and waters of Kongo and the Lowcountry. Indeed, arriving in a new land, as detailed in this chapter, was only one part of a much larger experience. The other part, one that has not been adequately explored until now, involved the transformation of a strange new land into a place where people could belong and establish communities. Through this process, African-descended people took a landscape of enslavement that was the early Carolina Lowcountry and recreated it as a land of the living, where they nurtured their bonds with African nature spirits and each other.

3

African Spirits of the Land and Water

The earth, sky, ocean and Nzadi river have always existed, and all that moves, moves in this framework....Lemba is the spirit of peace....He guards us, and must be respected and obeyed.
— Cabinda Origin Story

Where your ancestors do not live, you cannot build your house.
— Kongo proverb

The land is eternal. The earth withers in the dry seasons but flourishes with the coming of the rains. The sky bears the winds that bring the rains and shuffles the clouds to hide and then reveal the sun's rays. The ocean sends wave after wave crashing on the shore, taking from one spot and depositing on another. The Nzadi River flows forever, its currents constantly pushing new waters along its banks to eventually join the vast sea. The land does not stay still, yet it endures. "All that moves, moves in this framework."[1] The origin story that begins with the land as the fundamental framework for all that moves quickly turns from an account of the physical environment to a detailed description of the genealogy of myriad spirits that emerged from and then presided over the land and water. More important, the story tells of the relationship between these spirits and the people living in their domains. Lemba, along with the others, guards us. In return, the spirits "must be respected and obeyed." This is the fundamental order of existence with the physical land of the living intertwined with the spiritual land of the dead.

---

[1] Quoted in Janzen, *Lemba*, 302–3.

The Kongo proverb reflects another aspect of the interdependence of both worlds.[2] It expresses a vital concern for those who arrived in lands where they had no blood ties to the inhabitants and no established connections to the spiritual world. No ancestors in the new land meant no graves, and no graves meant no access to the land of the dead. This represented a serious crisis as the interment of ancestors in the soil provided sacred sites that served as shrines for their descendants and as markers of the spiritual sanction for the living to inhabit the territory. Further, the notion that the ancestors "live" on the landscape reveals the extent to which Kongo people understood that ancestors maintained a presence in the daily existence of their descendants, directing power from the spiritual realm to help their kin and remind them of their obligations to the dead. So, how did the Kongo people taken to new lands during the era of the trade in captive Africans cope with this crisis? Their ancestors had remedied that problem already, as they too had been strangers in new lands long before. They called upon the most distant ancestors imaginable, so ancient in many cases that these spirits remained immobile, although exceptionally powerful, in the waters and remarkable features of the landscape. These spirits were not the ancestors of particular lineages linked by shared blood. Instead, these spirits acted as the surrogate ancestors of every person who entered their territories, and they governed their domains with the proper amount of rain and a suitable supply of animals and fish so that the living could obtain sustenance. People in West-Central Africa knew them by many names, such as the nkisi, *nkita*, and simbi. While people applied specific names to these spirits in familiar domains, they knew that the spirits existed in all territories regardless of what inhabitants already occupied those lands and waters and what these indigenes called the spirits found there. They also knew that as long as newcomers established relationships with the spirits of any domain, they could find a place in the land of living and maintain their ties to the land of the dead.

It is particularly telling that African-descended people in the Lowcountry continued to use the Kongo terms kalunga and *finda* to refer to the sea and the forest, respectively.[3] In their original Kongo context, both kalunga and finda served as basic labels for features of the physical landscape, but they also carried spiritual meanings that referenced

---

[2] Quoted in Georges Balandier, *Daily Life in the Kingdom of Kongo: Sixteenth to Eighteenth Century*, trans. Helen Weaver (London: George Allen and Unwin, 1968), 253.

[3] Turner, *Africanisms*, 193, 196.

the most fundamental ideas about the connections between the land of
the living and the land of the dead. The appearance of these terms in the
twentieth-century Lowcountry provides linguistic confirmation that the
perceptions of the natural environment among African-descended people ultimately derived from the spiritual and environmental cultures of
the African newcomers discussed in the previous chapter. Another core
component of this cultural legacy was the continued use of the name
simbi for nature spirits and the acknowledgment of their significant roles
in the spiritual culture of people of African descent even as the identification with Christianity claimed increasing and eventually dominant
influence throughout the nineteenth century. The fact that kalunga and
finda represented key domains for the living to interact with the simbi
(and other nature spirits) indicates the extent to which a comprehensive
Kongo understanding of the spiritual landscape shaped culture in the
Lowcountry.

The presence of the simbi in South Carolina revealed a link to a body
of ideas and practices concerning nature spirits that formed a fundamental aspect of West-Central African and West African cultures for innumerable generations. Just as nature spirits have comprised a very old element
of these cultures, they have reflected the historical experiences of the
communities that formed and maintained relationships with them. We
have knowledge about nature spirits that portrays them as timeless, like
the natural environment, as implied in the Cabinda origin story, yet also
attaches them to specific times, places, events, and people. As seen in the
previous chapter, nature spirits figured centrally in ideologies supporting
the settling of new lands, encountering people in those lands, and reconstituting communities in these circumstances. Relationships with nature
spirits transformed dramatically with the economic, political, and social
changes wrought by contact with the Atlantic world, and it was within this
context of shifting meanings associated with nature spirits that millions
of captive West-Central Africans entered the African-Atlantic diaspora.
We will look in this chapter at the historical development of the place of
nature spirits in the cultures of West-Central African communities and
assess how the involvement of Kongo societies in trans-Atlantic trade
shaped perceptions of the simbi. While older notions of nature spirits as
beneficent patrons of the well-being and prosperity of societies remained
intact, some people began to reconceptualize the simbi as agents of the
Atlantic trade that profited from the captivity of Africans. This led to
a novel reworking of the relationship between communities of the living and the simbi, as people began to "hunt" the simbi and make them

captives for the purposes of controlling their power to serve the interests of their captors. In essence, some of the people caught in a world increasingly shaped by Atlantic commercial forces sought to enslave the simbi. The examination in this chapter of the foundational ideas and practices related to nature spirits in West-Central Africa and the various innovations sparked by Kongo's immersion in the Atlantic world will provide a basis for interpreting the introduction of the simbi to the Lowcountry in the next chapter and contemplating subsequent transformations of the Lowcountry simbi in the last two chapters.

KONGO SPIRITUAL LANDSCAPES

The nature spirits of West-Central Africa during the era of the trans-Atlantic trade in captive Africans included a number of entities that shared their most fundamental characteristics and at the same time possessed attributes unique to their particular manifestations in various regions. While individual nature spirits had their own names and locations, people typically understood them as belonging to broad categories, such as the nkisi of the Loango Coast and the Lower Nzadi, the nkita of Kongo, and the kilundu of Angola. In addition to employing these terms, which appear in various forms in seventeenth- and eighteenth-century writings by European merchants, missionaries, and compilers, West-Central Africans have attached other labels – most notably simbi – to nature spirits that appear in later sources, and have often used the terms interchangeably, especially in areas where spiritual cultures from different regions intermingled along the paths of commerce, migration, and cultural contact.

Father Giovanni Antonio Cavazzi's experiences in mid-seventeenth-century Angola led him to remark on these interactions: "From time immemorial, all the people of Congo have venerated idols [i.e., nature spirits], but they change the names and the cult according to their whims. In recent times, they had learned from the Jagas [an eastern Kimbundu-speaking group] many things about their ministers and have communicated to them, in turn, many other things concerning their gods."[4] Cavazzi's dismissive remark about the "whims" of the Kongo people unintentionally reveals how nature spirits functioned as sites of cultural innovation

[4] Giovanni Antonio da Montecuccolo Cavazzi, *Descrição histórico doe três reinos Congo Matamba e Angola*, trans. and ed. by Graziano Maria da Legguzzano (Lisboa: Junta de Investigações do Ultramar, 1965), 2: 58.

rather than as expressions of mindless caprice. Further, the communication between Kongo people and the Jagas undermines assumptions that absolute boundaries between the spiritual cultures of West-Central Africa existed and that we can treat these spiritual cultures as sealed constructs. Extensive exchanges and mutual influences were commonplace in times well before and after Cavazzi's observation.[5] The historical processes that resulted in the spread of people and elements of their spiritual cultures has created a diverse sacred landscape inhabited by various nature spirits that bears witness to the many overlapping patterns of cultural interaction over long periods of time. Underneath this diversity, however, the spectrum of nature spirits that includes the nkisi, nkita, and simbi derives from a core body of ideas and practices with a remarkably deep history.

Notions about the existence and roles of these entities extend back thousands of years to the Niger-Congo cultural tradition that originated in West Africa, and from which the earliest Bantu languages and cultures derived. Along with a creator source and ancestral spirits, nature spirits figured as one of the early categories of ethereal beings in this distant tradition.[6] Early Bantu perceptions of the interactions of living people with the realm of spiritual powers focused on nature spirits and the spirits of individuals who died long before the lifetimes of the living. People employed consecrated objects (so-called charms) to channel spiritual powers to influence aspects of their lives, notably as protection from the predatory use of spiritual power by others and for the purpose of protecting villages. Spiritual experts composed these objects and delineated the proper behavioral prohibitions that ensured the efficacy of the objects. Experts also divined the sources of misfortune and cured with the appropriate remedies based on information revealed through dreams and oracles, particularly poison tests that revealed individuals who attempted to harm others through the malevolent manipulation of spiritual power. These ideas, objects, and practices coalesced in the performance of rituals, often involving entire communities, that represented one of the most meaningful expressions of spirituality in these societies.[7]

---

[5] For the few attempts to account for the historical development and spread of a particular set of spiritual ideas and practices in West-Central Africa, see Janzen, *Lemba*; John M. Janzen, *Ngoma: Discourses of Healing in Central and Southern Africa* (Berkeley: University of California Press, 1992); and Klieman, "Of Ancestors and Earth Spirits," 48–59.

[6] Vansina, *Paths in the Rainforests*, 298; and Ehret, *Civilizations of Africa*, 50.

[7] Vansina, *Paths in the Rainforest*, 95–9, 273, 297–301. I have excluded the linguistic reconstructions attached to these ideas, objects, and practices because Vansina's reconstructions are based on a classification of Bantu languages credibly disputed in Christopher

Later Bantu-speaking communities in West-Central Africa retained the core elements of this early Bantu spiritual culture, although innovations in terminology and emphases on certain aspects over others developed in different areas among different groups. Certainly, over the many generations speakers of Bantu languages have regularly drawn on a rich body of concepts that underlay concerns about many aspects of daily life, particularly health and fertility, to redefine old ideas and create new practices to connect with nature spirits in ways that have reflected the evolving purposes of the spirits in the minds of the people who have venerated them.[8] The nkisi, nkita, and simbi in Kongo emerged from this ancient and dynamic Bantu cultural tradition.

The central role of nature spirits derived from the reliance on the natural environment for every aspect of support for communities of the living. This dependence has also informed a larger understanding of the interface between the visible and the invisible realms that has been conceptualized in the very material terms of the natural environment. The broad cosmological explanation of this relationship expressed in the twentieth century has centered on the example of the rising and setting of the sun in a world comprised of primeval earth and water (Figure 1). In the land of the living (*nsi a bamôyo*), the earth resembles a mountain in water from which the sun rises on one coast, passes overhead, and then sets on the other coast. In between the setting and the next rising, the sun journeys through the land of the dead (*nsi a bafwa* or *Mpemba*), which consists of a mountain in water, as well. The two mountains connect at a shared base resembling mirrored images, as the two realms of the land of the living and the land of the dead, and forming complementary inversions of each other. The journey from one to the other requires passage through the water (*n'langu*, *m'bu*, or *kalunga*), which serves as both a window or door and a great barrier between the two lands. Movement through the water establishes connections between the realms of the living and the dead and represents processes of transformation.[9]

The path of the sun through the lands of the living and the dead symbolizes the course of a person's life. According to this scheme, the setting

Ehret, "Bantu Expansion: Re-Envisioning A Central Problem of Early African History," *International Journal of African Historical Studies* 34, 1 (2001): 5–41. See also David Schoenbrun, "Representing the Bantu Expansions: What's At Stake," *International Journal of African Historical Studies* 34, 1 (2001): 1–4.

[8] Vansina, *Paths in the Rainforest*, 98.

[9] A. kia Bunseki-Lumanisa Fu-Kiau, *N'Kongo ye Nza Yakun'Zungidila: Nza-Kôngo (Le Mukongo et le Monde Qui L'entourait)* (Kinshasa, Zaire: Office National de la Recherche et de Dévelopment, 1968), 117–20.

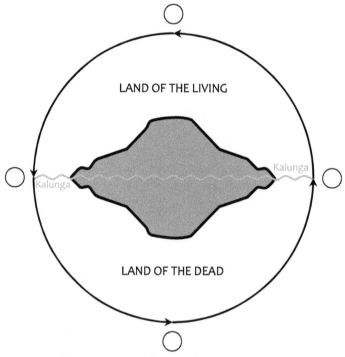

FIGURE 1. The Spiritual Landscape of Kongo Cosmology.
Source: Author's rendering of description in Fu-Kiau, *N'Kongo ye Nza Yakun'Zungidila*, 117–20.

of the sun represents a person's death, while the rising signifies "the continuity of life" and "rebirth." As such, physical death does not mean the end of life. It marks the crossing of the person into the land of the dead with the expectation of transformation and return through rebirth.[10] Explanations of this kind have provided core elements in old initiation societies such as Lemba and Kinkimba. According to the Kongo scholar Fu-Kiau, who has experienced and described the meanings of initiation, "To explain the passage from life to death (= the descent into Mpemba = rebirth) the *nganga* [expert] uses the image of the sun rotating around the earth."[11] In the Kinkimba society, the rotation of the sun is likened to four points in the lives of initiates. The first point represents the rising of the sun, morning, and beginning or birth. At this stage, the father presents the

---

[10] Fu-Kiau, *N'Kongo*, 120. Emphasis, capitalization, and punctuation given in the original.
[11] Fu-Kiau, *N'Kongo*, 122.

initiate to the initiating expert, the *nganga*.[12] The second point represents the pause of the sun at its apex as well as maturity with its responsibilities. This stage includes the initiate's instruction by the nganga in the highest levels of knowledge. The third point represents the setting of the sun, death, and transformation. The nganga completes the transmission of knowledge to the initiate, who in turn becomes a nganga. The fourth point represents midnight and existence in the land of the dead, leading thereafter to rebirth at the first point. These four moments constitute the endpoints of two axes that in graphic form render the image of a cross, which has served as a core design in Kongo iconography.[13]

An element of this model that requires particular attention given the historical circumstances in which West-Central Africans endured captivity and transport to the Americas is the transitory water of kalunga. The symbolic realm of kalunga, which could manifest physically in any body of water including streams, rivers, and pools in addition to the ocean, took on a reality unimagined before the trans-Atlantic trade in captive Africans. Especially for those who crossed it, the sea as kalunga had to assume new meanings that incorporated both the suffering and survival of the experience, ideas often expressed in images and ideas related to water spirits in the form of mermaids, as we will see in Chapter 6. Those who remained in West-Central Africa came to imbue the Atlantic and the people and places in close contact with its strange voyagers with meanings normally associated with the land of the dead. People expressed this transformed awareness of kalunga through their understandings of nature spirits, particularly in those areas affected deeply by Atlantic trade. In this way, ideas and practices associated with nature spirits provided a context for people to make sense of the historical and contemporary dynamics of social change.[14]

The articulation of a cosmological model by initiated experts offers a broad perspective of Kongo spiritual culture essential to understanding the place of people in the relationship between the land of the living and the land of dead, and how that relationship has been conceptualized and consecrated through the activities of the living in the natural

---

[12] *Nganga* eludes easy translation into English. For the present discussion, the glosses "priest" and "doctor" could be added to the meaning "expert" given in the text.

[13] Fu-Kiau, *N'Kongo*, 122–3 (designs appear on 91, 93–6).

[14] Bentley, *Pioneering on the Congo*, 1: 252; Wyatt MacGaffey, "The West in Congolese Experience," in *Africa and the West: Intellectual Responses to European Culture*, ed. Philip D. Curtin (Madison: University of Wisconsin Press, 1972), 49–75; and MacGaffey, *Religion and Society*, 43.

environment. However, people do not live their spiritual cultures through abstractions or models. Instead, the many thoughts and deeds of the living that addressed their daily spiritual needs have taken diverse forms and usually entailed interactions with spirits of the land and water. This begs the questions of where such spirits fit within the cosmology outlined above and how these entities have manifested in the everyday workings of the spiritual cultures of the living.

Any attempt to generalize the various ideas about the simbi and nature spirits in Kongo cultures encounters the complexities that arise from the fact that these concepts have not originated and been revised exclusively through the filters of institutions that have determined which notions retain authoritative status and which do not. Ideas and practices have emanated from the collective imagination of Kongo societies that have shared cultural and linguistic roots, of course, but these communities have also devised variations that have reflected the concerns of different communities in different places and times.[15] Still, we can cautiously represent some of the core principles that people have associated with the place of the simbi within the land of the dead and in relation to the land of the living in a modified version of the Kongo cosmological graphic discussed above. Elaborations on and divergences from this model appear in great detail in the remainder of this chapter.

The simbi and other nature spirits have inhabited those features of the landscape that connect the land of the living with the land of the dead because they ultimately emanated from the spiritual realm. Some are said to have first appeared as beings who existed before the advent of people. Primordial nature spirits included three described in an oral tradition from Cabinda recorded in the twentieth century that emerged from the waterfall at the second cataract of the Nzadi River. These three – Kuiti-Kuiti (the "most powerful of all, creator of all, master of the world"), Bati Randa ("ruler of animals with tails and their creators, who is in charge of rain and water"), and M'boze ("chieftess of prayer") – begat numerous other spirits. For example, the powerful spirit Bunzi was born to M'boze after Kuiti-Kuiti killed M'boze (his sister/wife) in a jealous rage, as she had been impregnated by her son Kanga. Kuiti-Kuiti paired Kanga and Bunzi as husband and wife and sent them to live downriver. Kanga and Bunzi had a mermaid daughter known as LuSunzi in Ngoyo and Tchi

---

[15] "Collective imagination" comes from Jan Vansina, *How Societies Are Born: Governance in West Central Africa before 1600* (Charlottesville: University of Virginia Press, 2004), 268.

Kambizi in Loango. LuSunzi then created other spirits, including Bingo (Buanga), Lemba, and Kalunga to meet the needs of the people in her domain and maintain social order.[16] In many Kongo communities of the interior, Bunzi held the special status of being the "chief of the bisimbi" and "the oldest of the bisimbi," who came from "the deep of the ocean" (that is, from kalunga) and dispersed other simbi across the land through the rains.[17]

In some cases, primordial nature spirits were progenitors of people, as seen in the case of Né-Mbinda Né-Mboma, another son of Kuiti-Kuiti. When Né-Mbinda Né-Mboma expressed his desire to take a wife, Kuiti-Kuiti ordered him to marry his mother, M'boze, and they begat albino twins. Kuiti-Kuiti took these children and carried them to Europe, where the twins had their own children (the ancestors of Europeans).[18] Additionally, the primordial spirit Bunzi paired with Ne M'binda (the "first man") to produce the triplets who became the first kings of Loango, Kakongo, and Ngoyo.[19]

While the primordial simbi had their ultimate origins in the spiritual space and deep temporality of the land of the dead, from which they could generate other spirits and children among the living, some nature spirits developed from people who entered the land of the living and there became nature spirits. This process is represented in Figure 2 by the spiral in the land of the dead, which symbolizes the continuing sequence of redeath and rebirth within the spiritual realm that leads to the transformation of a person into a simbi or other nature spirit.[20] For certain people, the transformation occurred by simply crossing from the land of the living to the land of the dead. According to a seventeenth-century tradition from Angola, the two kilundu spirits Navieza and Cassumba originally came from the Upper Ganguela region of the interior in the form of people afflicted with disease. They departed their homeland and eventually found refuge in an "isolated hut" in the Kisama region, where they died and transformed into local spirits who protected devotees from

---

[16] Janzen, *Lemba*, 302–3.

[17] Laman, *Kongo*, 3: 36; and Wyatt MacGaffey, *Kongo Political Culture: The Conceptual Challenge of the Particular* (Bloomington: Indiana University Press, 2000), 188, 190.

[18] Joaquim Martins, *Cabindas: História, Crença, Usos e Costumes* (Cabinda: Comissão de Tourismo da Cámara Municipal de Cabinda, 1972), 110–13.

[19] English translation provided in Janzen, *Lemba*, 302–3.

[20] This spiral is based on the graphic presented in Kimbwandende kia Bunseki Fu-Kiau, *African Cosmology of the Bântu-Kôngo: Principles of Life and Living* (Brooklyn, NY: Athelia Henrietta, 2001), 19.

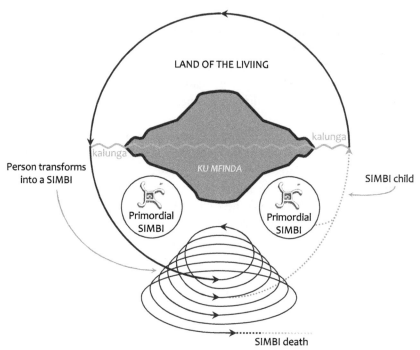

FIGURE 2. The Simbi in the Spiritual Landscape of Kongo Cosmology.
Source: Author's rendering of description in Fu-Kiau, *N'Kongo ye Nza Yakun'Zungidila*, 117–20, and Fu-Kiau, *African Cosmology of the Bântu-Kôngo*, 19.

the infirmity that drove them to leave home.[21] An early twentieth-century account from Kongo described another process through which a person became a nature spirit and a sacred medicine named Mbola:

Once upon a time there was a man who lived to a very great age. He died and was buried in his grave. After burial he lived for a long time in the land of the dead and grew old there. He died once again, but found himself no closer to his relatives there in the land of the dead, so he thought, "What am I to do in this second death? I should become an *nkisi*." So he betook himself to a stream.[22]

This nature spirit then appeared in the dreams of a man who happened to cross the stream, and taught him the procedures for assembling and consecrating the materials needed to employ the power of the spirit for

[21] Cavazzi, *Descrição*, 2: 67.
[22] Original text (Cahier 390) by Nsemi Isaki and translated by MacGaffey in *Kongo Political Culture*, 123–4.

healing and other endeavors.[23] Another account of the same path to achieving the status of nature spirit stated:

Those sojourning in the otherworld live for a very, very long time. When they grow weak from age, they shed their skins as snakes do, are rejuvenated, and become sturdy and strong. Then they live again, weaken, shed their skins, and are renewed once more. After shedding their skins five or six times they become water *simbi* and go to live in pools, wherever there are very hard rocks, and there they settle with those who have previously become *bisimbi*.[24]

The appearance of simbi who derived from people blurs the supposed line between nature spirits and ancestors. In the strictest sense, ancestors consist of the dead with lineal ties to the living and usually include those who lived recently enough to have had personal relationships with their surviving kin. Their proximity to the living, then, defines their realm of influence (those connected by blood or kinship) and their interests in the affairs of people (the state of their lineages). As we have seen in the example of Mbola, however, an ancestor could choose to become a nature spirit, paradoxically, in order to get closer to his people. Implicit in this account is the increased distance from the living represented by the long period in the land of the dead and the ancestor's second death. With the passing of time, his descendants among the living no longer knew him and likely neglected to venerate him. While an ancestor could afflict the living with some misfortune to remind them of their obligations, this ancestor pursued a different spiritual path and became a spirit that did not rely on a restricted group to maintain communication between both sides of kalunga. The stream provided the ideal medium to reach any person among the living who encountered the stream, and only a nature spirit (in this case an nkisi) could employ this habitation to affect those in the land of the living.

Above all, we must keep in mind that perceptions of the connections between nature spirits and ancestors have been fraught with complicated and conflicting notions both between and within local spiritual cultures. For some, the simbi originated as nature spirits indigenous to the local waters and the land, although they also shared a fundamental connection with living people in that they represented "men of the water as we are

---

[23] MacGaffey provides an extensive analysis of Mbola in *Kongo Political Culture*, 115–33.

[24] Original text (Cahier 133) by Kunzi Yelemia and translated by MacGaffey, *Religion and Society*, 74.

men of the earth."[25] An elaboration on this perspective held that the simbi existed as "wandering ancestors on banks of the waters" both "upstream [and] downstream."[26] This put the simbi in the same spiritual continuum as recently deceased ancestors (*bakulu*), although the "wandering" designation and the locations "upstream" and "downstream" suggested temporal remoteness along with the kind of spiritual transformation characteristic of the simbi and other nature spirits regardless of their supposed relationship to an earlier human existence. People in the eastern Kongo region of Mbata were less ambiguous in their understanding of the origins of the simbi, regarding them as the distant ancestors from the beginning times that became spirits of the water and ravines that served as protectors for the living. They have also been thought to have derived from the great chiefs of long ago or as God's intercessors similar to Roman Catholic saints.[27] Similar ideas prevailed in the central Kongo region, where people generally thought of the simbi as having originated with the ancestors of the earliest times who died accidentally or violently, such as those who perished by drowning, falling from a precipice or the top of a palm tree, or suicide by hanging.[28] While they had their ultimate origins as people, they had a status distinct from the spirits of the recently deceased who had retained their ties to their lineages. Following this line of thought, the simbi have existed at the most distant point in the continuum of being for people, such that they have surpassed corporeal existence to become "invisible physical forces."[29] These variations have reflected not only expected local differences but also the evolving layers of thought about ties to the land of the dead derived from many generations of engaging these concerns.[30]

The passage from person to nature spirit through the intermediary stage of ancestor reveals the close connection between the living and the simbi that not only obscures distinctions between the nature spirits and ancestors but also between nature spirits and the living. This is demonstrated most dramatically in the birth of simbi children. Indeed, the simbi could enter the realm of the living in fully human shape as people born with unusual conditions or in unusual circumstances, most notably

[25] Joseph Van Wing, *Études Bakongo: II, Religion et Magie* (Bruxelles: Académie Royale des Sciences d'Outre-Mer, 1938), 16.

[26] Wing, *Études Bakongo*, 19.

[27] Heusch, *Roi de Kongo*, 206, 214.

[28] Wing, *Études Bakongo*, 18, 120; and Buakasa, *Impense du Discours*, 221, 239, 264.

[29] Buakasa, *Impense du Discours*, 239–40, 299–300.

[30] For differing interpretations of these variations, see MacGaffey, *Religion and Society*, 72–82; and Heusch, *Roi de Kongo*, 222–8.

twins, albinos, and dwarves. Individuals like this played significant roles in Kongo spiritual culture as living embodiments of the simbi with special power and authority.[31]

People in Soyo regarded such special children as embodiments of the simbi, too, but also recognized another category of children known as *ki lombo* as manifestations of the simbi. A ki lombo child was a natural leader, so to speak, in that this child was the first of several simbi children born to one woman. As the first of a series of simbi, the ki lombo child revealed his status as a leader by exhibiting at birth certain physical traits associated with political power. A ki lombo child had two "ropes" or "vines" (not the umbilical cord) that came down from the shoulders like shoulder straps and crossed on the infant's chest, a "cap the color of blood" made of the caul that adhered to the head like a skullcap, and an extra digit on a hand. The last feature, the extra digit, symbolized a twin brother (another sign of the simbi) and a hunter's sack, the latter of which served as an emblem of leadership in Soyo. The three attributes of the ki lombo child – the crossed ropes, red cap, and hunter's sack – together represented the core symbols of the Soyo nobility and their claims to power.[32]

When the simbi decided to incarnate as children, they picked their parents from the women who drew water from the river or the men who touched the bottoms of rivers or lagoons with their poles as they propelled boats from one shore to the other. Additionally, the appearance of running water, snakes, and the simbi in the dreams of a pregnant woman presaged the birth of the child as a manifestation of a simbi. Following the birth of simbi children, all the other parents of simbi children (who had the status as nganga simbi) gathered to assess the meaning of this most recent manifestation and begin the necessary observances and ceremonies. As spiritually potent beings, simbi children received special treatment and provided essential assistance for people in life and death. In addition to bestowing their blessings on favored people, their dreams revealed future events and methods to help others evade misfortune or illness typically caused by the malevolent use of spiritual force. Further, the simbi officiated ceremonies of atonement conducted to address the distress caused by disasters that affected the entire community. When they died, the body of the incarnated simbi was wrapped in cloth in a

---

[31] MacGaffey, *Religion and Society*, 87; Heusch, *Roi de Kongo*, 135–7; and MacGaffey, "Twins, Simbi Spirits, and Lwas," 211–16.

[32] J. Troesch, "Le Nkutu du comte de Soyo," *Aequatoria* 24, 2 (1961): 41–7.

squatting position and interred close to their former home, located near a river. This house then served as a pilgrimage site for those seeking the benefits of the simbi's power.[33]

While this description of the simbi and their human incarnations in Soyo comes from the twentieth century, key aspects relate directly to the early eighteenth century observations of the missionary Lorenzo da Lucca in the same region. Lorenzo noted that the birth of twins occasioned the gathering of other mothers and fathers of twins. The association formed by those affected by the birth of twins kept as powerful objects a knife, hoe, and small container of liquid. These objects had to be replaced if touched accidentally by outsiders in order to avoid some misfortune caused by the transgression. At the gathering, members of the group used the knife, hoe, and container in their communal meal, in which the oldest woman placed a small amount of food in the hands of each member, who positioned their hands "one on top of the other in the shape of a cross." This proceeded in silence without the usual sounds of clapping or talking on such occasions. The ritual meal served to promote good health as it prevented illness from swelling and protected the participants from death. Further, members of this group did not consult outside experts in instances of illnesses but treated each other. In another notable practice associated with twins, those who gathered the first harvest of vegetables conscientiously set aside a portion for the mothers of twins to eat to ensure their well-being and defend them from misfortune.[34] Another eighteenth century source mentions the spiritual power of the mothers of twins, stating that people respected them more than other spiritual experts and considered them infallible as oracles. Those who could not realize their desires through the work of the other experts then turned to the mothers. If the intercession of a mother of twins failed, people then resigned themselves to the fact that *Nzambi nzolelequo*, or "God does not want it," and thus accepted the futility of pursuing the matter any further.[35]

While these early written sources on twinning in Kongo do not explicitly link the children and their families to the simbi, aspects of this account warrant particular notice because they mention features expressly associated with the simbi in later times. Clearly, the parents of twins were

---

[33] Weeks, *Among the Primitive Bakongo*, 113–15; and Troesch, "Nkutu du Comte," 43–6.

[34] Lucca, *Relations*, 138–9.

[35] Giacinto Hyancinthe, *La Pratique Missionnaire de PP. Capucins Italiens, dans le Royaumes de Congo, Angola et Contrées Adjacentes*, 1747 (Louvain: Éditions de L'Aucam, 1931), 125–6.

the equivalent of the nganga simbi, and their group resembled the associations connected to the simbi and other nature spirits such as Bunzi, Funza, and Lemba.[36] Further, the objects of the knife and hoe represented consecrated instruments made by blacksmiths, who held an especially significant role in West-Central African spiritual cultures for their association with nature spirits and positions of leadership (which depended on the sanction of nature spirits). Knives, hoes, blacksmith hammers, and similar metal objects have featured prominently in rituals associated with the simbi, as in the consecration of the *minkisi* Mbenza and Mbola, which among other purposes served to ensure the fecundity of women.[37] Additionally, people associated with twins and blacksmiths employed their powers in healing and ensuring well-being, one of the key functions of the simbi in Soyo. [38] Finally, the setting aside of the first vegetable harvest for consumption by mothers of twins put these women in a category of spiritually powerful people connected to the simbi that included political leaders and priests of nature spirits.[39] The link made between the fecundity of the mothers of twins and the continued fertility of the land in this practice acknowledged the need for people to maintain their relationships with the simbi, who provided for both.

This discussion of Figure 2 and its representation of the simbi and other nature spirits in the spiritual landscape of Kongo cosmology shows that West-Central Africans perceived nature spirits as primordial entities, created and begotten beings as well as transformed versions of people who once lived. This wide array of ideas about the origins of nature spirits has ensured that no simple hierarchy or system of classification of spirits could adequately account for the varied stations and roles of nature spirits in West-Central African cultures. The variance of thought on the origins of the simbi has been reflected in the proper forms for pluralizing the term "simbi" in spoken and written Kikongo. In some cases, people have referred to the simbi as *basimbi*, the "*ba-*" prefix usually indicating multiple people. This usage concurs with the understanding that the simbi derived from once-living people or were in some sense part of the human community. Yet people have also employed the "*bi-*" prefix

---

[36] MacGaffey, "Twins, Simbi Spirits, and Lwas," 211–26.

[37] Laman, *Kongo*, 3: 102–4, 129–31; Wyatt MacGaffey, ed. and trans., *Art and Healing of the Bakongo Commented by Themselves: Minkisi from the Laman Collection* (Bloomington: Indiana University Press, 1991), 53–63; and MacGaffey, *Kongo Political Culture*, 115–33.

[38] Lucca, *Relations*, 140.

[39] Hyancinthe, *Pratique Missionnaire*, 125–6.

to render *bisimbi*, which typically denotes nonhuman or even inanimate status. This corresponds with the notion of the simbi as primordial entities manifested in the features of the physical landscape. Both are correct, then, as the simbi have embodied the connotations of the two noun classes. Just as Figure 2 acknowledges both natures of the simbi, the neutral English plural form "the simbi" used in this work allows us to respect the complex essence of the simbi communicated through both basimbi and bisimbi.

The overlapping and interconnected existence of the simbi with the nkisi and nkita that appear in sources from the nineteenth century and after suggests that the earlier record of the nkisi and nkita can provide a context for imagining the place of the simbi during the era of the trans-Atlantic trade in captives. As such, an examination of the characteristics and roles of these cognate spirits supplies a historical grounding for the extended consideration of the simbi that follows.

The nature spirits of the lands and waters on the north side of the Nzadi River represent an interesting case in that the prevailing term for these entities, nkisi, has multiple meanings and variant forms throughout West-Central and Central Africa. Most students of the Kongo culture and the Kongo-Atlantic diaspora know of the nkisi as consecrated objects (minkisi), commonly glossed as "charms" or "fetishes."[40] The nature spirits called nkisi (or in the proper plural form, *bakisi*), however, have not been effectively addressed in the diaspora scholarship even though the term "nkisi" most often appears in the Americas in reference to West-Central African nature spirits (e.g., *enkisi* in Cuba and *enquice* in Brazil), not consecrated objects. This may result from the difficulties posed by the intricate interlacing of spirits, ideas, and objects associated with the term in some societies along with the range of meanings found in different contexts throughout West-Central Africa. Nevertheless, the nkisi nature spirits have influenced inhabited lands and waters stretching from the Atlantic coast through the forests and mountains of Mayombe to the central areas of the Kongo cultural realm.[41]

During the era of the trans-Atlantic trade in captive Africans, inhabitants of the Loango Coast and Lower Nzadi regions applied the term

---

[40] For minkisi in Kongo and the diaspora, see Wyatt MacGaffey and Michael D. Harris, *Astonishment and Power: Kongo Minkisi and the Art of Renée Stout* (Washington, DC: National Museum of African Art, 1993); Thompson, *Flash of the Spirit*, 117–31; Thompson, *Face of the Gods*, 105–45; MacGaffey, *Art and Healing*; MacGaffey, *Kongo Political Culture*, 78–133; and Young, *Rituals of Resistance*, 105–33.

[41] Janzen, *Ngoma*, 201; and Vansina, *How Societies Are Born*, 51–2 n.97.

mukisi (nkisi in more recent usage) to four related realms of meaning. Mukisi referred to nature spirits, objects consecrated to nature spirits, people seen as embodying remarkable spiritual power, and power from the spirit world.[42] A seventeenth-century account, attributed to Olfert Dapper, described the shrines, objects, people, and practices connected to fourteen of the nkisi of Loango, although the author noted that many others existed for which he did not have enough information to discuss adequately. According to this source:

> [The people of Loango] invoke household and country demons, to which they attribute different virtues; one presides over the rains, another over the winds, storms, and agriculture, this one commands the fish of the river, that one wills the sea creatures. There is one who maintains health, the others protect from illnesses and unfortunate mishaps. Some are said to be protectors of families, some others have the power to reveal mysteries and foretell future things.[43]

In addition to having influence over various aspects of life, people accorded certain nature spirits exceptional status, especially in areas such as the coastal kingdoms on the north side of the Nzadi River where key spirits were regarded as patrons of rulers and their lands. A Dutch document from the 1640s noted, "Each region has its particular *moquisis* that prevail over the others. Thus in Loango, they venerate *kykocke*, in Zary, *Bonsy*, in Pombo, *kitouba*, in Cacongo *imbomba*".[44]

Early inventories of the nkisi provide historical background for a few of the same spirits that also appear in ethnographies from the nineteenth and twentieth century. This material confirms a degree of continuity but also indicates that the institutions and numbers of followers of nature spirits waxed and waned according to various factors.[45] Despite the numerous changes, important concepts about the nkisi and the identities of certain nkisi have remained at the forefront of the spiritual cultures of communities in the Loango coast and lower Nzadi River regions. The distinction in Dapper's book between "household and country demons" points to one of these enduring features. These kinds of demons apparently refer

---

[42] Olfert Dapper, *Description de l'Afrique, contenant Les Noms, la Situation & les Confins de toutes ses Parties, leurs Rivieres, leurs Villes & leurs Habitations, leurs Plantes & leurs Animaux; les Moeurs, les Coûtumes, la Langue, les Richesses, la Religion & le Gouvernment de ses Peuples* (Amsterdam: Wolfgang, Waesberge, Boom and van Someren, 1686), 332–8.

[43] Dapper, *Description*, 333.

[44] Cappelle, "Brève description," 231.

[45] For examples of changes and the social conditions related to these changes, see Janzen, *Lemba*, 54–8.

to the two major categories of nature spirits in Loango, the nkisi (plural bakisi) and the *nkisi si* (plural *bakisi basi*). The nkisi include nature spirits not bound to a particular space and accessed by any person with the inclination to venerate them properly. The nkisi si inhabit a defined region or territory (as reflected in the designation si) with the appropriate shrines and priests and have specific attachments to certain clans, as they ultimately derived from deified ancestors.[46]

Although Dapper's account did not elaborate on this distinction, late eighteenth-century works penned by the Frenchmen Liévin-Bonaventure Proyart and Jean-Joseph Descourvières give additional information. Proyart described "Idols of the first order" as being "honored less as Gods than as interpreters of the Divinity" and physically represented by "roughly worked wood figures" kept in temples "neither more large, nor more richly decorated than ordinary houses." The inhabitants of Loango established these "idols" in towns, villages, "in the woods and in remote places," to which people made pilgrimages to consult them to receive blessings for their endeavors, particularly business ventures or marriage. The "idols" of the second order, the nkisi, included those that people maintained in their homes without the visible rites associated with the nkisi si, although people offered beverages to the consecrated statues and poured some of the drink on the ground before partaking themselves. Proyart and Descourvières associated these "idols" with items such as little anthropomorphic figures made of wood or ivory, fish teeth, bird feathers, and plant fibers that people wore for protection. Also in this category were branches of sacred trees along with pieces of broken pots installed in cultivated fields and in front of huts to guard crops and possessions.[47] The "idols of the first order" clearly comprised the nkisi si and those of the second order included nkisi, although neither author named these classes of "idols" as nkisi, and offered no identification of

[46] Frank Hagenbucher-Sacripanti, *Les Fondements Spirituels du Pouvoir au Royaume de Loango* (Paris: O.R.S.T.O.M., 1973), 30, 103–6; and Hersak, "There Are Many Kongo Worlds," 618–9.

[47] Liévin-Bonaventure Proyart, *Histoire de Loango, Kakongo, et Autres Royaumes d'Afrique* (Paris: C.P. Berton and N. Crapart, 1776), 191–3; and Jean-Joseph Descourvières, "Relation de la missión des prestres séculiers pour le Royaume de Loango et les environs," in *Documents sur une Mission Française au Kakongo, 1766–1776*, ed. Jean Cuvelier (Bruxelles: Institut Royal Colonial Belge, 1953), 53–4. Hippolyte-Louis-Antoine de Capellis noted similar objects and practices for Ngoyo in his report based on his 1784 voyage reproduced in François Gaulme, "Notes et Documents: Un document sur le Ngoyo et ses voisins en 1784: 'Observation sur la navigation et le commerce de l côte d'Angole' du comte de Capellis," *Revue Française d'Histoire D'Outre Mer* 64, 3 (1977): 368–9.

particular spirits. Nevertheless, the woods and remote places mentioned in these accounts likely referred to sacred groves (*chibila*) maintained as the centers for honoring the deified ancestors of clans.[48] In addition to the sacred trees, shrines, priests, and consecrated objects, sacred groves included "a spring or a lagoon or swamp or well of some kind containing or connected with perhaps the home of its snake," the snakes representing the nkisi si.[49]

In addition to making a distinction between bakisi basi and bakisi, people in Loango and nearby regions identified nature spirits as spirits of the land (*bakisi banthandu*) and water (*bakisi bamasi*). The spirits from both domains played crucial roles in the occurrence and treatment of illness and misfortune, although the spirits of the water appeared dedicated to addressing issues of fertility, such as the ability of women to conceive and carry babies as well as the state of health of infants.[50] Just to the south in Cabinda, the territory of the former kingdom Ngoyo, it does not appear that the land and water distinction held as much influence in the beliefs pertaining to the bakisi basi, although water origins remained important.[51] Further inland, people recognized the presence of the nkisi as either a distinct category of spirits or simply as individual entities within another set of nature spirits.[52] Additionally, northern and central Kongo communities by the early twentieth century tended to use nkisi and simbi interchangeably to name nature spirits, although it remains unclear how long inhabitants of these areas had done so.[53]

Like the nkisi, nkita nature spirits appear in seventeenth and early eighteenth century sources, although they appear predominantly in societies located in the eastern provinces of the kingdom of Kongo. The earliest

[48] Hagenbucher-Sacripanti, *Fondements Spirituels*, 31, 33, 52, 66.

[49] R.E. Dennett, *At the Back of the Black Man's Mind, Or Notes on the Kingly Office in West Africa* (London: MacMillan and Co., 1906), 97 (see pp. 96–101, 110–19, 139–46 for context). See also René Mavoungou Pambou, *Proverbes et Dictons du Loango en Afrique Centrale: Langue, Culture et Société* (Jouy-le-Moutier, France: Bajag-Meri, 1997), 94–7.

[50] Hagenbuscher-Sacripanti, *Fondements Spirituels*, 105, 113–40.

[51] Martins, *Cabindas*, 112, 113; and Carlos Serrano, *Os Senhores da Terra e Os Homens do Mar* (São Paulo: FLHC/USP, 1983), 56.

[52] Cavazzi, *Descrição*, 2: 60; Léo Bittremieux, *Société Secrète des Bakhimba au Mayombe* (Bruxelles: Librairie Flak Fils, 1936), 140; Wing, *Études Bakongo*, 119–21; and Mesquita Lima, *Os Akixi (Mascarados) do Nordeste de Angola* (Lisboa: Companhia de Diamantes de Angola, 1967), 81–90.

[53] John M. Janzen and Wyatt MacGaffey, *An Anthology of Kongo Religion* (Lawrence: University of Kansas Publications in Anthropology, Number 5, 1974), 59, 77; and MacGaffey, *Art and Healing*, 84.

written sources state that people known as *aquaquita* (nkita people) gathered in the *nzo a quimpazi* (house of *kimpasi*), where they had a wooden cross painted in many colors to "invoke a demon that they call *nquita* [nkita]," and become "filled with spirit of *nquita*." This association was identified as *Chinpassi Chianchita (Kimpasi kia Nkita)*, and the leaders carried the title of *Nganganchita (Nganga Nkita)*. [54] The ubiquity of Kimpasi groups and their meeting places in eastern Kongo and nearby lands resounds through the writings of European missionaries, who perceived Kimpasi as the greatest institutional rival to the firm establishment of Christianity and their claim to exclusive spiritual authority. Regarding the mission in Nkusu, one of the regions with extensive Kimpasi activities, Cavazzi recounted that the missionaries not only received sanction from the king of Congo to bring people together for catechism and baptize adults and children but, most importantly, to go throughout the province "knocking down the *Kimpasi* of idols and the signs of idolatry" as a key function of their "apostolic ministry." [55] The efforts of Roman Catholic priests to destroy the buildings and objects associated with Kimpasi often led to physical conflict as members of the societies vigorously defended their sacred institutions. [56]

Despite periods, particularly the tumultuous 1660s, when state support greatly facilitated the destructive endeavors of missionaries, Kimpasi and other initiation societies retained their relevance and preserved associations with the nkita into the twentieth century. [57] The nkita continued to animate the consecrated objects of Kimpasi and represent the focus of the institution, as initiates had to undergo *fwa nkita* (nkita death) and experience rebirth through the nkita, thus transforming into nkita people. Other initiation societies throughout the Kongo cultural realm

---

[54] Buenaventura de Corella, "Brève relation des rites païens, des cérémonies diaboliques et des superstitions du malheureux royaume du Congo pour informer les supérieurs," in *L'Ancien Congo et l'Angola, 1639–1655, d'après les Archives Romaines Portugaises, Néerlandaises et Espagnoles*, ed. Louis Jadin (Bruxelles: Institut Historique Belge de Rome, 1975), 1151–2; and Girolamo da Montesarchio, "Viaggio del Gongho ciò è Relatione scritta da un nostro Mesionario Cappuccino P. Girolamo da Monte Sarchio Della Prov(inci)a di Napoli morto in Arezzo il 29 Maggio 1669," in *La Prefettura Apostolica del Congo alla Metà del XVII Secolo*, ed. Calogero Piazza (Milano: Dott. A. Giuffrè Editore, 1976), 248–54.

[55] Cavazzi, *Descrição*, 4: 27.

[56] Cavazzi, *Descrição*, 4: 136–8; Marcellino d'Atri, "Giornate apostoliche fatted a me Fra Marcellino...nelle Messione del regni d'Angola e Congo...," in *L'anarchia Congolese nel sec. XVII: la relazione inedita di Marcellino d'Atri*, ed. Carlo Toso (Genoa: Bozzi, 1984), 199–203; and Hilton, *Kingdom of Kongo*, 195–7.

[57] Wing, *Études Bakongo*, 172–249; and Ngoma Ngambu, *Initiation dans les Société Traditionelles Africaines (Le Cas Kongo)* (Kinshasa-Zaire: Presses Universitaires du Zaire, 1981), 75–92.

drew upon the transformative power of the nkita while inducting their members, as well.[58] Additionally, the nkita provided the spiritual power employed in many consecrated medicines (minkisi), as they figured at the center of therapeutic initiation groups intended to remediate certain afflictions that entailed both biological ailments and social problems.[59]

THE SIMBI

The simbi have shared space with the nkisi and nkita throughout parts of the Kongo cultural realm, and individual simbi spirits have occupied places in areas normally dominated by the nkisi or the kilundu outside of Kongo.[60] Unlike the nkisi and nkita that originated within other communities, the simbi appear to have been an innovation within Kongo-speaking groups as a uniquely Kongo interpretation of the spiritual landscape. Unfortunately, the historical record for the simbi remains obscure in comparison to that for the nkisi, nkita, and kilundu. None of the seventeenth- and early eighteenth-century written sources identify the simbi by name, and the proper historical linguistic and comparative cultural work has not been done to suggest possible time ranges for the innovation or borrowing of the simbi in Kongo.

The earliest documentation of an entity called simbi comes from the early nineteenth century in a report from an English reconnaissance mission that mentioned a prominent rock outcropping inhabited by a "Seembi" (simbi) that presided over a particular section of the Nzadi.[61] The existence of the simbi cannot be doubted for earlier times, however, as captives from West-Central Africa carried the knowledge and

---

[58] John H. Weeks, "The Congo Medicine-Man and His Black and White Magic," *Folklore* 21, 4 (1910): 466–7; and Bittremieux, *Société Secrète*, 153–4.

[59] Bittremieux, *Société Secrète*, 153–62; Wing, *Études Bakongo*, 153–4, 256–72; Laman, *Kongo*, 3: 132; Gerard Buakasa, "Notes sur la kindoki chez les Kongo," *Cahiers des Religions Africaines* 2, 3 (1968): 158–61; Buakasa, *Impense du Discours*, 157–63; and Nolet de Brauware, "Les *nkita* comme pantomime des personages extraordinaire chez les Kongo du Bas-Congo," *Anthropos* 94, 4–6 (1999): 401–18.

[60] Hagenbucher-Sacripanti, *Fondements Spirituels*, 105; Alexandre Visseq, *Dictionaire Fiot-Française* (Paris: Maison-Mère, 1890), 157; Heli Chatelain, *Folk-Tales of Angola: Fifty Tales, with Ki-Mbundu Text, Literal English Translation, Introduction, and Notes* (Boston and New York: American Folk-Lore Society, 1894), 115, 117, 274, 283–4; and Virgilio Coelho, "Imagens, Simbolos e Representaçoes 'Quiandas, Quintas, Sereias': Imaginários Locais, Identidades Regionais e Alteridades," *Ngola* 1, 1 (1997): 147, 149.

[61] James Hingston Tuckey, *Narrative of an Expedition to Explore the River Zaire, Usually Called the Congo, in South Africa, 1816, Under the Direction of Captain J. K. Tuckey* (London: John Murray, 1818), 97, 302, 303, 380.

name of the simbi to the Americas, particularly the Lowcountry and Saint-Domingue, no later than the late eighteenth century, as that period marked the end of the transport of captive Africans to the latter colony. Additionally, a seventeenth-century dictionary of Kikongo recorded the use of the term *isimba ia nsi* to describe the prominent and distinguished members of society.[62] This appears related both in form and meaning to the terms *kisímbi kinsí* and *simbi kyansi* used in some Kongo dialects to mean "a very old person" or "a very old person who does not die," respectively.[63] As an early twentieth-century Kongo source explained, "Very old people are sometimes called bisimbi, as everything is decided by them. This power is accorded them because they are considered the basimbi (guardians) of the country."[64] Living elders, then, had been likened to the simbi in more recent times, which puts the seventeenth-century term in a cultural context that extends beyond the simple translation of the phrase. The term "isimba ia nsi" as used in the seventeenth century could very well represent an early reference to the core idea associated with the simbi or even an indirect mention of the simbi themselves, as the phrase (literally, "guardians of the land") mirrors exactly the titles reserved for nature spirits throughout the Kongo-speaking region.

The array of forms and meanings related to the term "simbi" in recent times provides an entry into the complex spiritual cultures in West-Central Africa that have intertwined people (living and dead), spiritual entities, spiritual forces, and objects within intricate relationships of multivalent, overlapping ideas and practices. Providing a succinct definition of the simbi within this context proves difficult. While the gloss "nature spirit" serves as an appropriate term for general use, it does not convey a comprehensive understanding of the essence of the simbi. Further, descriptions of the simbi reveal knowledge that does not readily conform to the meaning of spirits alone. This concern emerges clearly in an account written in the early twentieth century by a Kongo man, Kavuna Simon, about the multiple dimensions of the simbi:

What are *bisimbi*? They have other names, too. Some are called python, lightning, gourd or calabash, mortar or a sort of pot....They have many appearances of all kinds. Some are seen to be green, or red, black, perhaps in spotted or sparkling colors. The body in which they are appealed to is of three or four kinds: 1) the

---

[62] Joseph Van Wing and C. Penders, eds., *Le Plus Ancien Dictionnaire Bantu = Het Oudste Bantu-Woordenboek: Vocabularium p. Georgii Gelensis* (Louvain: J. Kuyl-Otto, 1928), 83.

[63] Laman, *Dictionnaire Kikongo*, 292, 899.

[64] Laman, *Kongo*, 3: 34.

body of a person 2) of a snake such as a python or viper 3) a calabash or gourd 4) of wood or pottery. Sometimes, a spark of fire.[65]

Another source described white hens, parrots (and birds whose coloring resembled parrots), driver-ants, twisted trees, and "various objects rising to the surface of the water" as physical forms of the simbi.[66] Additionally, as some of the simbi concluded their spiritual development in the land of the dead, they materialized in the land of the living as termite hills.[67] The simbi also took on quasi-anthropomorphic forms, as the following explanation attests: "The water bisimbi are white....The water bisimbi are short of stature...and have a fish tail, but a human face."[68]

In depicting the simbi as people, animals, organic and inorganic objects, and even the fleeting burst of energy from a fire, these accounts introduce a remarkable range of simbi forms and imply they represent something more than their many manifestations as particular spiritual beings or distinct physical objects. In the most fundamental sense of its meaning, the word simbi evokes a conceptualization of the energy or power that supports the existence and development of all life.[69] The etymology of the term reveals the essential meaning of the simbi for the people who relied upon the idea and entities designated as simbi. The name simbi derives from the verb *simba*, meaning "to hold, keep, preserve" as well as "to take hold of, to seize" and "to support."[70] The cluster of meanings attached to simba reflects key aspects of the relationship between people and the simbi. First, the simbi would often "seize," "hold," or "capture" people through possession or an illness to create a spiritual bond with those individuals.[71] Second, people did their own seizing as they "captured" the powers of the simbi by collecting the proper natural objects (such

[65] Kavuna Simon, translated by MacGaffey in *Kongo Political Culture*, 141. This can be seen readily in the amalgam of accounts included in the "Basimbi" chapter in Laman's *Kongo*, 3: 33–43.

[66] Laman, *Kongo*, 3: 36.

[67] Laman, *Kongo*, 3; 34.

[68] Laman, *Kongo*, 3: 33. It is worth noting that according to the missionary J.H. Weeks, the inhabitants of São Salvador regarded the people of the interior further up the Nzadi River as "half fish and half human" in *Among Congo Cannibals: Experiences, Impressions, and Adventures During A Thirty Years' Sojourn Amongst the Boloki and Other Congo Tribes, With A Description of Their Curious Habits, Customs, Religion, & Laws* (London: Seeley, Service and Co., 1913), 17.

[69] K. kia Bunseki Fu-Kiau, *Sîmbi Sîmba: Hold Up That Which Holds You Up* (Pittsburgh, PA: Dorrance Publishing, 2006), 1–5.

[70] Laman, *Kongo*, 3: 33; and Van Wing and Penders, *Plus Ancien Dictionnaire Bantu*, 297.

[71] The use of "seize," "hold," and "capture" comes from Laman, *Kongo*, 3: 33–6; and MacGaffey, *Art and Healing*, 88.

as stones) from simbi sites and incorporating these objects into sacred compositions (minkisi).[72] Third and most significant for this understanding of the simbi, their role in protecting, preserving, and supporting people who honored them elevated them to the ultimate guardians of the land and people. Indeed, the simbi "are found wherever people dwell. As the basimbi…safeguard the country, man could not exist anywhere without them….Their duty is to assist man."[73] As these statements attest, the dependency of people on the support given by the simbi has comprised the essence of their meaning, whether they manifested as spirits, people, objects, or forces associated with the natural environment. The rest of this section explores the diverse conceptions of the simbi and the ways people expressed their relationships with them.

A few simbi earned renown across regions, most notably Bunzi, described as the "chief of the bisimbi" and "the oldest of the bisimbi." Under various names such as Mpulu Bunzi, Mpulu Buzi, Mpulu Bisi, or Mangundazi, this great simbi affected the living through heavy rains and destructive floods.[74] Mpulu Bunzi, considered as male or female in different places, "lives in the deep of the ocean but travels in the rain to scatter bisimbi in the form of the red and white stones which ones discovers in gulleys and pools."[75] People credited Mpulu Bunzi with creating peculiar natural objects, most notably termite hills and unusual stones that represented the simbi. Additionally, Mpulu Bunzi provided the "power to cure diseases and support the people," typically through minkisi (consecrated objects), the first of which he composed "in the water," thus establishing the original bisimbi line of minkisi.[76]

For northern Kongo groups, the female Mpulu Bunzi featured in a tradition pitting her against her male rival, Mpangu Lusunzi, another mighty simbi. Mpangu Lusunzi took the physical form of an "upright stone stuck deep into the ground," described as "a white child with two eyes, that looks upwards and cannot sleep."[77] This spirit and his stone

---

[72] Laman, *Kongo*, 3: 35, 36; Buakasa, *Impense du Discours*, 268–9, 295, 300; MacGaffey, *Religion and Society*, 107–45; and MacGaffey, *Kongo Political Culture*, 50, 78–96. The descriptions in Buakasa and another account in the third volume of Laman's *Kongo* series (pg. 43) present the process of finding and capturing simbi as very much like the act of hunting.

[73] Laman, *Kongo*, 3: 33.

[74] Laman, *Kongo*, 3: 36; MacGaffey, *Kongo Political Culture*, 190.

[75] Lutute Esaya (Cahier 235), translated by Wyatt MacGaffey, *Kongo Political Culture*, 188.

[76] Laman, *Kongo*, 3: 69.

[77] Laman, *Kongo*, 3: 37; and MacGaffey, *Kongo Political Culture*, 188.

embodied a power so destructive that pregnant women did not dare to come near its presence for fear of having their pregnancies terminated. The tradition recounts Mpulu Bunzi's ultimate clash with her foe:

Once upon a time, (M)Pulubunzi...came across Pangu Lusunzi in the Nsinda grassfield. She saw Pangu Lusunzi standing there and asked him why he did so. He said, "Thus I made myself, not to lie down." She said, "Lie down!" Pangu Lusunzi said, "I refuse." After that they wrestled; Pulubunzi was strong and defeated Pangu Lusunzi, who broke in half about the middle. Upon this there came a heavy rain, a storm that lasted two days, with great peals of thunder. People passing by saw the stump of Pangu Lusunzi, cut off as though by a saw, and stood it up again.[78]

In this context, Mpangu Lusunzi appears to represent the threat of sterility and by metaphorical extension the danger of drought. Mpulu Bunzi, by contrast, embodies fertility through the rain that followed her victory of Mpangu Lusunzi and, as seen above, through dispersing her many children (the simbi) in the rains.[79]

Mpangu Lusunzi did not carry negative associations in all contexts, however. In point of fact, Lusunzi served as a basic designation for simbi in Mayombe and the southern Kongo region that had strong associations with extraordinary rocks, political power, and fertility. The rock linked to Lusunzi has occupied a particularly significant place in the spiritual and political culture of the Kibangu region since the seventeenth century. Further, the nature spirit Mwema Lusunzi was connected to a highly regarded political title because it derived from the Mpangu Luzunzi site. The investiture of a chief with Mwema Lusunzi included the recitation of certain praises: "As Mwema Lusunzi flourishes, so may the chief flourish. Where the simbi is planted, there also chiefship is planted. The chief is simbi, the chief is leopard."[80]

Whereas various forms of Bunzi and Lusunzi existed in multiple regions, most simbi inhabited specific locations and retained unique identities associated with those places. The most common sites for the simbi included watery domains such as streams, rivers, lagoons, springs, waterfalls, marshes, and whirlpools.[81] A number of these sites gained notoriety because of their powerful simbi residents. The simbi called Kidi-Kidi

---

[78] Lutete Esaya (Cahier 235), translated in MacGaffey, *Kongo Political Culture*, 188–9.
[79] For a fuller analysis of this tradition, see Heusch, *Roi de Kongo*, 277–9.
[80] Lutete Esaya (Cahier 235), translated in MacGaffey, *Kongo Political Culture*, 196.
[81] W. Holman Bentley, *Dictionary and Grammar of the Kongo Language, As Spoken at San Salvador, the Ancient Capital of the Old Kongo Empire, West Africa* (London: Basptist Missionary Society, 1887), 466, 503; Weeks, *Among the Primitive Bakongo*,

(named for the sound of splashing water) protected the dark waters that obscured stones on the bottom of a cave pool known by the same name as the spirits. This pool thus became an ideal spot for powerful people to leave their vital essence for safekeeping by the simbi. The "mighty chief" Nangoma Neuka created a bond with the simbi at Kidi-Kidi to ensure a long life, which he enjoyed until he drank water from the pool, which enabled him to finally die and join his kin in the land of the dead. Many other famous pools served that same purpose and earned reputations as dreadful, terrifying sites. To add to the danger, ritual specialists enlisted the most feared of predators, such as the crocodile and *mboma* python, to keep souls in their bodies and attack trespassers.[82]

Just as they used their power against malevolent trespassers, the simbi turned their might against each other at times. The mournful cries (*lwami*) that arose from a clash between five simbi provided the name for the waterfall Lwami, home to the single simbi that triumphed in the conflict. The other four simbi found refuge in another waterfall called Mbutani (derived from *butana*, "to multiply"). Other groups of simbi parted more amicably, such as the brothers of Bikungu, the elder simbi inhabiting the waterfall of the same name. His siblings decided to found their own "villages," which consisted of three separate pools along the descending path of the water as it tumbled over remarkably smooth rocks. Upon first beholding these beautiful waterfalls, visitors wail (*kunga*), which apparently provided the source for the name of the simbi and waterfall.[83]

In eastern Kongo, the waters of the simbi also comprised the pools where women left their manioc to soak before it could be prepared for consumption. In these same pools, the bursting of bubbles on the surface of the water represented nkita spirits released by the simbi, who blew on the water to send out their nkita emissaries to heal various afflictions. Additionally, the simbi took the form of the white catfish called *kisimbi ki ngola* that coiled around the ankles of those fishing in their waters, an event that required them to seek spiritual transformation through ritual therapy.[84] People in Mayombe bathed in the waters known to belong to the simbi in the hopes of restoring vitality or to ease the disabilities caused by birth defects, paralysis, and rheumatism.[85] The simbi

---

113; Bittremieux, *Société Secrète*, 155; Troesch, "Nkutu du Comte," 43–6; and Buakasa, *Impense du Discours*, 239–41.

[82] Laman, *Kongo*, 3: 38–40.

[83] Laman, *Kongo*, 3: 41.

[84] Heusch, *Roi de Kongo*, 206, 214.

[85] Bittremieux, *Société Secrète*, 155.

in southern Kongo were thought to guard springs and streams to maintain the potability of the waters for local people. Bitter water indicated that the simbi did not approve of the state of nearby communities and required some sort of remediation.[86]

People along the north bank of the Nzadi near the river port city of Boma saw the simbi as powerful and ultimately dangerous spirits that animated whirlpools and resided in the river's cataracts. The roar of the water crashing over the cataracts sounded like the simbi crying out, "Kill, kill," (*vonda, vonda*) according to the local inhabitants.[87] This idea may have derived from the fact that the stretch of the Nzadi between the waterfalls at Yelala and Boma were considered especially treacherous owing to the strong eddies that seized the largest ships and "twirled [them] about like toy boats."[88] The whirlpools appeared suddenly, pulling vessels down into their swirling currents, only to die just as swiftly and reappear nearby. These troubled waters churned and bubbled to such an extent near Tunduwa Point that Europeans took to calling this spot in the river Hell's Cauldron. John Weeks, who traveled along the Nzadi in the late nineteenth century, recalled one harrowing experience when the small boat that he and several others rowed to cross the river was sucked into a whirlpool. As they sank deeper into the vortex, they spun faster and faster, and "just as we thought the next turn or two would surely engulf us, the whirlpool filled and we were riding safely on the bubbling waters." Rather than laugh nervously as crews normally did to express relief and disguise their fear, these passengers were "hushed by the almost audible beating of our hearts, as we fully realized how near we had been to the unseen and the eternal."[89] It comes as no surprise then that many of the Africans familiar with the river frequently refused to accompany Europeans in these perilous waters, as they viewed them as abodes of powerful spirits.[90]

In addition to aquatic sites, the simbi inhabited extraordinary mountains that had unusual rock formations. Ngo Nuni rose so high that it provided a view of every other mountain in the region. This mountain and its simbi derived their name from the eagles that rested there. People in the region identified with the birds, mountain, and the simbi

---

[86] Weeks, *Among the Primitive Bakongo*, 113, 294; and Buakasa, *Impense du Discours*, 239–41.
[87] Schrag, "Mboma," 39.
[88] Weeks, *Among the Primitive Bakongo*, 299.
[89] Weeks, *Among the Primitive Bakongo*, 300.
[90] Tuckey, *Narrative*, 96.

as expressed in the motto, "I am crowned with the eagle. The leopard is quickly killed, but the eagle lives forever."[91] Next to Ngo Nuni stood Nkodo Masu, with its two large vertical rocks, abundant streams, and caves filled with the simbi and their animal allies, including porcupines, sloth monkeys, and birds, among others. The simbi Nkodo Masu was considered the head spirit among the Mangundazi group of simbi, which were collectively reputed to be the oldest of the simbi as confirmed by the presence of two exceptional rocks on the mountain.[92] Ngunga Nlembo had thirty-six peaks that extend straight up, each with its own simbi. The large mountain Kintadi had eight stones on its summit that the "old people called...the eight basimbi erected by Nzambi, that are impossible to budge."[93] The stones shaped like chests on Tadi ("the rock") served as homes for the simbi and containers for them to safely store their belongings.[94]

Many of these simbi mountains commemorated the travels throughout the land of the aforementioned Mpulu Bunzi to check on the "children" (simbi) distributed in earlier times. Kyavulu, Tadi, Nzingu-nzingu, and Nsangu stood as well-known resting places for Mpulu Bunzi that also housed powerful simbi. Nsangu was especially significant, as it served as a meeting place for all the simbi. At this gathering point, Mpulu Bunzi "walks the mountain to meet his followers and renew their trust in him after his long absence from their midst"[95]

A particularly well-known and remarkable location, Fetiche Rock, encompassed two of the natural features commonly associated with the simbi in this region: whirlpools and unusual rocks. Situated downriver of Boma, this site, known to local people then as Taddi Moenga (or "Taddy d'ya M'wangoo") and today as Ntadi Nkisi, represented a "magnificent scene." The large and steep formations hindered access from the river and presented a rock face that soared high above the water with its many eddies. Numerous crystalline formations included rocks with circumferences measuring 100–200 feet. The presiding spirit of this landmark and

---

[91] Laman, *Kongo*, 3: 42.

[92] Laman, *Kongo*, 3: 42. While the passage in Laman referred to Mangundazi as a group of spirits ("*ba Mangundazi*"), a text by Lutete Esaya (Cahier 232) identifies Mangundazi as an individual spirit (MacGaffey, *Kongo Political Culture*, 190). The name means "a person of great honor," and was also used in the phrase *mangundazi a mangundazi* ("king of kings"), which indicates that it was a title as much as personal name. See MacGaffey, *Kongo Political Culture*, 254 n42.

[93] Laman, *Kongo*, 3: 41.

[94] Laman, *Kongo*, 3: 41–2.

[95] Laman, *Kongo*, 3: 42.

nearby portions of the river was known as Seembi (simbi).[96] This may have been the unique name of the spirit, similar to the entity Nsimbi, who had a shrine downriver near the mouth of the Nzadi and served as the guardian over people in the vicinity.[97] Seembi could also have referred to the kind of spirit (simbi) that inhabited these rocks and was known specifically by the individual name of M'wangoo or Moenga. In either case, a simbi occupied this prominent site imbued with exceptional spiritual meaning.

Another feature of Taddi Moenga that enhanced its spiritual status was the presence of figures of people, animals, and symbolic shapes made on the surfaces of the rocks with a paste of sand and ashes. People considered the images sacred, although the purposes and meanings of the images were not revealed to John Hawkey, who documented the shapes and information about them in the early nineteenth century. According to Hawkey's informants, a "learned priest of Nokki" created the figures and taught other people about them. Several of the figures depict hunters taking on crocodiles, hippopotamuses, deer, and birds. Others portray animals alone, including elephants, crocodiles, lizards, buffalos, birds, and snakes. The figures that focus on people include images of men carried in hammocks by servants. Another set of shapes evokes representations of Kongolese thoughts on the movement of a person between the visible physical realm and the invisible spiritual realm within the process of maturation and transformation that forms the essence of existence (Figure 3).[98]

The spiritual significance of this part of the Nzadi River near Taddi Moenga was heightened by another natural feature on the other bank of the river. The rock formation known as Taddy Enzazzi (*Ntadi Nzazi*, meaning "lightening stone") stands atop a hill as a natural obelisk that resembles a human-made tower (Figure 4). This feature most certainly has been regarded as a spiritually potent object for a very long time, as noted in the early nineteenth century, and people have continued to venerate it into the present.[99] Nzazi as the spirit of thunder and lightning appears in oral traditions among the cohort of the most powerful nature spirits that included Mbumba Luangu and Mpulu Bunzi.[100] Also, Nzazi

---

[96] Tuckey, *Narrative*, 295, 380; and Zdenka Volavka, *Crown and Ritual: The Royal Insignia of Ngoyo* (Toronto, Ontario: University of Toronto Press, 1998), 146–7.

[97] Visseq, *Dictionaire Fiot-Française*, 157.

[98] Tuckey, *Narrative*, 380–3.

[99] Tuckey, *Narrative*, 97; and Volavka, *Crown and Ritual*, 146.

[100] Bittremieux, *Société Secrète*, 249–63.

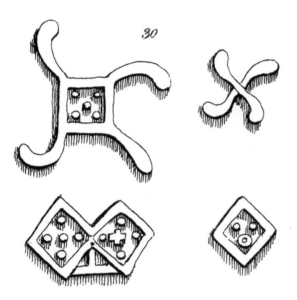

FIGURE 3. Images of shapes on "Fetiche Rock."
Source: Tuckey, *Narrative of an Expedition to Explore the River Zaire*, detail of Pl. IX, between pages 380 and 381.

has been associated with the great nature spirits "of the above" who have animated retributive minkisi. Like lightning and birds of prey, these spirits and their minkisi strike from the sky, their power very provocatively embodied in the well-known "nail fetishes" known as Nkondi.[101] These aspects of Nzazi appear in early written sources that describe the activities of the ritual experts dedicated to this spirit. The Nganganzasi (Nganga Nzazi) caused thunder to rumble during the dry seasons when it did not normally occur, and to resonate for exceptionally long times. Given the connection between thunder, lightning, and rain, people also believe that the Nganga Nzazi ensured the coming of rain with the help of consecrated objects.[102] Further, the Nganga Nzazi used his or her power over thunder and lightning as a spiritual weapon of attack and defense. Knocking two consecrated sculptures (*biteke*) together mimicked the noise of Nzazi's rumblings in the sky and provided the appropriate sonic context for the nganga to invoke Nzazi's force.[103]

[101] MacGaffey, *Art and Healing*, 97–104.
[102] Montesarchio, "Viaggi Apostolici," 193, 199.
[103] Luca da Caltanisetta, *Diaire Congolais (1690–1701)*, ed. and trans. François Bontinck (Louvain and Paris: Éditions Nauwelaerts/Béatrice-Nauwelaerts, 1970), 95.

FIGURE 4. Tadi a Nzazi (Lightening Rock).
Source: Tuckey, *Narrative of an Expedition to Explore the River Zaire*, 97.

Together Taddi Moenga and Taddi Enzassi marked the landscape of this portion of the Nzadi River as an especially significant location. The potent nature spirits found on the banks, in the waters, and near the cataracts upriver held an elevated status in local spiritual cultures. In her study of the sacred geography of the lower Nzadi, Zdenka Volavka concludes, "The region between Boma and Yelala has the prestige of being the religious core of the Kongoland. Myths portray it as the origin of the gods and people and as the cradleland of the godly invention of the way to constitute a group of kinsmen."[104] The prominence of the Seembi at Taddy Moenga within this "religious core of Kongoland" reveals, then, the centrality of the simbi in the spiritual thought of the region.

In general, much of the natural landscape provided domains for the simbi, most notably the forest that often surrounded the waters and covered the mountains where the simbi made their homes. Other features of the landscape associated with the simbi revealed additional ideas about their power. People credited the simbi with marking the terrain by creating ravines and chasms in hillsides while also occupying caves and other deep places.[105] These locations provided evidence of great force that transformed solid rock, a certain indication of exceptional spiritual strength, while at the same time embodying the notions of a deep descent and darkness, the combination of both identifying a site as a locus of intense spiritual power.

[104] Volavka, *Crown and Ritual*, 129.
[105] Weeks, *Among the Primitive Bakongo*, 294; and Troesch, "Nkutu du Comte," 43–6.

Certainly, the wilderness and dangerous places outside the safety of the domesticated realm served as ideal locations for nature spirits. The influence of the simbi, however, extended to the cultivated fields and villages, as well. The connection between the simbi and agricultural prosperity appeared in the late seventeenth century in an annual ritual that involved the Soyo nobility. The observance began with collective work in a field named Uri for the serpent spirit said to have inhabited a sacred grove in the middle of the field. Once the people finished preparing the field for planting, they gathered around the grove and invoked Uri to grant them bountiful rains as a reward for their devotion. The participants then accompanied the highest-ranking noble to his residence, where they celebrated with *malavu* (palm wine) and then returned to their own homes. The people were required to complete this rite before they could prepare clearings for planting and cultivate their own fields.[106] Failing to pay proper respect to local nature spirits led to agricultural hardship. In later times, people interpreted poor crops of peanuts and manioc as signs of the displeasure of the simbi with communities in their domains, while good conditions and good fortune revealed positive relations between people and the simbi.[107]

The representatives of nature spirits, the *kitome* or *kitombe*, occupied the highest spiritual office in Angola and Kongo in the seventeenth and early eighteenth centuries. Their primary duties included cultivating proper relationships between communities of the living and nature spirits to support agriculture. The kitome and his woman performed sacred songs that prompted the fields and seeds to provide large yields. Further, the kitome took up a hoe to initiate the breaking of the soil at the beginning of the planting season. For his services, the kitome received the bounty of the first harvests, thus acknowledging his role in relation to the territorial spirits for supporting the fertility of the land. Additional recognition of this special status came with rules that reserved the consumption of a certain kind of fish and other animals taken in the hunt for the kitome.[108] The relationship of the kitome to certain kinds of water also indicated their connection to nature spirits. One kitome in the Nsevo region of the kingdom of Kongo conducted public rituals to receive offerings on

---

[106] Lucca, *Relations*, 111–12. For more on the connection between nature spirits and snakes, see Troesch, "Nkutu du Comte," 47–8; Pambou, *Proverbes et Dictons*, 1: 94–4; and Janzen, *Lemba*, 302–3.

[107] Buakasa, *Impense du Discours*, 239–41.

[108] Cavazzi, *Descrição*, 1: 175–6; Buenaventura, "Relation," 2: 1152–3; Hilton, *Kingdom of Kongo*, 23–5; and Thornton, "Religious and Ceremonial Life," 78–9.

two large rocks and dispense sacred water taken from a nearby stream. Maintaining the sacred rocks in this central place, and presumably preserving the ritual, ensured that the spring of the stream would continue to provide water. While this account does not explicitly acknowledge the presence of nature spirits at this spring, the sacred rocks and water clearly represented these entities, which the inhabitants of this region knew as the simbi in later times.[109]

While the position of kitome did not continue to exist in most Kongo communities into recent times, the roles of spiritual experts (*banganga*) remained essential to sustaining ties between communities of the living and the simbi. Their activities often reflected these connections by linking the wilderness with the domesticated realm of the village. The process of consecrating the nkisi Mbenza required spiritual experts to go into the forest to find the simbi and their sacred objects. A simbi priest, along with other experts, initiates, and a drummer, entered the forest with the simbi nganga preceding them, although remaining within earshot. After finding the simbi, the priest cried out in an unusual voice with odd words to indicate his possession by the spirits. The rest of the group followed the noise to locate the nganga and the simbi object, in this case "an old, worn hoe-blade" that represented femininity and fertility. The assemblage acknowledged this discovery by singing a song celebrating the "the vision of the *yalumoni* [simbi]" accompanied by *ndungu* and *ngoma* drums and the *ngongi*-bell. The power of these sounds and the subsequent speaking of key phrases resonated throughout the forest so that "all the birds keep silence because of the chant reciting the praise-name of the *bisimbi*." The ritual experts then painted themselves with red and white clays along with earth from anthills. They also painted the simbi objects white and red, after which they returned to the village, where they conducted more initiation activities and where those possessed by the spirits "dance[d] beautifully."[110]

As these passages describing the work of initiated experts indicate, direct interactions with the simbi and other nature spirits usually required training and special knowledge. Those who served in positions as intercessors with the simbi underwent intricate processes to achieve this status. For example, the simbi Matengukidi (which meant "powerful in preventing, dissolving war") protected the pool of Bundi. Of the three celebrated spiritual experts who consecrated themselves to the simbi

---

[109] Cavazzi, *Descrição*, 4: 120.
[110] Lutete Esaya (Cahier 225), translated by Wyatt MacGaffey, *Art and Healing*, 58–63.

there, the ceremony established by the first, Ntembila Mbuka, outlined the process for allying with a powerful simbi. The objects used in the ritual included the initiate's saliva, hair, and nails combined with the heads from four snakes (the *ndimba, nduuna, buta,* and mboma snakes) and a stone tied up in certain vines. After throwing the stone into the pool, the snakes emerged in turn to lick the foreheads of the initiating nganga and the novice. The lick of the last snake, the mboma, imparted longevity to lives of the experts in accordance with the metaphor derived from the mboma's exceptional length and continuous growth. The head nganga then called on the snakes to, "Protect the life of your master" from those intent on doing harm to the soul of the consecrated nganga held in the stone. The nganga then cast a stone into the water, after which the snakes submerged, bringing on a heavy rain. Following the deaths of the three prominent experts consecrated to the spirit Matengukidi at the Bundi pool (the other two nganga were Me Nzudi and Malwanga), the waters diverged into three pools, each inhabited by one of the three experts, who became simbi.[111]

In many instances, only spiritual experts who knew how to properly approach simbi abodes could visit these powerful locations, which they did in order to collect certain objects for sacred compositions (minkisi), especially stones, tree roots, and the leaves of aquatic plants. Unwelcomed visitors who violated these waters risked having their feet assaulted by the many simbi that rested under the stones and roots in the springs. This led to afflictions including tumors, pustules, and internal pains, among other illnesses. Relief came only by composing the suitable nkisi to appease the simbi, as directed by the expert diviner, the *nganga ngombo.*[112] For people in some Kongo communities, the simbi acted as sources of illness, as seen in the idea that the term "simbi" derived from the verb simba, meaning "to touch," "to take hold of," and "to take firmly," all used as metaphors for causing sickness. This became most clear in instances in which the simbi punished those who sowed discord within families and communities. As one man stated regarding a dispute that split his family, "If the *simbi* notice the lack of love, they can become angry and take you."[113]

The basis of positive relations between nature spirits and communities of the living thus entailed proper knowledge and respect, the interventions of experts, and the efforts of all members of society to live in

[111] Laman, *Kongo,* 3: 40.
[112] Wing, *Études Bakongo,* 19–20, 189.
[113] Buakasa, *Impense du Discours,* 222, 270.

ways deserving of the beneficence of the simbi. Failure to do so invited misfortune. These requirements for maintaining bonds with the simbi to sustain the living found expression in the most elemental ideas about the basis for communities. This could be seen in the prescribed rites for the founding of a new village. Elders of the chief of the new village brought a branch of the *nsanda* tree from the old village that was planted in the new village under the direction of a nganga nkisi. The nsanda served as the village dwelling for the simbi, who protected the inhabitants and brought fertility and prosperity if the people maintained the order and laws mandated by the simbi and the elders. This relationship has been encapsulated in the phrase, "We respect the laws, the *simbi* will protect us; if we break the laws, they will strike us."[114]

An even deeper understanding of the importance of the simbi as the foundation for communities of the living appears in an explanation of the beginnings of the people of Soyo: "*Ntombe kuna kani/Nentombe kuna Nekongo katuta/Simbi ya nata* – Nentombe originated in Mbanza Kongo. The spirits [Simbi] dragged him to Soyo."[115] In this saying and the tradition associated with it, Nentombe represents a mythical figure who led his people from the east toward the coast in the Ntombe region and then north toward the mouth of the Nzadi. Once they reached this area near the river, Nentombe's people encountered indigenous groups and blended with them through marriage. The role of the spirits (simbi) in initiating the legendary migration of Nentombe and his followers reveals their place as the entities that ultimately sanctioned the settlement of new lands and supported the establishment of a new society; in this case, the blended populations of the autochthons and the newcomers that formed the ancestral community of the people of Soyo (the Basolongo). This predated the establishment of the state of Soyo, of course. That process involved the simbi, as well. Various traditions credit Ne Nzinga (Nezinga), the nephew of Nekongo (the originator of Kongo), as the founder of the state of Soyo. He migrated along a path similar to that taken by Nentombe and eventually encountered the Soyo dya Nsi, a "numerous and organized People" descended from Nentombe. Ne Nzinga's journeys took him to other locations, including a return to Mbanza Kongo, as he established the state and its noble lineages throughout the region. While traditions about Ne Nzinga differ in several ways (this has provided

---

[114] Buakasa, *Impense du Discours*, 239–41.
[115] Henrique Abranches, *Sobre Os Basolongo: Arqueologia da Tradição Oral* (Luanda: Fina Petróleos de Angola, 1991), 25. The differences in the punctuation in the Kikongo original and the translation appear in Abranches.

much material for disputes over the succession of the king of Soyo), one aspect has remained untouched by the disagreements over other details; Ne Nzinga was a simbi incarnated in the human form of a *ki lombo*. Ne Nzinga's status as a ki lombo affirmed his simbi nature and the approbation of the simbi for the establishment of his lineages as the ruling factions of Soyo, at least according to the traditions extolled by these lineages.[116] Chiefship and political status in other Kongo societies typically depended on the forging of close ties between the holders of titles and the simbi that provided chiefs and other leaders with the objects, protection, and powers necessary to function in their positions.[117]

While extant sources do not allow a substantial discussion of the simbi in the spiritual cultures of Kongo during the era of the trans-Atlantic trade in captive Africans, the documentary evidence from that period on the nkisi and nkita, coupled with the rich ethnography from more recent times, demonstrates a continuity of specific expressions and general themes related to nature spirits that requires us to consider the depth of knowledge about the simbi. Certainly, the people carried from West-Central Africa to the Lowcountry and other parts of the African-Atlantic diaspora came from communities that embraced ideas and practices related to those detailed in the preceding pages. This is not to say that African newcomers to South Carolina brought the precise concepts and behaviors discussed with them to their new surroundings. However, in the absence of positive evidence that would indicate otherwise, we must assume that they did indeed remain knowledgeable about the simbi and other nature spirits in a variety of ways that were likely very similar to those documented in sources from the mid-seventeenth century through the twentieth century. What became of that knowledge in the lives of African-descended people in the Lowcountry is addressed in the following chapters.

ATLANTIC TRANSFORMATIONS OF THE SIMBI

The West-Central Africans taken to the Lowcountry and other parts of the Atlantic diaspora came from societies submerged in the turmoil engendered by the trans-Atlantic commerce in captives. Their societies grappled with making sense of these struggles in spiritual terms, which

---

[116] Troesch, "Nkutu du Comte," 41–7; and Abranches, *Sobre Os Basolongo*, 25–7.
[117] Albert Doutreloux, *L'Ombre des Fétiches: Société et Culture Yombe* (Louvain: Éditions Nauwelaerts, 1967), 218; and MacGaffey, *Kongo Political Culture*, 188.

meant that their understanding of nature spirits reflected this process. Many people continued to rely on nature spirits in ways their ancestors did, but others began to attribute malevolent characteristics to the simbi by associating the spirits with enslavement in the Atlantic world.

Inhabitants of Kongo during the turbulent era following the dissolution of the old Kingdom of Kongo in the 1660s may have been more attuned than usual toward maintaining ties with the simbi and other local spirits. Frequent warfare and related predatory raiding forced many to abandon their normal settlements and take shelter in better-protected areas such as forests and mountains in places outside of the normal realm of habitation.[118] As we have seen, the simbi often resided in these secluded locations in the wilderness. Further, those fleeing conflict and likely enslavement had to leave the graves of their ancestors behind at the same time as they abandoned their villages and fields. Without access to ancestors' graves, the simbi served as the one source people could rely on for contact with the power of the invisible world. Those who were made captives and who had come from communities in this desperate condition would have been accustomed to turning to the simbi first when seeking direct connections to the land of the dead.[119] Certainly, those who crossed the Atlantic to arrive in early Carolina did not have any chance to access graves of ancestors in the new land. This would be possible only with the passing of time and the deaths of early African elders in the Lowcountry. Until then, the ties between the land of the living and the land of the dead existed through the simbi alone.

Additionally, for those communities stricken by the rapacity of other groups and other sources of misfortune, nature spirits provided support through the initiation institutions dedicated to them. Kimpasi societies grew during times of social distress, such as the series of droughts and the extended period of civil war in the late seventeenth and early eighteenth centuries following the fragmentation of the kingdom of Kongo.[120] The meanings connected to the term "kimpasi" adequately describe the essence of this society's existence. Kimpasi itself meant "place of suffering," and its root, *mpasi,* referred to "suffering," "sickness," "pain," "affliction," and "agony," among other similar meanings.[121] In this case,

---

[118] Thornton, *Kingdom of Kongo*, 7; and Miller, *Way of Death*, 37–8.
[119] The reorientation toward nature spirits and away from ancestors in areas profoundly disturbed by dislocation and demographic upheaval appears to have occurred in recent Vili and Yombe spiritual cultures. See Hersak, "There Are Many Kongo Worlds," 622.
[120] Hilton, *Kingdom of Kongo*, 26–8, 196–8.
[121] Wing, *Études Bakongo*, 2: 426; and Van Wing and Penders, *Plus Ancien*, 199.

we can interpret "suffering" as a reference to both the difficult ordeal that initiates endured to become healed and reborn as members of the society as well as to the original situation, in which serious hardships afflicted individuals and their communities. As West-Central Africans attributed the misfortunes of life to offenses perpetrated by people rather than to random coincidences or impersonal forces, the Kimpasi associations provided a means by which people came together as communities to redress collective problems through their relationships with nature spirits.[122]

As people perpetuated familiar aspects of their ties to nature spirits, evidence appears to show new perceptions of the simbi. People in the Lower Nzadi region connected the simbi directly to the Atlantic world as seen in figures found at the Taddi Moenga site discussed earlier. Some of the creatures portrayed at Taddi Moenga were thought of as animal allies of local nature spirits, particularly crocodiles, hippopotamuses, and snakes, yet they also posed threats to people on the river. Crocodiles and hippopotamuses, under the control of nature spirits or spiritual experts, overturned boats, sending passengers and goods to the bottom of the river or seized people from the riverbanks to entrap them in the Atlantic slave trade.[123] Additionally, a striking image shows a ship on the water that clearly represents trade with Atlantic merchants (Figure 5). The ship takes the form of a triangle on waves with a pole standing in the middle and emerging from the apex with a flowing flag on top. A man, presumably a European sailor, climbs the side of the ship. Within the vessel, we see on one side of the pole trade goods and on the other side a person, mostly likely a captive destined for enslavement in the Atlantic diaspora. This image along with the shapes of the animals located near it may have indicated a growing sense that dangerous creatures associated with the simbi served as predators, not protectors.

These associations of the simbi with Atlantic trade may have been commemorated in the figures on Taddi Moenga made by those initiated into the art, which reinforced the fundamental perception of the simbi around Boma as both particularly powerful and dangerous. The fact that Boma had become a major port for Atlantic commerce, including the trade in captives, by the beginning of the nineteenth century would have supported the perception that local nature spirits were behind the success of Boma merchants. The design of the port appeared to confirm this as well, with the prominence of ritual centers presided over by the experts

---

[122] This general interpretation comes from Thornton, *Kongolese Saint Anthony*, 56.
[123] Schrag, "Mboma," 39.

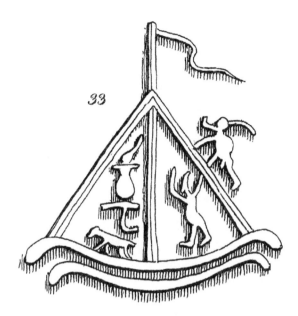

FIGURE 5. Image of ship on "Fetiche Rock."
Source: Tuckey, *Narrative of an Expedition to Explore the River Zaire*, detail of Pl. IX, between pages 380 and 381.

Ganga Empeenda (*Nganga Mpinda*) and Canga Lembamba (*Nganga Lembamba*) near the water to promote trade and protect the town from the detrimental influences of extensive contact with the strange visitors from kalunga.[124]

The image of the ship with its merchandise and captive on Taddi Moenga takes on additional meaning as we note that in the late nineteenth century some people in the interior regarded the faraway simbi of the sea (*ximbi ya mbu*) as instrumental in the workings of Atlantic trade, including the captivity of Africans. According to this view, the simbi worked with the Europeans as weavers of the cloth Europeans traded for enslaved Africans. According to a British observer who had been in West-Central Africa for three decades, "A large number of natives still believe...that we have found an opening leading to their [the ximbi ya mbu] oceanic factory, and whenever we need cloth, the captain of a streamer goes to this hole (*ntumpa*) and rings a bell; and the sprites, without showing themselves, push up the end of a piece of cloth, and the

---

[124] For the rise of Mboma as a port and the spiritual aspects of the town's design, see Schrag, "Mboma," 42–3, 50–79.

captain's men pull on it, one, two, three, or more days until he has all he requires."[125] The quality of the cloth, with its exceptionally fine textures, was considered possible only through the superior vision of the spirits, each of whom had a single eye with the concentrated acuity of two eyes. In exchange for this cloth, the simbi of the Atlantic required the dead bodies of Africans, who then became the servants of the spirits at the bottom of the sea:[126]

Those [dead Africans] thrown into the sprite-hole become the slaves of the sprites, making things for them and doing menial work. Enamel-war, cutlery, &c. are not manufactured by white people, but are the products of black men spirited away to the countries of the white men, where they are held in dire slavery and forced to make these things.[127]

The cognizance of Atlantic slavery among people in Kongo revealed in this statement appears remarkably accurate in describing the essence of enslavement and the work of Africans that produced directly and indirectly the material goods for Atlantic commerce. However, in reality this was coincidental. The key aspect of this description of the connection between the simbi and Atlantic slavery remained that the Africans traded by Europeans and enslaved by the simbi were dead. The implication in this narrative is that the deaths of these victims derived from the malevolent use of spiritual power (i.e., "witchcraft"). West-Central Africans have long interpreted the experience of captivity for sale into the Atlantic trade as a function of "witchcraft" that resulted in the spiritual death and enslavement of those victimized by this kind of predation. According to the information collected by Dapper in the late seventeenth century, people in Loango believed that, "there is no natural death, and that a person dies only by the malice and enchantments of his enemy, who by the same spells, revives him, carries him to desolate places and there puts him to work to enrich him."[128] In the early twentieth century, a missionary offered a fuller assessment of this understanding of "witchcraft":

The commonest opinion is that it is the man's own soul placed at the disposal of the devil...mainly for three evil purposes: disease, death, and slavery. The sole work of the witch is to cause sickness and death, which is done by drawing off the soul of the victim. That soul or spirit is then sold to white men who hide

[125] Weeks, *Among the Primitive Bakongo*, 294.
[126] Weeks, *Among the Primitive Bakongo*, 294–5.
[127] Weeks, *Among the Primitive Bakongo*, 294–5.
[128] Dapper, *Description*, 334.

them in their travelling trunks, water-tanks, salmon tins, etc., until they are able to despatch them to Europe, or to the bottom of the sea, or to some equally secure place far away where they spin cotton and weave cloth for their new taskmasters.[129]

These ideas about "witchcraft" and the simbi as forces in the enslavement of Africans existed within a larger conceptualization of the Atlantic world in which Europeans belonged to an essentially spiritual domain. Some people in certain eras viewed Europeans as deceased Africans transformed through their sojourn in the land of the dead (i.e., Europe and the Americas) or as simbi visiting the land of living to bring numerous goods and advanced technologies.[130] As such, we should expect to encounter narratives in which spiritual and material explanations of the trans-Atlantic trade were interwoven to express the meanings of captivity. Captivity and enslavement represented the spiritual condition of victims as much as they reflected legal and social status.

As mentioned earlier in this chapter, the word simbi has existed within a web of interrelated words and meanings that have usually referred to the concepts of holding, keeping, preserving, supporting, and seizing.[131] For the current discussion, we must include the meaning "to attack" reported for eastern Kongo communities. This adds a level of violence more pronounced than in the other expressions of seizing or capturing, which may reflect an eastern Kongo perspective of the simbi as primarily sources of misfortune rather than as spiritual benefactors. The simbi in this region grabbed the feet of the unwary that entered their waters and afflicted these people with illnesses such as tumors, pustules, and internal pains.[132] A similar idea prevailed in central Kongo communities, where the meanings associated with the word simba (the source of simbi) included "to touch," "to take hold of," and "to take firmly," all of which represented metaphors for causing sickness. Generally, throughout the various Kongo cultural regions, the "seizing," "holding," and "capturing" initiated by the simbi involved illness or possession for the purpose

---

[129] G. Cyril Claridge, *Wild Bush Tribes of Tropical Africa* (London: Seeley, Service and Co., 1922), 147.

[130] Wyatt MacGaffey, "Kongo and the King of the Americans," *Journal of Modern African Studies* 6, 2 (1968): 171–81; Hilton, *Kingdom of Kongo*, 50–1; MacGaffey, *Religion and Society*, 198–9; and MacGaffey, *Kongo Political Culture*, 27–30.

[131] Laman, *Kongo*, 3: 33; Laman, *Dictionnaire*, 899; and Wing and Penders, *Plus Ancien Dictionnaire Bantu*, 297.

[132] Wing, *Études Bakongo*, 19–20.

of creating spiritual ties with those afflicted, not simply to bring misfortune.[133] When the simbi took people, however, they did not always return them without strenuous interventions by the kin and communities of the captives. Led by spiritual experts, people gathered at the bodies of water where the simbi had seized their captives to perform the necessary songs, dances, and other rites. These activities included sending possessed divers into the waters to search for and retrieve the simbi captives or presenting the simbi with communal offerings of certain foods and animals.[134]

Ideally, the process of capture by the simbi and ransom by the living resulted in healing and other forms of spiritual transformation in which the returned captives brought knowledge and abilities from the realm of the simbi for use in the domain of the living. The spiritual dimensions of capture, however, took on additional meanings in ways that appear to reference the Atlantic trade and the changes it wrought. This notion of capture associated with the simbi came to entail domination and control and resembled forms of Atlantic enslavement.

A result of the perception that the simbi acted as agents of captivity for Atlantic merchants was the inversion of the captivity relationship between people and the spirits. This entailed a process of "domesticating" the simbi by "capturing" simbi objects found in the wilderness and using these captured objects to control the power of the simbi. People thus became predators of the simbi and reduced the powerful spirits to servitude.[135] The search in simbi domains for these objects proceeded much like a hunting expedition. Groups of banganga and their assistants attempted surprise attacks in the early morning light, stealthily approaching the elusive simbi, who made the search more challenging by fleeing from one "skin" (typically a stone) in a river to another "skin" in another river when the "hunters" came near.[136] Once captured, the simbi objects and the power linked to them formed the essence of the consecrated compositions (minkisi) used to direct spiritual power for the purposes of the living. The notion that the experts involved in composing and consecrating the minkisi dominated the spirits appears in the words a nganga uttered during this process:

[133] Laman, *Kongo*, 3: 33–6; and Wyatt MacGaffey, *Art and Healing*, 88.
[134] Laman, *Kongo*, 3: 35; and Joseph Van Wing and Cl. Scholler, eds., *Legendes des Bakongo-Orientaux* (Bruxelles: Bulens, 1940), 71–4.
[135] This sense of capturing the simbi is conveyed most strongly in Buakasa, *Impense du Discours*, 242–4, 268–9, 295, 300. For other references to the capture of simbi, see Laman, *Kongo*, 3: 35, 36; and MacGaffey, *Kongo Political Culture*, 80, 82.
[136] Buakasa, *Impense du Discours*, 268.

Mono yi rani?
Mono yi ta nganga
Mono yi mfunmu eno
Who am I?
I am the father *nganga*
I am your master[137]

The use of the two terms of seniority and authority, father (*tata*) and master (*mfumu*), reinforce strongly the concept of dominance in which the expert controlled the simbi and its power through the nkisi.

The explicit notion of capturing and essentially enslaving the simbi in spiritual servitude was not universal throughout the Kongo cultural realm, but appears to have been expressed in central and northern Kongo communities only. While similar processes of collecting and incorporating simbi objects in the ritual practices appear fundamental to Kongo spiritual cultures, they typically do not convey the same sense of captivity and domination. That sense has been reserved for the spirits of recently deceased people, particularly those known to have possessed much spiritual power, such as a "powerful chief or a great nganga" or "a well-known, powerful ndoki ["witch"]."[138] The process was described in the following passage:

When they go to the grave to take the nkuyu-spirit they carry with them a feast to soften his heart and let himself be taken. When the food has been set down on the grave, banganga withdraw to await events. As often as not, however, they look to see whether the nkuyu is beginning to eat. Last of all ngudi a nganga keeps watch and succeeds in catching the spirit. He calls for help to bind it or put it in the bastcloth to be incorporated with the "heart" of the sculpture [nkisi].[139]

The same process of capturing a spirit to empower objects composed to control spiritual power has existed in the diaspora, most notably in the Kongo-inspired spiritual cultures known as the *reglas de congo* in Cuba. The captured spirit then serves as an enslaved entity that, if fed and provoked appropriately, could acquire wealth and power for its master, the Tata Nganga who assembled and consecrated the nganga, the spiritually potent object that functions as the physical focus of the reglas de congo.[140] The connection of enslavement with spiritual status and spiritual work

[137] Buakasa, *Impense du Discours*, 243. The differences in the punctuation in the Kikongo original and the translation appear in Buakasa's text.

[138] Laman, *Kongo*, 3: 74, 92.

[139] Laman, *Kongo*, 3: 94.

[140] Cabrera, *Reglas de Congo*, 126–7; and Stephan Palmié, *Wizards and Scientists: Explorations in Afro-Cuban Modernity and Tradition* (Durham, NC: Duke University Press, 2002), 159–200.

appears throughout the African-Atlantic diaspora.[141] What does not appear, however, is the idea of a living person enslaving a nature spirit or any spirit other than that of a deceased person. Considering the remarkable power that derives from relationships with the simbi and similar nature spirits, we would expect the notion of capturing a simbi to form part of the spiritual practices in the diaspora if it had been a part of the spiritual cultures brought across the Atlantic. It seems reasonable, however, to assume that the idea of capturing these spirits had not yet been fully developed or had not taken root to the same extent as the concept of capturing the spirits of the dead when captive West-Central Africans reached the Americas. Instead, it likely emerged as a product of engagement with the Atlantic and found full expression at a later time.

The clear association of the simbi with the Atlantic trade in captive Africans indicates that West-Central Africans incorporated historical experiences and understandings of those experiences in their ideas and practices related to nature spirits. This was nothing new, as we have seen that accounts of the origins and development of nature spirits resembled historical narratives that recounted movements over land, sequences of transformations for spirits, and encounters with remembered people from earlier eras. An immense event such as the Atlantic trade in captives, with its consequences of great wealth and power as well as great violence, appeared ideally suited for association with the simbi, as these themes have predominated in accounts of the interaction between the living and nature spirits. What appears quite unexpected, however, was the transformation of certain nature spirits from benefactors to adversaries. It may be that certain groups perceived their vulnerability to captivity and the negative influences of Atlantic trade as a betrayal by the simbi. In response, these groups inverted their normal relationship with the simbi as an aggressive tactic in spiritual defense. This kind of response seems to have occurred in West Africa, specifically within Temne communities in Sierra Leone, where societies affected deeply by contact with the Atlantic world reconceptualized nature spirits as enemies in the wilderness rather than allies throughout the landscape. The result was the conversion of a spiritual culture that once embraced the presence of nature spirits in fields, villages, and homes into one that later reflected a more ambiguous connection that distanced these spirits from communities by relegating them to the bush and other dangerous areas.[142]

---

[141] J. Lorand Matory, "Free to Be a Slave: Slavery as Metaphor in the Afro-Atlantic Religions," *Journal of Religion in Africa* 37, 3 (2007): 398–425.

[142] Shaw, *Memories of the Slave Trade*, 46–69.

Some groups extended this approach further by diminishing significantly or abandoning altogether their ties to nature spirits.[143] In the equatorial rainforests of West-Central Africa during the eighteenth and nineteenth centuries, Fang societies in present-day Cameroon, Equatorial Guinea, and Gabon modified the ideas and practices associated with the ancient *bwiti* religious society to accommodate dramatic political, economic, and social changes that wracked the region in that era. The ancestors of these nascent Fang communities experienced considerable violence and captivity in their homelands, and undertook aggressive campaigns of migration and assimilation that encroached on weaker neighbors and led to the Fang emerging as major players in the highly competitive Atlantic commercial realm of the western rainforests. Unmoored to their original lands and especially brutal in their dealings with local communities, they revised the regionally dominant bwiti society. In doing so, they addressed far less the ties with local nature spirits and emphasized instead the spirits of their own ancestors. This provided Fang societies with greater spiritual authority by allowing them to circumvent the norms of the Niger-Congo principle of precedence discussed in Chapter 2.[144]

The most extreme expression of discarding relationships with nature spirits in West-Central Africa occurred with Imbangala (or Jaga) groups during the sixteenth and seventeenth centuries. The people identified as Imbangala earned a reputation as fierce, merciless combatants who sustained themselves through an itinerant, militaristic presence in central Angola. They venerated their warrior ancestors and their ferocious ways, while completely rejecting the kilundu that predominated as the regional nature spirits. As conquerors and bands sustained by predation on vulnerable societies, they grew no food of their own, raised no animals, founded no villages, and derived their wealth from subjecting others to captivity that ultimately delivered many to Portuguese merchants. Their very existence, however, likely derived from their exposure to the violence, exploitation, and enslavement that many people in Angola suffered with the growth of Atlantic trade. They enslaved others to keep from becoming enslaved themselves, and their destructive strategy required them to deny those aspects of spiritual cultures that supported the conceptions of life and community valued by most West-Central Africans. Their worldview simply could not admit any role for nature spirits.[145]

---

[143] Many thanks to Kairn Klieman for suggesting this line of inquiry and providing insights in her essay, "Of Ancestors and Earth Spirits," 57, 61 n108.

[144] Klieman, "Of Ancestors and Earth Spirits," 40–1, 56–8.

[145] Cavazzi, *Descrição*, 2: 37; Thornton, "Religious and Ceremonial Life," 82–3; and Vansina, *How Societies are Born*, 196–201.

Expressions of discord with nature spirits may have reached the Lowcountry through captives from Mende and Igbo communities. These West Africans introduced the common names for nature spirits in their home societies, ngafa and juju, respectively.[146] People in Mende communities have generally labeled spirits as *ngafanga* (plural form of ngafa), which have included both ancestral and non-ancestral spirits. Non-ancestral ngafa spirits have included those located in natural features and have served as the spirits at the heart of the essential initiation societies known throughout the region as Poro and Sande/Bondo.[147] The ngafanga appear closely related to the *krifi* (or *corofim*, in early written sources) spirits of the Temne discussed above. It may be that the ngafanga were once ubiquitous and beloved within early Mende villages, as the krifi were with Temne communities. By the nineteenth century, however, when the European visitors first documented ngafa spirits, they had become dangerous inhabitants of the wilderness, as had the krifi. Later accounts told of water spirits such as Jaloi, Jowei, and Tikpoi, all of whom claimed victims by capsizing boats and drowning those who fell into the water. An element of Jowei that may reveal an Atlantic connection includes the description of Jowei as having a woman's head with a body that consisted of a chain. The approach of people sent Jowei underwater, which made the sound of a chain slipping through water, similar to the dropping of an anchor. Other spirits of the wilderness inhabited the land, most notably those known collectively as *ndogbojusui*, who spent the days on a mountain and traveled the bush at night. People have described these spirits as men covered with hair or at least having long beards. Hunters and individual travelers were most susceptible to the deceptions of the ndogbojusui, who drew victims deeper into the forest where they often died of exhaustion.[148]

---

[146] For a broad survey of West African nature spirits based on twentieth-century ethnography, see Martha G. Anderson and Christine Mullen Kreamer, eds., *Wild Spirits, Strong Medicine: African Art and the Wilderness* (Seattle: University of Washington Press, 1989).

[147] K.L. Little, *The Mende of Sierra Leone: A West African People in Transition* (London: Routledge and Kegan Paul, 1951); M.C. Jedrej, "An Analytical Note on the Land and the Spirits of the Sewa Mende," *Africa* 44, 1 (1974): 38–45; and Anthony J. Gittins, *Mende Religion: Aspects of Belief and Thought* (Nettetal: Steyler Verlag – Wort und Werk, 1987).

[148] W.T. Harris and Harry Sawyerr, *The Springs of Mende Belief and Conduct: A Discussion of the Influence of the Belief in the Supernatural among the Mende* (Freetown: Sierra Leone University Press, 1968), 39–42, 45–7; and Little, *Mende of Sierra Leone*, 222–3.

For people within the Igbo cultural realm of present-day Southeastern Nigeria, the term juju came to serve as a general label for numerous forms of spiritual power, including nature spirits, objects consecrated to these spirits, shrines, and other centers of ritual activity, particularly those dedicated to settling disputes and discovering perpetrators of the malevolent use of spiritual power.[149] Additionally, the act of binding people in sacred contracts through the making of oaths required participants to "swear Ju Ju," thus ensuring that any violation of an agreement resulted in swift punishment by the spirits invoked in the pact.[150] Many of the spirits identified as juju helped communities secure good planting, large families, and the accumulation of material wealth.[151] Others, however, gained renown for their connections to Atlantic trade. The shrine and society associated with the Aro Chukwu spirit served as means for the Aro people to become the dominant brokers of commerce in the region, including the trade in captives from the interior to the coast.[152]

The negative meanings attached to ngafa and juju spirits appear to have taken hold among African-descended people in the Lowcountry, as these entities were described as "evil spirits."[153] Captives who entered the trans-Atlantic trade from societies in Sierra Leone and the Lower Niger River region certainly came from contexts in which the relationships between the living and nature spirits had to have experienced great change, as both regions endured major disruptions prompted by Atlantic commerce. West-Central Africans came from similar circumstances, although portrayals of the simbi as predators did not make the Middle Passage. This may have been the case because the interpretation of the

[149] On the origins of the use of the term juju, see Arthur Glyn Leonard, *The Lower Niger and Its Tribes* (London: MacMillan and Co., 1906), 290.

[150] For early written accounts, see Jean Barbot, *Barbot on Guinea: The Writings of Jean Barbot on West Africa 1678–1712*, ed. P.E.H. Hair, Adam Jones, and Robin Law (London: Hakluyt Society, 1992), 2: 694–5; and William Allen, *A Narrative of the Expedition Sent by Her Majesty's Government to the River Niger in 1841* (London: Richard Bentley, 1848), 1: 242. The phrase "swear Ju Ju" comes from Arthur Glyn Leonard, "Notes of a Journey to Bende," *Journal of the Manchester Geographical Society* 14, 2 (1898): 194.

[151] P. Aumary Talbot, *Tribes of the Niger Delta: Their Religions and Customs* (New York: Barnes & Noble, 1967 [1932]), 25–6, 55–7, 61, 92–4; and P. Aumary Talbot, *The Peoples of Southern Nigeria; A Sketch of Their History, Ethnology and Languages, with an Abstract of the 1921 Census* (London: Oxford University Press, 1926), 2: 43–4, 48, 107, 114–16, 135–7.

[152] Paul E. Lovejoy, *Transformations in Slavery: A History of Slavery in Africa*, 2nd ed. (New York: Cambridge University Press, 2000), 84–6; Chambers, *Murder at Montpelier*, 53–65; and A.E. Afigbo, *The Abolition of the Slave Trade in Southeastern Nigeria, 1885–1950* (Rochester, NY: University of Rochester Press, 2006), 38–9, 55–6, 61, 64–5.

[153] Turner, *Africanisms*, 193, 195.

simbi as malevolent agents of Atlantic trade did not overtake older, positive understandings of nature spirits, as seen in societies in Sierra Leone and the Lower Niger River region. In the Lowcountry and throughout the diaspora, favorable perceptions of the simbi as guardians and sources of spiritual aid remained intact. This allowed the simbi to become a key element of the emerging spiritual culture of African-descended people in the early Carolina Lowcountry.

While the diverse peoples taken from West-Central Africa and West Africa during the era of the trans-Atlantic trade in captive Africans did not possess a common language and culture, they did share basic understandings of the existence of nature spirits and the significance of these spirits for the living. Given that none of the African newcomers arrived with familiar lineal ties to the lands and societies in which they were enslaved, nature spirits would have been the first recourse for those seeking to reorient themselves within new physical and spiritual landscapes. The fact that newcomers shared this assumption about the necessity of reconnecting with nature spirits despite the many cultural differences among captives from West-Central Africa and West Africa indicates an especially significant arena in which Africans had common ground to work out a necessary accommodation for reconfiguring their ties to nature spirits in novel circumstances. Above all, this understanding allowed African newcomers brought to the Carolina Lowcountry to answer the challenge posed by the Kongo proverb, "Where your ancestors do not live, you cannot build your house," for, indeed, they knew that where the living found nature spirits they could build their houses.

4

African Landscapes of the Lowcountry

Heard about the Ibo's Landing? That's that place where they bring the Ibos over in a slave ship and when they get here, they ain't like it and so they all start singing and they march right down in the river to march back to Africa, but they ain't able to get there. They gets drown.

— Floyd White (St. Simon's Island, Georgia)

The story of Ibo's Landing has captivated many in the Lowcountry and beyond.[1] It has become enshrined in the mythic history of the struggles of African-descended people to define a past of resistance to captivity and claim a distinct cultural heritage defended by African ancestors.[2] A number of people have linked this narrative to the stories well-known through-out the Lowcountry of "flying Africans," who rejected enslavement and oppression by collectively taking flight to return to Africa. Phyllis Green of Charleston recounted one such story in which a group of Africans brought

---

[1] Georgia Writers' Project, Savannah Unit, *Drums and Shadows: Survival Studies among the Georgia Coastal Negroes* (Athens: University of Georgia Press, 1986 [1940]), 185.

[2] Silvia del Pilar Castro Borrego, "Recovering African American Spiritual History: The Myth of the Ibo Landing in Paule Marshall's *Praisesong for the Widow* and Julie Dash's *Daughters of the Dust*," in *Actas del XXI Congresso Internacional de A.E.D.E.A.N. (Associacíon Español de Estudios Anglo-Noteamericanos)*, ed. Fernando Toda Iglesia, Juan A. Prieto Pablos, María José Mora, and Teresa Lópiz Soto (Sevilla: Secretariado de Puclicaciones de la Universidad de Sevilla, 1999), 485–90; Alan J. Rice, *Radical Narratives of the Black Atlantic* (London and New York: Continuum, 2003), 94–6; Scott Romine, *The Real South: Southern Narrative in the Age of Cultural Reproduction* (Baton Rouge: Louisiana State University Press, 2008), 128–9; and Timothy Powell, "Summoning the Ancestors: The Flying Africans Story and Its Enduring Legacy," in *African American Life in the Georgia Lowcountry: The Atlantic World and the Gullah Geechee*, ed. Philip D. Morgan (Athens: University of Georgia Press, 2010), 253–80.

to James Island "'fore rebel time [the Civil War]" planned to end their captivity after the two-week period granted to them to become accustomed to
their new surroundings. "When they left by they self you hear a tapping,
tapping, tapping all day and all night. And they would not crack the teeth
to them [not talk to anyone]." When the time came for them to work and
the driver summoned the Africans by cracking his whip, "They come out
and they stretch out they hand just like they going to take the tools to
work like the rest. But when they stretch they hand they rise. At middle
day you could see them far out over the ocean. At sundown you could hear
[their] voice, but they couldn't see them no more. Them gone home."[3] It
may be that stories of flying Africans and the unfortunate captives in the
Ibo's Landing narrative addressed the same people and the same solution
to enslavement, although through different images. In one set of tellings,
they flew home; in another, they took their own lives by drowning together.
The reputation of captive Igbos as being especially inclined toward suicide
to escape enslavement and return spiritually to their homeland appears to
have informed the narratives of flying Africans and Ibo's Landing.[4]

In discussing the centrality of the "Ibo Landing myth" to her film
Daughters of the Dust, Julie Dash posited, "There are two myths and one
reality." The two myths, in her estimation, included the stories in which
the captive Igbos walked on water or flew to return to their African
homeland, while the reality involved the Igbos walking collectively into
the water to drown.[5] Even in the story of the drowned Igbos, however, we
find the core element of assigning meaning to captivity in this strange land,
which matters more as a process of mythmaking than as a report of a fact
or a discreet event in reality. The effort to locate the Ibo Landing story as
a historical incident that occurred at a specific place and time obscures
the full significance of this narrative in African-inspired Lowcountry culture. According to one source, Ibo Landing is on an island along the
Georgia coast, while another account claims it is on an island in Beaufort
County, South Carolina, and so on.[6] As Dash noted of her research, "I

---

[3] Interview with Phyllis Green (Charleston) by Cassles R. Tiedeman, "Negro Legends,"
Folder D-4-27B1, WPA-SCL.

[4] Gomez, *Exchanging Our Country Marks*, 118–20; and Michael A. Gomez, "A Quality
of Anguish: The Igbo Response to Enslavement in North America," in *Trans-Atlantic
Dimensions of Ethnicity in the African Diaspora*, ed. Paul E. Lovejoy and David V.
Trotman (London and New York: Continuum, 2003), 86–9.

[5] Julie Dash, *Daughters of the Dust: The Making of an African American Woman's Film*
(New York: The New Press, 1992), 30.

[6] Georgia Writers' Project, *Drums and Shadows*, 185; and Edward Ball, *Slaves in the Family*
(New York: Viking, 1998), 179.

found that almost every Sea Island has a little inlet, or a little area where the people say, 'This is Ibo Landing. This is where it happened. This is where this thing really happened.'" Dash concluded that the ubiquity of claims that the events in the Ibo's Landing story occurred throughout the Lowcountry stems from the fact that its "message is so strong, so powerful, so sustaining to the tradition of resistance, by any means possible, that every Gullah community embraces this myth."[7] According to historian Michael Gomez, the Ibo's Landing story communicates that "something more profound than simple suicide had taken place," because for the captive Igbos, "suicide was perhaps the ultimate form of resistance, as it contained within it the seed for regeneration and renewal."[8]

This understanding of Ibo's Landing as historical myth and not purely as historical event certainly explains its profound resonance with residents of the Lowcountry. The story, however, conveys more than a tradition of resistance represented in other episodes of Lowcountry history. The drowned Igbos did not physically strike out at their oppressors like the warriors led by Jemmy or Cato in the Gullah War (Stono Rebellion) in the 1730s, nor did they conspire to do so, as Denmark Vesey and his allies purportedly did in the 1820s.[9] The drowned Igbos did not run away and create a maroon camp in the woods. They chose to walk into the water together and die. Certainly, this was not a simple act of suicide or even one freighted with hopeful, transcendent meanings. It was a sacrifice, an offering to the land and waters to consecrate the landscape of the Lowcountry with the lives and spirits of captive Africans brought in chains to this shore. With this choice, the people in Ibo's Landing left no descendants among the generations that followed. As such, they could never become ancestors in a biological sense for those who populated the islands and coastal plain in later times, for the very people who would celebrate their memory in countless retellings of the Ibo's Landing story. Indeed, their sacrifice, and by extension their spirits, became part of the memoryscape, and this made them nature spirits.[10] They have remained

---

[7] Dash, *Daughters of the Dust*, 31.

[8] Gomez, *Exchanging Our Country Marks*, 120.

[9] Michael P. Johnson has raised doubts about the actuality of Vesey's plot, although many historians have responded with vigorous rebuttals. See Michael P. Johnson, "Denmark Vesey and His Co-Conspirators" *William and Mary Quarterly*, 3d Series, 58, 4 (2001): 415–76; and the several essays discussing Johnson's argument edited by Robert A. Gross in "Forum: The Making of a Slave Conspiracy, Part 2," *William and Mary Quarterly*, 3d Series, 59, 1 (2002): 135–202. For a broader analysis of the meanings attached to Vesey's plot, see Ford, *Deliver Us from Evil*, 205–97, 597–8n1.

[10] The use of "memoryscape" comes from Shaw, *Memories of the Slave Trade*, 46–69.

in the thoughts and words of African-descended people all along the coast where water meets land, where nature spirits prefer to make their abodes.

While the story of Ibo's Landing was inspired by an event that occurred very late in the history of the trans-Atlantic transport of Africans to the Lowcountry, this was not the first time that African-descended people assigned spiritual meaning to the landscape through the presence of nature spirits. Well before the drowned Igbos had even been born, West-Central Africans carried to South Carolina found the simbi in springs that provided plantations with fresh water. The Lowcountry simbi served much the same purposes in South Carolina as the Kongo simbi had in West-Central Africa. Above all, they provided a spiritual tie to the landscape that helped captives from diverse backgrounds coalesce into communities and gain access to the bountiful produce of the soils, forests, and waters of the Lowcountry. Further, the presence of the simbi confirmed that the Africans who settled Carolina during the earliest generations of colonization assumed the status of firstcomers in accordance with the Niger-Congo principle of precedence and despite the existence of European settlers and numerous indigenous groups. The Lowcountry simbi thus formed part of a larger relationship between African-descended people and the natural environment that entailed a deep engagement with the physical and spiritual dimensions of the landscape. This chapter explores both dimensions and explains the central role of the simbi in the formation of the African landscapes of the Lowcountry.

TAME AND WILD AFRICAN SPACES

The inclination to perceive the landscape in fundamentally spiritual terms appeared in the words of Sam Gadsden, a long-time resident of Edisto Island, who stated, "On some islands and in some parts of the country there is a wild part and a tame part." This distinction hinged upon the commitment of the inhabitants to spiritual unity, expressed by Gadsden's lifetime through a devotion to maintaining a Christian community. The "tame" parts consisted of those areas governed by Christian people, who marked their territory by building many churches. While white Christians may have introduced their understanding of the religion to Edisto first, it was through African-descended people that the island was "made one by its churches." According to Gadsden, "The colored people, after peace was declared [following the Civil War], they *covered* the island with churches."[11] The "wild" part included "the closed places in the swamp" where the immoral and disreputable escaped from the law and "civilized people." These wild places, of course, had no churches. In Gadsden's reckoning, the difference between tame and wild had less to do with the physical features of the natural environment than with the ways people associated the landscape with the spiritual state of the communities that lived there. Such a conception drew heavily from the core ideas concerning the relationship between people and the land brought to Edisto and the rest of the Lowcountry by African newcomers explored in the previous chapter.

Both the Ibo's Landing story and Sam Gadsden's perspective on tame and wild lands reveal meanings of the spiritual landscape of the Lowcountry as an African conceptual space that connected the visible, physical domain with the invisible, spiritual realm. As demonstrated in Chapter 3, nature spirits have served as a primary link between these two dimensions as the activities of farming, hunting, and fishing have been tied intimately with ideas and practices associated with nature spirits and other interactions with the powers of the invisible world. This association becomes crucial for understanding the enduring presence of the simbi in the Lowcountry. African-descended people relied on the land and waters for material sustenance and employed knowledge and techniques derived from their African ancestors to plant, hunt, and fish, as will be seen in this section. While identifying antecedents for this rich legacy represents an important endeavor, it remains incomplete without consideration of the spiritual aspects of these activities. African newcomers to the Lowcountry came from societies that based their knowledge and techniques on the insight that any efforts to grow crops or obtain animals depended on the support of nature spirits to succeed. As such, we must keep in mind that behind the visible ways that African-descended people produced food from the land and waters of the Lowcountry stood the invisible yet vital presence of the nature spirits, including the simbi. Just as people culled life-giving resources from the tame and wild domains of the natural environment, they engaged both realms as intertwined dimensions of the spiritual landscape consecrated by the drowned Igbo captives and protected by the simbi in the limestone springs.

In beginning to assess the material aspects of the relationship between the living and the natural environment, the tame and the wild, the visible and the invisible, we must listen to the ways that African-descended

---

[11] Gadsden, *Oral History of Edisto Island*, 39, 41. Emphasis in the original.

people talked about the growing, living things they depended on for nourishment. In this dialogue about the cultures of planting, hunting, and fishing, they maintained the use of seventy-two terms from African languages to identify plants and animals (Tables 7, 8, and 9). This inventory presents two patterns that offer us access to the foundations of the African-based food culture of the Lowcountry. First, more than half (56 percent, 40 of 72) derived from the Bantu languages, almost all of which came specifically from Kongo languages or dialects. This suggests that West-Central Africans played an especially significant role in naming the Lowcountry natural environment, in addition to the notable input of people from Greater Senegambia (speakers of Mande and Atlantic languages). Bantu, Mande, and Atlantic languages together account for more than 86 percent of the etymologies for plant and animal names. Second, twenty-three of the twenty-seven names for plants identified domesticated varieties, while forty of the forty-five labels for animals designated wild creatures. This indicates that the entire inventory of words maintained internal consistency as a naming system for sources of subsistence. The plant terms referred most often to food plants cultivated in personal gardens since the early days of slavery, while the animal words generally identified creatures acquired through hunting and fishing. While neither the tame plant nor wild animal inventories exhaust the range of plants and animals eaten, they certainly represent the major categories of subsistence sources exploited by African-descended people.

The use of African names in this way reveals that this set of terms served cultural purposes in addition to providing convenient labels. The fact that a number of these words named plants and animals that featured prominently in distinctively African or African-Atlantic foodways supports the interpretation that the foods and the terms that named them reveal "the ways that enslaved Africans used the production of food to resist imposed diets and to exercise choices over what served as their daily sustenance" as well as to expose "the symbolic meanings of specific foods and foodways."[12] The terms for domesticated plants provide an especially instructive example in this regard. We must keep in mind that all of the twenty-three words identified plants for which English-speaking non-Africans already had terms, even for a plant entirely novel to them such as *hibiscus esculentus*, as the word okra eventually became

---

[12] Judith A. Carney and Richard Nicholas Rosomoff, *In the Shadow of Slavery: Africa's Botanical Legacy in the Atlantic World* (Berkeley: University of California Press, 2009), 47.

incorporated into English usage in the Americas starting in the late seventeenth century. The application of African names for these plants represented conscious and repeated choices by African-descended people to not only name the plants in African ways but to define the gardens in which they grew the plants as African spaces. Further, the enduring relevance of the collection of African plant names, along with the definition of the space in which people cultivated the plants as expressions of identity, indicate that African-descended people continued to perceive planting in African ways. As seen in the previous chapter, these perceptions required the proper relations with spiritual benefactors, most notably nature spirits, to support the fertility of the land.[13]

Both material and spiritual concerns with the fertility of the land certainly remained prominent in the minds of African newcomers as enslaved people in the Lowcountry as well as in other parts of the diaspora. These newcomers not only bore the burden of producing export crops to enrich enslavers but also assumed the responsibility for providing much of their own food to compensate for meager planter allocations.[14] According to an early eighteenth-century account, "There are many planters who, to free themselves from the trouble of feeding and clothing their slaves allow them one day in the week to clear ground, and plant for themselves as much as will clothe and subsist them and their families."[15] A German settler noted in the mid-eighteenth century that after enslaved people finished daily plantation work, they "are given as much land as they can handle" for their own crops and "plant for themselves also on Sundays."[16] Further, enslaved people were observed "working in their own private fields, consisting of 5 or 6 acres of ground, allowed them by their masters, for planting of rice, corn, potatoes, tobacco, etc. for their own use and profit, of which the industrious among them make a great deal."[17] These subsistence activities

[13] Stuckey, *Slave Culture*, 64–5; and Gomez, *Exchanging Our Country Marks*, 266.

[14] Morgan, *Slave Counterpoint*, 134–48.

[15] "Instructions of the Clergy of South Carolina," SPG, quoted in Klingberg, *Appraisal of the Negro*, 7.

[16] Johann Martin Bolzius, "Johann Martin Bolzius Answers a Questionnaire on Carolina and Georgia," ed. and trans. Klaus G. Loewald, *William and Mary Quarterly*, 3d Series, 14, 2 (1957): 259.

[17] "A Curious New Description of Charles-Town in South-Carolina...," *The Universal Museum*, I (September 1762), 477, quoted in Morgan, *Slave Counterpoint*, 187. This arrangement remained a key feature of food production for enslaved people in the South Carolina and Georgia Lowcountry through the end of slavery. See handwritten entries for 1–2 June 1797, and 31 May 1798 in *The Carolina and Georgia Almanac, for the Year of Our lord, 1798, and 22–23 of American Independence* (Charleston: W.P. Young,

fed African-descended families and provided opportunities for some to "turn their crops into money" through trade and marketing, which occurred with a frequency and a volume substantial enough to prompt the passage of numerous laws in the eighteenth century that attempted to restrict this commerce.[18] Nevertheless, enslaved people continued to be a major source of provisions in the markets of Charleston, especially during those seasons when diseases such as yellow fever inhibited the travels of whites.[19]

Not only did African-descended people need to grow their own food, they chose to plant crops in the Lowcountry that had been well established in the Atlantic agriculture complex for some time following the dispersal of numerous cultivars by Europeans. A wide variety of plants and the methods of their cultivation crisscrossed the Atlantic between regions of Africa, South America, the Caribbean, and North America and became basic features of the planting culture of the Lowcountry.[20] According to a mid-eighteenth-century survey of agriculture in the South Carolina Lowcountry, enslaved people "plant for themselves corn, potatoes, tobacco, peanuts, water and sugar melons, pumpkins, bottle pumpkins (sweet ones and stinking ones which are used as milk and drink vessels and other things)."[21] To this list, other sources from the period noted the presence of yams, tania, millet, sorghum, sesame, pepper, okra, and rice in foods consumed by African-descended people.[22] Some of these, while ultimately American in origin, became prominent features of

1798), Allard Belin Plantation Journal, SCHS; and Charles Alfred DeSaussure, "The Story of My Life Before the War Between the States," Charles Alfred DeSaussure Papers, SHC.

[18] George Fenwick Jones, ed., "John Martin Boltzius' Trip to Charleston, October 1742," *South Carolina Historical Magazine* 82, 2 (1981): 104; Morgan, *Slave Counterpoint*, 358–76; and Philip D. Morgan, "Work and Culture: The Task System and the World of Lowcountry Blacks, 1700 to 1880," *William and Mary Quarterly*, 3d Series, 39, 4 (1982): 569, 571.

[19] François André Michaux, *Travels to the Westward of the Allegany Mountains, in the States of the Ohio, Kentucky, and Tennessee, in the Year 1802* (London: Richard Phillips, 1805), 7. See also, McCandless, *Slavery, Disease, and Suffering*, 227–36.

[20] For spread of an array of plants throughout the Atlantic basin with special attention given to Africa, see Stanley B. Alpern, "The European Introduction of Crops into West Africa in Precolonial Times," *History in Africa* 19 (1992): 13–43; and Monique Chastanet, *Plantes et Paysages d'Afrique: Une Histoire à Explorer* (Paris: Éditions Karthala, Centre de Recherches Africaines, 1998); Carney, *Black Rice*; and Carney and Rosomoff, *In the Shadow of Slavery*, 46–154.

[21] Bolzius, "Questionnaire," 259.

[22] Wood, *Black Majority*, 119–21; Morgan, *Slave Counterpoint*, 141–2; and Edelson, *Plantation Enterprise*, 65–8.

the planting cultures in West-Central Africa and West Africa long before captive Africans were first transported to South Carolina. Africans carried to the Lowcountry, then, had extensive experience in growing and preparing plants from their traditional agricultural expertise and the Atlantic agricultural complex. They brought this knowledge as well as their preferences for these crops with them. Indeed, they were "delighted with all their African food," as noted in the 1720s by the naturalist Mark Catesby.[23]

Plants first cultivated in Africa and brought to the Lowcountry (Table 7), either directly or in some cases through the Caribbean, included pepper (*dungu*), okra (*okra, gumbo*), sweet potatoes/yams (*sadi, jambi, sômbo,* and *yam/yambi*), gourds/calabash (*seka, senswa,* and *tumbu*), sesame (*bene*), and rice (*kala/kôlo, malo/melo, kafa/gafa,* and *moliku*). Identified by African-descended people with the Kongo term dungu (*ndungu*), "negroe pepper," sometimes called Ethiopian or Guinea Pepper, was considered "a good Ingredient in dressing Turtle."[24] Pepper grown by enslaved people must have been admired by enslavers, as Elias Ball, while visiting in England, wrote back to family in St. John's Berkeley to "tell Old Tom as I know he plants a good deal of pepper I wish [to] thank him to send me some...pounded and corked up in a pint Bottle."[25] Pepper also served to flavor soups that featured okra that people cut into pieces and boiled with tomatoes. Non-Africans readily acknowledged that the flowering plant that produced the key ingredient of these soups was "brought by the Negroes from the coasts of Africa and is called okra by them."[26] By the early nineteenth century, white Carolinians had also embraced this "much esteemed" plant in their cuisine, as the African-descended people who grew and prepared the food eaten by enslavers commonly included the "pods and seeds of this plant" in "making soup during the summer."[27] The two African words used in the Lowcountry, okra (Igbo – *okro*) and gumbo (Kimbundu – *kingombo*), for this single plant also appeared in other parts of the diaspora, with okra functioning as the most common designation in English-speaking locations while gumbo took firm root in

[23] Catesby, *Natural History*, 2: 45.

[24] Eliza Lucas Pinckney, *The Letterbook of Eliza Lucas Pinckney, 1739–1762* (Chapel Hill: University of North Carolina Press, 1972), 28.

[25] Elias Ball to Elias Ball, 26 February 1786, Ball Family Papers, SCL.

[26] Luigi Castiglinioni, *Luigi Castiglinioni's Viaggio: Travels in the United States of North America, 1785–87*, ed. and trans. Antonio Pace (Syracuse: Syracuse University Press, 1983), 171–2.

[27] John Drayton, *A View of South Carolina as Respects her Natural and Civil Concerns* (Spartanburg, SC: The Reprint Company, 1972 [1802]), 86.

TABLE 7. *African Names for Plants*

Bantu Terms	
dungu	pepper
gûmbo	okra
guba	peanut
kapoke	a green plant that is boiled and used for food
makaña	tobacco
munse	sugar cane
pinda (pɪnda)	peanut
sadi	a sweet potato having a reddish skin
seka	pumpkin leaf, gourd leaf
senswa	calabash
sôya	marsh grass
tumbu	calabash
wandu	a bean which grows on poles
Mande/Atlantic Terms	
bɛne	benne, the sesame
fa	a tree resembling cedar
jambi	a reddish sweet potato
kala (kôlo)	rice
malo (melo)	rice
ñebe (ñebɛ)	lima bean
sômbo	a red sweet potato
sûbi (sɪbi)	lima bean
Kwa	
adobɛ	a kind of grass used for covering roofs
kwabena	a thorny bush resembling the palmetto
moliku	rice
Other	
okra	okra [Benue-Congo]
kafa (gafa)	rice [Chadic?]
yam (yambi)*	sweet potato [Bantu, Mande/Atlantic, Kwa]

Source: Turner, *Africanisms*; and LDTP.

Louisiana to name the stew made with the plant.[28] In any case, captive Africans cultivated the plant throughout the African-Atlantic world and attached an array of African names to it.[29]

[28] John Fanning Watson, "Notitia of Incidents at New Orleans in 1804 and 1805," *American Pioneer*, II, 5 (May 1843): 233; Douglas B. Chambers, "Tracing Igbo into the African Diaspora," in *Identifying Enslaved Africans: The "Nigerian" Hinterland and the African Diaspora*, ed. Paul Lovejoy (London: Continuum, 2000), 64, 70n43; and Douglas B. Chambers, *Murder at Montpelier*, 168–9.

[29] Carney and Rosomoff, *In the Shadow of Slavery*, 94, 97, 124, 135.

In addition to the names of plants, the African contribution to the vocabulary describing agricultural activities includes the verbs *saya* ("to bank the earth") and *tima* ("to dig"), both of which derived from Kongo languages. While these terms may describe actions not directly related to planting (such as digging a burial pit), they certainly cover two of the most important aspects of preparing the soil for agricultural purposes. Taken together, these terms describe the monumental task performed by generations of enslaved people who moved earth to create and maintain the banks that drained the swamps and sustained the canals and rice fields of the Lowcountry's plantations. Understood in this sense, the retention of these terms reveals the particular importance of the West-Central African majority in the original construction of the hydraulic infrastructure throughout the first century of plantation agriculture. We may even suppose that these terms remained in use among West-Central Africans who emerged as the veterans (and "drivers") of the workforce and initiated later-arriving Africans into the rigorous regimes of early Lowcountry plantations.

The terms saya and tima apply to work in the gardens, as well. The tasks of digging and banking figured as especially important in the planting and harvesting of tubers and peanuts. Luigi Castiglioni explained the cultivation of yams:

A raised and sandy terrain near marshes having been chosen, it is tilled in April by Negroes, who make many little mounds with the soil. On each of them are planted five or six batate [yams], which are covered with a bit of earth. When they have grown, they are weeded; and they require no other care until the harvest of the roots, after which they can be preserved for several months provided they are in a dry place and kept from freezing.[30]

Shadrack Hall of Sapelo Island, Georgia, described the process further:

We make a bed, plant the potato, then it come, it comes a rind. Then we cut the rind and put it in the ground. Then that grow the potato. Then as the potatoes grow, then we hoe. We hoe that potato as high as we want it to. Then when the fall of the year come, then we dig it in. And after we dig it in, then we make a bank, or a little house, put it in it, then that will keep for the winter.[31]

Preparation of the soil and planting for peanuts, also called ground nuts, followed the same double furrow method as for yams. Harvesting

---

[30] Castiglinioni, *Viaggio*, 171.
[31] Interview with Shadrack Hall, Sapelo Island, Georgia, 29 July 1933, LDTC.

entailed digging the plants out of the furrows and setting groups of plants up in shocks to cure.[32]

The expertise of enslaved people in growing peanuts appears to have been unrivaled, and they recognized the peanut's commercial value long before enslavers considered the plant worth their consideration. The Lowcountry planter George Izard noted to his brother, "I know nothing of the culture...of this plant – but might not the negroes be encouraged to raise a large quantity of these for which they should receive a reasonable price?...My ground-nuts are not as large as most of those which are sold by the African hucksters."[33] An early nineteenth-century observer noted that peanuts were "planted in small patches chiefly by the negroes, for market."[34] Economic pressures, however, forced enslavers to see the utility of this crop so familiar to enslaved people.[35] Whites also embraced it as part of their diets, even as a familiar food that reminded them of home. In addition to requesting Old Tom's pepper as we saw earlier, Elias Ball noted in his letter from England, "a fue [few] ground nuts will be acceptable to his young mistress" there, as well.[36]

As with okra and a number of other food plants, whites acknowledged that peanuts reached the plantations of the Americas through the agency of Africans. Writing in the early eighteenth century, Hans Sloane noted the connection between the trade in captive Africans and the extension of the peanut into the Atlantic world: "I saw in this Harbour and Bay a Ship come from *Guinea*, loaded with Blacks to sell....I was assured that the *Negroes* feed on Pindals, or *Indian* Earth-Nuts, a sort of Pea or Bean producing its Pods under ground. Coming from *Guinea* hither, they are fed on these Nuts or *Indian*-Corn boil'd whole twice a day."[37] Similar to other foods used to provision the vessels that carried Africans to the Americas, the peanuts used to feed captives had been grown in

---

[32] For an extended explication of peanut cultivation in the U.S. South, see C. Corbett, "Peanut," in *Cyclopedia of American Agriculture: A Popular Survey of Agricultural Conditions, Practices and Ideals in the United States and Canada*, ed. L.H. Bailey (New York: MacMillan, 1907), 2: 515–19; and Lewis Cecil Gray, *History of Agriculture in the Southern States To 1860* (Washington: Carnegie Institution of Washington, 1933), 1: 194, 2: 828.

[33] George Izard to Henry Izard, 26 June 1807, Ralph Izard Papers, SCL.

[34] David Ramsay, *The History of South-Carolina from its First Settlement in 1670, to the Year 1808* (Charleston, SC: David Longworth, 1809), 289.

[35] Chaplin, *Anxious Pursuit*, 156–7.

[36] Elias Ball to Elias Ball, 26 February 1786, Ball Family Papers, SCL.

[37] Hans Sloane, *A Voyage to the Islands Madera, Barbados, Nieves, S. Christophers and Jamaica.* (London: Printed by B.M. for the author, 1707), 1: lxxiii.

Africa by Africans, with many of these farmers undoubtedly numbering among the unfortunates fed with this crop on the voyage. Agriculture in the Loango coast region of West-Central Africa relied heavily on the peanut, for, "After manioc there is nothing that the Negroes cultivate with more care than the *pinda*."[38]

In 1769, William Watson, a member of the Royal Society of London, provided additional details concerning the prevailing understanding of the origins, spread, and uses of the peanut:

I lay before you some pods of a vegetable, and the oil pressed from their content...the produce of a plant well known, and much cultivated, in the Southern colonies, and in our American sugar islands, where they are called ground nuts, or ground pease. They are originally, it is presumed, of the growth of Africa, and brought from thence by the negroes, who use them as food, both raw and roasted, and are very fond of them. They are therefore cultivated by them in the little parcels of land set apart for their use by their masters. By these means, this plant has extended itself, not only to our warmer American settlements, but it is cultivated in Surinam, Brasil, and Peru....[I]n southern climates its produce is prodigious.[39]

Another aspect of this account reveals how African-descended people once again made the most of the limited resources afforded them by enslavers, as "rich land is not necessary for its cultivation, as light sandy land, of small value, will produce vast crops of it."[40] The ingenuity of African-descended people in propagating peanuts demonstrated that the land considered worthless by enslavers, which certainly rendered it ideal to be "set apart" for enslaved cultivators, proved to be of great utility for growing an edible crop, a source for oil, and a source of feed for "swine and poultry, which are very fond of the ground pease; and, when they are permitted to eat freely of them, soon become fat."[41]

While the English terms for peanuts included "ground peas," "ground nuts," and eventually "peanuts," two African words, *guba* and *pinda*, named the plant among African-descended people that later became Anglicized as goober, goobers, goober peas, goofer, pinder/pindar, and pinders.[42] Both of these words came to the Americas with West-Central

---

[38] Proyart, *Histoire de Loango*, 16.

[39] William Watson, "Some Account of an Oil, Transmitted by Mr. George Brownrigg, of North Carolina," *Philosophical Transactions of the Royal Society of London*, 59 (1769): 379–80, 380–1.

[40] Watson, "Some Account," 381.

[41] Watson, "Some Account," 381.

[42] These variations on names for the peanut were collected as part of the American Linguistic Atlas Project under Hans Kurath. Information gathered for the South Atlantic

Africans who knew the Atlantic peanut as *nguba* and *mpinda*. This terminology for the peanut reveals the dynamics of cultural exchange and transformation in the African-Atlantic world. The earliest varieties of the plant originated in South America. The Portuguese transported it to Africa during the early phases of contact. As its cultivation and consumption spread along various trade routes in West-Central Africa, the crop took on different names. The term nguba originated in the lower Nzadi region and gained currency throughout the region, both in northern Angola and in communities connected in the vast Nzadi River trade network. Variations of the term pinda derived from an Amerindian word that West-Central Africans acquired as they adopted the crop, which proliferated throughout the Ogooué River trade network centered in present-day Gabon, although spreading as far south as the Loango coast and Kongo-speaking communities near the Nzadi River.[43] The plant impacted Kongo societies (where people used both words) to such an extent that peanuts became one of the more important food crops as well as a significant item in sacramental offerings.[44]

These terms appeared in Jamaica by the late seventeenth century, where an Anglo-Jamaican planter and naturalist first saw, "Pindalls... growing in a negro's plantation" and noted that, "some call them gub-a-gubs; and others ground-nuts."[45] Given the presence of the crop and the terms in English Caribbean, it is possible that the cultivar and terminology had been "brought from the Antilles" to the Lowcountry, as supposed by Castiglioni.[46] Still, the West-Central Africans who established the plant and its names in Jamaica came from the same body of captives that included those taken to South Carolina, even those who took a more circuitous path through the intercolonial trade described in Chapter 2. No reason exists to suppose that West-Central Africans in the Lowcountry

States research region (and the rest of the United States) has been made available in a searchable database under the direction of William A. Kretzschmar, Jr., at the University of Georgia (<http://us.english.uga.edu/>).

[43] Kairn A. Klieman, "Hunters and Farmers of the Western Equatorial Rainforest: Economy and Society, 3000 B.C. to A.D. 1880," (PhD Dissertation, University of California – Los Angeles, 1997), 227–31. It appears that the term pinda remained attached to the plant in South Asia, too. See Lyman Carrier, *The Beginnings of Agriculture in America* (New York: McGraw-Hill, 1923), 80.

[44] Lucca, *Relations*, 76; Caltanisetta, *Diaire Congolais*, 105–6; and Laman, *Kongo*, 3: 148, 149, 155, 157.

[45] Henry Barham, *Hortus Americanus* (Kingston, Jamaica: Alexander Aikman, 1794), 145–6. This was a later publication of Barham's unpublished manuscript.

[46] Castiglinioni, *Viaggio*, 172.

did not know peanuts in the same way as their countrymen in Jamaica and other parts of the African-Atlantic diaspora, where it appears that captive Africans independently initiated peanut cultivation, as well.

The example of peanuts identified as both guba and pinda raises the issue of the meaning behind the use of multiple terms for the same crop. We may imagine a certain amount of duplication or incidence of synonyms common in all languages. Yet the presence of an internally coherent set of African words in a language whose usual vocabulary relied on English terms suggests that conscious choices, not some kind of randomness or lack of imagination, informed the initial retention and continuing reproduction of these names. The African labels for cultivated plants reflected the cultural importance of these names for the identities of those who employed them, which contributed to the use of multiple African terms such as the words from Mande, Atlantic, Chadic, and Kwa languages for rice (respectively, kala/kôlo, malo/melo, kafa/gafa, and moliku) retained in the Lowcountry.[47] In a similar example, the four terms for yams (sadi, jambi, sômbo, yambi) come from languages in the Mande, Bantu, and (possibly) Kwa phyla. Certainly, the yams that Africans grew back home were not the same species of tubers grown in the Lowcountry, which included varieties of sweet potatoes instead. The differences between a yam and a sweet potato so significant to botanists, however, had little relevance to African-descended people who employed the same methods to cultivate, harvest, and eat both. It is possible that these terms named different species, although the glosses for three ("red," "reddish") suggest similar if not the same species. Above all, however, speakers of Mande, Bantu, and Kwa languages were more concerned with meanings of cultivating, harvesting, and eating the yam-resembling sweet potatoes and so retained these words to identify the significance of the plants in human, not botanical, terms. The multiple terms represent the multiple African influences on knowledge about a significant crop grown by African-descended people throughout the entire African-Atlantic diaspora. Rather than reduce this plural heritage into one African term, create a new word, or dismiss African names altogether for an English label, the Lowcountry-born descendants of Africans chose instead to retain the multiple names, thus retaining the meanings of the plants as living markers of identity linking the speakers to their African-born ancestors.[48]

---

[47] Wood, *Black Majority*, 35–62; Littlefield, *Rice and Slaves*, 74–114; Carney, *Black Rice*, 76–8, 92–4, 150–3; and Edelson, *Plantation Enterprise*, 53–91.

[48] On the relationship of food to identity in African Lowcountry culture, see Josephine Beoku-Betts, "'She Make Funny Flat Cake She Call Saraka': Gullah Women and Food

The meanings of the cultivars with African names had much to do with the spiritual nature of planting, as discussed for Central Africans and West Africans in the previous chapter and seen in references to later cultural practices related to harvests in the Lowcountry. Harvests offered memorable occasions for the gathering of food and people on plantations. Tony Washington recalled, "Folks seem to get heap of enjoyment out of the work in the old times. For instance, picking peanuts and gathering corn were just getting ready for big times! How about that peanut boiling, come Saturday night, when you eat peanuts out of the big kettles? Yum!"[49] Concerns about the fertility of the land culminated in communal celebrations following the reaping of bountiful crops. These events focused on the standard components of African-Atlantic spiritual rituals by including drumming, singing, and dancing, as recalled by Katie Brown in coastal Georgia: "Harvest time was time for drums. Then they have big times. When harvest in, they have big gathering. They beat drum, rattle dry gourd with seed in them, and beat big flat tin plates. They shout and move round in circle and look like march going to heaven. Harvest festival, they call it."[50]

On Sapelo Island, Georgia, Nero Jones remembered, "We use to have big time at harvest. We pray and sing the night through. When the sun rise we go out and dance. We have big beating of drums and sometimes we dry the gourds and leave the seed in them."[51] The spiritual component of these events was best expressed by Henry Williams of St. Mary's, Georgia: "We has a big time long about when crops come in and everybody bring something to eat what they makes and we all gives praise for the good crop and then we shouts and sings all night."[52] The practice of the "shout" represented the most significant collective ritual among African-descended people in the Lowcountry, and its place in harvest festivals attests to the fundamentally spiritual nature of these celebrations.[53]

African-descended people even infused the celebrations of white Carolinians with their notions of the great significance of the fertility of

Practices Under Slavery," in *Working Toward Freedom: Slave Society and Domestic Economy in the American South*, ed. Larry E. Hudson, Jr. (Rochester, NY: University of Rochester Press, 1994), 211–31.

[49] Orland Kay Armstrong, *Old Massa's People: The Old Slaves Tell Their Story* (Indianapolis, IN: Bobbs-Merrill, 1931), 30.

[50] Georgia Writers' Project, *Drums and Shadows*, 159.

[51] Georgia Writers' Project, *Drums and Shadows*, 165.

[52] Georgia Writers' Project, *Drums and Shadows*, 186–7.

[53] For the most extensive examination of the cultural context of the "shout," see Stuckey, *Slave Culture*, 3–97.

the land. Christmas time in the Carolina Lowcountry afforded enslaved people a respite of several days from the normal work routine and a chance to share the abundance of their own gardens with their enslavers. A telling of the holiday festivities on a St. John's Berkeley parish plantation described "numbers of negroes, dressed in their best...sauntering down the avenue – the women in bright calicoes and head-handkerchiefs, and the men in more pretentious suits than white woolen [*sic*]....The women brought little offerings of eggs, ground-nuts (peanuts), and occasionally a chicken; and all said 'Merry Chris'mus!' to every member of the family that they saw."[54] The grand weddings of enslavers also presented African-descended people, particularly the "negro women of the families of the bride and groom," an opportunity to demonstrate their mastery of their own food production and cooking. The remembrance of events at Pooshee plantation, also in St. John's Berkeley parish, included the midnight meals that followed the wedding ceremonies, in which enslaved women prepared, "Without fail a large 'fanner basket'...daintily but bountifully filled with all they had and sent to 'Missus an' Mossa an' de chillen.'" The food gifts in fanner baskets "were teeming with plates of hot, steaming rice, boiled fowl or chicken, pork, potatoes, black-eyed peas, etc."[55]

The fact that enslaved people shared with their enslavers their own food, not plantation stores, and included precious meat, certainly was a "custom that may surprise some," as the author of the account of the wedding feast attested.[56] We can see in these events both enactments of subservience (tribute to the enslaver) and inversions of power relations (enslaved people control the food of enslavers). Still, these interpretations may be secondary to a deeper cultural understanding that made such practices imperative from a spiritual standpoint. These offerings signified that the fertility of land under the care of African-descended people, enriched by the agricultural knowledge of African ancestors and fertilized by blessings from the spiritual domain, superseded the racial social order of enslavers. The fertility of the land was bigger than slavery, and African-descended people knew and showed it in ways incomprehensible to those who enslaved them.

[54] Anne Simons Deas, "Two Years of Plantation Life," 60–1, Anne Simons Deas Papers, SCL.

[55] Samuel Wilson Ravenel, "Christmas at Pooshee Plantation, Berkeley County, S.C.," 16, Charles Stevens Dwight Papers, SCL.

[56] Samuel Wilson Ravenel, "Christmas at Pooshee Plantation, Berkeley County, S.C.," 16, Charles Stevens Dwight Papers, SCL.

The mention of meat in the fanner baskets alludes to another aspect of the tame realm of African-based agriculture in the Lowcountry. In addition to the provision gardens, enslaved people kept their own animals, which like the produce of their plots provided sustenance and surplus for sale to plantation owners or at market. Lowcountry planters often paid enslaved people for hogs and fowl, as did Elias Ball, who bought fowl from Abraham and hogs from Maree and Johny.[57] In his 1760s account book, Henry Ravenel recorded numerous payments to enslaved people such as Pompey, Harculus, Amey, Gibbey, Hector, and Mary for hogs and fowls.[58] This practice continued into the antebellum period. Several enslaved people regularly sold hog meat to John Willson between 1848 and 1855.[59] Ben Sparkman paid several enslaved men (including Prince, Frank, Lindy, Leevy, Lewis, Tom, and Tim) for hogs and other produce during the 1850s.[60] While these planters paid cash, Joseph Palmer exchanged cloth for fowl with Ben, Flora, Phoebe, Jane, and Maria in 1818.[61] Sam Polite (enslaved in Beaufort County during his childhood) recalled, "You can have chicken, maybe hawg. You can sell egg and chicken to store and Master will buy your hog. In that way slave can have money for buy thing like fish and whatever he want."[62]

The West-Central African influence on this area of domestic production was marked, as well. Of the five African words for domesticated animals retained in the Lowcountry (*budi, gulu, kuti, bidibidi*, and *sanxisa*), all came from Bantu languages. Most notably, four of the terms named the animals most commonly raised and sold by enslaved people. Both *gulu* and *kuti* referred to pigs (the latter referred specifically to "a small pig"). The terms *bidibidi* ("a small bird or a small chicken") and *sanxisa* ("hen") named domesticated fowl. The last term, *budi* ("goat"), labeled an animal that apparently did not figure heavily in production for sale to planters or in the market, but that certainly inhabited many plantation yards.

---

[57] Plantation Account Book (1720–1787), 26 January 1728, 7 April 1728, and February 1735, John Ball Papers, SCHS.

[58] Fowls – 3 October 1763, 3 July 1764, 16 July 1764, 15 December 1764, 24 November 1764, January 1767, 15 October 1767, March 1768; Hogs – June 1764, 15 October 1764, 7 December 1764, 3 February 1767, Henry Ravenel Ledger, 175–1783, Thomas Porcher Ravenel Papers, Reel 1, Series B, RASP.

[59] Entries listed under "Truck purchased of Negroes," John O. Willson Papers, SCL. Willson purchased beef on several occasions, as well.

[60] Ben Sparkman Plantation Journal, SHC. See also, DeSaussure, "Story of My Life," Charles Alfred DeSaussure Papers, SHC.

[61] Joseph Palmer Account Book, SCL.

[62] Rawick, *American Slave*, vol. 3, pt. 4: 272.

TABLE 8. *African Names for Animals (Excluding Birds)*

Bantu Terms	
beɴ	rabbit
boma	large brownish snake
budi	goat
di'okolo	tadpole
gembo	bat
gone	rat
gulu	pig
jamba	elephant
kandi	rabbit
kaɴka	large fish resembling the catfish but larger
kuti	small pig
pudi	wide, flat, scaleless saltwater fish
puku	rat
xiji	rat
Mande/Atlantic Terms	
koima	alligator
landu	a striped lizard
toti	frog
wamaʊt	catfish (literally "large mouth")
Other	
kuta	tortoise (pan-Niger-Congo distribution)

Source: Turner, *Africanisms*; and LDTP.

As with plant names, the African terms for domesticated animals entailed cultural meanings beyond simple labels, which we find in Lowcountry ideas about the spiritual qualities attached to these animals. Pigs reputedly had a "guffer-eye" (one endowed with the ability to see the invisible realm) that allowed them to perceive the advance of storms, which they signaled by running back and forth in the direction of the coming wind.[63] Goats intimidated malevolent spirits, providing a good reason to tie one close to the front door to protect the home.[64] The crowing of a rooster after sunset warned of trouble or death.[65] Some poultry could protect people by finding harmful charms buried on their land. Many people in the Lowcountry kept "guinea fowls" in their yards

[63] Bound Volume (p. 118), John Bennett Papers, SCHS.
[64] Maulsey Stoney (Edisto Island, SC), interview with C.S. Murray, Folder D-4-27A(1), WPA-SCL.
[65] Chlotilde R. Martin (Beaufort County, South Carolina), "Animal Behavior and Meanings," D-4-27B, WPA-SCL; and M.H. Work, "Some Geechee Folk-Lore," *Southern Workman* 35 (1905): 635.

because "they is the only fowl what can scratch up conjures [charms]."[66] Similarly, coastal people had "frizzle" chickens for the same purpose. According to Rosa Sallins of Harris Neck, Georgia, "They dig up conjure what is laid down for you and let you know when somebody is after you."[67] Their role as anti-hoodoo agents earned frizzle chickens the title of "doctor".[68] These fowl could also locate hidden or lost objects, as noted by Horace Campbell of St. Mary's, Georgia: "They keeps chicken 'cause frizzle chicken is a wise chicken. It sure can find what you can't find."[69] These beliefs combined with the retention of two Bantu terms for chickens and the verb *takula* meaning "to scratch" (associated particularly with the scratching of fowl in Kongo languages) reflects the West-Central African perception of the hen and cock as intermediaries between complementary realms such as earth and sky, low and high, day and night, and by extension the land of the living and the land of the dead. Because of their remarkable spiritual status, people allowed the fowl to move in and out of their homes free to scratch up unseen (and potentially threatening) items, a practice that African-descended people in the South Carolina and Georgia Lowcountry considered effective, as well.[70]

While a few of the animals with African names inhabited the tame domain of gardens and yards, the vast majority lived in the wild swamps, forests, fields, and waters of the Lowcountry. Many of the land creatures, birds, and fish included in the African inventory named the sources of much-needed protein for African-descended people. From the earliest days of settlement, enslaved hunters displayed their prowess.[71] An act in the early eighteenth century awarded bounties to enslaved people for killing large predators such as wolves, panthers, bears, and wild

---

[66] Jessie A. Butler (Charleston, SC), "Negro Superstitions," Folder H-4-6, WPA-SCL.

[67] Georgia Writers' Project, *Drums and Shadows*, 129–30. See also, Harry Middleton Hyatt, *Hoodoo – Conjuration – Witchcraft – Rootwork: Beliefs Accepted by Many Negroes and White Persons, These Being Orally Recorded Among Blacks and Whites* (Hannibal, MO: H.M. Hyatt, 1970), 2: 990.

[68] Garland Rice of Burton, South Carolina, in Chlotilde Martin, "Folklore," Folder D-4-27B(1), WPA-SCL.

[69] Georgia Writers' Project, *Drums and Shadows*, 187. See also, Georgia Writers' Project, *Drums and Shadows*, 125 (Liza Basden), 140 (interview with Alec Anderson), 171 (interview with George Smith), 194 (interview with Shadwick Rudolph).

[70] René Devisch, *Weaving the Threads of Life: The Khita Gyn-Eco-Logical Healing Cult among the Yaka* (Chicago, IL: University of Chicago Press, 1993), 63.

[71] For the larger social and cultural context of African-descended hunters in the South, see Stuart A. Marks, *Southern Hunting in Black and White: Nature, History, and Ritual in a Carolina Community* (Princeton, NJ: Princeton University Press, 1991); and Giltner, *Hunting and Fishing*.

TABLE 9. *African Names for Birds*

Bantu Terms	
bobobo	woodpecker
bidibidi	small bird, small chicken
kelele	marsh bird with white and black stripes on its wings
kilombo	black and white marsh bird
kimbi	hawk
kimbimbi	quail
kiŋkwawi	partridge
kulu	blue and white marsh bird
kusu	parrot
xiele	large blue, white, and black marsh bird
sanxisa	hen
tukumpanda	tall, bluish bird smaller than a heron
wela	pigeon
Mande/Atlantic Terms	
degati ᴏᴜl	barn owl
fulafafa	woodpecker
Hu'hu	owl
jaja	blackbird
kakatulu	large bird, mockingbird
kamba'boli	gray/brown/speckled bird
kulu	blue and white marsh bird
pojo	heron
saŋgalo	wild duck
wulisãkpãkpã	woodpecker
Other	
elukeluke	grayish-brown marsh bird (Benue-Congo)
eriaria	white and brown marsh bird (Benue-Congo)
hihi	owl (Atlantic, Kwa, Bantu)

Source: Turner, *Africanisms*; and LDTP.

cats.[72] Additionally, conventional wisdom held that a "dextrous negro, will, with his gun and nets, get as much game and fish as five families can eat"[73] Many planters employed enslaved men exclusively as hunters and guides for their hunting parties.[74] Other enslaved people took up the hunt

[72] Thomas Cooper, ed., *The Statutes at Large of South Carolina* (Columbia, SC: A.S. Johnston, 1837), 2: 216.
[73] *American Husbandry: Containing An Account of The Soil, Climate, Production and Agriculture, of the British Colonies in North America and in the West-Indies* (London: Printed for J. Bew, 1775), 1: 428.
[74] Duncan C. Heyward, *Seed from Madagascar* (Chapel Hill: University of North Carolina Press, 1937), 117–27.

as a matter of necessity. In general, plantation rations in the Lowcountry included very little meat, if any.[75] To compensate for this want, some men used the time after they completed their daily tasks to seek out prey.[76] The experience obtained during these excursions gave some men the knowledge and inclination to abscond, such as a fellow called Jack, considered "very expert in hunting." Also, an African renamed Titus, adorned with "country marks down the sides of his face," failed to return to his Santee River plantation after leaving for a hunt.[77]

The older fathers, many of them Africans, taught young males the art of the hunt. Aaron Ford, born during the last years of slavery, stated, "I remember my grandfather all right. He the one told me how to catch otters. Told me how to set traps."[78] In addition to traps, novice hunters in the Lowcountry learned to use snares, guns, and dogs to bag a variety of birds, small mammals, and even alligators. Other animals commonly caught by enslaved people included rabbits, opossum, raccoons, otters, and squirrels.[79] One industrious hunter, Charles Ball, set traps in the swamps of the Lowcountry three nights a week up to three miles from his residence. His efforts yielded two or three meals of raccoon, opossum, or rabbit every week.[80] Some hunters knew how to trap more elusive game such as fox. One of these experts, Gabriel Myers, used a dead mouse dangled from a strand of spider web to bait the trap buried under a thin layer of sand. Additional bait included charred yams, which Myers claimed the fox could not resist. Master hunters recognized that each animal responded to particular lures and adjusted traps appropriately.[81]

Certainly, much of the knowledge of the terrain and creatures that dwelled there derived from the direct, local experience of African-descended hunters and early interactions with Native communities. The

---

[75] Bolzius, "Questionnaire," 235–6; and Charles Ball, *Slavery in the United States: A Narrative of the Life and Adventures of Charles Ball, A Black Man* (New York Kraus Reprint, 1969 [1837]), 107, 274–6.

[76] On the task system and its impact on enslaved people, see Morgan, "Work and Culture," 563–99; and Judith A. Carney, "From Hands to Tutors: African Expertise in the South Carolina Rice Economy," *Agricultural History* 67, 3 (1993): 1–30.

[77] *SCG*, 1 May 1749; *South-Carolina and American General Gazette*, 3 April 1777. See also *Georgia Gazette*, 5 April 1765.

[78] Rawick, *American Slave*, vol. 2, pt. 2, 62; vol. 3, pt. 4, 57; vol. 2, pt. 2, 75. See also, John Campbell, "'My Constant Companion': Slaves and their Dogs in the Antebellum South," in Hudson, *Working Toward Freedom*, 57–8.

[79] Rawick, *American Slave*, vol. 2, pt. 1: 156–57, 185, 191; vol. 2, pt. 2: 75, 138, 166; vol. 3, pt. 3: 159; vol. 3, pt. 4: 71, 101, 128, 234.

[80] Ball, *Slavery*, 262–3, 274.

[81] Archibald Rutledge, *God's Children* (Indianapolis and New York: The Bobbs-Merrill Company, 1947), 127.

linguistic and archaeological evidence, however, suggests that knowledge about taking animals derived in some part from the expertise of earlier African fathers and mothers. The faunal remains of wild land mammals that appeared regularly at sites once occupied by enslaved people and that retained African names in the Lowcountry indicate a significant presence of rabbits and rats. The continued use of five names for these creatures (*ben* and *kandi* for "rabbit"; *gône*, *puku*, and *xiji* for "rat") derived from Bantu languages demonstrates the particular role of West-Central Africans in the transmission of African-based knowledge regarding these animals. While the consumption of land mammals such as rabbits, opossum, raccoons, and squirrels appears normal for people who benefitted from the efforts of hunters, the eating of rats may seem exotic. This was nothing unusual for West-Central Africans as well as for West Africans for that matter. West-Central African children learned to dig up and trap rats as part of their early education. This served people well, especially in times of drought and famine when regular food sources were scarce.[82] Even under ideal circumstances, rats constituted one of the regular, albeit small, sources of meat in a plant-based diet for most West-Central Africans. This continued in the early Lowcountry, as Johann Martin Bolzius wrote during the 1750s that enslaved people "sometimes roast mice" when they desired meat.[83] The extensive presence of rats, which often burrowed in the banks around rice fields and lived in nearby forests, made them a readily accessible source of protein.[84] The absence of consistent stocks of meat from domestic animals coupled with the adequate supply of rats on and near plantations certainly allowed West-Central Africans, other Africans, and their descendants to indulge their fancy for rat meat.[85] African-descended communities in the

[82] Cavazzi, *Descrição*, 1: 119; and Balandier, *Daily Life*, 161. Laman, *Kongo*, 1: 100, provides descriptions of techniques and traps used in capturing rats among early twentieth-century Kongo people.

[83] Bolzius, "Questionnaire," 236. On the overall composition of the diet of enslaved people in the Lowcountry that mirrors the plant-to-meat proportions in West-Central Africa, see Cavazzi, *Descrição*, 1: 50–98. See also Bolzius, "Questionnaire," 235–6; Ball, *Slavery*, 107; and Laman, *Kongo*, 1: 50–63.

[84] Heyward, *Seed from Madagascar*, 167; Mamie Garvin Fields, *Lemon Swamp and Other Places: A Carolina Memoir* (New York: Free Press, 1983), 128–9, 133; Julia Floyd Smith, *Slavery and Rice Culture in Low Country Georgia, 1750–1860* (Knoxville: University of Tennessee Press, 1985), 50; and Stewart, *What Nature Suffers to Groe*, 161.

[85] For the presence of rats in faunal remains, see Michael Trinkley, ed., *Archaeological and Historical Examinations of Three Eighteenth and Nineteenth Century Rice Plantations on the Waccamaw Neck* (Columbia, SC: Chicora Foundation, 1993), 197–201; Natalie Adams, Michael Trinkley, and Debi Hacker, eds., *In the Shadow of the Big*

Lowcountry were not unique in this regard. Enslaved people in Jamaica (and apparently some Anglo-Jamaicans, as well) ate and traded rat meat on a regular basis.[86]

In addition to land mammals, enslaved people caught wild birds for food. West-Central Africans taught their Lowcountry progeny to utilize the Kongo *kulula* trap in this pursuit. These bird traps, regarded as "very simply constructed" by the mistress of a Georgia plantation, served to catch species such as partridge, pigeon, and quail, some of the birds most often taken and eaten by enslaved people. People in the Lowcountry continued to call these birds by names derived from their Kongo equivalents – *kimbimbi, kinkwawi,* and *wela* – long after the end of slavery.[87] Additionally, birds known by names from Mande and Atlantic languages figured prominently in the faunal remains recovered from former plantation sites.[88]

The African names for fish identified another wild source for protein. African-descended people employed multiple methods to obtain fish including poisoning, trapping, netting, and line fishing.[89] A 1726 act criminalized the first technique, in which "many persons in this Province do often use the pernicious practice of poisoning the creeks in order to catch great quantity of fish." The act included a specific provision for punishing enslaved people convicted of violating this law, that they "be publickly whipped, not exceeding thirty-nine lashes."[90] The method of trapping fish made good use of the tidal action on the waterways that drained into the ocean, as witnessed in the early 1760s: "Those living upon the rivers, by stopping of creeks with reeds and small canes tied closely together, on the ebbing of the tide, take abundance of fish."[91] Early evidence of

House: Domestic Slaves at Stoney/Baynard Plantation, Hilton Head Island (Columbia, SC: Chicora Foundation, 1995), 103–8; and Michael Trinkley, ed., *Archaeological Investigations at Haig Point, Webb, and Oak Ridge, Daufuskie Island, Beaufort County, South Carolina* (Columbia, SC: Chicora Foundation, 1989), 172–92.

[86] Sloane, *Voyage to the Islands,* 1: xxv; Patrick Browne, *The Civil and Natural History of Jamaica* (London: Osborn and Shipton, 1756), 484; Edward Long, *The History of Jamaica* (London: T. Lowndes, 1774), 2: 414; and Cynric Williams, *A Tour Through the Island of Jamaica in the Year 1823* (London: Hunt and Clarke, 1826), 203.

[87] Frances Anne Kemble, *Journal of a Residence on a Georgia Plantation in 1838–1839* (Athens: University of Georgia Press, 1984 [1863]), 58; and Rawick, *American Slave,* vol. 3, pt. 4: 71.

[88] For the presence of birds in faunal remains, see Trinkley, *Archaeological and Historical Examinations,* 199; Adams, Trinkley, and Hacker, *In the Shadow of the Big House,* 105; and Trinkley, *Archaeological Investigations,* 175.

[89] Wood, *Black Majority,* 122–3, 201–2; and Morgan, *Slave Counterpoint,* 138, 240–3.

[90] Cooper, *Statutes at Large,* 3: 270.

[91] "Curious New Description of Charles-Town," quoted in Morgan, *Slave Counterpoint,* 242.

expertise in fishing with nets appears in an advertisement from 1737 for a fugitive from Wando Neck plantation named Moses, who was "well known in Charlestown, having been a Fisherman there some time, & hath been often employed in knitting of Nets."[92] For line fishing, African-descended people fashioned "lines of very strong grass to which they affix a small piece of wood, sharpened at both ends, but thick in the middle; they bait this in such a manner that the fish must take it both ends, and when once they shut their mouths upon it, they cannot again extricate themselves from it, and so are catched."[93] The proficiency of fishermen of African descent was clearly evident by the 1730s, as one observer noted, "I've known two Negroes take between 14 & 1500 Trouts above 3 feet long."[94]

As with the domesticated animals, African-descended people in the Lowcountry imbued wild animals with spiritual meaning. A rabbit that crossed one's path to the right portended good luck, although crossing to the left meant misfortune.[95] Rodents gnawing on clothes, the flight of a rattlesnake from one's path, the "barking" of certain lizards (known colloquially as puppy-dogs) foretold death.[96] Birds more than any other kind of animal delivered messages of death, as did the mourning dove, whippoorwill, hoot owl, and screech owl with their calls.[97] The presence of buzzards, a bird closely associated with conjure or hoodoo, in the skies near a person's house foretold the death of a member of that household.[98]

---

[92] *SCG*, 5 November 1737.

[93] James Barclay, *The Voyages and Travels of James Barclay, Containing Many Surprising Adventures, and Interesting Narratives* (London: Privately printed for the author, 1777), 27.

[94] Undated letter by James Sutherland, Coe Papers, SCHS, quoted in Wood, *Black Majority*, 201.

[95] Information supplied by Ola Cohen for Pheobe Faucette (Hampton County, South Carolina), "Folklore," WPA-SCL.

[96] Jessie A. Butler (Charleston, South Carolina), "Superstition," Folder H-4-6, WPA-SCL; Henry C. Davis, "Negro Folk-Lore in South Carolina," *Journal of American Folklore* 27 (1914): 246; Bernice Gordon in Newbell Niles Puckett, *Folk Beliefs of the Southern Negro* (Chapel Hill: University of North Carolina Press, 1926), 480, 481; Georgia Writers' Project, *Drums and Shadows*, 101 (interview with F.J. Jackson).

[97] Chlotilde R. Martin (Beaufort County, South Carolina), "Superstitions that Predict Death," "Animal Behavior and Meanings," Folder D-4-27B; Phoebe Faucette (Hampton County, South Carolina), "Folklore," "Folk Customs and Folk Lore – Negro Superstitions Relating to Sickness," Folder D-4-27B; Sarah Boylston (Allendale County, South Carolina), "Folk Customs and Folk Lore," Folder F-2-18A, WPA-SCL.

[98] Bound Volume (p. 22), John Bennett Papers, SCHS; and Georgia Writers' Project, *Drums and Shadows*, 4 (interview with Dye Williams), 109–10 (interview with Peter McQueen), 157 (interview with Lawrence Baker), 184 (interview with Floyd White); and Rawick, *American Slave*, vol. 3, pt. 1: 292 (interview with Lizzie Davis).

The case of a wild boar that scavenged near a plantation along the Santee River during the annual flooding of the nearby swamp was seen by many as a sign of pending misfortune, as well. This creature, the most feared among all animals in the swamp, had killed several dogs and menaced plantation inhabitants, thus necessitating a communal hunt for the creature. Although eventually tracked down by the plantation hunting dogs and shot by Scipio, "a hunter of no mean ability," the killing of the wild boar did not undo the sinister consequences of the beast's presence. The African-descended people of the plantation considered the "boar's visit as a true prophecy of trouble to come," which followed a few months later with the lethal appearance of anthrax among the livestock.[99]

The pursuit of wild animals often took African-descended hunters into the forests and swamps filled with dangerous animals like the wild boar. There they required assistance from the spiritual domain to render protection and enhance the chances for taking game, as did the Native hunters, who first prowled through the same forests. This spiritual dimension of the hunt had also been understood quite well by the African newcomers to the Lowcountry because they came from societies in which these ideas shaped behaviors related to hunting. Within these societies, a good hunt depended on the support of ancestors and nature spirits who governed the forests and provided sanction for people using these domains. A failed hunt clearly indicated that either the hunters had violated a rule placed on their activities or people in the larger community had neglected their obligations to the spirits of the invisible realm, both of which needed ritual redress. These spiritual concerns, along with the demands of the hunt itself, encouraged hunters to carry empowered objects composed to promote safety and success. In West-Central Africa, certain spiritual experts, such as those known by the titles *nganga-ngudi-a-nambua* and *mpombolo*, earned renown for their abilities to enchant animals to draw them to hunters for the kill and make the necessary consecrated objects.[100] The most effective objects included parts of the animals sought by the hunters. For example, hunters of elephants wore elephant tail hairs in pouches around their necks for protection and strength in addition to keeping the bones of these animals in their homes.[101]

African-descended hunters in the Lowcountry employed a similar approach in their quest to collect "stones" taken from the bodies of predators. Foremost among these predators was the eagle, which

[99] Rutledge, *God's Children*, 46–8.
[100] Cavazzi, *Descrição*, 1: 201.
[101] Lucca, *Relations*, 128–9, 244.

according to Alec Johnson of Waverly Mills, was "the ruling bird of the element [nature]."[102] Sam Keith commented on the exceptional abilities of the eagle as the "Only bird can fly across Atlantic and Pacific Ocean. Carry the stone!"[103] In clarifying the significance of the stone associated with the eagle, Rich Knox of Murrells Inlet stated, "Eagle got lode-stone. In her head. Onliest way to get that been to kill eagle. Lode-stone. They know when fish hawk out fishing. They knows when anything coming to the nest."[104] While some claimed that a person could procure a stone from an eagle's nest, a story about Charles Green's quest on Edisto Island supported the position that the stone came from the body. After Green had climbed to the top of a tree to search an unoccupied eagle's nest, he found nothing. The bird returned just as Green decided to descend to the ground, and, "That been devil then, sure enough." During the ensuing struggle between eagle and man, Green pulled out his knife and "juck the bird in the throat." The stone "pop out the eagle throat and fall plop on the ground," which Green then retrieved, as the eagle had flown away "screeching 'cause he done lose he power." From that day on, Green kept his powerful eagle stone stowed away and "wrap in a leaf from the Bible."[105] Those who possessed an eagle stone were reputed to be able to attract not only game but "almost any object you can name." Further, a man with an eagle stone never lacked money, no matter how much he spent, and he could not be kept in jail.[106]

Less potent although still highly desired, were stones acquired from the heads of fish. While the eagle stone had universal power, the fish stones only attracted the kinds of fish from which fisherman had taken them. A successful fisherman such as Robert Samuel of the mainland town of Meggett usually kept a tobacco sack filled with a variety of well-polished fish stones. In describing his collection, Samuel noted, "This one here the black bass stone. See how big he is? This belong to whiting and this to croaker. The big rough one come from Catfish." The size of most

[102] Alec Johnson (Waverly Mills, SC), interview with G.W. Chandler, "Baptisin' to Chapel Crick, Waverly Mills S.C.," Folder D-4-36A, WPA-SCL.

[103] Sam Keith, interview with G.W. Chandler, "Interviews with Negroes," Folder D-4-36, WPA-SCL.

[104] Rich Knox (Murrells Inlet), interview with G.W. Chandler, "Sturgeon," Folder D-4-36A, WPA-SCL.

[105] George Brown (Edisto Island, SC), interview with C.S. Murray, "Charms," Folder D-4-27A, WPA-SCL.

[106] George Brown (Edisto Island, SC), interview with C.S. Murray, "Charms," Folder D-4-27A; G.W. Chandler, "About Eagles and Hags," Folder D-4-36A, WPA-SCL.

fish stones corresponded with the size of the fish, as with the pebble-sized stone from the small yellow-tail ("Ain't you see how little he is?") or the big stone from the drum fish. According to Rich Knox, the "big old drum" was so large it "took two mens to tote." Further, fishermen had to "scale him with a hoe. Stand straight up and down and scale him like hoeing."[107]

Like eagle stones, fish stones served as fertility objects. Fishermen had to observe several practices derived from a larger awareness of fertility to ensure the bounty of their catches. In addition to abstaining from fishing on certain unlucky days, fishermen were cautious to avoid conversations with older women and to keep older people from touching their fishing lines before going out. By contrast, a conversation with a "noung gal" (young gal) enhanced the chances of a good haul.[108] With these practices, we can see the risk that contact with the infertile (older women especially) had on the effort to find sustenance from the natural environment, an idea firmly rooted in West-Central African and West African cultures, as well.

Further, the stones taken from eagles and fish in the Lowcountry corresponded closely with West-Central African ideas about the physical manifestations of nature spirits, particularly the simbi, as discussed in Chapter 3. Certainly, people accessed the simbi stones differently, as they came directly from rivers and pools or stood as remarkable rocks on the landscape, but the basic form (a stone) and the function (fertility) remained the same. Both came from the natural environment and empowered people with the spiritual force of the invisible world to ensure successful hunting and fishing.

BANTU SPIRITUAL LANDSCAPES IN THE LOWCOUNTRY

Engagement with the physical domain of the wilderness entailed spiritual meanings, as we have seen with the ideas and practices associated with hunting and fishing. These meanings extended beyond the particular land mammals, birds, and fish encountered in the search for food to include larger realms of the natural environment as especially powerful spiritual spaces. This included the forest, at once a place in the land of the living

---

[107] George Brown (Edisto Island, SC), interview with C.S. Murray, "Charms," Folder D-4–27A; and Rich Knox (Murrells Inlet), interview with G.W. Chandler, "Sturgeon," Folder D-4–36A, WPA-SCL.

[108] George Brown (Edisto Island, SC), interview with C.S. Murray, "Charms," Folder D-4–27A, WPA-SCL.

for hunting and other mundane activities as well as a domain of contact with the invisible forces of the land of the dead. African-descended people in the Lowcountry commemorated this expanded understanding by retaining the Kongo word finda (*mfinda*) to name the forest. In doing so, they claimed the forest as part of the African landscape of the Lowcountry and used the conceptual vocabulary derived from a specifically Bantu heritage.

This claim had been established quite early, as Africans and Lowcountry-born people of African descent engaged the natural environment "beyond the banks" of the plantations in ways more like the Native inhabitants of the region than the European newcomers.[109] When John Lawson attempted to travel into Native territories to make commercial connections, he employed Native guides for much of the journey, except in a telling instance in the stretch of the Santee River settled by French immigrants. This section was, according to the trader, "the most difficult Way I ever saw, occasion'd by Reason of the multitude of Creeks lying along the Main, keeping their Course thro' the Marshes, turning and winding like a Labyrinth, having the Tide of Ebb and Flood twenty Times in less than three Leagues going." To navigate this wild space between the cultivated plantations of the growing colony, the trader could not depend on the Native escorts, but instead relied on a "Negro to guide us over the Head of a large Swamp."[110] This enslaved man was intimately familiar with both the waterways and the settlements linked by them. His was not just knowledge of the natural environment but also of the emerging landscape that took on increasingly novel dimensions through the presence of so many African and European newcomers. With time, African-descended boatmen emerged as the true masters of the flow of people and goods on the waterways that linked the habitations and markets of the Lowcountry.[111]

As expansive as the plantation zone became, this massive reformation of the landscape did not obliterate the wilderness; the older natural environment still prevailed. As one European observer in the late eighteenth century remarked, the "whole face of the countryside is covered with woods, except the plantations, which are like islands in a sea of

---

[109] The term "beyond the banks" and the perspective it conveys of the landscape comes from Stewart, "Rice, Water, and Power," 47–64; and Stewart, *What Nature Suffers to Groe*, 136, 178. For activities in the wilderness, see Wood, *Black Majority*, 117–19; and Edelson, "Nature of Slavery," 26–31.

[110] John Lawson, *A New Voyage to Carolina; Containing the Exact Description and Natural History of That Country* (London: Printed in the Year 1709), 20–1.

[111] Morgan, *Slave Counterpoint*, 236–40.

forest."[112] For many Carolinians, especially those invested in the plantation enterprise, the wilderness represented a threat to their ambition toward dominating the Lowcountry. Governor James Glen made a point of asserting, "Blessed be God [the land] is not to be viewed...in its uncultivated condition, overgrown with woods, over run with wild beasts, and swarming with native Indians...but as an undoubted part of the British dominions, as one of the fairest provinces belonging to our imperial Crown."[113] Certainly, colonial control of the territory had been well established by the mid-eighteenth century, but the glowing appraisal of a landscape given over entirely to the cultivation of British masters existed in aspiration more than in fact. Glen's buoyant description may have been excessive compensation for the fear of lack of control that gripped the colony following the Stono Rebellion in 1739. After that tumultuous event, whites lamented "the unhappy Effects of an Insurrection of our Slaves within our Selves (an intestine Enemy the most dreadful of Enemies) which we have just Grounds to imagine will be repeated," so that "many of our Inhabitants are determined to remove themselves and their Effects, out of this Province; insomuch, that upon the whole the Country seems to be at Stake."[114]

Whites continued to fear retributive violence of enslaved people and often equated it with the presence of the wilderness, which stood symbolically both as the antithesis of cultivation and domination and provided a safe haven for those who resisted enslavement. Self-emancipated people frequently took to the woods, sometimes as individuals attempting to reestablish the personal ties severed by the separation of family and friends through sales or disciplinary actions or, occasionally, as maroon bands striving toward lives unfettered by bondage.[115] For African-descended people in general, the wilderness outside of the plantation represented a realm in which they could assert their autonomy and initiative, even for those who did not directly challenge the institution of enslavement such

---

[112] Philip J. Staudenraus, ed., "Letters from South Carolina, 1821–1822," *South Carolina Historical Magazine* 58, 4 (1957): 210.

[113] James Glen, "Governor James Glen's Valuation, 1751," in Merrens, *Colonial South Carolina Scene*, 178–9. See also Silver, *New Face on the Countryside*, 138, 147–8.

[114] J.H. Easterby, ed., *The Journal of the Commons House of Assembly, September 12, 1739-March 26, 1741* (Columbia: Historical Commission of South Carolina, 1952), 2: 97–8.

[115] *SCG*, 9 February 1734; *South Carolina Gazette and Country Journal*, 14 October 1766, 25 February 1772; *Charleston Morning Post, and Daily Advertiser*, 26 October 1786; *Georgia State Gazette or Independent Register*, 28 October 1786, 19 May 1787; and Morgan, *Slave Counterpoint*, 525–30.

as maroons and those who emancipated themselves through escape.[116] Although the uncultivated realm beyond the banks and between the plantations remained a contested domain, where struggles between slavery and freedom played out, the wilderness became an indisputable feature of the black Lowcountry's sacred landscape.

One means by which African-descended claimed the wilderness as spiritual space was by naming it finda and populating it with the spirits of special animals and certain people. The association of the word and place finda with the realm of the dead in Kongo spiritual culture remained fundamental to perceptions of the forest in the Lowcountry. For all the inhabitants of the Lowcountry, including every person of Native, European, and African descent, the physical realm of the Lowcountry was as much the land of the dead as it was the land of the living. Mortality for these three cohorts exacted heavy tolls from all families and communities, especially during the colonial era when the numbers of newcomers initially stabilized and then grew only through the continuous influx of both captive and free immigrants.[117] Those oppressed by the cruelty of enslavement imbued the landscape with the spirits of people claimed by the violence of captivity, including those who took their own lives like the Africans in the Ibo's Landing story.

The haunting encounter between two enslaved men, Charles Ball and a West-Central African named Paul, in a Lowcountry swamp in the early nineteenth century provides another account of violence and loss that, like the story of Ibo's Landing, blurred the demarcation between the land of the living and the land of the dead. Ball's recountings of his times in the swamp cultivating plots of vegetables and catching a variety of game, particularly turtles, described an entirely physical world of trees, water, and innumerable creatures, until one Sunday, "in a very solitary part of the swamps," Ball "heard the sound of bells, similar to those which wagoners place on the shoulders of their horses." Such an unexpected sound unnerved Ball, and with much fear he heard the bells jingle a few times more as they drew nearer. He then "saw come from behind a large tree, the form of a brawny, famished-looking black man, entirely naked, with his hair matted and shaggy, his eyes wild and rolling, and bearing over his head something the form of an arch." Although he understood that he saw a man bound in chains and an iron collar, to which had been affixed the rod that arched over his head and held the bells that sounded

---

[116] Brown, "Walk in the Feenda," 305–17.
[117] Coclanis, *Shadow of a Dream*, 64–7; and McCandless, *Slavery, Disease, and Suffering*, 18–58.

whenever he moved, Ball did not seem convinced that the figure indeed represented a living person. Instead, from his vantage point hiding in the vegetation, he saw the figure carrying a staff with a spear point as an "it," a "strange spectre." Ball imagined that the "black apparition" was "an inhabitant of a nether and fiery world" whose shackles hissed as the being knelt by a pool and dipped his hands to collect water to drink. In desperation, Ball voiced a prayer for deliverance, drawing the attention of the "black apparition," who, just as alarmed as his observer, ran into the water and begged him "to have mercy upon him, and not carry him back to his master." Ball then recognized that this "object" was a man and "a poor destitute African negro, still more wretched and helpless than myself."[118]

In talking with the African, Ball learned that the man, Paul, had arrived from "Congo" five years before, separated from his mother, wife, and four children. He saw Paul's back scarred and speckled by many whippings from the hand of a cruel enslaver, which prompted Paul to take to the swamp on several occasions. The chains, collar, and bells were his latest punishment that ensured he could not survive long in the wilderness without being caught. After much conversation about Paul's miseries, Ball provided him with fresh turtles and eggs, built him a fire to cook the food, and left him with the promise of returning in a week to bring a file to free Paul from his iron bonds. On the following Sunday, he made his way back to the site where he and Paul had sat by the fire talking, but did not find Paul waiting for him as planned. Hoping that Paul had escaped and fearing that he had been caught, Ball heard the noise of ravens and saw a turkey-buzzard followed by an eagle overhead. Experience told him that the carcass of an animal lay nearby and "called all these ravenous fowls together." In finding the source of the frenzy, Ball walked into an overwhelming stench swarming with various birds of prey feasting on a corpse suspended from a sassafras tree. It was the "lifeless and putrid body of the unhappy Paul hung suspended by a cord made of twisted hickory bark, passed in the form of a halter round the neck, and firmly bound to a limb of the tree." The bells that plagued Paul in life frightened away the birds that alighted on him to feed on his flesh, which "preserved the corpse from being devoured," although Paul had already been "much mangled and torn." Ball returned to the grizzly scene months afterward during his regular sojourns into

---

[118] Charles Ball, *Slavery in the United States: A Narrative of the Life and Adventures of Charles Ball* (New York: John S. Taylor, 1837), 325–7.

the forest, where Paul's body continued to hang until nothing but bones remained.[119]

Charles Ball ended his account of Paul from Congo by noting that he told his enslaver of the hanging corpse (without telling about the rest of the encounter), although no one, including Paul's enslaver, bothered to remove Paul's remains.[120] The enslavement of Paul, the separation from his family, the brutality unleashed on his living body, the desperation that culminated in his suicide, and the neglect of his corpse evinced the greatest evils of captivity in Ball's narrative. Even with Ball's promise of liberation from the burdens of the irons that Paul bore, Paul may have realized that he could not live in the swamp indefinitely. It may have been a refuge, one that he had resorted to for nearly six months once before, but it offered only temporary respite. The Africans in the Ibo's Landing narrative knew their captivity would end only when their bodies ceased to be of value to enslavers. Paul likely came to the same conclusion and used the tree and bark cord to find a similar liberation. The location where Paul took his own life became a kind of memorial for Ball, a place he visited to confirm once again that the violence of enslavement claimed its African-descended victims and marked the landscape with their mortal remains.[121]

Paul's decision to end his life in the forest may have engendered another level of anguish because in his time in West-Central Africa, he likely knew the finda as a cherished space where he spent much of his youth collecting plants, trapping small animals, practicing the hunt, and otherwise learning to become a Kongo man. As a father in Kongo, he may have already begun to introduce his own children to the resources and powers of the finda before he had been made a captive. He certainly knew the finda as the spiritual domain where people journeyed after death and made their villages to become ancestors and sources of access to the power of the spiritual world for the living. Surely this was not how he had expected to spend his last days in the forest, bound in irons and then hanging lifeless from a tree. Did he even hope to enter the spiritual finda as an ancestor for his children in Kongo once his physical being expired? Did the finda in the Lowcountry even connect with the finda in Kongo?

Another West-Central African brought to South Carolina in the nineteenth century seemed to think so. A man known as Gullah Joe lived near

[119] Ball, *Slavery*, 328–31, 334–7.
[120] Ball, *Slavery*, 336–7.
[121] Ball, *Slavery*, 337.

the swampy forests of the Congaree River and in addition to telling a friend about his experiences of being enslaved and transported across the Atlantic as a child, expressed his thoughts of returning home:

I is a old man now, but I has a longing to walk in the feenda. I wants to see it one more time. I has a wife and children here, but when I thinks of my tribe and my friend and my daddy and my mammy and the great feenda, a feeling rises up in my throat and my eye well up with tear.[122]

Along with his parents and his people, Gullah Joe thought of the forest, "the feenda," as the place that was his home. Considering that he was "a old man now," he likely thought that his father, mother, and many of his friends had already transitioned into the spiritual finda. His longing to "walk in the feenda" and once again see those he parted from so long ago may have indicated that he looked forward to his own journey to the spiritual finda.[123]

Yet a certain tension arises in his statement, "I wants to see it one more time." The great spiritual finda awaits almost everyone, especially those with descendants in the land of the living like Gullah Joe, and it would be only a matter of time for him to enter it. He desired, however, to see it "one more time" while he still lived. Indeed, he offered his lament in response to the question, "Is you satisfy?" with life in South Carolina. He replied, "I would be satisfy if I just could see my tribe one more time. Then I would be willing to come back here." If given the opportunity, he would have gone back to see the people and land of his ancestors, but he would also have returned to the people and place of his life after crossing the Atlantic, the land of his descendants. In only a few words, Gullah Joe exposed the heart of his ties to the people he loved and his understanding of his place in the land of the living and the land of the dead. He wanted to be in the finda of his childhood and his homeland, the finda that existed in the physical, visible realm. He awaited the time when he would "walk in de feenda" of the land of the dead, the spiritual forest that reunited him with his ancestors back in Kongo and maintained his connection with his descendants in South Carolina.

Paul's ties to the Lowcountry finda, however, were far less certain. His children were not in South Carolina, but in Kongo. He apparently did not have any children on this side of kalunga to link his blood to this land as

---

[122] Edward C.L. Adams, *Tales of the Congaree*, ed. Robert G. O'Meally (Chapel Hill: University of North Carolina Press), 278.

[123] This interpretation of Gullah Joe's comments comes from Young, *Rituals of Resistance*, 176–7.

an ancestor. This did not mean, however, that he could not become part of the spiritual finda of the Lowcountry. We can assume that his desperate situation drove him to take his life, but in the same instance his knowledge of Kongo spiritual culture also gave him a certain understanding of the consequences of this act. While he could not expect to bridge the physical and spiritual forests of Kongo and the Lowcountry as both a descendant and an ancestor as Gullah Joe could, did he anticipate becoming a simbi or nkita, as many back home in Kongo said happened to those who died violently or by suicide? We cannot know how Paul transformed in the land of the dead, but we do know that the Lowcountry was home to the simbi. Maybe he became one of these simbi, watching over other sons and daughters of Africa held captive on this shore of kalunga, protecting them from the misfortune that he could not himself avoid or even wreaking vengeance on enslavers for the injustices they visited upon others.

THE "CYMBEE"

Because the spiritual cultures of West-Central Africans and West Africans centered around ideas and practices that emphasized interaction with the natural environment in both physical and spiritual ways, the presence of the physical forest ensured that the spiritual meanings of the forest remained relevant to African-descended people. We must imagine that the African newcomers arrived in a land already filled with spirits and shrines that only needed to be found. Locating them, of course, was inevitable, and they certainly expected to find the abodes of spirits in the most obvious locations. Certain natural features, as discussed in Chapter 3, provided these abodes, most notably bodies of water and forests. Among the bodies of water that had an especially strong association with nature spirits, springs and the pools formed by them comprised the ideal places to encounter the simbi. Fortunately for captive West-Central Africans, one of the early areas of settlement in the Lowcountry abounded with springs that served not only as sources of fresh water, but also as the homes of many simbi.

Some may have felt justified in describing the Lowcountry in very general terms as a flat, even featureless, landscape, although such a claim remains unsupportable by the diversity of vegetation and landforms seen in the coastal plain and the tidewater zone.[124] One of the more remarkable

---

[124] Silver, *New Face on the Countryside*, 14–19; Gregory Carbone and John J. Hidore, "Climate, Vegetation and Soils," in *A Geography of the Carolinas*, ed. D. Gordon

aspects of the landscape once found near the upper reaches of the Cooper River was a collection of springs unusual for the Lowcountry, although far more common in the interior portions of South Carolina, including the sandhills and piedmont regions that appeared as land elevation increased in the long approach to the Appalachian Mountains.[125] These springs in St. John's Berkeley parish emanated from the network of underground channels worn through the limestone substratum. According to one observer, "Springs of this kind, when deep in the visible opening & throwing up large quantity of water, are known by the name of *fountains*."[126] The fountains themselves inspired awe, as they not only spewed water or rose and fell regularly but held icy cold water that rolled as though boiling.[127] The springs impressed plantation owners enough that some named their plantations after these features, including Fair Spring and The Rocks.[128]

Just as some Carolinians exhibited much interest in the springs as aspects of the region's geology, African-descended people attached meaning to the springs as spiritual sites. An early written account from 1843 documented "a superstitious belief universal among the negroes" that, "Each of these fountains, of considerable depth & size, is believed to be the habitation of a kind of water sprite, or supernatural being called a Cymbee."[129] Other nineteenth-century sources noted that the upper portions of St. John's Berkeley parish and neighboring areas had a notable number of springs with cymbee residents, including Pooshee plantation, Woodboo plantation, Moore's Fountain, The Rocks plantation, Eutaw Spring, the Crawl Branch Springs, Belvidere plantation, and Lang Syne plantation. Even Wappoo plantation near Charleston along Wappoo

Bennett and Jeffrey C. Patton (Boone, NC: Parkway Publishers, 2008), 41–4; and Richard D. Porcher, "Inventory of Botanical Natural Areas in Berkeley, Charleston and Dorchester Counties," Technical Document for the Office of Ocean & Coastal Resource Management (Columbia, SC: South Carolina Department of Health and Environmental Control, 1995).

[125] Drayton, *View of South Carolina*, 49–51; and William Gilmore Simms, *Geography of South Carolina* (Charleston, SC: Babcock and Co., 1843), 34, 35, 78, 89, 100, 108, 114, 123, 124, 126, 133.

[126] Ruffin, *Agriculture*, 164. For the extent of the subterranean network, see F.S. Holmes, "Notes on the Geology of Charleston," *Charleston Medical Journal and Review* 3, 6 (1848): 665–9.

[127] Bound Volume (pp. 62B and 112B), John Bennett Papers, SCHS; and "Pooshee," *Names in South Carolina* XII (1965): 35–6.

[128] For an accounting of the plantation neighborhood in the nineteenth century and the origins of plantation names, see Frederick A. Porcher, "Upper Beat of St. John's, Berkeley," *Transactions of the Huguenot Society of South Carolina* 13 (1906): 31–78.

[129] Ruffin, *Agriculture*, 166.

Creek had its own cymbee, although the greatest concentration appeared in the inland districts in the vicinity of the headwaters of the Cooper River. People gave the springs unique names, such as Jack's Hole and Tidal Hole on Pooshee, and also identified the cymbees with names that included The Evil, One-Eye, and the Great Desire of the Unrotting Waters.[130]

The earliest source noted that, "Each fountain has a different cymbee, the size, appearance & habits of each varying some what from others."[131] Descriptions of the cymbees referred to aquatic attributes such as webbed feet or partial fish anatomy. The cymbee at Pooshee appeared as a female and similar to a mermaid, while another took female form with long brown hair that obscured all other features. Additionally, the size of the cymbees corresponded with the dimensions of the spring they inhabited. Circumstances for sightings of the cymbees differed, as well, as the one at Woodboo emerged only at midday ("when the sunshine is 'right up & down'"), while others appeared during the darkness of night. Their behaviors during these sightings had them "in a sitting posture, on any low bridge, or plank, crossing the water, or on the margin of a steep side."[132] The cymbee at Pooshee, however, had been seen once "running around & around the fountain."[133]

More central to accounts of the cymbees than their appearance and activities was the attitude toward them among people of African descent. Those who lived on plantations with springs and used them in their daily lives regarded them with a severe form of respect that often manifested as outright fear. Those who shared information about their sightings of the cymbees communicated that their experiences frightened them a great deal, even though they had not suffered direct harm from the encounter. More dangerously, these informants invited misfortune, as people believed that "it is bad luck any one who may see a cymbee to tell of the occurrence, or refer to it; & that his death would be the certain penalty, if he told of the meeting for some weeks afterwards."[134] Also, lone individuals who ventured to a spring to fish, bathe, or wash clothes risked drowning or possession by the resident cymbee. Although not immediately lethal, possession stoked insatiable desires that we can imagine led

---

[130] Bound Volume, pp. 62B and 112B, Bennett Papers, SCHS.
[131] Ruffin, *Agriculture*, 166. The following descriptions come from Ruffin, *Agriculture*, 166–7; and Henry William Ravenel, "Recollections of Southern Plantation Life," *The Yale Review* 25 (1936): 776.
[132] Ruffin, *Agriculture*, 166.
[133] Ruffin, *Agriculture*, 167.
[134] Ruffin, *Agriculture*, 166.

to the decline if not ultimate demise of the afflicted.[135] The best defense against these negative encounters required that people visit the springs in groups, as related in a nineteenth-century account:

On Saturday nights you may hear a strange rhythmic, thumping sound from the spring, and looking out you may see by the wild, fitful glare of lightwood torches dark figures moving to and fro. These are the negro women at their laundry-work, knee-deep in the stream, beating the clothes with heavy clubs. They are merry enough when together, but no one of them will go alone for a "piggin" of water, and if you slip up in the shadow of the old oak and throw a stone into the spring, the entire party will rush away at the splash, screaming with fear, convinced that the "cymbie" is after them.[136]

Drinking the waters of fountains, although often perceived as a source of beneficial if not miraculous curative power, could present another source of danger if a cymbee inhabited the spring.[137] A common practice entailed taking some of the water into a calabash (drinking gourd) and pouring it out on the ground in a manner that suggested skimming and disposing of any spiritual residue before drinking the water.[138] Although not directly attributed to the influence of the cymbees at Eutaw Spring, awareness of their presence there may have shaped the perception that "those who drink constantly of it are subject to the Ague and Fever."[139] These examples demonstrate that the power to bring misfortune to those who displeased them in any way allowed the cymbees to influence a variety of behaviors of African-descended people in regulating access to and activities at the springs. For most, it appears that the most appropriate dealings with the cymbee springs required people to approach in groups, use the waters with great care, and show the proper respect by disturbing the springs as little as possible.

Planters, however, had much less regard for the sanctity of the springs. During the early nineteenth century, the owner of Pooshee plantation

[135] Bound Volume, 112B, Bennett Papers, SCHS.
[136] Robert Wilson, *Half Forgotten By-Ways of the Old South* (Columbia, SC: The State Company, 1928), 157. The account originally appeared in *Lippincott's Magazine* in 1876.
[137] For the curative purposes of spring waters, see the interesting letter from Marks Lazarus to Lewis M. Ayer, in which Lazarus requests that an enslaved woman named Sarah be allowed to bathe in and drink from the springs on Ayer's plantation to find an elusive cure for her "very soar leggs." Marks Lazarus to Lewis M. Ayer, 3 April 1797, Lewis Malone Ayer Papers, SCL. See also the letter from Paul Hamilton to Ayer, 14 April 1797, Lewis Malone Ayer Papers, SCL.
[138] Bound Volume (p. 112B), John Bennett Papers, SCHS.
[139] William Blanding Diary, 26 June 1810, William Blanding Papers, SCL.

"enclosed his fountain with masonry & confined & raised its water, an old half breed Indian of the neighborhood, who was half negro in blood, & wholly in habits & superstition, remonstrated with him, upon the ground the cymbee might be made angry & leave her haunt, & that then the spring would be dried."[140] In another example, the proprietors of Lang Syne plantation at the confluence of the Congaree and Wateree Rivers installed a hydraulic ram to convey water from a spring to the big house. The spring also hosted the cymbee known as The Evil, which alone gave good reason to avoid the spring and the woods along the path to the spring in the evening. The pump exerted such an effect that at night the African-descended inhabitants of the plantation not only steered clear of the spring but also walked beyond earshot of the hydraulic ram's noise. The device itself, driven automatically by gravity and the energy of moving water, would have appeared as though operated by the cymbee. Just as likely, people may have wished to stay as far away as possible from the intruding technology in the spring and evade the wrath of the offended cymbee during its nocturnal appearances.[141] The planters' disregard for the cymbee, however, did not alter the perceptions among African-descended people of proper conduct concerning the spirits and their springs. As seen through the eyes of those raised in the African-inspired cultural traditions of the Lowcountry, the cymbees remained fearsome and potent "guardian spirits of water."[142]

The apparent dread of the spirits should not overshadow another fact about the relationship between African-descended people and the Lowcountry cymbees: More than they feared the wrath of the cymbees, people of African descent worried that the cymbees would leave their springs. The limestone springs of the Lowcountry were known to "suddenly disappear entirely," and on such occasions "the negroes believe that the cymbee has died, or has been offended & abandoned her residence."[143] A dried spring not only represented the loss of a crucial source of fresh water that served so many mundane purposes, it meant that access to the potent spiritual resident of the spring ended, as well. This concern was significant enough that the "old half breed" man felt compelled to oppose a planter owner to protect the simbi's abode. Just as the good water from springs supported the lives of those on the plantations, the existence of the cymbees ensured the continued direct connection with the land of

---

[140] Ruffin, *Agriculture*, 167.
[141] Bound Volume (p. 61B), John Bennett Papers, SCHS.
[142] Ravenel, "Recollections of Southern Plantation Life," 776.
[143] Ruffin, *Agriculture*, 167.

the dead and its powers, which upheld the physical and material well-being of people in the land of the living. Further, the dangerous nature of the cymbees signaled that these possessed great power as guardians of their springs and of the people in their territories, much like the simbi of Kongo. We will explore this connection in the next chapter.

Key characteristics of the cymbees indicate that these spirits derived from the Kongo simbi, most notably the transparent etymology of the term. Their occupation of springs corresponded with a favored habitation of the Kongo simbi. Further, the penchant of the cymbees for possessing people who encountered their waters also resembled a basic trait of the simbi in West-Central Africa. For these reasons and others that will be examined in greater depth in the following chapters, it appears reasonable to proceed with the supposition that the cymbees were in point of fact simbi. In order to reflect this profound connection with entities from Kongo yet retain a sense of the historical and geographical distinctiveness of the spirits in South Carolina, these entities will be referred to as the Lowcountry simbi.

While the relationship of the Kongo simbi and the Lowcountry simbi is clearly evident, the historical and cultural significance of the Lowcountry simbi to people of African descent must be inferred, as the contemporary written records do not explicitly yield this information. The author of the earliest description of the cymbees noted that "descriptions were very loose & meagre."[144] From this observation, we cannot leap to the conclusion that all understanding of the Lowcountry simbi was "very loose & meagre," but only that the author of this statement and the invaluable account that accompanied it had access to little information. Recall that those who provided details about the Lowcountry simbi indicated that firsthand knowledge of the spirits required secrecy, the violation of which entailed bad luck or even death. This reflected a principle valued in many cultures of West-Central Africa and West Africa concerning access to certain forms of spiritual knowledge. Only those who achieved full initiation into specific institutions of knowledge (often referred to as "secret societies") received full instruction in particular areas of expertise and swore oaths to keep such knowledge from being exposed to the uninitiated on pain of death.[145]

The circumstances of enslavement and racial politics in the Lowcountry introduced another barrier to the communication of cultural knowledge.

---

[144] Ruffin, *Agriculture*, 166.

[145] These institutions are discussed further in the next chapter. For insights into the principle of secrecy in other circumstances in the Lowcountry, see Powell, "Summoning the Ancestors," 262–3.

Outsiders – almost always of European descent – who observed and recorded aspects of the culture of African-descended people saw only what they were allowed to see, in large part because insiders did not wish to indulge outsiders who typically expressed little more than contempt and condescension for what they witnessed. Further, the accounts of the Lowcountry simbi come to us through stories recorded by witnesses whose objectives did not extend much beyond portraying African-descended people as superstitious and irrational, as seen in the description of the women washing clothes at the spring on a Saturday night. Recounting tales of mermaids with flowing hair who terrorized simpleminded people certainly went a long way toward supporting this prejudice. Additionally, the authors of the sources had little interest or training in providing the ethnographic detail necessary to adequately document beliefs and practices related to Lowcountry simbi.[146] Existing accounts, however, include enough insights to permit reasonable conjecture about the nature of the Lowcountry simbi based on a deeper knowledge of the historical and cultural contexts of the Lowcountry and West-Central Africa.

As noted already, the earliest documentation of the Lowcountry *simbi* comes from the 1840s, yet the account described knowledge of them as "universal among the negroes," which suggests that African-descended people had recognized the existence of the spirits for some time already. Further, given that the enslaved population of upper St. John's Berkeley parish had been predominantly Lowcountry-born for several generations before the 1840s, it seems unlikely that a common belief based specifically on an aspect of Kongo spiritual culture would have been introduced, widely disseminated, and then embraced within the numerically dominant non-Kongo and non-African inhabitants of the area's plantation communities. This assumption, and it is only that, although certainly a reasonable one, about the introduction of a "universal" aspect of the spiritual culture of this district of the Cooper River rests on the supposition that the most likely context in which knowledge of the simbi became entrenched in the Lowcountry was one in which captives from West-Central Africa were present in numbers significant enough to deeply influence the larger culture of the enslaved community and corresponded well with fundamental ideas about the existence of the simbi. This requires that we look to a time before the early nineteenth century, and even before the mid-eighteenth century.

---

[146] The work of John Bennett appears to be exceptional in this regard. Both his published and archival materials exhibited a nonjudgmental tone and appeared based on attentiveness to detail absent in the other stories.

Contemplating the first precondition for the establishment of the Lowcountry simbi involves a return to the demographic context addressed in Chapter 2. Although that discussion did not examine importation and population figures in detail after 1750, the second half of the era when captive Africans arrived as part of the "legal" trade across the Atlantic included numerous West-Central Africans. Certainly, the last large influx of captive Africans that occurred between 1783 and 1808 included more than 20,000 West-Central Africans, who comprised more than 40 percent of the new captives imported during this period. Yet a large proportion of these captives in the early nineteenth century figured in the inter-American trade, particularly to the newly acquired port of New Orleans, and never remained in the Lowcountry for any length of time.[147]

Some of the new captives remained in the Lowcountry, as seen in plantation registers from areas that experienced rapid growth with the increase in cotton planting such as St. Helena parish in Beaufort County, where the number of enslaved people rose more than 86 percent from 2,657 in 1800 to 5,741 in 1810.[148] A prime example of this trend appeared on John Stapleton's St. Helena Island plantation, where nearly half of the enslaved adults in 1810 had recently arrived from Africa.[149] People from West-Central Africa, particularly "Congo," numbered among those retained in the Lowcountry. An 1808 newspaper advertisement by the workhouse warden in Charleston recounted the story of an "African Boy of the Congo Nation." The warden wrote, "The boys account of himself (as from an interpreter) is, that he was stolen from the wharf with another of the same age, that they arrived here in a ship commanded by a capt. Clark, a French gentleman." An advertisement placed two months later revealed that the boy was about thirteen years old and had been in Charleston for almost one year.[150] The presence of the interpreter and the boy's ability to survive for a year without facility in the English language suggests the existence of a Kikongo-speaking community in Charleston.

---

[147] Voyages Database, *http://slavevoyages.org/tast/database/search.faces?yearFrom=1783 &yearTo=1808&mjslptimp=21300*. On the larger workings of the trade in this era, see McMillin, *Final Victims*.

[148] Philip D. Morgan, "Black Society in the Lowcountry, 1760–1810," in *Slavery and Freedom in the Age of the American Revolution*, ed. Ira Berlin and Ronald Hoffman (Charlottesville: University Press of Virginia, 1983), 96; and Rowland et al., *History of Beaufort County*, 348.

[149] List of Negroes belonging to Colonel Stapleton on his Plantation at St. Helena, 15 March 1810, John Stapleton Papers, SCL. See also examples from Port Royal Island and Tom's Island in the same county documented in William Joyner Receipt Book, SCL.

[150] *Charleston Courier*, 1 August 1808, 22 October 1808.

Advertisements for fugitives also attest to the dispersal of new West-Central Africans within the enslaved populations outside of Charleston during the first decade of the nineteenth century.[151]

The enslaved communities of St. John's Berkeley parish expanded during this time, as well, and well-documented plantations on the Cooper River indicate the arrival of new Africans during the first decade of the nineteenth century. With the reopening of the legal trade to South Carolina in 1804, the leading enslavers of the St. John's Berkeley parish, the Ball family, acquired Africans including twenty-three named men in 1804 and seven named women in 1805, placed on their Kensington, Hyde Park, and Midway plantations.[152] The backgrounds of captive Africans sent to these plantations were not noted in the records. Some of the men likely hailed from West-Central Africa, as almost 52 percent of the captives (3,093 of 5,961) taken to South Carolina in 1804 came on ships with people from West-Central African ports.[153] Indeed, a man known as Congo Joe arrived at Midway plantation some time between 1805 and 1808 and remained there at least until 1815, when he appeared on a blanket list for the last time.[154]

While many others certainly joined the enslaved communities on the Cooper River, accurate estimates remain elusive. A sense may be gained from the fact that one Ball family member apparently doubled the enslaved population on his plantation from 1790 to 1805, although African newcomers likely figured as only a portion of this increase given the practices of moving enslaved people between family plantations, purchasing people from family and neighbors, and settling inheritance claims.[155] Further, although some plantations expanded through the various processes of importation, redistribution, and natural increase the overall enslaved population of the St. John's Berkeley parish declined from 6,479 in 1800 to 6,210 in 1810.[156] Consequently, while some planters in the parish drew from the short but intense period of importation of new captives to South Carolina, it does not appear that this radically altered the composition of African-descended communities in the areas with the greatest presence

[151] *Charleston Courier*, 16 June 1805, 6 May 1808, 14 June 1808, 27 September 1808.

[152] Blanket Lists (January and November, 1804), Folder 1a, Volume 1, 1779–1817, John Ball and Keating Simons Ball Books, 1779–1871, Reel 1, Series J, Part 3: RASP.

[153] Voyages Database, *http://slavevoyages.org/tast/database/search.faces?yearFrom=1804&yearTo=1804&mjslptimp=21300.*

[154] Blanket Lists (1805, 1808, 1811, 1815), Folder 1a, Volume 1, 1779–1817, John Ball and Keating Simons Ball Books, 1779–1871, Reel 1, Series J, Part 3, RASP.

[155] Ball, *Slaves in the Family*, 261; and Cody, "Slave Demography," 41–2, 50–72.

[156] Cody, "Slave Demography," 40.

of the Lowcountry simbi. West-Central African newcomers to the parish would have refreshed or renewed existing ideas and practices that originated with earlier Bantu influences, but the introduction of the simbi in this demographic context seems highly unlikely.

Later cultural evidence supports this conclusion, as well. Lorenzo Dow Turner's collection of African-derived words used in conversation and as "basket names" given to children came largely from those communities on the sea islands of Beaufort County and coastal Georgia that grew significantly or formed for the first time during the last decade of the eighteenth century and the first decade of the nineteenth century. Turner documented in these communities the use of the Mende word gafa (*ngafa*) and Igbo term juju to name certain spirits, but simbi did not appear in any form in his extensive lists of vocabulary and names.[157] We may suppose that it would be far more likely for the many West-Central Africans among this last large influx of newcomers to introduce the simbi to these new and expanding communities in which they and other Africans formed a much larger cohort than in the demographic circumstances found in St. John's Berkeley parish during the same period. As the linguistic and ethnographic record attests, people did not use the term simbi to refer to water spirits in Beaufort County or coastal Georgia, which provides strong evidence for an earlier era for the introduction of the simbi to the Lowcountry.

Before moving to this earlier period, we must note that the enslaved communities that expanded rapidly in the two decades surrounding the turn of the nineteenth century did have biological and cultural ties to older communities based in the original Ashley-Cooper-Stono plantation zone. As discussed in Chapter 2, the expansion of the Lowcountry plantation complex into the southern parishes of South Carolina and throughout coastal Georgia after the mid-eighteenth century drew much of its "founder" populations from enslaved communities established in previous generations. These people not only played leading roles in creating new communities but also in transforming understanding of the meanings of the simbi that we will examine in the next two chapters. The absence of explicit references to spirits called simbi in these later settlements may have reflected later stages in the historical processes through which the Lowcountry simbi began to take on new identities in African-inspired

---

[157] Turner, *Africanisms*, 193, 195. Turner does not give an Igbo etymology for juju, but see Chambers, *Murder at Montpelier*, 53–65 for support of this origin.

spiritual culture as unnamed spiritual guardians, white soul babies, and mermaids.

In returning to the demographic context, the importation of captive Africans in the late-colonial period of the trans-Atlantic trade, roughly 1750–1775, included 9,879 West-Central Africans, who comprised 17 percent of the 57,617 newcomers. St. John's Berkeley parish planters augmented the numbers of enslaved people on their properties, as did other Cooper River planters such as Henry Laurens, who benefited from his original status as a trader in captives to expand the labor force on existing plantations he purchased and people new plantations he founded.[158] Further, Laurens expressed a hierarchy of preference for people from the different regions of Africa that likely influenced the purchasing practices of those with the commercial resources and personal connections needed to exercise such inclinations. Laurens stated, "Gold Coast or Gambias are best, next To Them The Windward Coast are prefer'd to Angolas."[159] It appears that powerful planters such as those in the Ball family could be selective, as the overwhelming majority, if not all, of the captives they bought in the 1750s and 1760s came from Gambia.[160] A list of males on the Ball family's Comingtee plantation in the late 1770s confirms the influence of this pattern on the composition of the African-descended community. The thirty-five males on the list included seventeen born in the Lowcountry, fourteen from Gambia, and four from Angola. The ages recorded in the list indicated that the Lowcountry-born males ranged from fourteen to forty-one years old and the Gambia men from twenty-six to forty-seven. Three of the Angola men (Tomwhit, Marcus, and Josey) were listed as fifty-five years old, likely an approximation.[161] The ages of the men imply that the Angola men had been purchased during the 1730s when West-Central Africans predominated numerically among African newcomers, while the Gambia men likely arrived on Comingtee after 1750.

---

[158] Edelson, *Plantation Enterprise*, 200–54.

[159] Henry Laurens to Smith and Clifton, 17 July 1755, in Philip M. Hamer, George C. Rogers, Jr., and Peggy J. Wehage, eds., *The Papers of Henry Laurens* (Columbia: University of South Carolina Press, 1968–85), 2: 295. On the issues of preferences, see Littlefield, *Rice and Slaves*, 8–11, 25; and Morgan, *Slave Counterpoint*, 66–8.

[160] Cody, "Slave Demography," 42–4.

[161] "A List of Males at Comingtee," c.1770s, Plantation Account Book, 1720–1787, John Ball Papers, SCHS. The name and age of the fourth Angola man appears smudged by water or damaged in some other way. The condition of the document has led other researchers to overlook this man and count only three Angola men. For analysis of the list, see Cody, "Slave Demography," 47–9.

The pattern exhibited on Comingtee along with the stated preference for "Gambias" among certain enslavers suggests that the Cooper River plantations were not probable destinations for large numbers of West-Central Africans at this time. As in the last era of the legal trade, those West-Central Africans who did arrive in St. John's Berkeley parish plantations in the late-colonial period would not have had the demographic or social standing necessary to establish the veneration of the simbi. That would have been the task of elders, such as Comingtee's Tomwhit, Marcus, and Josey or even those West-Central Africans who came before them. The significant presence of West-Central Africans in the founding generations from the 1680s through the 1740s discussed in Chapter 2 provided the ideal correlation of demographic and cultural contexts for the introduction of the simbi in the Lowcountry.

The lands around the headwaters of the western branch of the Cooper River near Pooshee swamp, where many of the recorded Lowcountry simbi inhabited springs, were within the bounds of the Wadboo or Watbu Barony, one of the original estates demarcated by the English colonists that carried an apparently Native name that would also later identify the plantation known as Wadboo or Woodboo. Wadboo comprised one of the areas where early Carolina planters claimed and settled lands during the first great wave of importation of captive Africans in the 1680s and 1690s.[162] The nature of the Cooper River's western branch favored early settlement by European colonists, as the waterway could "cary [sic] up a boat about 17 miles." As early as the spring of 1680, the western branch had "three Settlements upon it" with the expectation that it would "be forthwith strongly setled [sic] in all its parts, for Sir Peter Colletoun [Colleton] hat a Signoirie and his brother Mr. James a Barony about it."[163] While the growth of this area and the rest of what would be named St. John's Berkeley parish occurred most dramatically in the first twenty years of the eighteenth century, a significant number of landowners established their claims in the previous two decades. Between 1680 and 1704, 17 men received 18,502 acres through 39 grants in a neighborhood of Wadboo called Wantoot, many of them French Huguenots who had formed a numerically and culturally significant community in the area by 1693. Several of these French Protestant refugees, such as Peter (Pierre) de St. Julien and René Ravenel, were the first European newcomers to

[162] J.H. Easterby, *Wadboo Barony: Its Fate as told in Colleton Family Papers, 1773–1793* (Columbia: University of South Carolina Press, 1952), vii–ix.

[163] Maurice Mathews, "A Contemporary View of Carolina in 1680," *South Carolina Historical and Genealogical Magazine* 55, 3 (1954): 155.

claim lands with springs that housed the Lowcountry simbi.[164] Although no records exist that document the presence of African-descended people on the earliest plantations in Wantoot and neighboring areas, both branches of the upper Cooper River had plantations active in the cultivation of staple and experimental crops starting in the mid-1680s, without doubt employing growing numbers of enslaved people to provide the agricultural knowledge and labor needed for such endeavors.[165]

The West-Central Africans among the captive newcomers brought to the Lowcountry in the 1680s and 1690s would have been some of the first African-descended people to encounter the springs of Wadboo. The political instability and warfare that affected the communities formerly included in the collapsed Kingdom of Kongo ensured that many of the West-Central African captives boarded on English vessels bound for the Americas during this time came from Kikongo-speaking groups. As people steeped in Kongo spiritual culture, they had deep and intimate knowledge of nature spirits such as the simbi and the nkisi. When some of these Kongo captives arrived in Carolina and then journeyed up the Cooper River to begin the hard work of creating the plantations of their English and French enslavers, they found the springs and the simbi. The lasting memorial to their "discovery" of the water spirits in the springs was the name simbi itself. The Kongo men and women in early Wadboo were the first to find the spirits, and thus they were the ones to name them and teach their descendants and other newcomers about them. As such, even when many more Africans arrived in later times, especially the 1730s and after, the newcomers entered communities that had long ago established relationships with the Lowcountry simbi.

This assertion that the West-Central Africans introduced the Lowcountry simbi with the founding of the plantations in Wadboo during the 1680s and 1690s does not rest solely on the demographic context of the trans-Atlantic trade and settlement patterns of early Carolina. The cultural explanation is far more central. As mentioned above, Kongo people expected to the find the simbi in the Lowcountry because the natural environment was the domain of the simbi. Any spring, stream, river, ocean, or forest could be the home of a simbi. Kongo newcomers did not have to erect shrines or create priestly institutions to reconstitute their veneration of the simbi; they were already in the Lowcountry before the

---

[164] Terry, "Champaign Country," 41–70.
[165] John Stewart, "Letters from John Stewart to William Dunlop," *South Carolina Historical and Genealogical Magazine* 32, 1 (1931): 6–7, 21–3; and Stewart, "Letters," *South Carolina Historical and Genealogical Magazine* 32, 2 (1931): 85–7.

first African or European ever set foot on the land, just as the waterways and the trees predated the arrival of settlers from the other side of the Atlantic. This notion of the primordial essence of the simbi, or at least some of them, has been basic to Kongo understandings of these spirits, as examined in the Chapter 3. We have no compelling reason to assume that the same idea did not resonate with the Kongo men and women taken to Lowcountry in the seventeenth century or during the remaining eras of the trans-Atlantic trade to South Carolina.

Further, West-Central African newcomers not only expected to find the simbi in the Lowcountry, they needed them to survive in this new land. In West-Central Africa, the simbi helped people cope with the most serious difficulties of daily life and at the same time supplied the spiritual support necessary for individuals and communities to flourish. As newcomers, captive West-Central Africans in early Carolina needed the simbi to ensure that they could grow, hunt, and catch food for their sustenance. They needed the simbi to preserve the abilities of men and women to conceive and bear children. They needed them for protection against illness, as small pox, malaria, and yellow fever posed as virulent enemies of the living. Indeed, people enslaved in the Lowcountry had as much need for spiritual assistance in the essential aspects of life as did those who remained in West-Central Africa. It is possible to conceive that the needs of those carried across the Atlantic may have been even more acute given the emotional and physical tribulations that arose from the traumatic experiences of captivity and dislocation worsened by the demands imposed by enslavement.

While the impetus for forging relationships with the simbi in the Lowcountry may have been more pressing than usual, the necessity and process for doing so was not new in any way within the larger and older cultural background of West-Central Africans and West Africans taken to South Carolina. This recalls the discussion of the Niger-Congo principle of precedence in Chapter 2, in which we saw that the primordiality of nature spirits such as the simbi required that newcomers establish affiliations with local spirits in order to rightfully inhabit and prosper in a new land. Also within this process were efforts to include indigenous people, or at least the idea of indigenous people, as spiritual authorities whose incorporation within the ritual practices of the newcomers provided approbation for the occupation of the territory by newcomers. Of course, when European and African newcomers first reached the Lowcountry many people already inhabited the land, but the Lowcountry at the time of contact did not know peaceful stasis with Native groups long entrenched in ancestral territories coexisting in harmony with each other and nature. Instead, the Lowcountry included a number of small bands that European colonists demeaned with the label "settlement Indians" that found themselves caught in the swirling turmoil unleashed by the arrival of diverse newcomers from across the Atlantic and the influx of other indigenous people mobilized by the growing presence of Europeans, Africans, and Atlantic commerce.

One of the consequences of Carolina's founding in the midst of this dynamic setting was close contact between newcomers and many different groups of Native people in war, trade, diplomacy, and enslavement. For most African newcomers in the early Lowcountry, the predominant context for contact with Native people involved coexistence within enslaved communities, which began in the 1680s and reached its apex in the first decade of the 1700s (Table 1). The trade in captive indigenous people involved Native and European traders who traveled and maintained contacts throughout the southeast and brought between 30,000 and 50,000 bound people to Carolina, almost all of whom came from Florida and the Mississippi Valley. The intercolonial trade in captive Native people shipped from South Carolina flourished from the 1670s to 1715 to such an extent that Carolinian merchants exported more Native captives than they imported enslaved Africans.[166]

The number of enslaved Native people remained relatively small at the beginning of the eighteenth century, when an estimated 200 individuals formed 8 percent of the enslaved population. Within the next several years, however, enslaved communities experienced a dramatic change. Aggressive raids by Carolinians and their Native allies fueled the export trade in captive Native people and weakened the Spanish missions in La Florida. These raids devastated indigenous communities associated with the missions, particularly the Apalachee, Timucua, and Guale. People taken from these groups likely comprised a large majority of those retained in the Lowcountry as Carolinians sponsored and participated in multiple attacks between 1702 and 1705 that generated thousands of captives. The extent of the influx appears in the increase of Native people within enslaved communities from 200 people at the beginning of the eighteenth century to 1,500 people 10 years later. By 1710, Native people constituted 30 percent of the enslaved population. It also seems likely that the small number of Native captives in the previous two decades came from this same source. The Apalachee, Timucua, and Guale at Spanish missions had been targeted by indigenous allies of the English as early as the 1660s, although not on the scale seen in the early eighteenth century. Although the number of enslaved Native people in the Lowcountry rose to 2,000 by 1720, the export trade in captives had already begun to diminish due to the exhaustion of sources for captives in conjunction with the transition to deer skins as the key item of exchange between Native groups and European colonizers. The simultaneous growth of the importation of enslaved Africans reduced the proportion of Native captives to 14 percent of the bound population by the end of the 1710s. Within another generation, the once conspicuous presence of enslaved Native people diminished to the point of invisibility.[167]

The significant presence of Native people within the enslaved population raises questions about the early history of the simbi in the Lowcountry. How did West-Central African newcomers perceive the connection between the existence of indigenous groups and the introduction of the simbi? How did the spiritual cultures of Native captives shape perceptions of the simbi within the larger enslaved community? Answering these questions entails understanding the social and cultural backgrounds of captive Native people and considering how they and Africans may have interacted based on their approaches to cultural differences and new influences. As noted earlier, the European and African founders of Carolina arrived in a region undergoing remarkable changes owing to the rise of the enslavement of Native people in English colonies. Native communities, identities, and cultures shifted, in many instances quite radically, as the realm affected by raids expanded in the second half of the seventeenth century. The shock waves of instability that rippled throughout Eastern North America as indigenous groups entered into violent trade relationships with European newcomers transformed where and how people lived on the land. A few groups that acquired firearms from European colonizers became the primary agents for acquiring captives and flourished in the southeast from the early seventeenth century into the early eighteenth century at the expense of their neighbors. The English in Carolina relied on the Westo, Savannah, and Yamasee as raiders, all three of whom had entered the orbit of Carolina's expansion as refugees from other turbulent regions and chosen to become predators

---

[167] Gallay, *Indian Slave Trade*, 144–9; William L. Ramsey, "'All & Singular the Slaves': A Demographic Profile of Indian Slavery in Colonial South Carolina," in Greene, Brana-Shute, and Sparks, *Money, Trade, and Power*, 166–86; and John E. Worth, "Razing Florida: The Indian Slave Trade and the Devastation of Spanish Florida, 1659–1715," in Ethridge, *Mapping the Mississippian Shatter Zone*, 296, 299–306.

rather than prey for the sake of survival. While indigenous raiders remained relatively few in number, their activities "caused widespread dislocation, migration, amalgamation, and, in some cases, extinction of Native peoples."[168] The fact that predatory groups emerged from the same circumstances of hardship that dismantled the communities of their neighbors through their raids reveals the extreme instability facing all Native groups. Indeed, this pattern continued into the eighteenth century, as people of various cultural backgrounds formed "coalescent societies," including the new nations of the Creek, Catawba, Chickasaw, Choctaw, and Cherokee that would play key roles in the transformation of the southeast over the course of the next several generations.[169]

The creation of coalescent societies out of people who spoke different languages and had diverse geographical origins reveals instances of intense crises when older corporate bonds broke under duress. Cultural continuity appears unlikely in such desperate circumstances. Yet if we are to understand how those Native captives who became part of the enslaved communities in the early Lowcountry functioned culturally in their new surroundings, we must grasp the idea that they came from societies in which multilingual and polycultural accommodations reflected deep-rooted cultural principles and normal daily practice in times of either stability or stress. For several centuries, many indigenous people in the southeast lived comfortably within polycultural polities where inhabitants did not need to share the same material culture and language to coexist and cooperate. These polycultural societies were likely buttressed by "basic cultural understandings" shared by communities inhabiting lands that spread from the Mississippi River valley in the west to the Atlantic coast in the east.[170] This polycultural inclination became an

---

[168] Robbie Ethridge, "Creating the Shatter Zone: Indian Slave Traders and the Collapse of the Southeastern Chiefdoms," in *Light on the Path: The Anthropology and History of the Southeastern Indians*, ed. Thomas J. Pluckhahn and Robbie Ethridge (Tuscaloosa: University of Alabama Press, 2006), 208–9 (quote 208), 216; William Green, Chester B. DePratter, and Bobby Southerlin, "The Yamasee in South Carolina: Native American Adaptation and Interaction along the Carolina Frontier," in *Another's Country: Archaeological and Historical Perspectives on Cultural Interactions in the Southern Colonies*, ed. J.W. Joseph and Martha Zierden (Tuscaloosa: University of Alabama Press, 2002), 13–29; Eric E. Bowne, *The Westo Indians: Slave Traders of the Colonial South* (Tuscaloosa: University of Alabama Press, 2005), 2–3, 37–107; and Ethridge, "Introduction," 31–6.

[169] Ethridge, "Introduction," 36–42.

[170] Karen M. Booker, Charles Hudson, and Robert L. Rankin, "Place Name Identification and Multilingualism in the Sixteenth-Century Southeast," *Ethnohistory* 39, 4 (1992): 399–451; Charles Hudson, "Introduction," in *The Transformation of the Southeastern*

imperative following contact with the first European colonizers in the sixteenth century and increasing interaction with European colonial agents and settlers into the eighteenth century. As such, the combination of common cultural foundations and a polycultural template for making new societies prepared indigenous captives for novel contexts of cultural dialogue in ways quite similar to those understood by enslaved Africans. When Africans and Native people were thrust together in the crucible of captivity, they at least had a strong cultural capacity for building communities from disparate elements.

Evidence of the process in the early Lowcountry came through the biological intertwining of African and Native lineages as "mustees" (an Anglicization of the Spanish term *mestizo*) appeared in estate records and newspaper advertisements with greater frequency in the 1720s and 1730s. Naming practices provide another indicator of the integration of Native people into enslaved communities. Captive Native mothers gave their children, whether mustees or more rarely of full Native ancestry, English names and names common among African-descended people, as seen with mustees named Quacoo and Mingo, in addition to the "Indian boy" identified as Cuffey. Further, probate inventories in the 1730s noted the presence of Native men named Mingo, Hercules, Ceasar, Nero, and Sambo as well as mustee children with the common "plantation names" Cupid, March, and Caesar.[171]

Even beyond a baseline predilection for polycultural approaches to community formation, southeastern Native cultures shared foundational concepts that related well to the African cultures brought to the Lowcountry. More specifically, the perception of the essential spiritual basis for the fertility of the natural environment featured prominently in religions of Native communities. This emphasis appears to have played a central role in the large-scale public rites associated with the monuments of "Mississippian" era chiefdoms, which may have influenced local

Indians, 1540–1760, ed. Robbie Ethridge and Charles Hudson (Jackson: University Press of Mississippi, 2002), xv; and Hudson et al., "On Interpreting Cofitachequi," 476.

[171] Ramsey, "All & Singular," 171–2, 175–80; Inventories of Francis Guering (1730 – Mingo), John Betteson (1729 – Hercules), Jonathan Tamor (1731 – Caesar, Indian man), Henry Nicholes (1730 – Cupid, March), Vol. H, 1729–1731; Joseph Summers (1736 – Nero, Sambo), Moses Martin, (1734 – Caesar, mustee boy), Vol. CC, 1732–1736, RSP-SCDAH. Analysis of genetic evidence in current populations appears in E.J. Parra et al., "Ancestral Proportions and Admixture Dynamics in Geographically Defined African Americans Living in South Carolina," *American Journal of Physical Anthropology* 114, 1 (2001): 18–29.

variations of similar rites in the centuries before the arrival of Europeans.[172] Among the practices recorded by non-Native outsiders were the "green corn" ceremonies that comprised one of the most important communal rituals for a number of southeastern groups even after most of the Native inhabitants had been forced out of the region in the nineteenth century. These rites included the offering of ripening ears of corn and other activities oriented toward "celebrating the primordial origins of maize" and acknowledging that "maize was rooted not just in little hills of earth but in a mystery."[173] Coastal groups in the Lowcountry also made "a kind of Offering of first fruits when their Corn is ripe," according to the Anglican missionary Francis Le Jau in 1708.[174]

Native communities close to the Spanish in La Florida commemorated their dependency on the spiritual realm for the fertility of the land through their *juego de pelota* (ballgame). The Apalachee dedicated their game to the deified warrior figure known as Nicoguadca. The game involved all the inhabitants of a village and centered around a large pole that had an eagle's nest at the top as a goal and that served as the focal point of the rituals conducted in preparation for contests.[175] Stories told by the Apalachee about the origins of the game also reflected sacred understandings about the relationships between people and the sun, lightning, and rain cultivated through playing the game. In one of the myths, the originator and primordial champion of the game, Nicoguadca, explained to his living contemporaries, "When you have your fields sown....I will remember you and give you water. And, accordingly, when you hear it thunder, it is a sign that I am coming."[176] Ideas about the connection between Nicoguadca and the game prompted many to interpret lighting strikes on the poles as manifestations of spiritual power. The meanings attached

---

[172] Vernon James Knight, Jr., "The Institutional Organization of Mississippian Religion," *American Antiquity* 51, 4 (1986): 675–87; Thomas E. Emerson, "Water, Serpents, and the Underworld: An Exploration into Cahokian Symbolism," in *The Southeastern Ceremonial Complex: Artifacts and Analysis*, ed. Patricia Galloway (Lincoln: University of Nebraska Press, 1989), 45–92; and Susan C. Power, *Early Art of the Southeastern Indians: Feathered Serpents and Winged Beings* (Athens: University of Georgia Press, 2004), 74–6, 165–7.

[173] Joel W. Martin, *Sacred Revolt: The Muskogees' Struggle for a New World* (Boston: Beacon Press, 1991), 35–42 (quote p. 35).

[174] Le Jau, *Carolina Chronicle*, 45.

[175] John H. Hann, *Apalachee: The Land between the Rivers* (Gainesville: University Press of Florida, 1988), 71–87.

[176] Reverend Juan de Paiva, "Origin and Beginning of the Game of Ball that the Apalachee and Yustagan Indians Have Been Playing since Pagan Times until the Year of 1676," translated in Hann, *Apalachee*, 343.

to such events took on even greater significance within the uneasy coexistence of traditional spiritual cultures and the Catholicism promoted in the Spanish missions of La Florida.

The complicated spiritual context within the missions of La Florida affected the largest segment of the Native population enslaved in the Lowcountry, which included people from Apalachee, Timucua, and Guale communities captured in the first decade of the 1700s. Franciscans established more than 100 missions among these groups from the mid-sixteenth century through the end of the seventeenth century that served as religious and political centers for the Spanish and sites where the spiritual cultures of the firstcomers and newcomers converged. From the perspective of the missionaries, the implantation of Christianity in the new land appeared firm. According to a report from the 1630s, the indigenous communities included "more than 20 thousand souls baptized and more than 50,000 catechized among the catchumens." In addition to the regular masses and feast days honored by Timucua and Apalachee Christians, "those of Our Lady on Saturday they are most devoted to, as to her rosary, which they always wear around their neck like the religious." Indigenous Christians also "respected the Holy Cross with such great love that they never step on its shadow....Nor is it missing from their house."[177]

Evidence of burial practices at the missions indicates a thorough engagement with Catholicism among those Apalachee, Timucua, and Guale who embraced Christianity. Typical burials before the era of interaction with Spanish Catholics involved placing the deceased in mounds in a flexed position or collecting and burying the bones of the dead in bundles after an extended waiting period. Those placed in mission cemeteries reflected Catholic norms, although with notable variations likely derived from conventional indigenous practices. Most were placed on their backs with their legs extended fully and their arms and hands crossed over the upper body. Burial plots followed the alignment of the church structure, with the heads oriented toward the east. Although the direction of bodies did not correspond with the usual Christian practice (having the feet directed to the east to ensure that the resurrected believer would face the rising sun/Risen Son), the feet of the dead pointed toward the altar of the church and bodies of interred priests and friars. The most conspicuous indigenous element of these mission burials was the frequent presence of

---

[177] Francisco Alonso de Jesus and John H. Hann, "1630 Memorial of Fray Francisco Alonso de Jesus on Spanish Florida's Missions and Natives," *The Americas* 50, 1 (1993): 100–1.

grave goods. While many of these items consisted of Christian objects such as rosary beads, crosses, and medallions, they also included numerous glass beads, shells, animal bones, and other personal possessions that held traditional significance beyond Christian symbolism.[178]

Indications of traditional practices related to death reveal that the extended interaction with the Christianity of Franciscan missionaries and Spanish colonizers did not entirely replace older ideas even in the setting of missions dominated by this foreign spiritual culture. Similarly, Native communities connected to many of the missions maintained the sacred ballgame, which prompted responses from the representatives of the Church that ranged from practical tolerance to zealous repression. These examples serve to caution against the assumption that Native people in the missions became essentially cultural extensions of the Spanish colonial endeavor. Their presence and behaviors represented an aspect of continuous dialogue between the original people of the land and the European newcomers that never fully concluded with the complete "conversion" of a large segment of the Native population of La Florida to either Spanish religion or rule. That this dialogue remained active and contentious many generations after the arrival of the Spanish suggests that true conversion for little more than a few did not figure into the worldview of the Apalachee, Timucua, and Guale people. Indeed, they found spiritual sustenance in honoring Nicoguadca on the ball field while at the same time admiring the Virgin Mary in the chapel.[179]

The few fragments in the written record that reveal the religious inclinations of Native captives relocated to South Carolina during this early phase indicate a desire to sustain connections with Christianity, even the Protestantism of the English. As Francis Le Jau noted in 1710, "We have several Apalachi Slaves amongst us; all Indian traders tell me they were baptised, some Indians themselves have told me so, but being uncertain may I not baptise them upon condicion?"[180] In addition to attending to the Apalachee Christians among the enslaved, Le Jau also sought to minister to free Apalachee settlements recently established on the edges of the colony. He "found many grown Persons among them had been

---

[178] Bonnie G. McEwan, "The Apalachee Indians of Northwest Florida," in *Indians of the Greater Southeast: Historical Archaeology and Ethnohistory*, ed. Bonnie G. McEwan (Gainesville: University Press of Florida, 2000), 68–70; and Bonnie G. McEwan, "The Spiritual Conquest of La Florida," *American Anthropologist* 103, 3 (2001): 637–40.

[179] On the persistence of Native spiritual culture in Florida, see Patricia Riles Wickman, *The Tree That Bends: Discourse, Power, and the Survival of the Maskókî People* (Tuscaloosa: University of Alabama Press, 1999).

[180] Le Jau, *Carolina Chronicle*, 73.

baptised by Spanish Priests, and have Christian Names, and told me, if they had Priests, as they call them, they wou'd use them very well."[181] It appears that in the eyes of Apalachee newcomers in Carolina, the agents of Christianity, whether Catholic or Protestant, could serve their needs and allow them to continue to cultivate this aspect of their spiritual culture in a new land.

In many ways, the captives taken from those indigenous communities that had extensive experience with Catholic missions resembled African newcomers taken to the Lowcountry from the places in West-Central Africa where Luso-Atlantic influences had become part of the cultural environment. Captives from both Kongo and La Florida had been raised with the ideas of their ancestors that valued the creation of polycultural communities, especially in times of distress, and assigned great meaning to rites acknowledging dependence on spiritual powers for fertility. In addition to these deep-rooted cultural principles, both had lived in communities shaped by the interaction of traditional spiritual cultures and Roman Catholicism. It would be difficult to imagine that people from Apalachee, Timucua, and Guale societies did not draw upon these aspects of their backgrounds as newcomers from West-Central Africa did when they arrived in the Lowcountry as captives. While Native people may not have initially shared a language with Africans in Carolina, they certainly had much to contribute to a dialogue about spiritual culture in enslaved communities. Their experience with Christianity in La Florida afforded them common ground with West-Central Africans who originated in communities in Kongo and Angola that also engaged the Roman Catholicism of Jesuit and Capuchin missionaries. This does not mean that captive Native people and West-Central Africans attempted collectively to perpetuate a distinct Catholic community in the early Lowcountry. It does suggest, however, that Christianity formed part of what both groups knew about ways to access spiritual power.

The shared experience with Catholic Christianity may have shaped the encounters that enslaved Africans and Native people had regarding the simbi in the early Lowcountry. Just as Native Christians in La Florida exhibited a pronounced devotion to the Virgin Mary, many communities in Kongo displayed a pronounced attachment to Saint Mary. People in the province of Soyo expressed their devotion by linking Our Mother to nature spirits, as both Mary and the simbi were seen as embodying the spiritual dimensions of fertility. Indigenous Christians in La Florida

---

[181] Le Jau, *Carolina Chronicle*, 57.

may have made a comparable connection by associating the Virgin Mary with a fertility figure such as the Corn Woman encountered in southeastern Native mythologies.[182] The continued significance of the spiritual dimensions of the ballgame dedicated to Nicoguadca make clear that the Apalachee retained ancient concerns about fertility, and Mary may have been a cosmological tie between traditional and Spanish religions in the missions. She would have served a similar bridging purpose as enslaved people from West-Central Africa and La Florida attempted to create spiritual and communal bonds in their shared plight in the early Lowcountry. As these Africans and Native people turned to their common adoration of Saint Mary in this dialogue, the Kongo view of the Virgin as a nature spirit would have helped teach the Native newcomers the spiritual meaning of the simbi that inhabited the springs of Wadboo.

In the end, it appears that the interactions of Kongo captives and enslaved Native people from La Florida may have been instrumental in solidifying the standing of the simbi in the spiritual cultures found on St. John's Berkeley parish plantations because of the associations that many Africans made between indigenous people and nature spirits in accordance with the Niger-Congo principle of precedence discussed in Chapter 2. Certainly, those Native people relocated to Carolina as captives likely retained a generic status as firstcomers given that they represented direct descendants of the first people to settle the larger domain in which Africans later arrived as newcomers. As such, any role that Native people, even those from as far away as La Florida, played in affirming the prestige of the simbi (in this case through the African-Native dialogue about Mary and the simbi) afforded legitimacy to the simbi as the guardian spirits of Wadboo.

Within the closer confines of Lowcountry plantations, however, the meanings of firstcomer and newcomer status took on a different hue, although with the same effect of embedding the simbi in the landscape. The African elders from the founder generation in the 1680s were the true firstcomers of enslaved communities. They built these communities from nothing in a strange land and thus earned the respect due to exemplary elders of this kind. Further, these African elders and their Lowcountry-born children were the people who absorbed the deluge of Apalachee, Timucua, and Guale captives in the early eighteenth century and remade their established communities to incorporate the Native

---

[182] Charles Hudson, *The Southeastern Indians* (Knoxville: University of Tennessee Press, 1976), 149–55.

newcomers. However, this was a context in which traditional ideas about firstcomers, newcomers, the land, and nature spirits converged amid great violence and suffering and produced new combinations. As a novel hybrid of firstcomers and newcomers, captive Native people reinforced ideas that Africans had about the spiritual meanings of living in the early Lowcountry and provided additional sanction for the veneration of the simbi among diverse people brought from West-Central African and West African societies that remained tied to their shared Niger-Congo heritage.

Confirmation of this fundamental African-Native union in the veneration of the simbi appears in the person of the "old half breed Indian of the neighborhood, who was half negro in blood, & wholly in habits & superstition" on Pooshee plantation. Recall that he confronted Dr. Henry Ravenel, the owner of the plantation, to attempt to stop the desecration of the Pooshee simbi's abode.[183] His presence as a forceful defender of the simbi embodied the enduring relationship forged between Native and African-descended people through the Lowcountry simbi. The intermingled histories and cultures of Africans and Native people remained vital in numerous aspects of life in the Lowcountry as well as in other parts of the South long after the initial encounters of these peoples.[184] While this bond originated in the struggles and suffering of enslavement in early Carolina, the Lowcountry simbi emerged from the same context to provide spiritual sustenance for the first generations of captive Africans and Native people and affirm that the descendants of these firstcomers could claim the land as their spiritual home. The "old half-breed Indian" knew this, and risked his well-being to defend the Pooshee simbi's legacy.

As we have seen in this chapter, both the physical and spiritual realms of the Lowcountry were claimed as African spaces. The naming of the natural environment with African terms attests to this process of redefining the landscape. The forest was the finda and the sea was kalunga. The gardens and fields sprouted African plants, the wilderness teemed with

---

[183] Ruffin, *Agriculture*, 167.

[184] Martin, *Sacred Revolt*, 71–6; Leland Ferguson, *Uncommon Ground: Archaeology and Early African America, 1650–1800* (Washington, DC: Smithsonian Institution Press, 1992), 82–4; Faith Mitchell, *Hoodoo Medicine: Gullah Herbal Remedies* (Columbia, SC: Summerhouse Press, 1999); David Elton Gay, "On the Interaction of Traditions: Southeastern Rabbit Tales as African-Native American Folklore," in *When Brer Rabbit Meets Coyote: African-Native American Literature*, ed. Jonathan Brennan (Urbana: University of Illinois Press, 2003), 101–13; and Stephanie Y. Mitchem, *African American Folk Healing* (New York: New York University Press, 2007), 5, 59.

African animals, and the springs sheltered African spirits. This was not a static relationship, however, in which African-descended people thought of the natural environment and spiritual domain in unchanging ways. Just as the communities of those of African descent increasingly came to be composed of Lowcountry-born people, the Lowcountry simbi took on new identities, as well. The spirits retained fundamental characteristics of the old Kongo simbi, but changed enough that their new identities superseded their old names. They became white babies and mermaids.

5

Spiritual Guardians in the Wilderness

As strong as your house you shall keep my life for me. When you leave for the sea, take me along, that I may live forever with you.
    – Invocation for the simbi Mbamba

You want to find Jesus, Go in the wilderness, Wait upon the Lord.
    – Morris Hamilton singing "Go in the Wilderness"

When Morris Hamilton of Johns Island, South Carolina, thought about the meaning of joining the Christian community, he recalled in song the rigorous process he endured in his youth that entailed journeying into the spiritual realm to receive the affirmation that he had attained the forgiveness of his sins and his soul did indeed "get through." The people who experienced the same initiation called the ordeal "seeking" or "traveling." Those prepared and strong enough to complete the trial of seeking earned the reward of "coming through" or "liberation," in which their souls had been "set free." To reach this point, the young men and women who ventured forth in seeking had to "go in the wilderness" and enter the spiritual landscape. In the wilderness, they encountered spiritual beings of various kinds and ultimately found or received a white bundle that usually became a white baby. With this they achieved a spiritual transformation that allowed them to eventually "become Christian" and fully initiated members into the spiritual community of the "praise house."[1]

---

[1] The "praise house" has been the fundamental institution of Christianity among African-descended people in the Lowcountry. Historically, its membership and authority superseded that of the denominational churches (most commonly, the Methodist and Baptists churches), as it derived from the spiritual initiatives of African-descended people rather

The conversion process was not conventional according to the prevailing norms of Protestant Christianity in North America during the nineteenth century. Seeking in the Lowcountry entailed a long period of spiritual guidance by a senior member of the Christian community. This period of supervision emphasized intensive prayer and the interpretation of dreams and visions, rather than the formal catechism associated with the institutional Christianity of the Roman Catholic and mainline Protestant churches. The framework for this Lowcountry Christian practice came from West-Central African and West African initiation societies, revealed in part by the stages of seeking in which the initiate endured seclusion in the wilderness and returned after a dramatic spiritual transformation. The West African associations known as Poro and Sande have been examined as likely precursors for Lowcountry seeking, although West-Central African antecedents have received much less attention.[2] African-derived names current in the Lowcountry as late as the 1930s included at least twenty titles and thirty-five initiation names used within Nkimba, Ndembo, Kimpasi, and Lemba, the four major initiation societies found in Kongo since the era of the trans-Atlantic trade in captives. This alone suggests that people inducted into these societies numbered among those transported across the Atlantic and reconstituted these associations to the extent that many Nkimba, Ndembo, Kimpasi, and Lemba titles and names remained in use among African-descended people in the Lowcountry.[3]

Additionally, as discussed in Chapter 3, Kongo initiation societies consecrated their members to nature spirits. Evidence of this same purpose for Lowcountry seeking appeared in the role of the white beings that helped seekers find white bundles and babies. Most significant within this combination of beings and objects were the white babies, which according to one woman who completed seeking in the nineteenth century, represented the source of spiritual renewal: "Your soul, your soul is the baby."[4] The combination of white beings, bundles,

---

than from outsider missionaries or denominational institutions. See Creel, *Peculiar People*, 233, 276–81, 298–301; and Alonzo Johnson, "'Pray's House Spirit': The Institutional Structure and Spiritual Core of an African American Folk Tradition," in *Ain't Gonna Lay My 'Ligion Down: African American Religion in the South*, ed. Alonzo Johnson and Paul Jersild (Columbia: University of South Carolina Press, 1996), 8–38.

[2] Creel, *Peculiar People*, 285–95; and Kuyk, *African Voices*, 83–8, 113–15.

[3] The specific Lowcountry names and citations in Turner's *Africanisms* appear in Tables 10 and 11. For general overview of the major Kongo initiation societies, see Ngoma, *Initiation*.

[4] LDTC, Disc 12–3274 A1.

and babies in the spiritual landscape of the wilderness indicates that this stage in seeking signified an encounter of transformation through the simbi, as the experience corresponded closely with events in the Kongo initiation societies dedicated to nature spirits. Indeed, the white babies symbolized, I contend, another manifestation of the simbi that seekers had to "find" and "clean" in order to consecrate themselves to these spirits and reach spiritual "liberation." The connection of the simbi with Christianity did not occur first in the Lowcountry, however. People in Kongo already associated the Virgin Mary with nature spirits, and the elaboration of the simbi as white beings, bundles, and babies in the seeking process marked a continuation of the spiritual dialogue between traditional Kongo culture and European Christianity in a new context in the Americas.[5] Despite all of these novel reconfigurations of the simbi, they remained at root guardians of the land and people who inhabited it.

The journey to Christianity as both an individual and collective historical experience for African-descended people may at first appear to be a distant step away from the spiritual culture that included and honored the simbi. Yet once we come to understand the role of the simbi as both guardians and agents of spiritual transformation, we see the essential place of the Lowcountry simbi in the individual conversion of seekers and the larger transition of the spiritual culture from the traditional religions of Africans to the Protestant Christianity of their Lowcountry-born descendants. In turn, the simbi were transformed, as well, becoming unnamed entities in the journeys of seekers from those intermediate generations during the shift from traditional to Protestant Christian orientations. As this long, uneven change led to the dominance of Protestant Christianity as the spiritual framework in the late nineteenth and early twentieth centuries, the simbi, even as anonymous but essential beings and objects in the seeking process, faded away to be abandoned and forgotten by later generations. Moreover, the spiritual landscape that was once fundamental to the physical and metaphorical experience of seeking and liberation devolved into a purely symbolic realm. The relationship with the simbi and spiritual landscape had turned such that Christians of African descent no longer sang about how they would "go in the wilderness" as their ancestors

---

[5] For documentation of the link between the Virgin Mary and nature spirits, see Hyancinthe, *Pratique Missionnaire*, 142–4. The influence of Catholicism in Kongo and Angola is addressed in Thornton, "Religious and Ceremonial," 83–90; and Heywood, "Portuguese into African," 98–102.

did, but instead sang of how they have "come out the wilderness" to find salvation.[6]

GUARDIANS OF SPRINGS AND SOULS

As guardians of the land, the Kongo simbi not only governed the physical environment but also protected the inhabitants of their domains. While it may appear contradictory at first glance, the true measure of the ability of the simbi to safeguard people was not confirmed in their acts of beneficence. Instead, it was revealed in their extraordinary power to harm or take the lives of those who transgressed their authority or sought to injure people under their guardianship. Relationships with nature spirits were not merely one-way flows of benevolent blessings from the spirits to the living. Any contact with the powers of the spirit world required caution and entailed obligations ranging from general respect and one-time offerings to rigorous adherence to codes of prescribed observances and prohibitions. A Roman Catholic missionary's account in the early eighteenth century noted that before crossing a river, people called out, "Malicious spirits who are the lords of this river, grant us safe passage, because we have great faith in you."[7] The modifier "malicious" in this phrase conveys something more meaningful than the expected bias of the Christian priest. It was the recognition by those crossing the river that the spirits inhabiting the water had the power to take life just as they had the ability to preserve it. This showed that the power of the spirits was at once dangerous and necessary. As a twentieth-century source explained, the role of the simbi as potent conduits between the land of the dead and the land of the living was authenticated through frightening displays of violence in the natural environment:

Truly [the simbi] have great power and authority, for their power is revealed by the force they show in the water and in the gullies. They stir up very high winds and unleash tornadoes, so that the bodies of people are filled with fear and trembling. They break people's courage and render it feeble, weak, limp, petrified, hollow and fevered; they are stunned and grovel in terror. This is how the *bisimbi* show their strength: if they see someone come to draw water from the pool where they reside, they rise to the surface and cover it with foam and turbulence, turning and twisting. So the person drawing the water is scared stiff when she sees how

---

[6] A different interpretation of the relationship of these verses is found in Bernice Johnson Reagon, *If You Don't Go, Don't Hinder Me: The African American Sacred Song Tradition* (Lincoln: University of Nebraska Press, 2001), 83–4.

[7] Lucca, *Relations*, 142.

the water boils in the pool. She may tumble into the water because she is dizzy. If she does not cry out so that those who remain in the village hear her, when next they meet her she may be dead.[8]

The fact that people attributed deaths by drowning to the simbi, whether as punishment for trespassing on restricted domains or because they decided to "seize" or "capture" a person and keep them in a simbi village (that is, retain people under the water), reflected the perception that the simbi held power over life and death, the most significant expression of mastery of spiritual power.[9] This power extended to general well-being, as seen in the statement by the Kongo writer Babutidi that, "The reason why a man remains alive is that he strictly follows the rules of the spirits; for example, when he has been treated by one and told not to eat such-and-such. If he breaks no rules he will live into old age."[10] Clearly, transgressing the rules of the spirits led to illness and early death, as the simbi demanded the proper respect and behavior from the people to whom they extended their blessings.

People relied on this aspect of the power of the simbi by entering into direct relationships with the spirits to ensure good health and long life. Sources from the early twentieth century described a common means of forging an alliance with a simbi that involved people approaching bodies of water known to house powerful simbi and consecrating themselves to the simbi by "hiding their souls" in the waters. One of the great spirits, Mpulu Buzi, created the waterfall Mbembe, where twenty-nine of his simbi children dwelt in the pools at the bottom of the waterfall. People who trespassed into the pools lost their lives, as this was a spiritual preserve where others hid their souls under the guardianship of the simbi.[11] The simbi provided protection for the souls of people in other locations considered their abodes, particularly the forest, which held many associations with the land of the dead.[12] In the following account, the spiritual realms of the water (represented by the sea shells) and the forest were linked in the efforts to safeguard and preserve souls:

Mbamba is a large sea-shell. Finding many of these shells, the people in the old days consecrated them their bisimbi. They hid their souls in the shells and dug

---

[8] Kavuna Simon, translated by MacGaffey, *Kongo Political Culture*, 141.
[9] Laman, *Kongo*, 3: 35–6; MacGaffey, *Art and Healing*, 88; and MacGaffey, *Kongo Political Culture*, 220–4.
[10] Babutidi, translated by MacGaffey in *Art and Healing*, 33.
[11] Laman, *Kongo*, 3: 40.
[12] MacGaffey, *Kongo Political Culture*, 27–8, 77.

them down in the woods with only the tips showing above ground, addressing them as follows: "As strong as your house you shall keep my life for me. When you leave for the sea, take me along, that I may live forever with you." The sea is the indestructible town of the basimbi. The builders of that town created an eternal realm.[13]

It was in this role as protectors of people's souls that the simbi fully manifested their status as guardians. As people struggled to maintain their physical and spiritual vitality, they turned to the simbi as their strongest spiritual allies.

The descriptions from Kongo of the "boiling" simbi waters, violence unleashed by the simbi, and fear attached to approaching simbi abodes resonate strongly throughout the accounts of prohibitions and warnings associated with the springs where the Lowcountry simbi resided. This suggests that the Lowcountry simbi guarded their waters for the same purposes as their Kongo counterparts. For people in the Lowcountry, the sight of an individual lurking in a spiritually potent place aroused much suspicion and fear, as he or she undoubtedly planned mischief and engaged in some effort to bring misfortune to another person.[14] The fear associated with individuals visiting simbi springs may have reflected the idea the waters held something worth protecting by means of the dreadful power of the Lowcountry simbi. African-descended people in South Carolina certainly retained the notion that people could make and use containers to keep or trap the force of the living as well as the dead. Some may have followed the example of their Kongo ancestors and entrusted the simbi to preserve their souls in the springs that housed these water spirits.[15] In addition to protecting their springs, then, the Lowcountry simbi likely served as spiritual guardians for the living, as did the Kongo simbi.

During the course of the nineteenth century, the spiritual culture of African-descended people increasingly incorporated Protestant Christianity. In this journey, the simbi retained their role as guardians. To say that the Protestant forms of Christianity, specifically the Methodist and Baptist denominations, that gained followers in this era comprised a "new faith" is not to claim the absence of previous contact with Christianity in the Lowcountry or even in Africa. Certainly, the missioning by the Anglican Church and the efflorescence of the First Great

---

[13] Laman, *Kongo*, 3: 37.
[14] Bound Volume (p. 27), John Bennett Papers, SCHS.
[15] Thompson, "Bighearted Power," 61.

Awakening in South Carolina provided eighteenth-century precedents for later Christianization. The bearing of these efforts, however, did not appear to substantially alter the spiritual orientation of the vast major- ity of enslaved people, in part because such endeavors did not result in numerically or culturally significant converts. Nevertheless, Protestant Christianity defined almost entirely the religious milieu of Carolinian society. Consequently, Protestant Christianity was accessible to African- descended people. Even if they did not participate formally in its institu- tions, they could see, hear, and in some cases read Protestant Christian expressions of ritual and belief.[16]

These early contacts with Christianity in the Lowcountry came at the discretion of enslaved people, as enslavers did not persecute Africans for continuing familiar spiritual practices (at least those that did not appear to promote uprisings) and did not attempt to thrust the prevailing reli- gious orthodoxy upon them. Limited efforts by Anglican missionaries to attract converts among enslaved people received inadequate material support and engendered outright hostility among planters, who perceived time and energy spent on spiritual work as time and energy lost for plan- tation work. On this attitude, Anglican clergy in South Carolina lamented in the early eighteenth century that, "The masters of slaves are generally of the opinion that a slave grows worse by being a Christian; and there- fore instead of instructing them in the principles of Christianity...they malign and traduce those that attempt it."[17] The indifference of enslav- ers to the spiritual culture of those they enslaved continued for some time, as Christianity did not form part of a concerted "civilizing mis- sion" to reform "heathen" enslaved people and justify enslavement as morally uplifting until the 1830s. In sum, the spiritual lives of enslaved Africans and their Lowcountry-born descendants remained their own for several generations. Even after the more strenuous efforts to introduce Christianity during the nineteenth century, African-descended people in the Lowcountry tended to cultivate Christianity according to their own sensibilities.[18]

[16] Creel, *Peculiar People*, 68–74; Frey and Wood, *Come Shouting to Zion*, 62–80; Olwell, *Masters, Slaves, and Subjects*, 103–39; and Laing, "Heathens and Infidels," 197–228.

[17] "Instructions of the Clergy of South Carolina given to Mr. Johnston on his coming away for England," Society of the Propagation of the Gospels Manuscripts, quoted in Klingberg, *Appraisal of the Negro*, 6.

[18] Creel, *Peculiar People*, 67–109, 167–251, 259–302; Joyner, "Believer I Know," 18–46; Alonzo Johnson and Paul Jersild, "Introduction," in Johnson and Jersild, *Ain't Gonna Lay My "Ligion Down,"* 4; and Lacy K. Ford, *Deliver Us from Evil: The Slavery Question*

The spiritual backgrounds of Africans carried to South Carolina also included varying levels of exposure to Christianity. Many captive Africans, especially those brought from West-Central Africa, came from societies influenced by the missions of Roman Catholic orders such as the Jesuits and the Capuchins. These endeavors introduced a number of Christian concepts, observances, and symbols to Kongo and Angola. While it remains debatable what proportion of the overall population claimed a specifically Roman Catholic identity, most people in highly evangelized areas such as Kongo at one time or another participated in Christian rites, whether as individuals in baptism or in larger community settings through attendance at mass and celebration of feast days.[19] Exposure to the Christianity of Roman Catholic missionaries, however, did not result in a comprehensive conversion of the Kongo people or even of the kingdom's nobility, who readily embraced the political implications of such an alliance in a manner suitable to the European priests. The priests invariably complained of "paganism...idolatry...vain observances, superstitions and other diabolical customs" and bemoaned the nobility's enduring commitment to plural marriage among the many spiritual failures they assigned to the people of Kongo.[20] That fact that the same inventory of "bad customs" appears in the early literature of Roman Catholic missionaries as well as that of their nineteenth- and twentieth-century Protestant counterparts suggests that these forms of Christianity augmented but did not fundamentally subvert the spiritual cultures of Kongo and West-Central Africa.

One area of confluence between Roman Catholic Christianity and Kongo spiritual culture that even the European missionaries considered a good custom was the veneration of powerful spirits in the figure of the Virgin Mary. The coastal region of Soyo provided remarkable examples of such interactions of local and European Christian spiritual cultures. The people of Soyo, more so than any other society of the Lower Nzadi region, have cultivated a long and continuous relationship with European Christianity. A Dutch visitor in the early seventeenth century commented that the capital Mbanza Soyo had "five or six churches." Further, the people of Soyo "are mostly Christian and go to mass every day and twice

in the Old South (New York: Oxford University Press, 2009), 8, 92–4, 231–2, 242–5, 251–67, 463–80, 527–32.

[19] Thornton, "Religious and Ceremonial Life," 83.

[20] The quote comes from the title of chapter 9 in Hyacinthe, *Pratique Missionnaire*, 116. The chapter records the most common "bad customs" that missionaries expected to encounter (pp. 116–30).

a day when it rains...and everyone goes the whole day with a book in hand and with a rosary."[21] By the late seventeenth century, Mbanza Soyo had as many as eight churches, and the inhabitants participated fully in the celebrations of Roman Catholic Holy Days and honoring the dead interred on church grounds.[22]

For Europeans arriving in Soyo after a long journey on the Atlantic, one of the first sites encountered in the new land revealed that the spiritual culture of the region represented both local and European traditions. The promontory called Padrão presented a significant hazard for ships entering the Nzadi and at the same time exhibited a landmark of the European presence in Soyo. On this spit of land named after the stone standard planted there by Portuguese explorers led by Diogo Cão in the 1480s, the newcomers erected a large cross to commemorate their landing. It was borne by a great stone (the stone considered by later generations as the original Padrão). Although the condition of the monument in the decades that followed is not known, by the mid-seventeenth century a small church that stood at this location housed a stone statue also identified as Padrão. Not long after this, however, the English reduced the remaining stone structure to pieces after firing their cannon at the site in retaliation for a perceived slight by Soyo.[23]

While the basic story of Padrão may appear limited to describing the establishment and dynamics of the European presence in Soyo, the people of Soyo have understood the site and relics associated with it in very different terms. In the mid-seventeenth century, local people did not attribute the existence of the Padrão stone in the chapel to Cão. Instead, they said that it came from the sky. This idea features prominently in traditions recorded in the twentieth century that posit a divine origin for the stone and Christianity in Soyo. According to these traditions, God sent Saint Mary and Saint Anthony to Soyo from Heaven. When Diogo Cão landed at Padrão, he encountered a tall stone on which were Mary and Saint Anthony. Cão wanted to bring both saints back with him to Portugal, but Mary wished to stay in Soyo. She thus remained on the beach within a highly ornate and beautiful box. The sea claimed the box

---

[21] Pieter van den Broecke, *Pieter van den Broecke's Journal of Voyages to Cape Verde, Guinea and Angola 1605–1612*, trans. J.D. La Fleur (London: Hakluyt Society, 2000), 59.

[22] Andrea da Pavia, "Viaggio apostolico alle missioni del Padre Andrea da Pavia, predicatore cappuccino, 1685," in "Andrea da Pavia au Congo, à Lisbonne, à Madère. Journal d'un missionaire capucin, 1685–1702," ed. and trans. Louis Jadin, *Bulletin de l'Institut Historique Belge de Rome* 41 (1970): 439–54.

[23] Pavia, "Viaggio apostolico," 456; and Cappelle, "Brève description," 221.

from the beach and carried it to a location that suffered from drought. A fisherman found the box but did not have the strength to take it to his home. His woman, however, carried it with ease. Santa Maria brought the couple prosperity although the land did not produce crops and the people struggled. As news of the sacred box and its blessings spread, the king heard about it and decided to seize it. The fisherman avoided conflict by volunteering the Saint to the king and telling the story of the box. The king determined that the inhabitants of Soyo would guard Saint Mary as a Christian people, after which they built a chapel in a single day, in which they kept the Saint under the protection of the prevailing nganga nkisi (the priest consecrated to the nature spirits). Only the head expert (also known as *kintumba*) could enter the Virgin Mary's chapel, known as the Nzo a Nkisi (House of the Spirit), while the people made their prayers and offerings to the nkisi Santa Maria outside of the chapel.[24]

One of the fundamental elements of the Santa Maria traditions in Soyo remains the assertion that Christianity came to Soyo directly from God in the holy personages of Saint Mary and Saint Anthony, not from European conquerors or missionaries. Cão did not bring or erect the sacred stone at Padrão; he found it there already inhabited by the two saints. Additionally, the sea delivered the sacred box of Santa Maria to the people of Soyo. This may reflect ideas about the sea as a primary source of spiritual power, as seen in traditions about the great spirits such as the Bunzi or even Kalunga from Angola.[25] As such, while Santa Maria would be associated with terrestrial waters and rain only, the origin in the sea comports well with larger narratives about access to the forces of the spirit world. At this point, it is essential to make clear that the conflation of Santa Maria with the box that contained her reflects the basic understanding of the inextricable connection between spirits and the objects consecrated to them. Once in the hands of the people of Soyo, Mary

[24] Cappelle, "Brève description," 221. This version of the Santa Maria tradition combines material discussed in Abranches, *Sobre Os Basolongo*, 72, 74.

[25] For more on the spirit Kalunga, see Cavazzi, *Descrição*, 2: 64; C. Tastevin, "Culte des genies. Ba kisi ba n'si," in Volavka, *Crown and Ritual*, 292–5; Martins, *Cabindas*, 111; Joseph C. Miller, *Kings and Kinsmen: Early Mbundu States in Angola* (Oxford: Clarendon, 1976), 59–63; and Óscar Ribas, *Ilundu: Espíritos e Ritos Angolanos* (Porto: União dos Escritores Angolanos, 1989), 31, 179. Kalunga as a spirit and concept appears in the diaspora, as well. See Arthur Ramos, *O Negro Brasileiro: Ethnographia, Religiosa e Psychanalyse* (Rio de Janeiro: Civilização Brasileira, 1934), 84–5; Edison Carneiro, *Negros Bantus: Notas de Ethnographia Religiosa e de Folk-lore* (Rio de Janeiro: Civilização Brasileira, 1937), 77; Cabrera, *Reglas de Congo*, 128; and Todd Ramón Ochoa, "Versions of the Dead: *Kalunga*, Cuban-Kongo Materiality, and Ethnography," *Current Anthropology* 22, 4 (2007): 473–500.

bestowed her fertility on the people who honored her, a blessing considered the most important power offered by nature spirits. The association of this power with the female entity Santa Maria and the woman of the fisherman (who could bear the sacred box, unlike her man) shows that the tradition addresses the fecundity of women, another primary concern of nature spirits. Finally, the establishment of the Nzo a Nkisi and the role of the Nganga Nkisi speak to the notion that key aspects of Christianity could be perceived as consonant with older Soyo spiritual culture (and not necessarily as foreign elements) and that the traditional authority of local experts remained entrenched and superseded that of European missionaries. The history of missionaries in Soyo reveals a more complicated story than this, but the key features of this tradition also played out in the twists and turns of Soyo's long engagement with Christianity and its European representatives.[26] In the end, this tradition recounts how the Virgin Mary became the patron nature spirit of Soyo. Aside from the clear Christian references, it represents a most typical account of the creation of a relationship between the people of a territory and a powerful, dominant nature spirit dedicated to protecting them.

Another remarkable connection between the simbi and Santa Maria occurred in Soyo in relation to the sacred site of the church Our Lady of Pinda. In the mid-eighteenth century, this "country chapel" stood outside of Mbanza Soyo and hosted a mass every week for those who made the journey to worship in front of an altar that featured a bas-relief of the "very Holy Virgin." A Capuchin priest restored the figure, as it had suffered damage over the years. The return of the image to the chapel following repairs occasioned a large procession and celebration for Santa Maria that included vast offerings of legumes, manioc, millet, tobacco, eggs, fruits, and other produce of the land. The event came during a terrible famine that had already claimed many lives, but the people continued to add to the "extraordinary heap of alms offerings to Our Lady." The procession and offering had been intended to ask for rain in addition to rededicating the image to the chapel. The generosity of the suffering people was rewarded by a "prompt and abundant" rain that not only ended the famine but also resulted in an unprecedented bounty in which the crops of millet rendered twice the normal harvest. Aside from the fact that the role of Santa Maria in this communal offering accorded with the role given to the simbi, the traditional meaning of the site and event

---

[26] Richard Gray, "'Come vero Prencipe Catolico': The Capuchins and the Rulers of Soyo in the Late Seventeenth Century," *Africa* 53, 3 (1983): 39–54.

appeared in the fact that the "pagans of the kingdom of Angoi located on the other side of the great river Zaire" joined the event, as well. They brought their own offerings of food and cloth in addition to sick people to seek healing from Santa Maria.[27] While the priest regarded the participation of the neighboring "pagans" astonishing, it appears less so when we consider that Santa Maria represented in their minds, as well as in the perceptions of many of the Christians in Soyo undoubtedly, a powerful nature spirit, a "guardian of the land" that rewarded their obedience and loyalty with plentiful rain. In short, the Holy Virgin Mary was a simbi.

A reflection of the confluence of the simbi and Santa Maria in the Lowcountry may have played a part in the timing of the Gullah War (or the Stono Rebellion in scholarly parlance). The beginning of the military component of the conflict corresponded with the celebration of the day of Nativity of the Virgin Mary.[28] Moreover, the initial gathering of the African combatants took place near the Stono River, suggesting that the fighters may have sought the support of water spirits such as the simbi before taking action. Sanction and assistance from the forces of the land of the dead featured prominently in warfare in West-Central Africa as well as in freedom wars throughout the African-Atlantic diaspora.[29]

Still, any lasting influence of Roman Catholic doctrine and observances brought by Kongo people to the Lowcountry does not appear readily in historical sources or later cultural practices. Kongo captives deeply committed to Roman Catholicism did not form or perpetuate a distinct Kongo Catholic community in a way that drew the attention of Anglican and state authorities (other than those connected to the Gullah War). Certainly, many of those who exhibited a strong devotion to Roman Catholicism fled to the sanctuary of Spanish St. Augustine, diminishing the likelihood of the formation of this kind of community.[30]

---

[27] Hyacinthe, *Pratique Missionnaire*, 142–4.

[28] Smith, "Remembering Mary," 527.

[29] Cavazzi, *Descrição*, 2: 45. For examples from the larger African-Atlantic diaspora, see João José Reis, *Slave Rebellion in Brazil: The Muslim Uprising of 1835 in Bahia*, trans. Arthur Brakel (Baltimore, MD: Johns Hopkins University Press, 1993); Terry Rey, "Ancestors, Saints, and Prophets in Kongo-dominguois Root Experience: A Revisionist Reading of Transatlantic African Resistance," in *Africa and the Americas: Interconnections during the Slave Trade*, ed. José C. Curto and Renée Soulodre-La France (Trenton, NJ: Africa World Press, 2005), 215–30; Dianne M. Stewart (Diakité), *Three Eyes for the Journey: African Dimensions of the Jamaican Religious Experience* (New York: Oxford University Press, 2005), 65–8; and T.J. Desch Obi, *Fighting for Honor: The History of African Martial Art Traditions in the Atlantic* (Columbia: University of South Carolina Press, 2008).

[30] Landers, "Gracia Real," 9–30; and Landers, *Black Society*, 29–60.

Further, while South Carolina had relatively open policies concerning Protestant Christian affiliations, the Carolinian public and state extended an uneasy tolerance toward Roman Catholics of any nationality.[31] In a world in which Roman Catholic Spanish and French settlers presented a threat to British colonial interests in North America, the religious rivalry would have resulted in close scrutiny of any group that openly presented itself as Roman Catholic. This meant that, at best, expressions of Roman Catholic doctrine and practice among Kongo newcomers had to have taken place in the covert spiritual domain shared by almost all African-descended people. Any kind of a distinct Roman Catholic identity that arrived with Kongo Catholics, then, could not find fertile soil in a hostile Anglican land and left no scions.

Despite the difficulties in maintaining Kongo Catholicism in South Carolina, the interaction of Kongo and Roman Catholic spiritual cultures in West-Central Africa did leave a legacy in the Lowcountry. This legacy had less to do with the continuity of Catholic doctrine and observances than with the extension of the notion that the simbi could be found in the religions of Europeans. The fact that many in Kongo could see that the faith taken there by missionaries recognized and honored the power of nature spirits, as in the example of the simbi Virgin Mary, may have established a foundational understanding among Kongo people in general that the other cults of Europeans, including Protestant Christianity, acknowledged the same idea. When the evangelists of the Second Great Awakening and later missionary endeavors brought their teachings of an expert healer and powerful spirit named Jesus, the Lowcountry-born children and grandchildren of the Kongo ancestors were ready to hear about this remarkable nganga who became a simbi.

SEEKING AND SPIRITUAL TRANSFORMATION

The individual experience of becoming Christian called seeking or coming through as a core feature of Christian ritual among African-descended people first emerged in the nineteenth century as a consequence of the missionary efforts sponsored primarily by Methodists and Baptists. The terminology for the experience came from the practice of Methodist missionaries concluding their meetings with calls for

---

[31] James Lowell Underwood, "The Dawn of Religious Freedom in South Carolina: The Journey from Limited Tolerance to Constitutional Right," in *The Dawn of Religious Freedom in South Carolina*, ed. James Lowell Underwood and W. Lewis Burke (Columbia: University of South Carolina Press, 2006), 1–57.

people to show their commitment to "seek Jesus" and become "seekers of religion."[32] As with so much in the evangelization endeavors of white Christians at this time, the actual outcome of the introduction of the Methodist seeking process did not conform to the expectations of the missionaries. Instead, it appears that African-descended people incorporated seeking Jesus into existing ideas and practices of spiritual transformation that derived from Lowcountry manifestations of African spiritual cultures, a pattern also seen in other customs connected with the developing Christian culture, most notably the communal rite known as the ring shout.[33]

The earliest description of the practice later known as seeking comes from Methodist missionary reports produced in the 1840s:

When one of these people becomes serious, or "begins to pray" as he would say, – and this is seldom the result of preaching, but most commonly a "warning in a dream," – it is customary for him to select, by the direction of "the spirit" of course, with some church member influence, as his spiritual guide. Females are often chosen. Soon after the "vision" in which his teacher is pointed out, he makes known to him his revelation and puts himself under his instruction. These are of a two-fold nature, answering to the two-fold character of the teacher. He is now a prophet to teach him how to conduct himself, and particularly how to pray. He is also "an interpreter of visions" to whom the seeker relates all his "*travel.*" This word *travel*...is one of the most significant in their language, and comprehends all those exercises, spiritual, visionary and imaginative, which make up an "experience."...These travels may differ in some things; and in others they all agree. Each seeker meets with warning – awful sights or sounds, and always has a vision of a white man who talks with him, warns him, and sometimes makes him carry a burden, and in the end leads him to the river. When the teacher is satisfied with the travel of the seeker, he pronounces "he git thru"; and he is ready for the church. This decision is never questioned by the neophyte. "I prayed under him," say the latter; "he is my spiritual father." Thus the case is settled. The man's religion is endorsed by an authoritative *imprimatur* and heaven is sure. Meanwhile perhaps there has been no solitary conviction of the true nature of sin, no genuine repentance to embitter sin to the soul, no distant apprehension of the sacrifices of the Savior and the merit of his death as the atonement of sin, and the great procuring cause of pardon; in a word, no distant element of Christian experience involved in the whole affair.[34]

---

[32] Creel, *Peculiar People*, 285–6.

[33] On the African influences for seeking, see Creel, *Peculiar People*, 285–95; and Kuyk, *African Voices*, 83–8, 113–15. For the ring shout, see Stuckey, *Slave Culture*, 3–97; Creel, *Peculiar People*, 297–302; and Gomez, *Exchanging Our Country Marks*, 264–74.

[34] *Southern Christian Advocate*, 30 October 1846 and 30 October 1847, quoted in Creel, *Peculiar People*, 286.

This account reveals that the African-descended people in the Lowcountry at this time named their experience of spiritual transformation "travel," not "seeking." The terminology of "seeker" in the passage conformed to the language of the missionary. The fact that people retained "travel" in later periods and also adopted "seeking" from the lexicon of missionaries supports the interpretation that local approaches to initiation into Christianity described in this passage had been built upon previous practices, reflecting a continuum of spiritual culture, not a rupture. The clarity of this observation appears in the remark that there seemed to be "no distant element of Christian experience" in the process. Outward expressions of doctrine, which the missionaries considered essential to the proper conversion to Christianity, were not fundamental to spiritual transformation and did not figure in any significant way in the early formulations of Christianity of African-descended people.[35]

The missionary account documents the basic outline of the process of seeking and getting through that remained largely intact into the twentieth century. It neglects a few features, however, that can be gleaned from the reports of African-descended people born in the mid- and late nineteenth century, who knew the experience firsthand. At the same time, it records aspects that appear in these later accounts of successful seekers that have not yet been adequately interpreted by scholars, most notably the meanings of the encounter with the white man during the seeker's travel.

When using the larger base of sources, we can see that the process of joining the Christian community entailed multiple steps within three major phases. These phases included the preparatory stage that began with sanction by the Christian community and preliminary guidance by a spiritual leader; the wilderness and getting through period of isolation and visions; and the final phase of formal instruction by the spiritual leader, public acceptance into the community of Christians, and baptism. The discussion that follows focuses on the wilderness and getting through sequence as the key phase of spiritual transformation. Further, this period corresponds with the travel experience mentioned in the early missionary account. Overall, the process of seeking, beginning with acceptance of the candidate through full membership, lasted between two weeks and three months depending on the initiate's progress.[36]

[35] Creel, *Peculiar People*, 260–4.
[36] Elsie Clews Parsons, *Folklore of the Sea Islands, South Carolina* (New York: American Folk Lore Society, 1923), 204–5.

Upon reaching a certain age (typically thirteen to fifteen years old), the prospective seeker sought approval to begin initiation by demonstrating a commitment to the process and establishing a relationship with a mentor. This ensued after proving the sincerity of intent as described by the Reverend July C. Brown, an Edisto Island resident, who recalled:

On meeting night about five or six of us would go and bunch to together at meeting house. We go and go and go. Then, we go and go every night. And at last one night, they see us continually coming. They call for mourners, and we bowed to the mourner's bench, and they were people pray for us, and we'd set out one by one, we got to go repent.[37]

The next step in this first phase centered on the dreams of the seeker that identified an elder as a spiritual mother or father, also known as a leader or teacher. The elder's primary role consisted of interpreting the many dreams and visions of the initiate during the next stage of prayer. In many cases, the seeker then had to convince the elder of his or her dedication by showing continued interest and having additional dreams that confirmed the connection between the initiate and the elder. When Mollie Robinson became a spiritual mother herself, she confirmed a seeker's dream of her by identifying a correspondence between the seeker's dream and her own dream of the seeker. In one instance, a silver leaf needle in her dream corresponded with a silver object in a seeker's dream, thus authenticating the spiritual link between the two.[38] For other seekers, "Some teachers know before the child comes."[39] Once this relationship had been established, the elder put the initiate "out to work" and into the next major phase, which included activities that represented the key stages of spiritual transformation for the seeker.

After the seeker received the commission to go out to work, the seeker endured the intense phase that required initiates to seclude themselves, pray, have visions, and consult with their leaders. Seekers typically described this phase as the time for them to "go in the wilderness." A sacred song from the Lowcountry intoned:

You want to find Jesus,
Go in the wilderness, go in the wilderness, go in the wilderness.
You want to find Jesus,
Go in the wilderness,

---

[37] LDTC, Disc 12–3272 B1.
[38] Mollie Robinson, St. Helena Island, South Carolina (c.1920s), Guy Benton Johnson Papers, SHC.
[39] Anonymous source quoted in Parsons, *Folklore*, 204.

Wait upon the Lord.
Going wait upon the Lord, going wait upon the Lord, going wait upon
    the Lord,
Till my soul come to me.

As Morris Hamilton of Johns Island explained, "That's the only way you can find Jesus; go in the wilderness and wait on him until he come."[40] The words of the song reveal the key elements of the second phase of seeking. Initiates had to leave the safety and familiarity of home to go into the wilderness (typically the forest or a secluded field), often alone at night, where they "worked" (prayed).[41] Those who could not go to the woods attempted to replicate the meaning of the forest as best as they could. A young woman named Handful was relocated to Charleston from her country home around the time of her seeking period. Although she could not go into the forest, every evening at dusk she went into the yard and "would kneel down in the midst of whatever shrubbery she could find or beneath a tree, and pray."[42] Clearly, aside from being a physically isolating place necessary for an intense experience of praying, the wilderness stood in the spiritual landscape as a metaphor for transition. Further, it was in the spiritual landscape of the wilderness that seekers encountered various white beings and objects as well as more familiar Christian figures to help them in their quest. We will analyze the meanings of this part of seeking in more detail.

The wilderness period could entail much hardship, as fasting was common, and neophytes had to check in continuously with their spiritual mothers or fathers to affirm the validity of their dreams and visions. While fasting was not considered essential, many felt that it helped their individual efforts to advance through the process. As one successful seeker phrased it, "I could have eaten all right, but I was determined I was going to find the Lord." Another was more resolute in stating, "Certainly I fast. Can't think of religion and eating all to same time." The fasting could last

---

[40] Hymn and quote from Interview with Morris Hamilton, Johns Island, South Carolina, 24 May 1932, LDTC, Disc 12–3305 A1. The theme of going into the wilderness for salvation in this song evokes the biblical accounts of Jesus being tested in the wilderness after his baptism (Matthew 4: 1–11; Mark 1: 12–13; Luke 4: 1–13). Although these stories provide a clear Christian context for seeking, the Lowcountry process inverted the baptism-wilderness sequence in the scriptures, as the wilderness phase came first and baptism occurred last.

[41] Zackie Knox of Murrell's Inlet, South Carolina, as recorded by Genevieve W. Chandler (Georgetown, South Carolina), "Seeking and Comin' Through," WPA-SCL.

[42] Jessie A. Butler (Charleston, South Carolina), "Seekin'," WPA-SCL.

for stretches of "three or four days at a time without food or drink" or as long as one to two weeks in a few instances.[43] In addition to coping with fasting and the isolation in the wilderness, the candidates had to satisfy their spiritual parents that they had been maintaining their commitment and had the proper visions and dreams necessary to move forward. Sam Doyle noted, "As long as you're on the wrong road, that teacher knows. You can't fool 'em." His spiritual mother was Nancy "Nanny" Newton, who apparently supervised seeking for many people (as many as 2,000, according to Doyle). Another of Nanny Newton's spiritual children, Gertrude Green, remembered her experiences: "They know when you ain't doing nothing. So she tell my mother that I was doing nothing. It was true. They could *see*."[44] Although she had been in the process for three months already, Nanny Newton made her "stop praying" and attempt seeking again later when she was fully dedicated to it. For many seekers the only option was to "turn back," to try again on another occasion.

Others persevered, and their spiritual work progressed appropriately even though it may have required an extended period of time. The Reverend Brown recalled of his ordeal, "I had to seek a long time. I seek ninety days, three months before...getting...liberation."[45] The experience of liberation or getting through at the end of the wilderness period marked the most important point of spiritual transformation for the initiate. As one seeker described her getting through experience, she heard a voice say, "your sins are forgiven and your soul set free" as she prayed in the woods before sunrise.[46]

Once the seeker's spiritual mother or father had validated the getting through experience the period of seeking in the wilderness ended, and the leader undertook direct instruction of the initiate. The next test for the initiate involved an exam at the praise house, in which the elders judged the quality of a seeker's transformation. This was no mere formality. According to Demus Green of Beaufort County, "Twelve committee talk over you and find out if you're guilty or ain't guilty or not. Whether you got it or you ain't got it. If you ain't got it, you go back. They send

---

[43] Quotes from anonymous interviews included in Samuel Miller Lawton, "The Religious Life of South Carolina Coastal and Sea Island Negroes" (PhD Dissertation, George Peabody College for Teachers, 1939), 148.

[44] Sam Doyle and Gertrude Green quotes from Penn Community Services Oral History Project (Penn Center, St. Helena Island, South Carolina), quoted in Kuyk, *African Voices*, 86.

[45] LDTC, Disc 12–3272 B1.

[46] Mollie Robinson, Guy Benton Johnson Papers, SHC.

you back. You got to be ready."[47] The northern teacher Laura M. Towne observed an examination on St. Helena Island in 1862:

After church Father Tom and his bench of elders examined candidates for baptism and asked Ellen to record their names....Each candidate, clothed in the oldest possible clothes and with a handkerchief made into a band and tied around the forehead, stood humbly before the bench. Father Tom, looking like Jupiter himself, grave, powerful, and awfully dignified, put the most posing questions, to which the candidates replied meekly and promptly. He asked the satisfactory candidate at last, "How do you pray?" Then the soft, musical voices made the coaxing, entreating kind of pray they use so much. A nod dismissed the applicant and another was called up. There were sixty or seventy to examine.[48]

Although seekers endured the wilderness in relative isolation and then stood before the elders to be judged on the merits of their individual spiritual transformation, the larger examination rite included all the seekers (the sixty or seventy in Towne's recollection). As such, examination before the elders brought the seekers together and reestablished the connection of individual seekers with the larger community from which they had been separated as they prayed in the wilderness.

Those judged ready moved on to baptism and received the hand of fellowship for membership in the church community. The rite of baptism was entirely communal, as large groups of initiates gathered along with many family members and friends along with numerous other observers (Figure 6). A northern teacher recorded the event of a baptism on St. Helena Island in 1863:

The ceremony was performed by the roadside near a bridge where the road crossed the creek. "Siah" "leader" at "Good William Fripp's" took the arm of Mr. Phillips [the white minister] and together they entered the water. Around on every side were hundreds of people arrayed in their Sunday best. Their shiny black faces surrounded by bright turbans and white turbans...–near the water stood a large band of singers and they sent up hymn after hymn during the exercises. Mr. Phillips and Siah went into the water. The Pastor extended his hands and his whole flock of candidates went forward into the water. Each one seemed to be attended by several friends or relatives, who besides being bodily support carried dry clothing, shawls, cloaks and overcoats....They all gathered about the minister and Siah. Mr. Phillips took them in turn – each by one shoulder while Siah laid hold of the other and together they immersed them, over one hundred and forty.

[47] Demus Green, "Conversation" (interviewed by Alice D. Boyle, 1975), Alice D. Boyle Collection, SFC.

[48] Laura M. Towne, *Letters and Diary of Laura M. Towne, Written from the Sea Islands of South Carolina, 1862–1884,* ed. Rupert Sargent Holland (Cambridge: Riverside Press, 1912), 79.

FIGURE 6. River baptism, by Beulah Glover (Photographs 12239.9b), Courtesy of South Caroliniana Library, University of South Carolina, Columbia.

As fast as they had been baptized they stepped to the shore, though before they reached there, their friends received them and shuffled them up...and hurried them off into the bushes. It took a long time to get through with so many, but after a while it was over and we all went back to church. All the candidates came out in shiny robes....There was a great difference in their looks when they came into the church the second time. Then we had a long service after which the right hand of fellowship was given and...the sacrament was administered to them.[49]

The significance of the baptism in a natural, flowing body of water imbued the rite with much spiritual meaning in addition to the inherent meaning of the baptism itself. Immersion into these waters provided a merging of the physical and spiritual in an ideal location for just such a connection to occur. The continuum of seeking in the wilderness through baptism in the creek or river ensured complete engagement with the spiritual landscape and the two features of the natural environment where the land of the living intersected with the land of the dead. People needed to experience the entire seeking process and come through the wilderness and the water to be considered a full-fledged, trustworthy church member and a Christian. Demus Green remarked with justifiable pride, "I was

---

[49] David Thorpe to John Mooney, 25 January 1863, David Franklin Thorpe Papers, SHC, quoted in Creel, *Peculiar People*, 293–4.

a member of the church. I been pray and baptized, you know. Been out there in the wilderness and pray, too."[50]

As other scholars have noted, the seeking process in the Lowcountry derived many of its elements and principles from institutions of initiation known to the early generations of captive Africans brought to the western shores of the Atlantic. Margaret Washington pioneered this approach with her argument that the Poro and Sande initiation societies found in Sierra Leone, Liberia, and Guinea provided the framework for seeking.[51] Given the many captives carried from this region of West Africa and their clear influence on the culture of African-descended communities in the Lowcountry, her careful analysis of the parallels between induction into the Poro and Sande societies and the practices linked to seeking remains persuasive. Still, before we can conclude that Poro and Sande supplied the dominant if not only antecedent for Lowcountry seeking, we must keep in mind that initiation societies similar in many ways to Poro and Sande have existed throughout West Africa, West-Central Africa, and other regions of the continent. Certainly, the elements of coming of age, seclusion in the wilderness, having visions and dreams, receiving guidance from parent-like tutors, and reentering the community with a new status of membership represented the continuation of a general model of initiation schools and societies. This was clearly the case for communities in the western portions of Central Africa, where the considerable number of Kikongo-speaking captives taken to the Lowcountry originated. Following Washington's lead, Betty Kuyk and Jason Young have shown correspondences of the Kongo initiation societies such as Lemba and Kimpasi with Lowcountry seeking.[52] The pervasive influence of African initiation societies affected other aspects of culture among African-descended people. Beneficial and burial societies existed in many manifestations such as the Sons and Daughters of I Will Arise, African-American Order of Owls, Household of Ruth, Sons of Zion, Brothers and Sisters Oyster Society, and The Brother and Sister of The Weeping Mary.[53] Further, T.J. Desch-Obi has shown that Lowcountry brotherhoods, closed to outsiders, perpetuated the knowledge and principles of various forms of martial arts and spirituality from Central Africa and West Africa.[54]

---

[50] Demus Green, "Conversation" (interviewed by Alice D. Boyle, 1975), Alice D. Boyle Collection, SFC.

[51] Creel, *Peculiar People*, 288–90.

[52] Kuyk, *African Voices*, 95–143; and Young, *Rituals of Resistance*, 78–80, 95.

[53] Chlotilde R. Martin, "Negro Burial Societies," Folder D-4–27B, WPA-SCL; and Kuyk, *African Voices*, 52–69.

[54] Obi, *Fighting for Honor*, 102–8.

The present analysis of seeking extends this earlier work by offering evidence of the continued influence in the Lowcountry of Kongo initiation societies, including Lemba and Kimpasi as well as Nkimba and Ndembo. More central to this study of the place of the simbi in Lowcountry spiritual culture, the significance of nature spirits (the simbi and others) in these initiation societies supports the contention that the simbi remained fundamental elements of the spiritual transformation experienced through seeking.

The most prominent initiation associations in the greater Kongo cultural realm have included Kimpasi, Lemba, Ndembo, and Nkimba. These groups maintained their status as large initiation societies until the twentieth century, although others that followed similar procedures and fulfilled comparable purposes flourished in earlier times, as well.[55] The initiation societies served several functions, among them the establishment of bonds between people whose only connection to each other came through the experiences, rituals, and knowledge shared in the initiation process. Initiates lived these bonds through the acquisition of new names, learning of secret coded languages, performance of special songs and dances, and adherence to particular prohibitions concerning food and behaviors unique to any given initiation association. In most cases, the groups accepted members from all sectors of the general population, including both males and females, although the financial costs of certain groups, especially Lemba, put membership out of reach for many people. The more immediate circumstances that called for the presence and services of these societies included the need to prevent or confront the malevolent uses of spiritual power and their effects on the fertility, health, and prosperity of society members and the community in general. Most important, nature spirits (and in some cases ancestors) provided the foundation of spiritual force accessed by initiation societies in this perpetual struggle.[56]

The best documented of these societies during the era of the transAtlantic trade in captive Africans were the Kimpasi associations. The Kimpasi societies consecrated initiates to the nkita, nature spirits closely linked to or conflated with the simbi in later periods, as discussed in Chapter 3. The central importance of the nkita to Kimpasi was such that the term served as synonym for the society and the society's experts and

---

[55] Laman, *Kongo*, 3: 256.
[56] This summary derives from the sources consulted for the analysis of Kimpasi, Lemba, Nkimba, and Ndembo in the following paragraphs.

initiates in addition to its original form as the name of the nature spirits. In a secluded location called the *nzo a kimpasi* (house of kimpasi) or simply the kimpasi, the society's leaders – the nganga nkita – led neophytes, both males and females, in the rites through which they became "filled with the spirit of the *nquita* [nkita]" and transformed into "*nkita* people."[57] People were typically drawn into these societies by spirits, who visited various circumstances upon people that required them to seek spiritual and physical healing from the specialists of particular initiation societies such as Kimpasi. The manifestations of these communications from the spirit world included all kinds of maladies, which in themselves represented symptoms of deeper afflictions derived from a spiritual force. The early descriptions of Kimpasi noted that it was "intended for the treatment of sick people," who were "cured" as part of their initiation.[58] As such, the suffering and healing that formed the complementary core principles of initiation societies placed nature spirits at the center of West-Central Africans' efforts to understand and remedy the most pressing concerns of daily life.

The early European sources on Kimpasi offer significant although not copious details of the process of initiation that yield insights beyond the intentions of the missionary chroniclers. One account noted, "The *nequita* celebrate their gatherings in remote places and principally at the bottom of valleys, where the rays of the Sun do not reach to reveal their wicked vile acts."[59] This location of the nzo a kimpasi not only placed the initiation rite in a private setting in the spiritual realm of the natural environment (the wilderness of mfinda) but also near a stream or river, which formed the key feature of the bottom of valleys. To the Christian missionaries, the bottom of valleys below the reach of the sun's light mirrored the darkness of the evil essence of the society and its nkita "demon." To members of Kimpasi, however, the valley with its river represented the definitive location where people could move from the land of the living to descend into the land of the dead. It was there that initiates encountered and then became nkita spirits. A number of sticks "coarsely worked and painted" in the general shape of human figures stood in a semicircle in front of the kimpasi house, which represented the "wall of the king of

---

[57] Cavazzi, *Descrição*, 1: 98, 4: 138; and Corella, "Brève relation," 1151–2.

[58] Bernardo da Gallo, "Rapport de Bernardo da Gallo au cardinal Giuseppe Sacripanti, préfet de la Propagande," in "Le Congo et la secte Antoniens. Restauration du Royaume sous Pedro IV et la 'saint Antoine' congolaise (1694–1718)," ed. Louis Jadin, *Bulletin de l'Institut Historique Belge de Rome* 33 (1961): 464; and Cavazzi, *Descrição*, 1: 198.

[59] Cavazzi, *Descrição*, 1: 99.

Congo" that could not be trespassed by the uninitiated.[60] The initiates approached a semicircular assemblage, at which point the experts placed a consecrated rope for each initiate to pass over many times to the point of collapse. The group then carried the initiates into the kimpasi house, where they were revived and then swore an oath to remain loyal members of the society.[61] The bare outline of the initiation described by Christian missionaries certainly lacked many of the elements of process, but at the very least included a mention of the ceremonial death and rebirth of the initiates at the kimpasi house.[62] Once the initiates had been consecrated to the nkita, they reentered normal society accorded the respect and fear that their powerful association commanded in Kongo at that time.

Another prominent society, Lemba, originated in some areas with guardian nature spirits (or in other regions with ancestors) and spread throughout many of the communities located primarily on the northern side of the Nzadi River.[63] This society emerged no later than the seventeenth century, when Europeans on the Loango coast noted the presence of Malemba as an important political and social institution. In that time, Malemba included rites that linked this *"mokisi"* (nature spirit) to the king and the general well-being of the land and its inhabitants. By the nineteenth century, however, Lemba lost this particular attachment to royalty and appeared geared toward the spiritual needs of those closely associated with the regional commerce fed by Atlantic trade. Lemba emphasized fertility and marriage, while providing an institutional framework for resolving legal disputes and conducting trade among its members throughout the region. The primary function of Lemba, the enlargement of families through childbearing and marriage (a core ritual component of initiation in some variants of the society), appears in an origin story from the Cabinda region on the Atlantic coast: "*Lemba* is the spirit of peace, as its name indicates. In *Lemba*, Nzambi is asked, 'Nzambi *Lemba*, give us fecundity.' He guards us, and must be respected

[60] The reference to the "king of Kongo" here was not necessarily an allusion to the head of the Kingdom of Kongo, as Cavazzi imagined. Instead, Kongo has been a synonym for Kimpasi, as the society was also known as Fwa Kongo (the Kongo death). See Herbert Ward, "Ethnographical Notes Relating to the Congo Tribes," *Journal of the Anthropological Institute of Great Britain and Ireland* 24 (1895): 288–9; and Wing, *Études Bakongo*, 172–3.

[61] Cavazzi, *Descrição*, 1: 99; and Montesarchio, "Viaggio," 252–3.

[62] Other details about the kimpasi altar and plants associated with initiation appear in Atri, "Giornate apostoliche," 201–2.

[63] The spiritual source of Lemba varied in the different local versions of society throughout the region. See Janzen, *Lemba*, 183, 234, and 303; and Fu-Kiau, *N'Kongo*, 133–47.

and obeyed."[64] Further, as seen in this passage, the name Lemba evoked healing principles with its meaning "to calm," which found additional expression in the frequent use of *lemba-lemba* leaves in sacred medicines.[65] Both themes of promoting family and health appeared in the terminology of membership in Lemba and the special relationship created in the association. The leaders bore the titles of tata and *ngudi*, meaning "father" and "mother," respectively, while the initiates assumed the status of *mwana*, "child." In explaining the relationship, a nineteenth-century source stated, "Whoever is initiated into the secrets of *Lemba* can as 'Tata *Lemba*' pass on the order to a 'mwana *Lemba*', and when the latter, the *Lemba* child, becomes ill, he must come to his spiritual Father *Lemba* to be healed through his medicine."[66]

These descriptions of Kimpasi and Lemba delineate the basic contours of initiation societies in general, so information about Nkimba and Ndembo appears below only when it has direct bearing on the analysis of seeking. In any case, the historical and comparative study of initiation societies in Kongo reveals change over time and variation over space, but also indicates remarkable continuity in the core practices and principles within and among these societies. The interrelated characteristics of the societies were such that even the names by which the societies were known overlapped. For example, some eastern Kongo communities called the society Kimpasi ki ndembo, while central Kongo peoples identified Ndembo as Kimpasi and Nkita after the nature spirits that formed the spiritual focus of both the Ndembo and Kimpasi societies. Additionally, people used the term Kongo as a name for both Kimpasi and Ndembo.[67]

While these associations focused on initiating groups of candidates, the same process of initiation on a smaller scale accompanied the consecration of individuals to certain spirits, through which an initiate became an expert (nganga) in the composition of a nkisi (the general name for a complex that links the spirit, people, objects, and practices associated with a particular body of spiritual knowledge). Once the initiate acquired their nkisi, they became members of the community of experts with the

---

[64] Janzen, *Lemba*, 303.

[65] Janzen, *Lemba*, 3; and MacGaffey, *Art and Healing*, 136.

[66] Adolf Bastian, *Die Deutsche Expedition an der Loango-Küste* (Jena: Hermann Costenoble, 1874) 1: 172, translation given in Janzen, *Lemba*, 57. For explanations of Lemba ritual that shows the use of this terminology, see Laman, *Kongo*, 3: 113; Wing, *Études Bakongo*, 433–8; Ngoma, *Initiation*, 146; and Janzen, *Lemba*, 106–30.

[67] Wing, *Études Bakongo*, 172–3; and Ngoma, *Initiation*, 97.

same nkisi. Further, while experts of particular minkisi and members of the various initiation societies carried titles particular to their disciplines, they all bore the generic title of nganga, as their consecration to the forces and knowledge of the spiritual domain allowed them to influence the workings of the physical world.[68] The initiation process differed in scale, but the end result appeared quite similar. Both the group and individual models for initiation into spiritual associations continued to proliferate into the twentieth century, although the prominent initiation associations suffered during the colonial era from the efforts by European administrators and missionaries to undermine their influence.

We may suppose that initiation societies took on even greater meaning in the Atlantic diaspora, as the continuation of parent-child and sibling terminology among members replicated the familial model typical of these societies and represented a revealing choice for group association in the conditions of enslavement, where blood-based kinship was regularly undermined. Initiation societies thus provided a means for creating relationships with new nature spirits and between people with no prior connection, both vitally important to dislocated and distressed Africans. Further, these societies served as institutions within which elders trained the young in specific sets of knowledge and behaviors brought from Africa and considered worth maintaining in new lands.

Evidence of the continuing relevance in the Lowcountry of the principles and rituals associated with African initiation societies can be inferred from the vast inventory of African names retained in coastal communities in South Carolina and Georgia. While a few scholars have analyzed plantation records to assess naming patterns, cultural change, and possible African origins for certain names, the collection of African names recorded by Lorenzo Dow Turner in the 1930s remains an underutilized source in reconstructions of early Lowcountry cultural history.[69] As noted by Turner and subsequent scholars, African naming patterns reflected cultural values beyond the simple act of attaching labels to people. Personal names in many African societies have related to situations of birth (such as the timing or coincidence with significant events) and

---

[68] The composition of minkisi was the same process by which people went through the process of becoming an expert. For examples and explanations of both processes, see MacGaffey, *Art and Healing*; and MacGaffey, *Kongo Political Culture*, 78–133.

[69] Wood, *Black Majority*, 181–6; Cody, "There Was No Absalom," 563–96; John C. Inscoe, "Generation and Gender in Carolina Slave Naming Practices: A Challenge to the Gutman Thesis," *South Carolina Historical Magazine* 94, 4 (1993): 252–63; and Thornton, "Central African Names," 727–42.

originated with terms from regular speech that conveyed meanings associated with the named person.[70] People have devised names from the full range of vocabulary in their languages, not from a relatively small, distinct set of personal names that had no meanings in regular speech. As such, names have conveyed cultural information in ways unfamiliar to the European-based naming practices that have predominated in the Americas. Further, the acquisition of multiple names, often corresponding with life transitions (such as adulthood, marriage, childbearing) has appeared commonly in West-Central African and West African societies. The layering of names remained current in the Lowcountry when Turner conducted his research, as most people had a "real" or "true" name and a nickname or "basket" name. The first kind was usually a common English name that was used for "official purposes" (at school and in interactions with outsiders), while the second name was typically of African origin and employed among family and friends.[71] This aspect of Lowcountry naming suggests that any study of records that included only real or true names (the sources typically used by historians who have examined this issue) cannot fully account for the deeper cultural patterns in naming practices. A more thorough analysis of the cultural contexts for names documented in Turner's invaluable research thus appears warranted.

Naming arises as one of the central issues in assessing continuities between Kongo initiation societies and Lowcountry practices related to spiritual transition, as the taking of new names featured prominently in the rites of Kimpasi, Ndembo, Nkimba, and to a lesser extent in Lemba. The superficial understanding of initiation societies held by European observers during the era of the trans-Atlantic trade in captive Africans has resulted in a thin record of titles and names associated with these institutions. At the very least, Christian missionaries noted titles such as nganga, most often to identify spiritual experts generally, and nkita to name the members of Kimpasi. We must rely on the inventory of names that appear in more recent ethnography to explore possible continuities in naming practices. This certainly poses problems for those concerned with the historical value of these sources. We should keep in mind, however, that many of the titles and names employed in initiation societies have carried meanings specific to the purposes of those societies. We may expect, then, a certain degree of consistency in these titles and names that did not apply to everyday naming practices outside of the initiation

---

[70] Turner, *Africanisms*, 31–42.
[71] Turner, *Africanisms*, 40.

institutions. While we cannot uncritically assert that these same titles and names existed in older manifestations of Kimpasi, Ndembo, Nkimba, and Lemba, we also cannot discount the probability that they did appear in earlier times. The argument for cultural change requires as much evidence as the case for cultural continuity. The contemporary evidence is simply too scarce to support conclusively either interpretation in this instance. We may suppose that the parallel appearance in more recent times of the titles and names in both Kongo and the Lowcountry suggests at the very least that they did indeed exist during the era of the trans-Atlantic trade in captive Africans, although we may not be able to determine their meanings within the cultures of either region during that period. In any case, the presence of the names and titles in the Lowcountry shows that bearers arrived in the Lowcountry and their appellations were deemed worthy of passing on to subsequent generations. Whether the titles and names figured specifically into initiations in the Lowcountry or simply became part of a larger body of African-based names cannot be determined from the names alone. Nevertheless, the significance attached to them in the Kongo initiation societies and the large number of titles and names retained in the Lowcountry suggest that we acknowledge fully their possible relevance to African-descended people and their spiritual culture in the Lowcountry.

Table 10 indicates that African-descended people in the Lowcountry incorporated as many as twenty titles associated with Kimpasi, Ndembo, Nkimba, and Lemba into their repertoire of African-derived names. On the most basic level, the names for each of the four societies remained in use as the male names Paxi (based on the southern Kongo variant of Mpasi), Dembo, Kimba, and Lemba.[72] Most notable among the Lowcountry names derived from the titles was Nganga, the basic title for a spiritual expert in much of West-Central Africa and a male name in the Lowcountry.[73] In the realm of Lowcountry spiritual culture commonly referred to as "conjure" or "root," the English meaning of nganga remained in use in the title Doctor, which possessed greater meaning as an allusion to expertise than to any pretense of practice in the more limited arena of biomedical diagnostics and treatment. Although the English gloss for nganga came to predominate in the terminology of conjure, the fidelity of the term's form as a personal name marks it as exceptional among the African linguistic retentions. Most communities throughout

---

[72] Turner, *Africanisms*, 123, 147, 73, 110.
[73] Turner, *Africanisms*, 140.

TABLE 10. *Kongo Initiation Titles and Lowcountry Personal Names*

Lemba	Kimpasi	Ndembo	Nkimba	Lowcountry Names
Nganga	Nganga	Nganga	Nganga	Nganga
Ngudi Nganga	Ngudi Nganga	Ngudi Nganga	Ngudi Nganga	Gudi, Nganga
Nganga Lemba	–	–	–	Nganga, Lemba
Mwana Nganga	–	–	–	Mwana, Nganga
–	Nganga Kimpasi	–	–	Nganga, Paxi
Tata ma Lemba	–	–	–	Tata, Lemba
Malemba	–	–	–	Malemba
–	–	Ndembo	–	Dembo
–	–	–	Nkimba	Kimba
–	–	–	Zungu	Zungu
–	Ma Lubondo	–	Mbondo	Bondo
–	Na Kongo	–	Kongo	Kongo
–	Mfwa–Wasi	–	–	Fwa, Wasi
–	Nsumbu	–	–	Sumbi*
–	Mavuzi	–	–	Wuji
–	Mbila	–	–	Mbila
–	Ma Binda	–	–	Binda
–	–	Mavakala	–	Mawakala
–	–	Masamba	–	Samba
–	–	Ntiamwa	–	Tiama

Note: The term marked with an asterix was retained in conversational vocabulary, not as a personal name.
Sources: Bittremieux, *Société Secrète*, 46, 47, 77; Turner, *Africansims*; and Ngoma, *Initiation*, 78–9, 103, 108, 123.

the African-Atlantic diaspora have typically dropped the initial "n" sound from the many Bantu words that they preserved in their vocabularies. People in the Lowcountry thus rendered *goma* from ngoma to identify a drum and *tumbu* from *ntumbu* to label a calabash.[74] However, out of the thousands of African names and words retained by Lowcountry communities, only eight items exhibited the initial "n" sound, six of which derived from Bantu terms, including Nganga. The retention of an uncommon form that did not fit well within the prevailing norms of Lowcountry

[74] Turner, *Africanisms*, 194, 203.

speech indicates that this name held unusual significance for those who continued to use and those who bore it.

In Kongo, Nganga appears as part of several titles, including Ngudi Nganga, shared by all of the initiation societies and other titles specific to Kimpasi (Nganga Kimpasi) and Lemba (Nganga Lemba and Mwana Nganga). The combination of terms did not occur in the Lowcountry, although the components remained as the male names Nganga, Gudi, and Lemba and the female names Muana (Mwana) and Paxi.[75] The compound title Ngudi Nganga carried special significance as the term for the most senior experts who oversaw the initiation of new members in the major associations as well as the consecration of new experts in the composition of minkisi. The use of ngudi in titles for ritual specialists appears in a seventeenth-century missionary account from Angola that notes the *ngudi-a-nzima, ngudi-a-nsusi, ngudi-a-mbanza,* and *ngudi-a-nturi,* who provided the proper attention for twins and their parents. The title *ngudi-a-mbaca* named dwarves and "pygmies," considered exceptionally potent agents of spiritual power, as they stood as the "major authority among the *nkita* [Kimpasi members]." We must note here that West-Central Africans often perceived twins, dwarves, and "pygmies" as manifestations of the nature spirits that served as the spiritual patrons of the initiation societies.[76] Further, the core meaning of *ngudi* is "mother," although its usual application to titles has evoked the sense of "progenitor" with the association of seniority and power regardless of the gender of the title-bearer.[77]

The larger reference to concepts of the family in titles appeared most clearly in Lemba with its basic delineation of the participants in initiation as the Lemba Fathers (Ngudi Nganga and Tata ma Lemba) and Lemba Children (Mwana Nganga) mentioned above. Familial terminology permeated the titles and roles of the experts in Nkimba and Kimpasi, as well, from which African-descended people in the Lowcountry derived several personal names. Women played two of the most important roles in Nkimba as Mama Mbondo, the "mother of all the Bakhimba [members of the society]" and Mama Kongo, who initiated the members and guarded the "knife of power."[78] The names Bondo and Kongo remained in use in the Lowcountry, although the latter only as a male name. Mama

[75] Turner, *Africanisms,* 91, 123, 133, 140, 147.

[76] Cavazzi, *Descrição,* 1: 200, 255.

[77] Wing and Penders, *Plus Ancien Dictionnaire Bantu,* 254; and Laman, *Dictionnaire Kikongo,* 693.

[78] Bittremieux, *Société Secrète,* 77–9.

Mbondo maintained especially high status as a spiritual mother, as commemorated in an Nkimba song for initiates:

> *Mama Mbondo butidi muan' e!*
> *kabutidi muana, muana weka i ngongo:*
> *kàmba ulèla kilela-muan' e!*
> *ndèdila wau, yimòna kuam' e!*
> Mother Mbondo gave birth to a child, oh!
> She gave birth to a child, the child was dirty:
> Look, take care of the child, oh!
> Take care of it for me, that I might see it![79]

This song not only explained the role of Mother Mbondo but also implored those charged with looking after her spiritual children to do so with great care and to keep them from becoming unclean.

Those who directed the Kimpasi initiation, the *nganga zi kimpasi*, included the master initiator, the *ngudi nganga*, also known as Na Kongo and M'fwa-wasi and retained in the three Lowcountry names Kongo, Fwa, and Wasi.[80] While the ngudi nganga presided spiritually over the initiation, the actual work of conducting the rituals fell to the Nsumbu ("buyer"). This title did not remain in use in the Lowcountry as a personal name, but the term *sumbi*, also of Kongo origin, had the same meaning as "purchaser" in conversational vocabulary.[81] The Mavuzi served as the Nsumbu's assistant, whose title may have been preserved in the Lowcountry male name Wuji.[82] The Mbila, whose title meant literally "call," served to respond to the ngudi nganga's calls and to provide guidance in the performance of the initiation. Although this position was held only by men in Kongo, the title existed in the Lowcountry as the female name Mbila. Among the roles played by women in the initiation, the Ma Binda acted as the "mother keeper" by guarding the "forces" involved in the rituals, and the young woman known as the Ma Lubondo or the "mother lullaby" pacified the initiates as they endured the hardships of the process. The female names Binda and Bondo in the Lowcountry derived from these titles.[83]

---

[79] Bittremieux, *Société Secrète*, 77.
[80] Ngoma, *Initiation*, 78; and Turner, *Africanisms*, 89, 114, 178.
[81] Ngoma, *Initiation*, 79; and Turner, *Africanisms*, 201.
[82] Turner, *Africanisms*, 182.
[83] Lu- in Lubondo is a singular prefix the renders the terms literally as "one lullaby." As such, we can expect the prefix to be dropped, which is almost always the case in the Bantu names and terms retained in the Lowcountry as in other regions of the diaspora. Ngoma, *Initiation*, 79; and Turner, *Africanisms*, 64, 67.

At a certain point during their training and trials in the Kongo initiation societies, candidates took new names to signify their places in the associations and to link themselves through their new names to the spirits connected to the societies. Thirty-five initiation names from Kongo remained in use well into the twentieth century among African-descended people in the Lowcountry (Table 11). From the Nkimba society came seventeen names, nine for males and eight for females. In the Lowcountry, five of the male Nkimba names remained in use as male names (Lute, Kela, Kongo, Bela, and Gidi), while the other four became female names (Baka, Lusala, Landa, and Sunda). Five of the female Nkimba names retained their use for women and girls (Bondo, Keba, Sungila, Tumba, and Kuta), with two crossing gender to name men and boys (Lambi and Fuka). The female Nkimba name Mbanda-Samba formed two separate names in the Lowcountry, one (Banda) used for males and the other (Samba) for females.[84] The ten names attached to Ndembo initiates provided two Lowcountry male names (Mawakala and Kanga) that derived from male Ndembo names as well as three Lowcountry male names (Zanza, Lemba, and Lembeka) that originated in female Ndembo names. Three female Ndembo names were maintained for women and girls in the Lowcountry as Bondo, Binda, and Baka, while three other female Lowcountry names (Samba, Lema, and Tiama) came from male Ndembo names.[85] The contribution of Kimpasi initiation names included nine female names and six male names. These became ten male names (Bangula, Lumbu, Lute, Leka, Zanza, Wuji, Lemba, Banda, Zengi, and Lambi) and six female names (Beya, Bondo, Binda, Samba, Bila, and Senga) in the Lowcountry.[86] Five of the male Kimpasi names retained use as names for men and boys in the Lowcountry, while two compound Kimpasi names for males (Mavuzi-Lembi and Mbanda-Samba) corresponded with four Lowcountry names that split their gender between the male names Wuji and Banda and the female names Lemba and Samba. Five of the eight female Kimpasi names remained female names in the Lowcountry, but the other three converted to male names.

As seen in this brief review of Kongo initiation names and their retention in the Lowcountry, several names were shared by the four societies, which reflected commonalities in their core aspects as well as mutual

[84] Bittremieux, *Société Secrète*, 29, 65, 79; and Turner, *Africanisms*, 58, 61, 67, 88, 90, 107, 118, 121, 126, 163, 173.

[85] Ngoma, *Initiation*, 106; and Turner, *Africanisms*, 58, 64, 67, 105, 122, 123, 130, 155, 169, 188.

[86] Turner, *Africanisms*, 59, 60, 62, 64, 67, 121, 122, 123, 125, 126, 155, 158, 182, 188.

TABLE 11. *Kongo Initiation Names and Lowcountry Personal Names*

Kimpasi	Ndembo	Nkimba	Lowcountry Names
Bangula (m)	–	–	Bangula (m)
Beya (f)	–	–	Beya (f)
Lubondo (f)	Lubondo (f)	Mbondo (f)	Bondo (f)
Lumbu (m)	–	–	Lumbu (m)
Lutete (m)	–	Lutete (m)	Lute (m)
Mabinda (f)	Mabinda (f)	–	Binda (f)
Maleka (f)	–	–	Leka (m)
Manzanza (f)	Manzanza (f)	–	Zanza (m)
Masamba (f)	Masamba (m)	–	Samba (f)
Mavuzi-Lembi (m)	–	–	Wuji (m), Lemba (m)
Mavuzi-Mbila (m)	–	–	Wuji (m), Bila (f)
Mbanda-Samba (f)	–	Mbanda-Samba (f)	Banda (m), Samba (f)
Na Nzambi-zengi (m)	–	–	Zambi (m), Zengi (m)
Nlambi (f)	–	–	Lambi (m)
Senga (f)	–	–	Senga (f)
–	Lema (m)	–	Lema (f)
–	Lembe (f)	–	Lemba (m) [Lembeka (m)?]
–	Mbaka/Baka (f)	Baka (m)	Baka (f)
–	Mavakala (m)	–	Mawakala (m)
–	Nkanga (m)	–	Kanga (m)
–	Ntiama (m)	–	Tiama (f)
–	–	Kikeba (f)	Keba (f)
–	–	Kikela (m)	Kela (m/f)
–	–	Kinsungila (f)	Sungila (f)
–	–	Kintumba (f)	Tumba (f)
–	–	Kongo (m)	Kongo (m)
–	–	Lambi (f)	Lambi (m)
–	–	Lubela (m)	Bela (m)
–	–	Lusala (m)	Lusala (f)
–	–	Makuta (f)	Kuta (f)
–	–	Malanda (m)	Landa (f)
–	–	Masunda (m)	Sunda (f)
–	–	Mfuka (f)	Fuka (m)
–	–	Ngidi (m)	Gidi (m)

Note: "(f)" denotes female name, "(m)" denotes male name.
Sources: Bittremieux, *Société Secrète*, 29–30, 65, 79; Wing, *Études Bakongo*, 232–5; Turner, *Africansims*; and Ngoma, *Initiation*, 106.

influences. In a few cases, such as with Masamba, Mbaka, and Kongo, the gender associations of the names varied according to the particular society. While consistency in the correspondence of gender for the names in Kongo and the Lowcountry lends greater credibility to the argument that these names reveal some level of continuity of the initiation societies in the Lowcountry, the variability in Kongo suggests that changes in name gender should not be unexpected in the diaspora. Further, the significant imbalance in the proportion of males to females carried across the Atlantic to the Lowcountry would have created circumstances in which the gender-shifting of names would have been considered appropriate for those perpetuating these societies in which men, women, boys, and girls had key roles. Even with these stipulations, the high degree of fidelity to the original gender and forms of fifty-five titles and names reflects the enduring legacy of Kongo initiation societies in the Lowcountry.

THE SIMBI AND THE WHITE BABY

The experiences of the initiates in the wilderness included visions in which some encountered Jesus and angels, while many also described meeting "white" people or people "in white." These white beings acted as guides throughout the spiritual journey and at times as guardians against impeding forces (such as "the devil"). The most important function of these white beings was to present the seeker with a "bundle," typically wrapped in white cloth. Upon closer inspection, many initiates recognized this white bundle as a baby. The white bundle and white baby embodied the soul of the seeker, the finding of which formed the essential stage in the spiritual transformation of "getting through" and attaining "liberation." These features commonly appeared in the seeking narratives of older people, as recorded in the early 1930s. They mirrored and expanded the account given by missionaries in the 1840s, in which the seeker "always has a vision of a white man who talks with him, warns him, and sometimes makes him carry a burden, and in the end leads him to the river."[87] The presence of the simbi and the retention of Kongo initiation titles and names in the Lowcountry suggest that we look to aspects of Kongo spiritual culture to interpret the meanings of this stage in the seeking process. As we have seen in Chapter 3, the simbi have figured at the core of Kongo ideas and practices related to spiritual transformation.

---

[87] *Southern Christian Advocate*, 30 October 1846 and 30 October 1847, quoted in Creel, *Peculiar People*, 286.

It was in this realm of Lowcountry spiritual culture that the simbi went from their more familiar state as inhabitants of springs to beings and objects in the wilderness visions and dreams of seekers.

The meanings of the white beings, bundles, and babies during seeking in the wilderness have been either entirely overlooked or inadequately analyzed by scholars to this point. This may be because white beings can be easily understood in Christian terms as angels or Eurocentric representations of Jesus, whom some seekers did explicitly claim to encounter in their visions and dreams. If we see these as Christian symbols, they cannot be African-inspired, some might say, and thus hold little value as expressions of African spiritual cultures in the Lowcountry. Yet even this reasonable, standard interpretation of white beings needs to be reexamined. Interpretation becomes more complicated with the white bundles and babies, as these have no ready Christian analog. Neither do they appear to fit within generalizations of the cosmologies of African societies, giving an additional reason for their scholarly neglect. On closer consideration, however, knowledge of the simbi in Kongo and the Lowcountry provides an interpretive context necessary to assess the meaning of the beings, bundles, and babies. Before moving to such an assessment, we must first put the significance of white as a descriptor of beings and objects into a proper context.

The Protestant Christianity that took root among African-descended people in the nineteenth-century Lowcountry came burdened with the racism and ethnocentrism endemic in the religion of whites, who sought to use Christianity as a means to control enslaved people and then as a method to disassociate freed people from their ancestral African-inspired culture. Historian Michael Gomez has asserted, "It is an unassailable fact that American Christianity is directly responsible for the psychological impairment of many within the African-based community" because the "white slaveholder's promotion of a white god aloft in white splendor...was imagery sufficient to convey to the African a message of unmitigable disadvantage."[88] We should then expect to see "whiteness" in Christian experiences equated with the power and images of people of European descent. Indeed, we do. Charlotte Sherold of Charleston told a WPA interviewer, "The Lord must be white, because I never saw any other kind of people rise and redeem!"[89] Her statement alleged the link

---

[88] Gomez, *Exchanging Our Country Marks*, 244–5.
[89] Interview with Charlotte Sherold (Charleston) conducted by Martha S. Pinckney, Folder D-4-27B, WPA-SCL.

between spiritual power and instrumental power that inevitably found a place within the Eurocentric Christianity embraced by many of African descent.

While these words confirm the racial pathology inherent in some perceptions of Christianity, the meanings of spiritual whiteness among African-descended people cannot be reduced simply to references to European-descended people and their ideologies of dominance. The Reverend C.S. Ledbetter, pastor of the Plymouth Congregational Church in Charleston during the 1930s, commented, "The negro thinks of every-thing in Heaven as being white…solid white mass, with white gates which are opened and shut by St. Peter. The negro's conception of God is also a white mass. This white mass never takes a form and God is never impersonated in our pageants. He is only referred to and exists always in the mind."[90] The Reverend's remarks, made in the context of southern urban Christianity in the 1930s, may convey more of a theological under-standing than the ideas that circulated among lay people. Nevertheless, he could be read to suggest that whiteness to African-descended people in a fully Christian context did not emanate entirely from the Eurocentric foundations of the church in North America.[91] For example, Maria Bracey of Charleston offered her thoughts on heaven and its relation to the racial order of this world during the same era. In her estimation, "It's beautiful up there….They be no black and white; we be all alike then, and have wings and play the harp. The fine white folks of Charleston gonna be surprise when they miss and go down there, where the black and white folks burn together."[92] While believing in the popular Christian imagery of the heavenly wings and harp, Maria Bracey did not accept the idea that the power and status of whites in this life corresponded with power and status in an afterlife. Further, she insisted that the racial order did not pertain in the afterlife. The segregation of her day did not exist in either heaven or hell, and the "fine white folks" who dominated society and supported its iniquities would "miss" going on to an antiracist reward for the righteous.

Additionally, we should be aware of alternate concepts of whiteness in the Christianity of African-descended people, based on the knowledge that in many African spiritual cultures, including those of West-Central

---

[90] Interview with the Reverend C.S. Ledbetter (Charleston) conducted by Ethel M. Cohen, Folder D-4–27B, WPA-SCL.

[91] Sobel, *Trabelin' On*, 108–22.

[92] Interview with Maria Bracey (Charleston) conducted by Cassels R. Tiedeman, Folder D-4–27A-1, WPA-SCL.

Africa, whiteness has defined the color of the land of the dead and of those people, beings, and objects that have traversed the spiritual divide to appear in the visible, physical domain of the living.[93] Most notably, as we have seen already, the simbi and allied nature spirits have typically appeared as white in color and have manifested among the living as albinos.[94] This color association did not enter into the spiritual culture of West-Central Africans and West Africans through European Christian missionaries, whose ideas about whiteness and holiness may have coincided with African ideas in very general terms. The concept of white as the color of the spiritual realm has been too firmly entrenched in traditional spiritual practices in too many contexts, especially those far removed from the intrusive reach of European Christianity, and imbued with too many local meanings to have originated in a relatively recent introduction by foreign missionaries. Therefore, white beings in the visions and dreams of seekers should not be assumed to have represented the same whiteness as understood and embodied by people of European descent. In the end, we must acknowledge the uncomfortable coexistence of both Eurocentric and African-derived semiotics, especially during a transitional era in the religious history of African-descended people, when Christianity began to emerge as the dominant spiritual framework.[95]

The seekers who encountered Jesus or angels, clearly representative of the Christian tradition, said so and did not confuse or confound these figures with the unnamed white beings that appeared in their visions. Mary Smalls of James Island ascribed to Jesus the central role in the seeking process, stating that, "Jesus Christ put he hand down and reach your soul out and then you...must pray and go in the wilderness and Jesus Christ show your soul, it become a living baby."[96] This account was exceptional in that no other seeking story from the set of narratives analyzed here mentioned that Jesus removed the soul of the seeker and then led the seeker to the soul. Hester Milligan of Edisto Island drew heavily

---

[93] The most thorough analysis of the color in white in Kongo spiritual culture remains Anita Jacobson-Widding, *Red-White-Black as a Mode of Thought: A Study of Triadic Classification by Colours in the Ritual Symbolism and Cognitive Thought of the Peoples of the Lower Congo* (Stockholm: Almqvist and Wiksell International, 1979), 188–219. See also, Robert Farris Thompson and Joseph Cornet, *The Four Moments of the Sun: Kongo Art in Two Worlds* (Washington, DC: National Gallery of Art, 1981), 43; Thompson, *Flash of the Spirit*, 134–5, 138; MacGaffey, *Religion and Society*, 52; and Stuckey, *Slave Culture*, 35.

[94] Martins, *Cabindas*, 110–13; and Heusch, *Roi de Kongo*, 156–8, 213–15, 219–21.

[95] Sobel, *Trabelin' On*, xxii.

[96] LDTC, Disc 12–3367 A1.

from Christian imagery in recalling have seen "Jesus walking through a big red bakestone house...and I walk with him and the master" until they reached "a great big white house" with an angel on each side of the entrance to the house. Once inside, they stood over "a big Bible," which Jesus "fling open" and then pronounced "your soul has set free and your sins forgiven."[97] These were the only accounts that made explicit references to unambiguous Christian figures.

Hester Milligan's vision in the wilderness continued and corresponded more closely with the other descriptions of the seeking experiences, which always focused on white bundles or white babies. She recounted that after the absolution given by Jesus in the white house, he "come down" accompanied now by her leader and met with "the devil" on the left and "a white man standing 'pon the right hand side." The leader and the unidentified white man advised her to "come over this side, there's not life to that side, your left hand side; there's life to the *right* hand side." In describing her choice, she said, "He come over here to me and I gone over to the white man," who then "carry me all through a great big house.... It look like it was gold all around" and included "all the little angels" in many white rooms. She concluded:

The last thing I see been a white man. He say "Give her the big bundle." And when I take the bundle, I see a great big gutter, like a creek; like a river. And the riverside been so pretty! The water been calm. And when I take the big white bundle, he say, "You go now and cast the big white bundle just as far as you can get it." And I gone and I cast it over the riverside; and he say: "Oh!" he say, "daughter!" he say, "your soul is set free now, ain't it?"[98]

Morris Hamilton also encountered a white being: "I saw in the vision that the white man come and bless me and keep me naked...and he gave me...a baby, said 'You take care of that baby, you mind him until I come.'"[99]

Other seekers did not encounter unnamed white guides, but experienced similar spiritual struggles as each received her or his white baby. Hagar Drayton of James Island recalled:

I befind myself been in a battle when I going cross the river, and after I going cross the river I had a little bundle in my hand, and I dash the bundle in the river. And

---

[97] The "master" who accompanied the seeker and Jesus was not clearly identified in the interview, though it could be God the Father given the strong Christian references in the rest of the account. LDTC, Disc 12–3270 A1.

[98] LDTC, Disc 12–3270 A1.

[99] LDTC, Disc 12–3305 A1.

I didn't know what he is. And I went to my leader and I tell my leader and my leader says, "Well, my daughter," he says, "that's your sense." He says, "Now you must go on and fight and fight and fight until you get the prize what is for you." And I went on and I fight and I pray on and I fight and then I come get my last look. My last look was a baby. And the baby was dressed down in white. And he tell me must come to my leader and my leader would tell me...what to do...with the baby and the baby was clean and I go on to my leader, and my leader tell me say, "Well, you get through."[100]

In the end, the common feature of all of the recollections about seeking visions remained the white baby. While some seekers provided detailed narratives of journeys and ordeals as evidence of earning the right to receive the baby, others described their prelude to encountering the baby as a period of less vivid although no less intense prayer and contrition. Hester Fludd of James Island remembered her time of dedicated prayer as one of relatively peaceful yet diligent effort, with visions of digging up white objects from the soil. After enough of this kind of "working in the field," she stated, "And god bless my soul, my soul, I see then I had a baby and the baby come white dressed right neat nice and God tell me my sin is forgiven and the soul is cut free."[101]

As noted in two of the accounts above, the baby embodied the soul or as one seeker told it, the sense (spiritual intelligence) of the seeker. Other seekers provided further explanations. Rosina Cohen of Edisto Island claimed that, "When you seek religion you compelled to see that baby. And what is the baby? Your soul, your soul is the baby."[102] Morris Hamilton remarked that:

[He was given] a baby that is...my soul. When I started out to pray and...then I accomplish my work, I saw a...baby....This is your baby and you hold that baby until I come. And don't turn it loose...hold him, and wash him white....That's the soul...that's the soul. When you going to die, you know, when you going to die, then that's the soul God...take that baby from you, that's the soul. Man soul is the baby, as I understand it.[103]

In this passage, we find the notion that the baby is central not only in the spiritual birth of the seekers but also in the transition into death, although the meanings of the baby in the death phase were not addressed by others interviewed for their seeking experiences.

[100] LDTC, Disc 12–3333 B1.
[101] LDTC, Disc 12–3341 B1.
[102] LDTC, Disc 12–3274 A1.
[103] LDTC, Disc 12–3305 A1.

The features of these accounts that support the interpretation of the beings and objects in the visions as expressions of the simbi include the spiritual landscape of the visions, the prominence of the color white, and the physical forms of bundles and babies. Further, the context and aspects of spiritual transformation for seekers in the Lowcountry reflected in many ways Kongo institutions of spiritual transformation in which initiates became consecrated to nature spirits such as the simbi.

In addition to physically going into the wilderness to do the necessary work for liberation, seekers entered a spiritual landscape within their visions. The accounts quoted above frequently mentioned a key place in this spiritual landscape, a river, as the site where the seeker found the white bundle or the white baby. Others included additional details about their interaction with the river. The Reverend Brown recalled, "I was given a bundle...[with a] calico ribbon...and then I got down to the river with the bundle....I was commanded to go through a little narrow gate to go through that river."[104] The narratives of Hester Milligan and Hagar Drayton also included the act of "casting" or "dashing" the bundle into the river, which apparently represented a step necessary for some before encountering the baby. In this context, doing some kind of action with the bundle, including throwing it into the river, resembled an invocation of sorts, an act entirely appropriate when reaching the abode of a simbi.

Within the context of initiation into Protestant Christianity, we may suppose that the river that often appeared in visions represented the Jordan River, especially since some seekers spoke of crossing the river in a way evocative of Christian symbolism. Crossing, however, seemed far from essential in seeking visions and did not even occur in some accounts. Additionally, the river in visions did not serve as a source of purifying waters or symbolize in some way the rite of baptism. Morris Hamilton supervised numerous seekers and told one, who had a vision of the ocean, that she could not "'complish that yet" and only "when you join, you cross Jordan River and get cross on the other side."[105] According to this spiritual father, the metaphorical crossing of the Jordan River came only at the end of the seeking process, followed by baptism and the hand of fellowship. The river in the spiritual landscape of visions marked a point of intersection where the fundamental transition of seekers took place through contact with the white bundles and white babies, not through contact with the waters of the river.

[104] LDTC, Disc 12–3272 B1.
[105] LDTC, Disc 12–3305 A1.

The ideas that Kongo people have had about the wilderness and rivers as settings for encounters with the simbi suggest that we should consider that African-descended people in the Lowcountry understood the spiritual landscape of seeking in similar terms. As we have seen, West-Central African experts (banganga) sojourned in rivers for extended periods of time as the guests and pupils of the simbi to gain spiritual knowledge for use back on dry land. Further, peculiar stones taken from the beds of rivers have often operated as simbi objects gathered by people intending to use the power of the invisible world to influence the happenings of our visible, physical world. Just as Kongo people associated the rivers with these qualities, we can readily imagine that African-descended people in the Lowcountry also saw rivers as an ideal location to find spiritually powerful beings and objects as manifestations of the simbi.

The color white that seekers used to describe the man, bundle, and baby mentioned in seeking narratives also indentifies these beings and objects as powerful things derived from the invisible realm of the spirit world and linked to the process of spiritual transformation. Fundamental to West-Central African and West African spiritual cultures long before contact with Eurocentric Christianity in the Atlantic world, whiteness appeared in sacred items in the possession of a nganga in eighteenth-century Soyo. These items included three wooden biteke and a box that contained white powder, parrot feathers, and seashells, among other objects. This nganga apparently employed the white powder in his dealings with clients by placing it on their tongues.[106] Additionally, the European missionary Luca da Caltanisetta encountered a group of banganga, who had "painted their bodies in various manners with a kind of earth, white like chalk, called *mpeso*."[107] This was especially significant in the prominent initiation schools found throughout the Kongo-speaking realm of West-Central Africa, particularly Nkimba.

Color symbolism indicating phases of spiritual transformation operated within initiation societies in general. This process of transformation has often been expressed in relation to the *dikenga dia Kôngo*, commonly referenced in scholarly literature as the Kongo "cosmogram," a graphic representation of the stages of life transitions and spiritual development. As discussed in the previous chapter, such summary presentations of Kongo cosmology have been portrayed with symbols of a spiritual landscape, and further iterations included color codes to explain the movement

---

[106] Lucca, *Relations*, 93.
[107] Caltanisetta, *Diaire Congolais*, 100.

through this landscape. The basic cross shape of the dikenga dia Kôngo indicated the four points of the path of the sun that also marked the key stages of personal maturation and spiritual transformation, each with its corresponding color. The first stage, kala, associated with the color black, defined the process of coming into being and entering the physical world. This point represented the rising of the sun, morning, beginning, and birth, which corresponded with the father presenting his child to the nganga (expert) for initiation. From there, the second stage, takula, represented by the color red, entailed the ascent of a person into maturity. This phase included the initiate's instruction by the nganga in the highest levels of knowledge. The third transitional stage, *luvèmba*, associated with the color white, marked the descent into the spiritual world through the transition of death. This point symbolized the setting of the sun and death, which corresponds with the completion of the nganga's transmission of knowledge to the initiate, who in turn became a nganga at this stage. In the land of the dead, the fourth stage, *musoni*, signified by the color yellow, represented the inherent energy (*ngolo*) of the person, who ideally experienced further development of knowledge and charged up to transform once again into rebirth. While this process appears cyclical at this level of explanation, we can better conceptualize it as more of a spiral in that the repeated progression through the four stages leads to continued growth.[108] Even in this more general conceptualization of the meanings of color, the key stage of spiritual transformation, that of the novice becoming an initiated expert (nganga), was represented by the color white.

In the Nkimba society found in Mayombe and other areas close to the coast, the color white marked every stage of the progress of the initiates. The first stage, following the construction of the initiation enclosure, involved singing and drumming, when the lead expert (ngudi nganga) used white clay to make lines around the arms and navels of the initiates. With all of the initiates marked, they underwent a "death" and "resurrection." The experts charged with resurrecting the dead candidates used white clay to make a circle on the ground, next to which they placed the novices on their backs, while the experts engaged in many more songs that referenced themes of regeneration and long life. After this had been completed for all the initiates, the lead expert mixed bananas and white

---

[108] This summary is based on Fu-Kiau, *N'Kongo*, 117–23, 133–48; Fu-Kiau, *Self-Healing Power: Old Teachings from Africa* (Baltimore, MD: Imprint Editions, 2003), 7–10, 63–6; and Fu-Kiau, *African Cosmology*, 25–36.

clay, which the initiates had to eat as their first meal as resurrected people. Completion of this meal led to the shaving of the heads and bodies
of the novices, who then received a thorough coating of white clay. Thus
covered in white clay, the initiates returned to their village to publicly
receive their Nkimba names amidst more singing. They ventured back
to the enclosure for the prolonged period of separation and instruction
in the various forms of knowledge particular to Nkimba. After enduring numerous ordeals and exams, those deemed worthy concluded the
wilderness phase by going to a stream where the experts immersed certain initiates three times in the waters, which led to all the novices then
washing the white clay from their bodies to prepare for the great revelry
and feasting that accompanied their return to normal society as experts
(banganga) of Nkimba.[109]

The initiation society of Lemba, variations of which existed in many
parts of the larger Kongo-speaking region, centered on the encounters
with the spiritual whiteness of mpemba as both clay and a distinct domain
of spiritual transition. Lemba in Mayombe was "enacted with white
chalk [clay], given during its consecration."[110] In Lemba in Manianga,
those prepared for the "the descent to Lemba" entered the final stage of
initiation which entailed direct encounters with spirits at a stream in a
valley (ndimba). As part of the spiritual landscape of initiation, the valley and stream provided a setting that symbolized the spiritual realm in
opposition to the Lemba lodge, located on a savanna hilltop where the
neophytes received the proper preparation for the last phase. Further, this
descent to Lemba represented a journey to Mpemba, the land of the dead
and the same name given to the white clay taken from river beds. At this
stage, experts wearing Lemba masks marked with white, red, and black
lines and adorned with black feathers encircled the novice while moving
their heads and singing songs that heightened the intensity of the moment
and explained the meanings of the masks:

> O! *Tala!*
> *Tala matebo!*
> *O nkuyu!*
> *E Mpungu-tulendo!*
> *Banganga, ka tuswama ko e?*
> *Bakulu ku mpemba!*

---

[109] Laman, *Kongo*, 3: 244–56. Bittremieux (*Société Secrète*) presents a more detailed and
   varied description of Nkimba, although the uses of white materials, especially white
   clay, conforms to the account in Laman.
[110] J. Konda, translated by Janzen, *Lemba*, 234.

Bukulu ku mpemba!
O! Mpemba!
Oh! Look!
Look at the demons!
Oh the devil!
God Almighty!
The nganga, are we not hidden?
Ancestors in Mpemba!
Ancestors in Mpemba!
Oh! Mpemba![111]

The initiates who could handle the fear and uncertainty of this experience passed the ultimate test of Lemba, which led to a stage in which the experts revealed the meanings of the initiation process to the novices, and the novices swore the Lemba oath.[112] The encounter with *matebo* and *nkuyu* (both evil spirits in this context) in addition to God Almighty and the ancestors (who, broadly speaking, included lineal ancestors and nature spirits) resembled the remarks of Charlotte Sherold of Charleston: "When you travelin'…you got to travel with good and bad spirits."[113] Contact with the devil and with the white man mentioned in the seeking or traveling accounts in the Lowcountry corresponded with the interaction with various spirits in the descent to Lemba. Additionally, the appearance of the stream or river in this phase of spiritual transformation indicated that the initiate had entered the white realm of Mpemba. It seems, then, that we must consider the white bundles and white babies encountered in the phase of seeking as material indicators of contact with the realm of spirits. In other words, we are dealing with minkisi (the bundles) and bisimbi (the babies).

Interpreting the bundles as minkisi requires a few words on the composition and meanings of minkisi. Scholars have sought to define minkisi generally, but the focus here is on a few key concepts.[114] First, minkisi have not served simply as "fetishes" or "charms" in the ethnocentric sense that prevails in the accounts of European Christian visitors to West-Central Africa. The physical objects that have formed the visible components of minkisi were not the sources of spiritual power that have allowed the makers, keepers, and consumers of minkisi to access the forces of the spiritual world to influence the happenings in the physical world. Instead,

[111] Fu-Kiau, *N'Kongo*, 139.
[112] Fu-Kiau, *N'Kongo*, 139–40; and Janzen, *Lemba*, 190–4.
[113] Interview with Charlotte Sherold (Charleston) conducted by Martha S. Pinckney, Folder D-4-27B, WPA-SCL.
[114] See especially, Young, *Rituals of Resistance*, 105–33.

the minkisi have served as the containers for the spiritual forces that exist in this physical world through the objects employed in the composition of minkisi. The objects themselves reveal both the meanings attached to the spirits that animate the minkisi and the purposes that inspired the composition of the minkisi. The second key point is that the materials that have served as containers have often been lengths of cloth bound up to form bundles or sacks as well as small pouches worn like amulets. While many contemporary observers and later scholars have fixated upon the anthropomorphic statues (biteke) that represent one category of nkisi containers, the bundle or bag has more often been the predominant container for minkisi, or at least the most common container within another container.[115]

People in seventeenth- and eighteenth-century Kongo routinely received small bags from spiritual experts that they wore around their necks. Others suspended pouches made from animal skins such as that of snakes, filled with shells, takula (powder made from red wood), and other objects.[116] Experts also prepared nkisi bundles made of cloth to put on stakes placed in fields to protect the crops from thieves.[117] Additionally, nature spirits communicated through banganga to help people redress serious community misfortunes (such as epidemics and excessive deaths) by instructing the inhabitants of afflicted villages to place palm nuts in raffia cloth bags and hang them from the forked stands. These sacks on the forked stands were then placed on a mound of offerings, comprising a *bumba kindongo* altar. Groups of nature spirits, represented by the multiple palm nuts in each cloth bag, thus worked with the living to resolve the problems of the community, revealing the meaning of bumba kindongo as a kind of "collective medicine." An assemblage of this kind could include as many as 200 bundles.[118] Unfortunately, accounts of nkisi bundles from the era of the Atlantic trade in captive Africans remain relatively scarce, as the attentions of foreigners seemed drawn more to the biteke forms of minkisi, which tended to better resemble European preconceptions of demonic "fetishes" and "idols."

Early twentieth-century descriptions of the nkisi Mbumba, most likely related to the eighteenth-century bumba kindongo, noted that it was "a very ancient, well-known and feared nkisi."[119] Its basic container consisted

[115] Laman, *Kongo*, 3: 72.
[116] Caltanisetta, *Diaire Congolais*, 71, 107.
[117] Lucca, *Relations*, 142.
[118] Caltanisetta, *Diaire Congolais*, 81–2.
[119] Laman, *Kongo*, 3: 100.

of a piece of raffia cloth that held so many items that the bundle had to be placed in a large basket. The extensive inventory of objects incorporated into the nkisi included much more than the palm nuts described for bumba kindongo, although nuts of various kinds comprised key medicines, as did white clay (mpemba). Further, the Mbumba bundle had small sea shells and a double bell attached to its exterior.[120] Its complicated composition in its twentieth-century manifestation reflected its antiquity, wide acceptance, and general applicability to treating a variety of illnesses. The name of the nkisi also revealed its spiritual source of power as the old and well-known nature spirit Mbumba. Another aged nkisi that included bundles and "derive[d] from bisimbi" was Mbenza, which utilized simbi stones as the key spiritual objects in addition to other medicines. During the composition of Mbenza, the experts searched for the simbi stones and other objects associated with the simbi. When one in the group of experts searching in the forest encountered a "beautiful white stone," the nganga called out, "A *mwana*! Oh! A child! A small fetish stone!" The experts then treated the simbi stone as a child, handling it delicately, ultimately placing it next to its "mother" (presumably the larger stone of Mbenza) in the container back in the village. Such a discovery allowed for the healing and initiation of the person for whom the experts had undertaken the composition of Mbenza.[121] Subsequent steps entailed the experts painting themselves white and red with clays, while painting the simbi stones white and singing:

> O mavundu mu
> Meeso ma ndubukila [ndwenga].
> Ngondo yo bakila
> Mpembe u yaya.
> Oh, lines around the eyes,
> the eyes of understanding.
> White it is,
> They mark with chalk.[122]

The composition of Mbenza also included wrapping the simbi stones in cloth and assembling the other medicine bundles within cloth.[123]

As old minkisi, both Mbumba and Mbenza served many purposes. Both, however, had gained renown for their utility in promoting fertility,

---

[120] Laman, *Kongo*, 3: 101; and MacGaffey, *Art and Healing*, 64–70.
[121] Bittremieux, *Société Secrète*, 141–2.
[122] MacGaffey, *Art and Healing*, 60. The differences in the punctuation in the Kikongo original and the English translation appear in MacGaffey's text.
[123] Laman, *Kongo*, 3: 129–31; and MacGaffey, *Art and Healing*, 53–60.

as they could "open the womb for a rich progeny."[124] In short, the simbi, color white, and medicine bundles coalesced in these minkisi to produce babies. This also may explain why the Mbenza stone was described as a child by its finder. These associations derived from fundamental and long-established concepts that certainly existed in earlier times, even if they had not yet been connected to the precursors or early versions of Mbumba and Mbenza. Further, recognizing these associations allows us to reveal the meanings of the white babies who appeared in the visions of seekers in the Lowcountry.

The examples of the position of Mama Mbondo in the Nkimba society, discussed earlier in this chapter, and the treatment of the Mbenza stone reveal the central importance of babies as spiritual beings and symbols in Kongo cultures. Indeed, throughout many Bantu cultures, infants and those with the appearance of infants (as in cases of dwarfism) have been associated with "exceptional spirituality."[125] In Kongo communities, twins and albinos have possessed this status along with direct connections to the simbi, as both kinds of children have been considered nature spirits. Those initiated into the societies dedicated to nature spirits underwent initiation in part because they were not born with a special relationship with nature spirits, unlike twins, albinos, and other "sacred children."[126] Through "nkita death" and rebirth in their initiation, however, they became reconstituted as "nkita people" (in terms specific to Kimpasi), thus achieving union with the nature spirits that they did not experience at birth.

In the interpretation presented here, the white beings and bundles represented manifestations of and containers for the power of the simbi, but it was through the white babies alone that seekers attained liberation. The fact that the white babies were described as the seeker's soul attests to a profound spiritual transformation focused on the babies, a transformation that could only be achieved in the wilderness (the land of the dead) and with these objects found there. I refer to the white babies as objects, because they did not embody persons or real babies, as the seekers made clear. The white babies represented spiritual things, not unlike the Mbenza stone, and in this context constituted bisimbi. The use of the

---

[124] Laman, *Kongo*, 3: 129.

[125] Klieman, "Of Ancestors and Earth Spirits," 47, 58. This may be another Niger-Congo legacy when considered along with Alma Gottlieb's study of children in Beng communities in Côte d'Ivoire, *Afterlife is Where We Come From: The Culture of Infancy in West Africa* (Chicago, IL: University of Chicago Press, 2007), 79–104.

[126] Laman, *Kongo*, 2: 6–8; and MacGaffey, "Twins, Simbi Spirits, and Lwas," 213.

plural form bisimbi here emphasizes the "thing-ness" of the simbi stones and the white babies in contrast to the clearer association with person-hood implied in the plural form basimbi (associated with "sacred chil-dren," for example). While a distinction between an object and person in spiritual matters such as this has not been as firm as we might imagine, the subtle difference here is key. The white baby object (the equivalent of a simbi stone) provided the "physical" embodiment of the simbi that a "normal" person needed to become consecrated to the spirit.[127]

Another aspect of the experience with the white baby elucidates this connection with bismbi and consecration to nature spirits. Most of the narratives also mention the white babies as clean or the seekers having to clean their babies. As Rosina Cohen recounted, "That baby is white and they tell you take that baby....Wash him off and make him clean and hand him to you. And then it bless my soul...wash off my baby nice and clean."[128] We can view this as symbolic of purity or the act of purification. Once a seeker received her baby, she knew that that her "soul is set free," liberated from an earlier life of sin and spiritual bondage. Additionally, the idea of cleaning or washing the baby reflected the same principle that informed the painting of simbi stones white, as with the Mbenza stone. The overlap of these concepts appeared in the retention of south-ern Kongo term *tunia* by African-descended people in the Lowcountry. In South Carolina, the word meant "very clean." It derived from the south-ern Kongo meanings of "excessive whiteness" and "cleanness" (tunia) as well as "whiteness, cleanness, purity" (*ntunia*).[129] According to several seekers who underwent the process in the late nineteenth or early twen-tieth century in Beaufort County, the recovery of white babies (or in one case, a white pigeon) was equivalent to the act of cleaning in the seeking visions.[130] In the end, cleaning the white baby served as an act of conse-cration that confirmed the union of the seeker and the spirit. This con-secration of the seeker through the white baby marked the fundamental transformation of the seeker – "your sins are forgiven and your soul set free" – not baptism, although that water rite remained essential to the process of "becoming Christian."[131]

We must consider that the appearance of the white baby resonates in some ways with exclusively Christian meanings. Certainly, the white

---

[127] On the "personhood of objects," see MacGaffey, *Kongo Political Culture*, 78–96.
[128] LDTC, Disc 12–3274 A1.
[129] Turner, *Africanisms*, 203; and Bentley, *Dictionary*, 402, 436.
[130] Kuyk, *African Voices*, 86.
[131] Mollie Robinson, Guy Benton Johnson Papers, SHC.

baby evokes the idea of rebirth that conforms with the familiar Christian notion of being "born again." The Christian concept of being born again, however, does not suit the larger context of the transformation within the seeking journey. The wilderness setting, the white beings, and the river as a place of spiritual interaction (not a water body of purification) contextualized the encounter with the white baby as far more reminiscent of Kongo perceptions of mfinda, kalunga, and the simbi. Further, the encounter with the white baby was not the outcome of "liberation," but its cause. Only after initiates found and cleaned the white baby did they receive forgiveness and attain liberation. Finally, and most importantly, none of the seeking stories described the white baby as the seeker reborn. While it is possible to view the white baby as a Christian symbol, we might better identify it as a meta-Christian symbol that could coincide with Christian concepts although its origins and core meanings derived from another source that seekers considered essential to the seeking. Substantiating this interpretation of the white baby as a meta-Christian symbol is the fact that the white baby ceased to be an aspect of the seeking process as the twentieth century progressed. The narratives that mentioned the white baby came predominantly from people who had undergone the seeking experience in the nineteenth century. The accounts of those who did their seeking well into the twentieth century recounted the appearance of the white baby far fewer times and not at all in more recent seeking experiences.[132] Had the white baby been considered essentially Christian and equivalent with being born again, we would expect it to remain central to the seeking process, which had taken on more obviously Christian symbols and meanings over the course of the twentieth century. In the end, the white baby retained meaning for those involved in the earlier stages of the transition to Protestant Christianity, yet lost significance for later generations who had much less experience with the older African-inspired spiritual cultures that informed the formation of the Christian ritual among African-descended people in the nineteenth century.

Interpreting the white bundles as minkisi and the white babies as bisimbi, indicative of the consecration and spiritual transformation of the seeker, allows us to reconceptualize the baptism rite as rebirth and

---

[132] While a quantitative assessment is not possible (and unwarranted given the individualistic nature and variation typical in seeking narratives), the eventual disappearance of the white baby is clear. See Lawton, "Religious Life," 150, 155; and Johnson, "Pray's House Spirit," 8–38. Johnson's essay addresses practices in the second half of the twentieth century and does not include any reference to the white baby.

reemergence. This understanding corresponds with Kongo processes of spiritual transformation in that the final stage of transformation entailed leaving the spiritual domain (the land of the dead) to reenter normal society. Just as the Nkimba initiates went into the river to wash the white clay from their bodies to mark the end of their spiritual journey and prepare to return to the village, Christian initiates in the Lowcountry experienced baptism as the means of washing off the physical and spiritual residue of their passage. The account of the 1863 baptism presided over by Siah and the Reverend Phillips included the details that the candidates appeared "dressed for the water in miserable looking clothing" with handkerchiefs on their heads. Those baptized were taken away to change clothes in private and then reappear next in public at the church "in shiny robes" with "a great difference in their looks when they came into the church."[133] Recall that the sins of seekers had been forgiven during the vision with the white babies, so the baptism rite did not confer absolution of sin. Instead, it served to cleanse the initiate of the sins that had already been forgiven. In this practice, the conjunction of the physical and spiritual landscape converged, as the baptism occurred when the tide ebbed back to sea regardless of the time of day. According to a Beaufort County minister in the 1930s, "They baptizes the candidate in the outgoing tide so the tide can carry the sins on out to the deeps of the sea. If you baptize in the incoming tide, the water will wash the sins right back up on them."[134] In the terms of Kongo spiritual transformation, the final water rite also represented passing through kalunga once again, this time to leave the land of the dead. Annette Lindsay's recollection of her baptism suggests that she may have experienced her baptism ritual in a similar way:

I baptize at Sandy Island....When I gone down in the water I see something white before me and I ain't know yet what it been but I never flutter at all, and I ain't been make sick from it. I ain't been baptize in a pool. I baptize in the big river. It the right thing to be baptize.[135]

The something white she saw in the big river provided a color indicator of the transition from the spiritual world through kalunga into her new life as a baptized Christian. With this last water rite, the initiate completed the process of spiritual transformation that satisfied both the

---

[133] David Thorpe to John Mooney, 25 January 1863, David Franklin Thorpe Papers, SHC, quoted in Creel, *Peculiar People*, 293–4.

[134] Lawton, "Religious Life," 27–8.

[135] Annette Lindsay (Charleston), interviewed by Cassels R. Tiedeman, Folder D-4–27A-1, WPA-SCL.

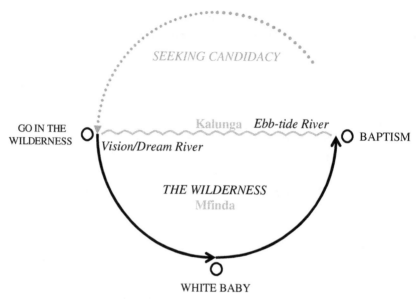

FIGURE 7. Seeking in the Lowcountry Spiritual Landscape.
Source: Author's original design.

model of the older Kongo institutions and that of the new Lowcountry Christian church.

The enduring importance of simbi figures in seeking may have been ensured because African-descended people conceptualized transformation in ways that maintained the Kongo spiritual landscape (Figure 7). From going in the wilderness to baptism, the process closely resembled the sojourn in the land of the dead for those undergoing initiation into the major societies or into the disciplines of spiritual experts. The first penetration of kalunga came in the encounter with the river in the dream or vision state while in the wilderness (the equivalent of the Kongo mfinda). This signaled that the real work of transformation was about to begin. Finding the white bundle and white baby and then cleaning the white baby marked the culmination of the white stage of transformation in mfinda. Once completed, the seeker began the journey back to the land of the living, the realm of the initiated and of Christian community, which was achieved through the second penetration of kalunga in the rite of baptism, conducted in a river affected by the power of the sea. In both physical and symbolic ways, the ebb-tide river baptism represented the engagement of the seeker with the transformative power of kalunga and the powerful spirits from that realm.

Scholars have credited Roman Catholicism with providing the personages of saints and cultic observances that African-descended people used
as "cover" for their veneration of African spirits, thus giving an institutional structure to preserve older beliefs in a new spiritual context.[136]
The example of the simbi-inspired figures in the Protestant Christianity
of the Lowcountry, however, reveals that African-descended people did
not need the props of the European cults of Jesus to devise the means
to uphold their dedication to the spirits who had protected their ancestors for countless generations. None of the Anglican, Methodist, or
Baptist missionaries spoke of the white beings, bundles, and babies in
their teachings about conversion. African-descended people incorporated these elements into their understanding of Protestant Christianity
because the meanings of the simbi-inspired figures in spiritual transformation were already established and helped make sense of the transition
into the new faith. The great irony of this development was that the same
Kongo spirits, who played key roles in the personal transformation of
seekers and the larger cultural transition into more conventional forms
of Protestant Christianity, ceased to be relevant to later generations once
the new faith had become the only faith.

The simbi remained for some time in the changing spiritual culture
of African-descended communities as Protestant Christianity emerged to
become the dominant religious framework in the Lowcountry, but they
did so only as unnamed entities and objects. This shift into anonymity
pointed toward the larger trend, in which the simbi faded altogether
from the key process of spiritual transformation. The loss was tied to the
changing significance of the spiritual landscape in the experience of seeking. By the 1930s, an exceptionally large proportion of younger seekers
(those still attending school) no longer sought to go to the wilderness by
spending their nights in the forests and fields of the physical landscape.
Instead, they prayed inside their homes, in their yards, in the church, or
in the praise house for their work, and in these man-made locations they
had the visions in which they found salvation.[137] Very few even called the
outside sites where some did their seeking the wilderness, unlike older

---

[136] Roger Bastide, *African Civilisations in the New World*, trans. Peter Green (New York:
Harper and Row, 1971), 152–70; Raboteau, *Slave Religion*, 87–8; and Young, *Rituals
of Resistance*, 6–7.

[137] Lawton, "Religious Life," 146–7; and Johnson, "Pray's House Spirit," 22, 28. Lawton's
chapter on "Methods of Admission to Church Membership" ("Religious Life," 129–84)
included much that showed significant generational differences in the experiences of
those joining the Christian community during the 1930s.

people, who continued to use the wilderness as the most common term for the domain of seeking. It should come as no surprise that seekers ceased to come into contact with the simbi figures and instead encountered unambiguously Christian entities almost always in the forms of God and Jesus.[138] The realm of seeking had become domesticated and conventionalized to the extent that the simbi no longer had a place in Lowcountry Protestant Christianity. With this, the simbi as unnamed spiritual guardians in the wilderness of seeking died one last time, never to be reborn again in the spiritual landscape of the South Carolina Lowcountry.

[138] For late twentieth-century seeking narratives, see Johnson, "Pray's House Spirit," 20, 27–8.

6

Mermaid Histories and Power

Oh, yes, Sir; it was a mermaid; they see her here in this here very shop, in a tub, in the cellar. All of them old people can tell you about her. Yes, Sir; that is the mermaid history.

– Araminta Tucker

What Araminta Tucker remembered as "the mermaid history" was no fairy tale. It was an event of social protest by African-descended people instigated by a spiritual crisis. This crisis took the form of an unrelenting deluge caused by a mermaid held captive in the city of Charleston, and it reflected the continuing struggle of black people to gain political recognition from white authorities during the nineteenth century. Why would Araminta Tucker describe the event and its circumstances as the mermaid history? What possible relevance could a mermaid have in any discussion of political action? Once again, awareness of the meanings that people have associated with the simbi in Kongo and other parts of the African-Atlantic diaspora provides the basis for understanding the transformation of the identity of Lowcountry simbi into mermaids. Just as people of African descent began to reconceptualize the simbi as guardians and white babies in the emerging expressions of Protestant Christianity, they also devised a way to discuss openly the spiritual basis of power in a racially oppressive society that did not readily tolerate the idea of such talk from those of a supposedly servile and subordinate caste. Indeed, stories of mermaids concealed an older and culturally grounded narrative strategy used to remember the past and critique the present in Kongo and the African-Atlantic diaspora as well as the Lowcountry.

Recall from Chapter 3 that stories of the simbi and other nature spirits linked these entities to the historical events of the land of the living. The renewal of relationships of the simbi with the living during the founding of villages commemorated and atoned for the physical and emotional violence visited upon the original inhabitants of the land by the earliest Kongo ancestors who settled there. The creation of the state of Soyo and its political geography have been explained by traditions of the journey of the simbi child Ne M'binda. Further south in Angola, accounts of the kilundu detailed the transformation of these spirits as a direct response to the traumatic events of an earlier era. Traditions documented in the mid-seventeenth century indicated that the kilundu initially existed as spirits of the dry land, but became spirits of the springs and rivers as a result of the conquests perpetrated by the Imbangala, discussed in Chapter 3. The intensely vicious invasion of the Jaga drove the original spirits of the land into the waters to take shelter. Only after the passage of much time did these spirits overcome their terror to reassert their power from their new abodes and defeat the invaders of their domains. Another tradition told of how the old spirits of the land fled from the terrible advance of the Jaga filled with grief over the killing of their devotees. As they wept, their powers flowed with their tears into the waters of the region, thus giving birth to the female spirits of the lagoons and the male spirits of the springs and rivers. Following this transformation of spiritual power, the people venerated these water spirits, asking the spirits to spare them from afflictions, particularly disease, and to give them comfort during troubles.[1]

Most important for this chapter, the experiences of the trans-Atlantic trade in captive Africans became intertwined with ideas about the simbi, as well. In Chapter 3, we saw how some West-Central Africans reimagined the simbi as something other than benevolent spirits that protected the natural environment and inhabitants of their domains. As the expanding Atlantic trade threatened communities throughout West-Central Africa over centuries, many began to perceive the simbi as agents of Atlantic commerce who manufactured the cloth traded by European merchants and seized the living to take them into the sea as laborers. In the turmoil of world upset by the trade in captives, however, people in Kongo also told stories of the simbi as saviors of children abandoned by their families, which may have reflected the great traumas connected to the increasing incidents of the kidnapping and selling of children into local forms of bondage and the trans-Atlantic trade. The same process of using evolving

[1] Cavazzi, *Descrição*, 2: 66.

relationships with nature spirits to explain past and present concerns played out in West African societies, as well.[2] This tendency may have been another legacy of the Niger-Congo ancestors shared by so many of the peoples in West-Central Africa and West Africa whose communities were ravaged by the trade in and enslavement of Africans in the Atlantic world. Ultimately, those consigned to the Middle Passage and American slavery carried with them the range of ideas about nature spirits and captivity. It is telling that African-descended people often chose to talk about these spirits as mermaids, and just as often they talked about them as champions of the oppressed and avengers of the enslaved. With their stories of mermaids, they remembered slavery, renewed their relationships with the simbi, and asserted understanding of the immorality of captivity and domination that had both spiritual and political meanings.

LOWCOUNTRY MERMAIDS

Lowcountry mermaids have appeared in two forms in the stories of African-descended people. One portrayed a river mermaid as a surrogate mother for a girl whose mother had died and whose father neglected her. Unfortunately, the girl's father shot the mermaid, and the girl drowned attempting to reunite with her slain guardian. This narrative grapples with the suffering caused by the violence of men, the vulnerability of children, fragile familial bonds, and the spiritual crises that arose from these trials and tribulations. Such themes have figured prominently in Kongo stories about children killed by their fathers, but who regained life, prosperity, and the unity of their families through the care and support provided by the simbi. The tragic ending of the deaths of the nurturing water spirit and the girl remains unique to the Lowcountry narrative, however. This mermaid represents a once-powerful spirit who could not rectify the suffering and oppression of one of her spiritual children. It evokes the concern seen in Chapter 4 that the Lowcountry simbi would die or leave their springs and thus abandon the living. It is hard not to see the violence and agony of enslavement woven into the fear of the simbi leaving and the heartrending conclusion to the story of the mermaid and the girl.[3]

---

[2] Robert M. Baum, *Shrines of the Slave Trade: Diola Religion and Society in Precolonial Senegambia* (New York: Oxford University Press, 1999); Elizabeth Isichei, *Voices of the Poor in Africa* (Rochester, NY: University of Rochester Press, 2002), 25–64; and Shaw, *Memories of the Slave Trade*, 46–69.

[3] The Lowcountry mermaid story is titled "The Mermaid" and appears in Parsons, *Folklore of the Sea Islands*, 137–8. The Kongo stories come from John H. Weeks, *Congo Life and*

The second form taken by Lowcountry mermaids appears in the telling of the mermaid history, in which captive mermaids punish the living for denying their liberty. Described by the white fiction writer and pioneering folklorist John Bennett as "an aged, reputable, and eminently respectable negro nurse of Charleston," Araminta Tucker provided the following account:

Yes, Sir; about that mermaid; I remember her well. I was a young gal then, Sir; the man what marry my daughter was porter in this here drug-store. Doctor Trott kept the drug-store then. That was a long time ago, Sir, before the war. It rain! My God, it de rain! Every day it rain more. Then they say, 'Twas because Doctor Trott got a mermaid in here; right here where I standing this minute. He got her in water; they going die if you ain't. These here mermaid been one-half fish tail, the other half woman. This here mermaid Doctor Trott had, done stray up here en a boat, somehow, I don't know. They say these mermaid have lovers on land, and they follow them up; I don't know about that. This mermaid been in this very shop; in a tub of water; and it rain; my God! Sir! How it de rain! It rain daily, until they ain't no dryness anywhere left. And then the people find out about this here mermaid; and they files complaints with the city; and the city force Doctor Trott to put that mermaid back; and if he ain't de put that mermaid back in the sea, and stop that continual rain, they going fine him; and if he ain't pay the fine, they going send him up the road; yes, Sir; they going send him up to jail. So Doctor Trott he though better of it, and he put that mermaid back. Oh, yes, Sir; it was a mermaid; they see her here in this here very shop, in a tub, in the cellar. All of them old people can tell you about her. Yes, Sir; that is the mermaid history. You is quite welcome, Sir. Any of the old folks could tell you about it, Sir.[4]

This description supplied one of the key sources for Bennett's stylized retellings of the event in two published forms, one in his novel *The Treasure of Peyre Gaillard* and another as the tale "The Apothecary and the Mermaid," both of which included information from multiple reports recorded by Bennett about mermaids and Charleston's "mermaid riot."[5]

Folklore (London: The Religious Tract Society, 1911), 406–9; and Suzanne Comhaire-Sylvain, *Qui Mange avec une Femme: Contes Zairois et Haitiens* (Bandundu, Zaire: CEEBA, 1973), 73–7. I have analyzed "The Mermaid" in greater detail in Ras Michael Brown, "'But the Mermaid Did Not Rise Up': The Death of a Simbi in the Carolina Lowcountry," *Southern Quarterly* 42, 4 (2010): 120–50.

[4] John Bennett, "Mr. John Bennett Replies to Certain Criticisms of His Novel, 'The Treasure of Peyre Gaillard' – That 'Mermaid Riot,'" *New York Times*, 26 January 1907. For an overview on Bennett's work on the culture and folklore of African-descended people in the Lowcountry, see Harlan Greene, *Mr. Skylark: John Bennett and the Charleston Renaissance* (Athens: University of Georgia Press, 2010), 90–142.

[5] John Bennett, *The Treasure of Peyre Gaillard* (New York: The Century Co., 1906); and John Bennett, *The Doctor to the Dead: Grotesque Legends & Folk Tales of Old Charleston* (New York: Rinehart and Company, 1943), 221–31.

In "The Apothecary and the Mermaid," Bennett included elements that enhanced the story for effect, of course, but also other details that reflected how African-descended people perceived the event. One that deserves special notice relates that some people thought that "the mermaid had a baby in the sea, and that, until she was released to go back to nurse her child, the rain would continue to fall."[6] Additionally, Bennett's explanation of the sources he used to construct his stories included the observation that the onset and duration of the rain described by Araminta Tucker resonated with the "common superstition of the Africans" in Charleston that the source of the deluge came from the capture of a mermaid. Further, Bennett stated, "Of my own knowledge I know the belief still to be general, even among fairly well-informed and intelligent colored people, that the forcible detention of a mermaid upon land produces torrents of rain only to be ended by the mermaid's return to the sea, whence she came." To many, this notion explained similar downpours, such as that experienced in 1906.[7]

The accounts of the mermaid history collected and employed to compose Bennett's tale "The Apothecary and the Mermaid" reveal that the African-descended and European-descended people who knew of the event regarded it as a fundamentally political incident. In Araminta Tucker's explanation, the efforts of African-descended people compelled city authorities to force Doctor Trott to release a captive mermaid. While Bennett appeared satisfied (at least in publication) with characterizing the meaning of the mermaid as a mere "common superstition," Araminta Tucker's story emphasized that the people rose because of the mermaid, and the city acted at the behest of the African-descended community to ensure the release of the mermaid and end the public crisis. While this

---

[6] Bennett, *Doctor to the Dead*, 225.

[7] Bennett, "Bennett Replies." The period for Araminta Tucker's mermaid history came a decade after the appearance of P.T. Barnum's traveling exhibit of the "Feejee Mermaid," which reached Charleston in 1843. Although the exhibit generated much attention and sparked heated debate over the authenticity of the "mermaid," its effect on African Americans in Charleston may have been less pronounced, as neither Bennett nor any of his African-American informants in Charleston drew connections between the exhibit and the "riot" or Lowcountry mermaids in general. See Greene, *Mr. Skylark*, 121, 304n20. For the context for the showing of the "Feejee Mermaid," see Sally Gregory Kohlstedt, "Entrepreneurs and Intellectuals: Natural History in North American Museums," in *Mermaids, Mummies, and Mastodons: The Emergence of the American Museum*, ed. William T. Alderson (Washington, DC: American Association of Museums, 1992), 32–4; James W. Cook, *The Arts of Deception: Playing with Fraud in the Age of Barnum* (Cambridge, MA: Harvard University Press, 2001), 73–118; and Molly Rogers, *Delia's Tears: Race, Science, and Photography in Nineteenth-Century America* (New Haven, CT: Yale University Press, 2010), 73–85.

incident did not address a particular political or economic end (objectives that we might consider appropriate materialist motivations), we can
interpret the mermaid as a symbol for collective action potent enough
to lead African-descended people to rise up, demand a response, and get
what they asked for. For African-descended people, the mermaid provided a site of memory, a figure at the center of events focused on captivity and emancipation through which they reconstructed their own history
of struggle and, in this case, triumph.

In the memories of white Charlestonians, however, this history
became the Mermaid Riot, a label that conveyed an entirely different
interpretation of the actions of African-descended people. Dr. William
Schwettmann, a subsequent proprietor of the shop (Apothecaries' Hall),
and William Ostendorf, a witness of the event, informed Bennett that
the Mermaid Riot transpired in the early 1850s, which corresponded
with the yellow fever epidemics in 1852 and 1854 that provided an environment of anxiety and unrest.[8] According to these informants, in this
context, "The lower classes of the city, the negroes, were in an excited
condition, to begin with." Based on these circumstances, a "mob of black
people...made desperate by superstitious fears, attempted to enter the
shop" by force. Further, "It became necessary, for safety, to call upon the
police and city authorities to disperse the excited mob, who were in so
restless, unsatisfied, and dangerous state of mind" that the group quieted
only after agreeing to have representatives from the African-descended
community (identified by Bennett in "The Apothecary and the Mermaid"
as Old Man Rutter, William Holmes, and Joe Cole) accompany the police
and a group of white men (labeled in Bennett's tale as "white men of the
gentry class") in searching the apothecary for evidence of the mermaid.
They found nothing, and the crowd that packed the streets surrounding the shop at the corner of Broad and King dispersed without further
incident.[9]

In all three of the accounts, the city leaders worked with representa-
tives of the black community to peacefully resolve the protest. Araminta
Tucker, however, did not include depictions of mobs and violence, while
Schwettmann and Ostendorf did assert such negative characterizations.
Bennett heightened the latter sentiment in "The Apothecary and the
Mermaid," in which the unrelenting rain and its destructive effects served

[8] On yellow fever epidemics, see Joseph I. Waring, *A History of Medicine in South Carolina,
    1825–1900* (Charleston: South Carolina Medical Association, 1967), 32; and McCandless,
    Slavery, Disease, and Suffering, 60–83, 106–24.
[9] Bennett, "Bennett Replies," 25

as a dark background for the more ominous expressions of collective unrest and action by African-descended people. The disparity in the portrayals of the activities of African-descended people arises most clearly in the fact that Bennett elected to call the event the Mermaid Riot even though his main informant, Araminta Tucker, dubbed it the mermaid history. As such, we can see that not only was the incident itself about political power, but so were the retellings.

As noted by Bennett, the belief that the captivity of the mermaid resulted in torrential rainfall remained current among African-descended people into the twentieth century. This idea existed outside of the environs of Charleston, as well. The same core theme figured in a conversation between Pauline Pyatt and Ben Horry recorded in Georgetown County about events that preceded the devastating hurricane of 1893:

> PAULINE: "Find a mer-maid and kept to Magnolia." (Pauline said, 'mere-maid') "Doctor Ward [Joshua J.W. Flagg] and them shut 'em up a month. Mer-maid. Had a storm ball. Heep a turning round. Keep a telling him (Dr. Arthur [Flagg]) storm coming. He wouldn't believe 'em. (Barometer – called by Uncle Isaac's wife, gatekeeper at Brookgreen, chronometer.) He wouldn't believe. And a cussing man! All the time cuss! Mere-maid got a forked tail just like shark. From here down (illustrating by pantomime) all blue scale like a cat-fish. Pretty people! Pretty a white woman as you ever lay your eye on."
>
> BEN: "Pretty, ain't she?"
>
> PAULINE: "Them stay in sea. They walk – slide long on tail." (twisting from her waist to illustrate.) Pretty. From they waist down to tail blue scale. You got a bathing house on beach. Leave bread in there. They sure eat bread....
>
> PAULINE: "Doctor Ward shut that mere-maid up. He been in that! When that storm was, he wasn't old. I go there now and talk bout that storm and he eye get full of water. Look at his Papa clothes....
>
> "Long as he have mere-maid shut up, it rain! People gone there to look at 'em. Long as keep 'em shut up it rain. That time rain thirty days. That just fore Flagg storm."[10]

This account attributed to the captive mermaid not only a heavy rain but the subsequent hurricane, as well. The storm's destructive force was such

---

[10] G.W. Chandler, "Uncle Ben Horry," in Works Project Administration, *Slave Narratives: A Folk History of Slavery in the United States From Interviews with Former Slaves*, South Carolina Narratives (Washington, DC: Federal Writers' Project, 1941), vol. 14, pt. 2: 320, 322. Though the given name of Doctor Ward in this account was actually Joshua John Ward Flagg, I will retain the use of Doctor Ward in this chapter, as this is what Pauline Pyatt and Ben Horry called him in their narratives.

that memory of the hurricane served as a fundamental temporal marker for those who survived it.[11]

Both the mermaid history and Flagg storm stories portrayed the bodies of the mermaids in classic Atlantic terms with a fish-like lower body and a woman's upper body. Pauline Pyatt went further in stating, "Pretty a white woman as you ever lay your eye on," but this is where the resemblance to the familiar European-derived mermaid ends. As seen in numerous spiritual cultures of the African-Atlantic world, images of the European mermaid have been adopted and transformed to represent ideas about water spirits firmly rooted in local cultures before and after contact with Europeans and their portrayals of mermaids. Additionally, the word "mermaid" itself should not distract us from the meanings of these figures in the narratives. Perhaps the use of the term mermaids by African-descended people may have been a narrative strategy by the tellers of mermaid stories to substitute a term that the hearers of the stories (in this case, people of European descent) already knew and could relate to an existing folklore familiar to the hearers. This strategy would have satisfied the basic objective of any good storyteller of reaching the audience. Just as likely, however, disguising nature spirits as mermaids allowed the storytellers to keep the real knowledge and meaning of these spirits within the oral traditions of the African-descended community, thus maintaining the boundary between insider and outsider fundamental in the exposure to spiritual knowledge according to African initiation institutions discussed in the previous chapter. Further, the reference to the appearance and name of the mermaid may have been pleasing for reasons that had little to do with any particular set of expectations or body of knowledge. It seems that in many places and times, people have simply enjoyed making images of and telling stories about mermaids.[12]

---

[11] Walter J. Fraser, Jr., *Lowcountry Hurricanes: Three Centuries of Storms at Sea and Ashore* (Athens: University of Georgia Press, 2006), 184–7; and Tom Rubillo, *Hurricane Destruction in South Carolina: Hell and High Water* (Charleston, SC: The History Press, 2006), 104–10.

[12] For mermaids in North American folklore, see Walker D. Wyman, *Mythical Creatures of the U.S.A. and Canada: A Roundup of the Mythical Snakes and Worms, Insects, Birds, Fish, Serpents, and Mermaids, Animals and Monsters That Have Roamed the American Land* (River Falls: University of Wisconsin-River Falls Press, 1978). The entities that appeared most like mermaids in the oral traditions of southeastern Native groups were river spirits, who consumed the bodies of dead people. See James Mooney, "Myths of the Cherokee," in *Nineteenth Annual Report of the Bureau of American Ethnology to the Secretary of the Smithsonian Institution, 1897–98*, ed. J.W. Powell (Washington, DC: Government Printing Office, 1900), 349–50. See also a story told by Pascagoulas on Mississippi's Gulf coast about a mythical "tribe" that "emerged from the sea" and

The physical and terminological resemblance of mermaids (and more recent representations of a widespread water spirit known as Mami Wata) in African-Atlantic spiritual thought, art, and practice to the European-Atlantic mermaid reflects a point of cultural connection and exchange, not an instance of a foreign culture introducing a completely new idea or overwriting existing cultures. Above all, the outward appearance and superficial identification of the mermaids in the mermaid history and Flagg storm stories remain, at best, incidental to the meanings of the mermaids in the narratives. What we will see when we place the Lowcountry mermaids in an African-Atlantic context is that they were actually African female water spirits, or more specifically simbi spirits. In considering how the dispersed kin of Lowcountry black people have constructed their associations of older African spirits with European-Atlantic mermaids, we gain insight into the ways the spiritual cultures of African-descended folk remained connected and the many forms that nature spirits took in the collective imaginations of diaspora communities.

AFRICAN-ATLANTIC MERMAIDS

As in the Lowcountry, the term "mermaid" appears as a common label for certain entities throughout Africa and in the African-Atlantic diaspora. These mermaids in many instances have only incidentally approximated European-Atlantic perceptions of mermaids, which indicates that ideas and words related to mermaids have served primarily as a lexical and cultural point of contact to open dialogue between the people of African and European descent in the Atlantic world when contemplating the meanings of the powerful female spirits of the water. Recent usage of the term supports this interpretation. People in West-Central Africa, West Africa, and in the Atlantic diaspora have employed mermaid and equivalent terms in other European languages (*sirène* in French, *sereia* in Portuguese, and *sirena* in Spanish) in ways not restricted to the specific definitions, concepts, and images associated with these words in European languages. Certainly, the use of mermaid terms accompanied the influence of European-based perceptions of mermaids in African-Atlantic cultures. Still, such an influence did not necessarily subvert or even change the core meanings of female water spirits in preexisting beliefs and practices.

"adored a mermaid" in Charles Gayarré, *History of Louisiana: The French Domination* (New York: Redfield, 1854), 1: 383–6.

An especially revealing example of this appears in Angola, particularly in the metropolitan area of Luanda, which has involved the rise in prominence of European-Atlantic mermaid terminology and images as representative of *kianda* nature spirits, typically associated with the many lagoons in the region as well as the coastal waters frequented by fishermen. The overlapping of the kianda with European-Atlantic mermaids appears to be rather recent, however, even though the areas around the city have comprised a zone of intense interaction between Angolan and Portuguese peoples and cultures since the founding of Luanda in the late sixteenth century.[13] Given this long history of interaction, the fact that the attributes of the European-Atlantic mermaid have not superseded the ideas and practices related to the original nature spirits suggests that terminology and imagery remained fluid enough to accommodate distinct notions of aquatic entities without resulting in displacement or even creolization for many generations.[14]

This dynamic also appears in the complicated interweaving of terms for local spirits, mermaids, and mami wata in many parts of the African-Atlantic world. Mami wata (and related names, all of which indicate "water mother") has gained general acceptance in numerous African-Atlantic societies as a way to name various manifestations of water spirits, frequently portrayed in the form of mermaids.[15] As with mermaid, mami wata has resonated in different ways in different contexts and spiritual cultures, very often as a focus of veneration or as a foil in African forms of Christianity and Islam. In recent times, people have come to use sirène and mami wata in Congo-Brazzaville and Congo-Kinshasa and sereia in Angola to identify not only those beings and images recognized as mermaids and Mami Watas in other parts of the African-Atlantic world but also nature spirits that have been known by specific local terms over many generations, such as simbi, nkisi, and kianda. As such, it is not

---

[13] Ruy Duarte de Carvalho, *Ana A Manda – Os Filhos da Rede: Identidade colectiva, criatividade social e produção da diferenta cultural: um caso muxiluanda* (Lisboa: Instituto de Investigação Científica Tropical, 1989), 283–301; Coelho, "Imagens," 127–91; and Dunja Hersak, "Mami Wata: The Slippery Mermaid Phenomenon," in *Sacred Waters: Arts for Mami Wata and Other Divinities in Africa and the Diaspora*, ed. Henry John Drewal (Bloomington: Indiana University Press, 2008), 344–8.

[14] This is especially remarkable as the creolization of Angolan and Portuguese cultures has been extensive since the sixteenth century. See Heywood, "Portuguese into African," 91–113; and Heywood and Thornton, *Central Africans, Atlantic Creoles*, 169–235.

[15] For an introduction to the many manifestations of mami wata, see Kathleen O'Brien Wicker, "Mami Water in African Religion and Spirituality," in *African Spirituality: Forms, Meanings, and Expressions*, ed. Jacob K. Olupona (New York: Crossroad, 2000), 198–222; and the collection of essays in Drewal, *Sacred Waters*.

unusual to encounter a nature spirit called a sirène in nothing more than a generic sense, as that spirit often has none of the characteristics typically associated with mermaids. While the use of the new terms does reflect foreign influences and has stimulated the creation of novel ideas and images expressed under the name mermaid or mami wata, it does not indicate the replacement of older concepts about nature spirits or even a fundamental alteration of the roles of these nature spirits in local spiritual cultures. A West-Central African nature spirit becomes a sirène or mami wata because people regard both kinds of entities as beings from the spiritual realm that inhabit the water, not because people necessarily imagined the local spirit to resemble the physical manifestations of the Atlantic mermaid or Mami Wata.[16]

This point is further amplified in certain parts of West-Central Africa in that local nature spirits of both genders have been labeled in recent times as sirène or mami wata. Additionally, the use of sirène has expanded to include those simbi that in some regions have been associated exclusively with forests, not bodies of water. Even more revealing of the process of broadening the scope of the new terms, people in the lower Kouilu River region have begun to subsume terms for spirits of the dead (*nkulu*) and ghosts (*ciniumba*) under the label of mami wata without reconfiguring their perceptions of these spirits to reflect the typical characteristics of Mami Wata.[17]

It is clear that we cannot assume that entities called mermaids have been essentially a European cultural invention and ideas and images about them were thus transmitted primarily by Europeans throughout the Atlantic world. Nevertheless, it is also clear that European mariners and cultural agents (missionaries, most notably) did communicate ideas and images about mermaids as they traversed the seas between Europe, Africa, and the Americas from the fifteenth century onward. This lore about mermaids is vast and ancient. The deity Derketo appears to be the first entity to resemble the prevailing perception of the mermaid as attested to by Lucian, who wrote, "I saw a likeness of Derketo in Phoenicia, a strange sight! It is a woman for half its length, but from the thighs to the tips of the feet a fish's tail stretches out."[18] This combination predominated as

---

[16] Hersak, "Mami Wata," 339–50.
[17] See Germain Tshinkela, *Le Miroir Mukongo* (Tumba: Signum Fidei, 1965), 43; Frank Hagenbucher-Sacripanti, *Sante et Redemption par les Genies au Congo* (Paris: Publisud, 1989), 22–3, 25, 91–2; and Nathalis Lembe Masiala, *Le Rite du Káandu chez les Basolongo du Bas-Congo (RDC)* (Paris: Publibook, 2008), 19–20.
[18] *The Syrian Goddess (De dea Syria) Attributed to Lucian,* trans. Harold W. Attridge and Robert A. Oden (Missoula, MT: Scholars Press, 1976), 21.

the physical representation of mermaids even as they had been understood to have diverse abilities, temperaments, and purposes. The most
enduring and widespread attribute linked to mermaids remained their
ability to seduce men with their beauty, which they enhanced with the
combs they ran through their long hair with one hand and admired with
the ever-present mirror they held in the other hand. Their loveliness drew
men and then led the beguiled to their destruction. At other times, their
irresistible voices called men from afar, especially sailors at sea, driving
them to ruin, as well. They have also appeared in Christian stories and
images as representations of "paganism."[19] Further, Christian monks in
medieval Europe produced bestiaries that employed popular mythologies to illuminate the many paths of sin that awaited the incautious, and
mermaids provided the ideal figure to illustrate the dangers of sexuality,
vanity, and worldliness.[20]

During the era in which European sailors initiated continuous exploration and commerce across the seas, they carried their knowledge of
mermaids with them.[21] The dangers of sea travel stoked fears that mermaids and their male counterparts would seize and sink ships in addition
to causing other troubles. According to one seventeenth-century commentator, "Some have supposed them to be devils or spirits, in regard
of their whooping noise that they make. For (as if they had power to
raise extraordinarie storms and tempests) the windes blow, seas rage, and
clouds drop, presently after they seem to call."[22] Additionally, aquatic
creatures new to Europeans, particularly manatees, provided fresh opportunities for sailors to revisit and enhance their perceptions of mermaids.
No less than Christopher Columbus, famed explorer of the Americas,
claimed to have seen mermaids in the Caribbean as he had in earlier
voyages along the coast of West Africa. Of those he encountered in the

[19] Gwen Benwell and Arthur Waugh, *Sea Enchantress: The Tale of the Mermaid and Her Kin* (New York: The Citadel Press, 1965), 63.

[20] Debra Hassig, *Medieval Bestiaries: Text, Image, Ideology* (New York: Cambridge University Press, 1995), 104–15; Carmen Brown, "Bestiary Lessons on Pride and Lust," in *The Mark of the Beast: The Medieval Bestiary in Art, Life, and Literature*, ed. Debra Hassig (New York: Garland, 1999), 53–70; and Debra Hassig, "Sex in the Bestiaries," in Hassig, *The Mark of the Beast*, 71–98.

[21] For several examples from published accounts, see Benwell and Waugh, *Sea Enchantress*, 93–7.

[22] John Swan, *Speculum mundi, Or A glasse representing the face of the world* (Cambridge: Printed by [Thomas Buck and Roger Daniel] the printers to the University of Cambridge, 1635), 375.

Americas, he noted in his journal that they "were not as pretty as they are depicted, for somehow in the face they look like men."[23]

Later observers have noted that these mermaids were likely manatees (a connection addressed further below), including another captain, Nathanial Uring, who dismissed the claims for mermaids and other "Falsities and Inventions that are too often found in Books of this kind...which are all made Stories, on purpose to impose on the World, and to get Money".[24] He addressed particularly the assertion by Christian missionaries in Central Africa that inland waters held "Water Monsters" including human-like fish, such as a female caught in a net and "big with young." According to the missionary Merolla, from whom Uring derived his information, "The colour of this Fish was black, it had long Hair and large Nails upon very long Fingers." Merolla then asserted that, "Throughout all the River Zaire there is to be found the Mermaid, which from the middle upwards has some resemblance of a Woman, as in its Breast, Nipples, Hands, and Arms, but downwards it is altogether a Fish, ending in a long Tail forked."[25] Uring countered, "This Creature that the good Father speaks of as the Mermaid, can be no other than the Manatee, it answering exactly to that Description, only he had made the Finns to be Hands and Arms," while the other human-like fish described above "are, I suppose, of the same sort; but being improved by the good Father, he made it of humane Shape."[26] While the fact that many mermaid sightings likely originated from the limited knowledge of some European observers of tropical aquatic animals, this should not overshadow the larger point that European sailors of various levels of erudition and experience acted as purveyors of European mermaid lore.

The circumstances in which Africans and Europeans began the long dialogue on nature spirits and mermaids remain obscure. It is likely that the earliest contacts included some interaction on this matter, as European sailors certainly carried ideas about mermaids with them on

[23] Christopher Columbus, *The Diario of Christopher Columbus's First Voyage to America, 1492–1493: Abstracted by Fray Bartolomé de las Casas*, trans. Oliver Dunn and James E. Kelley, Jr. (Norman: University of Oklahoma Press, 1988), 321.

[24] Nathaniel Uring, *A History of the Voyages and Travels of Capt. Nathaniel Uring* (London: Printed by W. Wilkins for J. Peele, 1726), x ("Advertisement To the Reader").

[25] Girolamo Merolla da Sorrento, "A Voyage to Congo, &c.," in *A Collection of Voyages and Travels*, ed. John Churchill (London: Printed for Awnsham and John Churchill, 1704), 1: 672.

[26] Uring, *History of the Voyages*, 66.

their voyages.[27] European mariners and merchants brought to Africa images of mermaids in many of their cultural artifacts and trade goods from the fifteenth century onward. Additionally, Catholic missionaries to Central and West Africa may have referenced mermaids in their moral teachings, as agents of the Church had long targeted these creatures as models of the evils of sexuality and vanity.[28]

This last point holds particular relevance in the intersection of African conceptions of nature spirits (especially those of the water) and European portrayals of mermaids. While European missionaries may have intended to cast the connection of mermaids with sexuality in a negative light, this would have taken on a different meaning for Central and West Africans, who have typically linked sexuality with procreativity and other favorable associations of fertility and prosperity rather than with "sin"or other broadly condemned behaviors. In more recent times, this European interpretation has gained currency among certain Christian groups in many parts of Africa.[29] For those more rooted in traditional spiritual cultures, this link has served as a draw for mermaid-related beliefs and practices. Even in this case, however, the larger moral concerns with the spiritual forces behind fertility and prosperity have remained significant.[30]

In searching for another point of contact in the initial stages of the dialogue, we find that an early context for the exchange of ideas about mermaids between West-Central Africans and Europeans involved an interesting confluence of concepts about the appearance and meaning of manatees. European visitors to Kongo and Angola typically made note of the presence of aquatic creatures local people called *ngulu-a-maza* ("pig of the water"), the Portuguese called *peixe-mulher* ("woman-fish"), and the French called sirène ("siren"). This was the manatee, which enchanted the Europeans to the extent that in their writings about Central Africa they needed to explain the relationship of the creature to their mythological beings. Upon close inspection, the ngulu-a-maza appeared strange but

---

[27] Henry John Drewal, "Introduction: Sources and Currents," in *Mami Wata: Arts for Water Spirits in Africa and Its Diasporas*, ed. Henry John Drewal (Los Angeles: Fowler Museum at UCLA, 2008), 33–8.

[28] Hassig, *Medieval Bestiaries*, 104–15; Wicker, "Mami Water," 200–1; and Drewal, "Introduction: Sources and Currents," 33.

[29] Wicker, "Mami Water," 201, 206–8; Bogumil Jewsiewicki, "Congolese *Mami Wata*: The Charm and Delusion of Modernity," in Drewal, *Sacred Waters*, 125–40; Birgit Meyer, "Mami Water as a Christian Demon: The Eroticism of Forbidden Pleasures in Southern Ghana," in Drewal, *Sacred Waters*, 383–98; and Rosalind I.J. Hackett, "Mermaids and End-Time Jezebels: New Tales from Old Calabar," in Drewal, *Sacred Waters*, 405–12.

[30] All of the essays included in Drewal, *Sacred Waters* attest to this.

not charmingly exotic, or as the Italian missionary Cavazzi phrased his understanding of the *pesce donna*, "beautiful in name, but horrendous in form."[31] A few features of the animal looked somewhat human, such as its arm-like fins that had five "fingers" and most notably its breasts, for which Europeans took to calling the water pig a "woman fish."[32]

West-Central Africans did not share romanticized ideas about this creature, but local expressions of the connection between manatees, mermaids, and water spirits appear to have emerged at some point after contact with Europeans. Near the trading center of Boma, people feared the *seliwata*, spiritually potent manatees said to resemble mermaids and cause death to those who looked into their eyes. Further, some oldtimers in the Niari River valley of the Republic of Congo have equated manatees with the spirit Mami Wata, often portrayed as a mermaid and frequently called sirène in that region, as in other parts of West-Central Africa. In Angola, fishermen near Luanda have considered the manatee a kind of mermaid and water spirit, as did others along Kwilu River, who called the manatee *qui-anda* (*kianda*), the same name given to the river spirits.[33] The connection between the animals, mermaids, and spirits, however, does not seem to be widespread or fundamental to West-Central African ideas about mermaids and water spirits. Nevertheless, the key point remains that the European conflation of the peixe-mulher and sirène with the manatee certainly opened a dialogue between Europeans and West-Central Africans about the intersections of ideas and practices related to spirits and animals (both natural and mythical). The fact that West-Central Africans as well as Africans in other regions readily adopted and adapted European terminology (particularly sirène and sereia) to discuss traditional concepts about nature spirits shows that a close agreement

---

[31] Cavazzi, *Descrição*, 1: 132.
[32] Dapper, *Description*, 277, 297–8; and Caltanisetta, *Diaire Congolais*, 5.
[33] Schrag, "Mboma," 39; Michel Ogrizek, "Mami Wata, les envoûtées de la sirène: psychothérapie collective de l'hystérie en pays Batsangui au Congo, suivie d'un voyage mythologique en Centrafrique," *Cahier O.R.S.T.O.M.* 18, 4 (1982–1982): 435; Hersak, "Mami Wata, 344; and H. Capello and R. Ivens, *De Benguela ás Terras de Iácca: Descripção de uma Viagem na African Central e Occidental* (Lisboa: Imprensa Nacional, 1881), 2: 387. The gloss of "peixe mulher (*Manatus*)" as qui-anda appears in Capello and Ivens and should be considered alongside the more common use of *dikunji* in Kimbundu. The link between the mermaid (*sereia* in Portuguese) and water spirits remains, as Angolans often use water spirit terminology, such as *kianda* or *kiximbi* in Kimbundu and *ximbi* in Kikongo, to name mermaids. See Antonio da Silva Maia, *Dicionário Complementar, Português-Kimbundu-Kikongo (Linguas Nativas do Centro e Norte de Angola)*, 2d ed. (Cucujães, Portugal: Depositária Editorial Missoes, 1964), 470, 573.

in previous understandings need not precede fruitful engagement. The dialogues about the meanings of manatees and mermaids that emerged from these early contacts likely initiated the flow of ideas and images that have culminated in the current expressions linked to Mami Wata, one of the more recent articulations of an older and ongoing discourse between African and European spiritual cultures.

While early written sources do not provide descriptions of mermaids among the nature spirits found in West-Central Africa, the historical ethnographic record from the nineteenth and early twentieth centuries offers evidence of the application of the term mermaid to nature spirits, a process that also involved the intermingling of European-based attributes of mermaids with existing concepts of nature spirits. The point is not to suggest that these particular manifestations of mermaids existed or were brought across the sea during the era when captive Africans were transported to the Lowcountry or any other part of the Atlantic diaspora. Instead, these examples demonstrate the ways that Africans have incorporated words and ideas related to mermaids into their spiritual cultures. At the very least, this offers us material with which we can assess how African-descended people in the Americas who themselves or whose immediate ancestors shared the same spiritual cultures of their African kin imagined their own associations between nature spirits and mermaids.

On the Loango coast, a female water spirit often described as a mermaid and known as Chicamasi-chi-Buinji or Mwe Chinkambisi once provided spiritual sanction for the governance of the Chilunga province, and has long been linked to the power of the sea. According to an oral tradition from Cabinda, she originated upriver in the Nzadi as the primordial female "spirit of the land" (nkisi nsi) MBoze, the mother of all nature spirits, and eventually settled closer to the coast at Boma. After parting acrimoniously from her male counterpart (Kuiti Kuiti), she fled to Loango and became MKambizi-ci-Buingi.[34] In general, she has been best known as Cinkambisi, which means "she who holds back the water."[35] The varied names attributed to this spirit overlap in their core reference to the water (*si* means "water" and *masi* means "of the water") and represent her complex nature as a powerful water deity in the spiritual cultures of the Loango Coast and Lower Nzadi.

---

[34] Laurent Mam Buko, "Ka binda. Un récit historique," in Volavka, *Crown and Ritual*, 289–90.

[35] Tavestin, "Culte des génies," in Volavka, *Crown and Ritual*, 294.

Chinkambisi occasionally came on land to retrieve certain articles, such as redwood, to groom herself, and became angry when people took these items from the shore. Such transgressions resulted in her generating a surge that prevented fishing and drowned those caught in the surf. Additionally, "When Chicamassi is vexed she comes ashore and takes one of twins or triplets, and drowns it in the sea." People poured libations of rum and tossed food offerings of fish or manioc into the sea to show their respect and appease her.[36] Her violent nature appears to have derived from her early life of suffering, according to those traditions that indicate that she originated as a living person, not a primordial nature spirit. One story recounts that a princess named Buinji had three malformed children, the oldest of whom was Chinkambisi. All three died a day after birth, which reduced the grieving Buinji to illness. Chinkambisi came to her ailing mother in a dream and told her to fish in the river Noumbi. A heavy rain lasting an entire day followed this dream, although it was the dry season. With her remaining strength, the mother sewed a small statue of a kneeling female figure into her fishing net. This statue became a sacred object of the clan that maintained the shrine for the spirit Chinkambisi. Soon after Buinji fulfilled her mission, she died to reunite with the children for whom she had mourned.[37] Another story reports that Chinkambisi cried incessantly throughout her childhood and drove her mother (not necessarily Buinji in this telling) to abandon her on a heap of garbage. Mermaids rescued her from this fate and endowed her with the great powers with which she has affected the lives of people ever since.[38]

In addition to exerting her authority from the sea, Chinkambisi has often played the role of a captor on land. She set out a variety of alluring foods along isolated stretches of paths to tempt people traveling alone. Those who attempted to partake of this bait simply disappeared forever. This attribute resembled the practice in Loango and the Lower Nzadi of "poigner" by those involved in the trans-Atlantic trade in captive Africans. This custom allowed rulers and other designated officials to claim the right to seize under any pretext people within their domains for sale into the trade. The unfortunate people caught in this trap included unwary and unprotected travelers from the interior who often followed

---

[36] R.E. Dennett, *Notes on the Folklore of the Fjort (French Congo)* (London: Folk-Lore Society, 1898), 8.

[37] Hagenbucher-Sacripanti, *Fondements Spirituels*, 65.

[38] Hersak, "Mami Wata," 341.

the merchant caravans to the coast.[39] Given her association with the rulers of Chilunga province, it is not surprising to see her penchant for snatching people linked with the practice of *poigner*, as the victims of either the spirit or the rulers found themselves dragged to the sea. Chinkambisi has also taken on characteristics much more familiar to African-Atlantic Mami Wata/mermaid figures. She has long been reputed to attract men of her choosing with her sensuality and promises of sexual pleasure in dreams and secret nocturnal meetings. These men, even those with wives already, who then did not remain sexually faithful to her alone invited great misfortune from Chinkambisi.[40]

Ultimately, Chinkambisi has held the reputation as a spirit deserving both respect and fear. Embodied in the destructive power of sea storms, she has demonstrated her nature as "extremely violent like a soldier with arms, ready to fight to protect the authorities. She favors her friends, offering them money; she destroys her enemies."[41] The same association with storms from the sea adhered to LuSunzi, the cognate spirit of Chinkambisi in Lower Nzadi societies. The connection to the Atlantic was so basic to her identity that the path to LuSunzi's shrine followed the direction that she travelled when "in the form of a cyclone, the deity rushed from the ocean to the forest."[42]

LuSunzi's role in Lower Nzadi spiritual culture differed from Chinkambisi, however, in that LuSunzi regulated the coming of sea storms and seasonal rains according to society's adherence to her moral codes of conduct.[43] Rather than afflicting individuals, often for arbitrary reasons as has been the case with Chinkambisi, LuSunzi extended her rewards and punishments to affect entire communities based on the actions of individuals that undermined the stability of those societies. This was given special emphasis in the laws of the old kingdom of Ngoyo, in which LuSunzi served as the spiritual source of certain rules that regulated sexuality and marriage. Most notably, her laws prohibited intercourse on the ground or in a house with open doors and windows, did not allow sex between

---

[39] Kabolo Iko Kabwita, *Le Royaume Kongo et la Mission Catholique, 1750–1838* (Paris: Éditions Karthala, 2004), 104.

[40] Hagenbucher-Sacripanti, *Fondements Spirituels*, 65.

[41] Janzen, *Lemba*, 303. People along the Loango coast have attributed misfortune (often in the forms of storms or loss of fresh water) to the displeasure of mermaids/water spirits with people who do not respect them and their habitats when locating oil storage facilities, plantations, and forestry operations. See Hersak, "Mami Wata," 341–2.

[42] Volavka, *Crown and Ritual*, 67.

[43] She shares these duties with Bunzi and Lunga. See José Martins Vaz, *No Mundo dos Cabindas: Estudo Etnográfico* (Lisboa: L.I.A.M., 1970), I: 50.

adults and young people who had not yet undergone the transitional ritual confirming sexual maturity, and forbade menstruating women from having sex or preparing food. Additionally, LuSunzi's laws required people to marry outside of their families (composed of those who shared maternal blood ties). Beyond acting as the "legislator of men," LuSunzi appeared in dreams to denounce "excesses of those who have her laws" and instruct "her priests in each village to condemn or absolve them."[44] Failure to abide by her exogamy law resulted in LuSunzi and her male counterpart Bunzi withholding seasonal rains in order to bring the punishment of famine to the land.[45]

People in Cabinda visually presented LuSunzi with two faces on her head, one black and the other white. Her body corresponded to this color scheme with one side black and the other side white as well. The explanation given for this appearance was "She came into the world to expound a doctrine of value and benefit for blacks and whites."[46] The fact that this explanation was recorded during the era when Cabinda was a colonial possession of Portugal highlights the understanding that LuSunzi's reputation as a spiritual lawgiver and judge of human behavior transcended the racial, social, and religious order of all human, including European, authorities.

Another mermaid, Ne-Vemba, resided inland in the southern Kongo region and had strong links to an earlier manifestation of the Ndembo initiation society. According to tradition documented in the mid-twentieth century, Ne-Vemba presided over an initiation school that prepared a select group of young males of noble or prominent lineage to serve the king of Kongo. The school occupied a secret location hidden in dense forests along the banks of the Nzadi. Ne-Vemba, known as the Wise Mermaid, remained in the river most of the time but emerged on occasion to bestow exceptional powers to the head priest of the school and those who passed the process of the initiation. The curriculum of this school focused on knowledge and behaviors necessary for sustaining the political, medical, and spiritual functions of the king of Kongo's office. The process of initiation began with the nocturnal abduction of the chosen young men and their transport to the clandestine camp. The secrecy of the school's site was paramount, as even a king of Kongo, who had not been initiated, could not know of its location or enter there. Further,

[44] Janzen, *Lemba*, 303.
[45] Martins, *Cabindas*, 111; and Vaz, *Mundo dos Cabindas*, 2: 158.
[46] Martins, *Cabindas*, 111–12. The English translation is my rendering of Martins's Portuguese translation of the KiKongo text.

those of low social status could not approach the school without risking their lives, although such an incident seemed unlikely given the isolation of the site deep in the forest. The apprenticeship lasted from three to five years and culminated in an event that included the appearance of Ne-Vemba to the initiate. Those who reached the completion of the school left the camp during the night (just as they first entered), before the formal conclusion of initiation, to bathe on the bank of the river and wait alone for Ne-Vemba. For those deemed worthy, Ne-Vemba arrived to provide the final teachings and transmit spiritual powers. Novices whom the Wise Mermaid considered inadequate in their knowledge and temperament did not return from this last test. The successful candidate reentered society to practice his vocation as an initiated expert (nganga) with the title of Ne-Dembo, understood to mean "Wise Son of the Mermaid" and "Wise Master."[47]

This short account of Ne-Vemba reveals aspects of the power of nature spirits (as mermaids in this case) relative to the instrumental power of those who dominated the political realm. Not only could an uninitiated king of Kongo not enter the compound of Ne-Vemba's school, the school operated without state support despite the institution's dedication to service of the king's court. These aspects represented an interesting accommodation of powers that had long featured as a key component of Kongo political culture. Leaders required the sanction of nature spirits to rule or hold certain chiefly titles, which meant that leaders and the institutions of the state had to maintain relationships with the priests and institutions connected to these powerful spirits. This relationship was most evident in the dependence of the ruling nobles of Kongo on the offices of the head priest of the local nature spirits, the kitome (or kitombe), in the era before the demise of the old kingdom of Kongo in the seventeenth century. These ties continued in later times at local levels and remained prominent in the political cultures of lower Nzadi states, particularly Ngoyo and Loango, until the colonial era. Without this accommodation, rulers lacked the necessary spiritual authority to ensure the well-being and prosperity of the land and its people. The fact that the spiritual institutions stood independent of the state structure indicates that in Kongo spiritual culture the authority of nature spirits was seen as connected to but apart from the instrumental forms of power wielded by the nobility and state institutions. Indeed, this spiritual authority exceeded that of the

---

[47] Serra Frazão, *Associações Secretas entre os Indígenas de Angola* (Lisboa: Editora Marítomo – Colonial, 1946), 287–94.

social and governmental hierarchy. Ne-Vemba's school with its purposes and prohibitions exemplified this conception of spiritual and physical power with the Wise Mermaid at the heart of the discourse.

The range of characteristics attributed to these West-Central African mermaids reflected overlapping ideas and images in the Atlantic dialogue about mermaids in the centuries following initial European contact with West-Central African societies in the fifteenth century. The key point of understanding is that, even with the existence of intersecting layers, the core meanings of the local nature spirits remained intact. The same dynamic appears to have played out in the African-Atlantic diaspora, as well.

Throughout the African-Atlantic diaspora, numerous female spirits prominent in African-inspired spiritual cultures have been considered mermaids to one extent or another. African-descended Brazilians have associated mermaid imagery with the female spirits of the water, which could be seen in the most important communities of spirits that derived from Nagô, Bantu, and Amerindian spiritual cultures. The various ideas and images derived from these backgrounds have coalesced in the identity of Yemanjá, who originated in the Nagô-Yoruba spiritual culture established in Bahia. Yemanjá has been called Sereia do Mar ("Mermaid of the Sea") and Sereia Mukunã ("Mermaid Who Remains in the Water"), and her most prominent objects include a round silver fan with the figure of a mermaid and a white stone taken from the sea.[48] The example of Yemanjá as a mermaid does not appear to imply any association with the European-Atlantic mermaid beyond being seen as a powerful female spirit of the sea. Even when invoked as a mermaid, Yemanjá retains her fundamental characteristic as a strong mother. Additionally, a song featured in the public celebration of Yemanjá in Bahia during the early twentieth century showed the variety of female spirits linked to the mermaid in proclaiming, "The Mermaid plays, the water mother (*mãe-dagua*) plays, Janaina plays, Dandalunda plays in the village."[49] This song not only described the possession of devotees (the reference to playing) by these spirits but also indicated the multiple names and identities associated under the identity of Yemanjá by referencing together the European-Atlantic mermaid, the African-Atlantic water mother (akin to Mami Wata), the Amerindian Janaína, and the Angola/Congo spirit

---

[48] Olga Gudolle Cacciatore, *Dicionário de Cultos Afro-Brasileiros* (Rio de Janeiro: Universitária, Instituto Estadual do Livro, 1977), 241, 267.
[49] Carneiro, *Negros Bantus*, 73.

Dandalunda. Oxum, another spirit with many followers in Brazil, has also been linked to Yemanjá and the other female water spirits through an explicit connection to the mermaid. An Umbanda song reveals this relationship in describing a "palace" found "in the depths of the ocean" inhabited by Oxum, the mermaid, Yemanjá, and "her children who have nowhere else to stay."[50]

Like their Brazilian counterparts Yemanjá and Oxum, the Cuban entities Yemayá and Ochún acquired associations with the mermaid. As a figure representing fertility and maternal affection, Yemayá has been portrayed as a woman or mermaid with very black skin, a large belly (owing to pregnancy), and protruding breasts.[51] Additionally, Yemayá has been seen as having "pearly scales from the waist down, a fish tail," and black pupils in "bulging, round, wide open" white eyes surrounded by eyelashes resembling spikes. She has silver hair as a sign of her old age, fertility, and motherly essence. Also, Yemayá maintains a "magnificent palace" on the bottom of the seas and hides her treasures there, as well.[52] The container for objects associated with Yemayá's qualities and power, known as a *sopera* (often in the form of a porcelain tureen), typically contains several items that represent fertility and health as well as a small mermaid figure to symbolize her "mysterious beauty."[53] In regard to Ochún, one of the *caminos* ("paths") associated with her comes in the form of Ochún Olodí (or Ololodí), who embodies notions of mature, domestic love similar to Yemayá. She lives on the bottom of the river, presides over waterfalls, and spends much of her time knitting, sewing, and embroidering. In addition to the needles, spools of thread, arrows, and machetes kept in soperas for her and representing the domestic and warrior sides of her personality, Ochún Olodí is symbolized by a mermaid figure.[54]

In Haitian spiritual culture, the mermaid has taken the form of the female spirit called Lasirèn ("mermaid" in Kréyol, derived from the French La Sirène) and has been frequently linked with the male spirit

[50] Quoted in Lindsay Hale, "Mama Oxum: Reflections of Gender and Sexuality in Brazilian Umbanda," in *Òsun Across the Waters: A Yoruba Goddess in African and the Americas*, ed. Joseph M. Murphy and Mei-Mei Sanford (Bloomington: Indiana University Press, 2001), 213. Translation of the song is provided by Hale.
[51] Castellanos and Castellanos, *Cultura Afrocubana*, 54.
[52] Lydia Cabrera, *Yemayá y Ochún: Kariocha, Iyloríchas y Olorichas* (Miami, FL: Ediciones Universal, 1996), 32.
[53] Castellanos and Castellanos, *Cultura Afrocubana*, 56; and Brown, *Santería Enthroned*, 219, 358n15.
[54] Cabrera, *Yemayá y Ochún*, 271; and Isabel Castellanos, "A River of Many Turns: The Polysemy of Ochún in Afro-Cuban Tradition," in Murphy, *Òsun Across the Waters*, 35.

Agwé Woyo (the loa of the sea) while also being regarded as a manifestation of the female spirit Ezili of the Waters. In this last role, Lasirèn, along
with the other expressions of Ezili, has maintained associations with the
Virgin Mary. Another connection has paired Lasirèn with Labalen, the
Whale, as "two marine divinities so closely linked that they are always
worshipped together and celebrated in the same songs."[55] The association
with the sea remains central, as Lasirèn prefers that her priests establish temples close to the sea. Those who have spent much time on the
open water, such as fishermen and sailors, have often thrown into the sea
offerings of bottles filled with sweet orgeat syrup to appeal for Lasirèn's
protection, especially in bad weather. Sailors also have claimed to have
glimpsed Lasirèn as she held on to the bows of their vessels or sang from
her perch on an islet.[56] The connection with water extends beyond the sea,
as some accounts note that Lasirèn has also inhabited the fresh waters
of springs and fountains. Lasirèn in these locations has been known to
take a liking to young boys who pass by her waters, especially on moonlit
nights. She captures them and raises them as her adoptive children in the
depths of the spring.[57]

The people who have venerated these spirits in Brazil, Cuba, and Haiti
have often employed the standard imagery of the European-Atlantic mermaid to portray Yemanjá, Oxum, Dandalunda, Yemaya, Ochún, Lasirèn,
and the others. Yet it becomes clear that the identification as a mermaid
in name and likeness represented an aspect of these spirits acquired
in the Atlantic context, but not a fundamental transformation of the
spirits. Ultimately, an African-Atlantic mermaid remained essentially a
female water spirit, who may or may not have had attributes similar to
a European-Atlantic mermaid but who nevertheless embodied the core
characteristics widely associated with female water spirits in several parts
of the diaspora.

THE SIMBI, MERMAIDS, AND CAPTIVITY

The common association of African-inspired spirits with mermaids provides a firm basis for interpreting the Lowcountry mermaids as manifestations of African-Atlantic spirits rather than European-Atlantic mermaids.

---

[55] Quote from Metraux, *Voodoo in Haiti*, 104. See also Herskovits, *Life In A Haitian Valley*, 279–80; and Milo Marcelin, *Mythologie Vodou (Rite Arada)* (Port-au-Prince: Éditions Haïtiennes, 1949), 103, 119–22.

[56] Marcelin, *Mythologie Vodou*, 119.

[57] Marcelin, *Mythologie Vodou*, 119.

While the key difference between the Lowcountry and other parts of the African-Atlantic diaspora remains that African-descended people in South Carolina have not maintained the veneration of these kinds of spirits to the same extent as people in Brazil, Cuba, and Haiti, it would be a mistake to overlook the presence of the Lowcountry simbi as a similar expression of the knowledge about the various forms taken by nature spirits. Features of the Lowcountry mermaid narratives suggest that we not only indentify these as stories about classic African-Atlantic nature spirits, but that we also recognize them as narratives that addressed the specific concerns of African-descended people. Indeed, the mermaid history and Flagg storm stories comment on the historical experiences of African-descended people, particularly in their interpretations of the consequences of captivity. Following a pattern established in West-Central Africa where nature spirits represented a domain of creative power employed to understand and influence life in the physical realm, these narratives drew deeply from the well of Lowcountry spiritual culture in an effort to explain the meanings of captivity. As we have seen in Chapters 4 and 5, one of the core sources for Lowcountry spiritual culture was knowledge about the simbi, which included much concerning the spiritual meanings of captivity and its consequences for the living. In order to extract these meanings from the mermaid history and Flagg storm narratives, we must consider further the immediate contexts surrounding the events they address.

People of African descent of both free and enslaved status in antebellum Charleston lived in a volatile context in which clashes over the control of the African-descended community simmered at most times and flared on occasion. According to one visitor to the city in the mid-1840s, the "negroes here have certainly not the manners of an oppressed race," a bearing that reflected a vibrant and assertive population willing to engage the limits of the dominant sector's rule.[58] Efforts by white authorities to control gatherings, movements, and commerce of African-descended people typically met with only partial success, although not for lack of effort. White Charlestonians marshaled considerable material and human resources to police the activities of people of color, particularly following the Vesey Conspiracy of 1822. During her visit to Charleston in 1838, Frances Anne Kemble noted "a most ominous tolling of bells and beating of drums, which...made me almost fancy myself in one of the old fortified frontier towns of the Continent, where...the guard set as regularly every

---

[58] Sir Charles Lyell, *A Second Visit to the United States of America*, 2d ed. (London: John Murray, 1850), 1: 297.

night as if an invasion were expected." Kemble continued, "It is not the dread of foreign invasion, but of domestic insurrection, which occasions these nightly precautions." She obliquely referred to the predominance of enslaved people in Charleston and averred, "I should prefer going to sleep without the apprehension of my servants' cutting my throat in my bed, even to having a guard provided to prevent their doing so."[59] At the beginning of the American Civil War, the Irish war correspondent William Howard Russell reported from Charleston that the "curfew and the night patrol in the streets, the prisons, and watch-houses, and the police regulations, prove that strict supervision, at all event, is needed and necessary."[60] The struggle over control of the African-descended community became even more precarious when segments of white society advocated expelling or even enslaving free people of color as tensions mounted toward the end of the 1850s and in the early 1860s.[61] Despite the initiatives taken by African-descended people to build upon the limited opportunities available in the bustling urban setting of mid-nineteenth-century Charleston, no day or night passed in which white authorities failed to buttress the mechanisms for holding African-descended people in captivity. Without doubt, the conspicuous presence of policing and patrolling forces served as a constant and public reminder of the social order.

Another very visible aspect of life in nineteenth-century Charleston was the public sale of enslaved people. Next to the post office in the busy market center surrounded by throngs of buyers and sellers of all kinds of goods and amid the calls of enslaved market women to, "Buy cabbage, mas'r....Buy sweet potatoes," the auction of men, women, and children proceeded as normal everyday business. A visitor from England in 1853 recorded in his diary "scenes of misery," including "Stout men, crying like children at being parted from their wives, and children clinging in vain to their mother; and more agonies than I have a mind to recapitulate."[62] Other travelers described similar scenes, such as that of a mother who cried out, "They have sold my babe, they have sold my babe," as she

[59] Kemble, *Journal of a Residence*, 39.

[60] William Howard Russell, *My Diary North and South* (Boston: T.O.H.P. Burnham, 1863), 132.

[61] Bernard E. Powers, Jr., *Black Charlestonians: A Social History, 1822–1865* (Fayetteville: University of Arkansas Press, 1994), 64–5; and Wilbert L. Jenkins, *Seizing the New Day: African Americans in Post-Civil War Charleston* (Bloomington: Indiana University Press, 1998), 22. See also, Marina Wikramanayake, *A World in Shadow: The Free Black in Antebellum South Carolina* (Columbia: University of South Carolina Press, 1973)

[62] Frederick Lehmann, 15 February 1853, in R.C. Lehmann, ed., *Memories of Half a Century: A Record of Friendships* (London: Smith, Elder and Co., 1908), 314.

struggled through the crowd to catch up with her child taken from her following an auction. The witness wrote that the woman "wept and raved... crying out in those tones of despair and anguish which nothing but a heart broken, crushed and wrung to the very core, can ever give utterance to."[63] Another mother endured such suffering while "pressing her infants closer to her bosom with an involuntary grasp, and exclaiming, in wild and simple earnestness, while the tears chased down her cheeks in quick succession, 'I can't leff my children! I won't leff my children!'"[64]

These "scenes of misery" played out so often that no enslaved person could forget for a moment that their ties to family and friends could be quickly broken following the brief exchanges of a barking auctioneer and the bidding of crowds of buyers. This concern appears in "The Apothecary and the Mermaid," as Bennett referenced one of the beliefs of African-descended Charlestonians that "the mermaid had a baby in the sea, and that, until she was released to nurse her child, the rain would continue to fall."[65] In this aside, we see the mermaid cast as a representative of the simbi, as she embodied the loving water spirit mother. The grieving mother in the case of the simbi mermaid was not only held in captivity but also separated from her child, not unlike the unfortunate mothers among the living who lost their children on the auction block. The mermaid then exacted her devastating punishment of continuous rain for being held captive and kept from her child, both terrible transgressions illustrative of moral offenses of enslavement.

We must note that Araminta Tucker's account and Bennett's "The Apothecary and the Mermaid" end with the liberation of the mermaid. Doctor Trott decided, after being threatened with jail, that his own captivity was not worth the price of keeping the mermaid, and "he put that mermaid back."[66] In Bennett's story, "the rain stopped, the sun came out and shone brightly; so all the people went home," apparently satisfied that the mermaid had been returned to the sea.[67] The mermaid history stood as a critique of captivity and a hopeful call for emancipation. It also served as a warning of the price to be paid for holding the mermaid in bondage. The forces of the spiritual realm coupled with those of nature

---

[63] Philo Tower, *Slavery Unmasked: Being A Truthful Narrative of a Three Years' Residence and Journeying in Eleven Southern States* (Rochester, NY: E. Darrow and Brothers, 1856), 114.

[64] James Stuart, *Three Years in North America*, 2d ed. (Edinburgh & London: Robert Cadell and Whittaker and Co., 1833), 110.

[65] Bennett, *Doctor to the Dead*, 225.

[66] Bennett, "Bennett Replies."

[67] Bennett, *Doctor to the Dead*, 230–1.

would punish the guilty captors as well as the rest of society for allowing the crime to continue until the captive had been set free. As with LuSunzi and other nature spirits, the power of the simbi transcended the authority and instrumental control of white society or any other political entity in the physical world. African-descended people in the Lowcountry knew this and drew upon the "common superstition of the Africans" to fashion a narrative about a mermaid that spoke of liberation and reckoning in a time and place when statements of this kind would not be tolerated.

In the Flagg storm story, we find a similar moral narrative that critiques captivity, but does not offer a resolution in emancipation. After all, the hurricane occurred almost thirty years after the end of slavery. This was a time, however, when the promise and gains of Reconstruction were unraveling. Changes in political power resulted in the disenfranchisement of African-descended people throughout the South, with South Carolina leading the way beginning in the late 1870s. By 1895, the state constitution formalized the legal portion of the process.[68] The very personal aspects of these struggles appear as powerful subtext for the Flagg storm narrative. The story tells of death as the consequence of captivity, death for both the captors and the captives. Doctor Ward initiated the misfortune by holding the mermaid captive and refusing to release her despite the thirty days of rain and the impending hurricane indicated by the spinning "storm ball." Arthur Flagg, Doctor Ward's father, did not heed the warnings of the coming storm to the extent that he failed to move his family and servants to a safer location out of reach of the storm surge. They paid the price, as Ben Horry, formerly enslaved by the Flaggs, noted, "All his [Doctor Ward's] family – thirteen head – drowned and gone right out to sea."[69] The Flagg family's tragedy (and responsibility, we may suppose) led people to remember the hurricane as the Flagg Storm or the Doctor Storm.[70] Compounding the misfortune, Doctor Ward's transgression in capturing the mermaid and Arthur Flagg's stubborn refusal to move to a safer location resulted in the deaths of the African-descended

---

[68] For the context of this shift and efforts of contemporaries to create narratives to explain or justify the reordering of society and politics in this era, see Walter B. Edgar, *South Carolina: A History* (Columbia: University of South Carolina Press, 1998), 407–29; Grace Elizabeth Hale, *Making Whiteness: The Culture of Segregation in the South, 1890–1940* (New York: Vintage, 1999); Leon F. Litwack, *Trouble in Mind: Black Southerners in the Age of Jim Crow* (New York: Vintage, 1999); and Michele Mitchell, *Righteous Propagation: African Americans and the Politics of Racial Destiny after Reconstruction* (Chapel Hill: University of North Carolina Press, 2004).

[69] G.W. Chandler "Uncle Ben Talks 'Bout The Old Doctor," Folder D-4-36a, WPA-SCL.

[70] G.W. Chandler, "Aunt Bobbitt Horry," Folder D-4-36, WPA-SCL.

servants of the family. According to Ben Horry's memory, "All that family drown out because they wouldn't go to this lady house on higher ground. Wouldn't let none of the rest go. Servant all drown! Betsy, Kit, Mom Adele! Couldn't identify who lost from who save till next morning."[71] Bobbit Horry recounted that unfortunate consequences were revealed, "After the water gone back," as those charged with recovering the victims "catch the servant body so here-and-there. Gone right out in the Gulf Stream."[72]

The Reverend Cato Singleton recalled the storm as well and portrayed it vividly as a divine act of destruction, when God "turn the sea loose." He and his wife knew the hurricane was coming and saw that "the sea been light up....He look same like fire....That sea make us think of judgment and hell." After the Reverend Singleton and his wife struggled their way to safety on higher ground, they joined others in a prayer meeting that lasted for the duration of the storm, through the night and into the next day. The preacher also recounted that Doctor Ward later claimed that the storm surge spoke, the water "moan and complain...He groan and resist" as God called the water to return to sea. As the water receded, Doctor Ward heard it say:

> I done my work!
> I done my work!
> I done my work!
> I done my work!

That work included drowning members of the Flagg family and their servants and killing many animals, as "Much corpse bin lie in the dead marsh the dead." The Reverend Singleton concluded his recounting by singing a song composed by another African-descended preacher in the area, the Reverend Albert Carolina:

> The wind so high
> He blow so hard
> We just don't know what for do.
> Then we recognize in it
> The wonderful power of God.
> Two hundred body
> Come floating by.
> We ain't know
> Just what for do.

[71] Chandler, "Uncle Ben Horry," 313.
[72] G.W. Chandler, "Aunt Bobbit Horry," Folder D-4-36, WPA-SCL.

Then we recognize in it,
The wonderful power of God.[73]

Within the accounts of the Reverend Singleton and Ben Horry, the tragic survivor of the Flagg storm, Doctor Ward, appeared as a figure at once haunted by his personal losses and redeemed to "exhort like Isiah [sic]" and explain "God's judgment on Jerusalem."[74] Yet even the Reverend Singleton's remembrance of Doctor Ward's redemption had him preaching not about being spared during the storm but about death and destruction as judgment for those who failed to obey God. The meaning of this collection of stories about the Flagg storm becomes much clearer when we recall Pauline Pyatt's narrative, in which the hurricane and its deadly power arose as retribution for Doctor Ward keeping the mermaid captive. The two captors in the stories, Doctor Ward and Arthur Flagg, refused to recognize the spiritual power of the sea and release their captives (the mermaid and the servants), and the result was death for the guilty as well as the innocent.

Just as the storms and droughts wrought by the mermaid LuSunzi and her companion Bunzi afflicted entire communities, including those individuals who assiduously observed the sacred laws and those who violated them, the punishments of the captive mermaids caused suffering throughout the society as a whole.[75] This aspect of the mermaid history and the Flagg storm stories reflected African-inspired perceptions of the origins and remedies for social problems, as seen in the bumba kindongo rite from eighteenth-century Kongo, discussed in the previous chapter. These troubles had spiritual causes and called for spiritual cures. Moreover, spiritual crises affected everyone within a society and thus required social remedies. In the end, the Lowcountry mermaid stories served the purpose of interpreting natural disasters as signs of spiritual distress instigated by a society's violation of the moral codes enforced by nature spirits. The punishments unleashed by the captive mermaids proved that every person, black and white, would feel the pain of the reckoning for these transgressions. To those who had endured enslavement and the racial order constructed to maintain that regime's iniquities,

---

[73] G.W. Chandler, "De Flagg Storm (Rev. Cato speaks)," Folder F-2–14a, WPA-SCL.
[74] G.W. Chandler, "De Flagg Storm (Rev. Cato speaks)," Folder F-2–14a; and "Uncle Ben Talks 'Bout The Old Doctor," Folder D-4–36a, WPA-SCL.
[75] A connection between LuSunzi and a mermaid figure in the work of Lowcountry artist Ralph Griffin is discussed in Kuyk, *African Voices*, 132–3.

the greatest betrayal of the simbi and their laws was keeping their sons and daughters in bondage.

The fact that the mermaid occupied the central role in the story of the Flagg storm, told almost seven decades after the end of slavery yet drawing upon the same theme found in the mermaid history about the early 1850s, reveals a profound continuity within the oral lore of African-descended people. This continuity was based upon a deep connection to the simbi in the spiritual culture that remained vital even as the religious orientation shifted toward Protestant Christianity. The Lowcountry simbi took on the identity of mermaids, as seen with other African spirits throughout the Atlantic diaspora, yet preserved their original power and authority as nature spirits. The Lowcountry mermaid narratives spoke of this transformation and enduring legacy in that they retained their core meaning as a critique of captivity and domination by telling of a powerful water spirit who visited punishment on a society that condoned the oppression of the children of the simbi. As long as people still told the mermaid histories to those who would listen, they continued to remember and honor the simbi.

Epilogue

In 1939, thousands of laborers from across the state of South Carolina found good-paying jobs in Berkeley County with the beginning of the material phase of the Santee-Cooper project after years of political wrangling in Charleston, Columbia, and Washington, DC. Supporters of the project intended the damming of the Cooper River to generate hydroelectric power, employment, and economic growth for the people of the Lowcountry and industry in Charleston. It also entailed the flooding of the lowest lands along the Cooper River, above Moncks Corner, to create Lake Moultrie and Lake Marion. The area to be inundated by the flood waters included most of the springs inhabited by the Lowcountry simbi.[1]

While the construction of the dam employed the latest machinery, the work of clearing the Santee-Cooper basin relied on the muscle power of men and mules to reduce the dense forests of cypress and other hardwoods to thousands of acres of stumps. Two years of clearing with cross-cut saws and hand axes and hauling away the trees strapped to mules transformed places people had once known as Biggin Swamp, Ferguson's Swamp, Hog Swamp, Hanover, Indianfield, Wantoot, Woodboo, and Pooshee to a barren landscape, stripped of the flora and fauna that made the local lands and waters bountiful spots for hunting and fishing. Higher areas of the basin served as productive farmland, typically for families

[1] Edgar, *History of the Santee Cooper*; T. Robert Hart, Jr., "The Santee-Cooper Landscape: Culture and Environment in the South Carolina Lowcountry" (PhD Dissertation, University of Alabama, 2004); and Elizabeth Marie Harvey Lovern, "Cultural Models, Landscapes, and Large Dams: An Ethnographic and Environmental History of the Santee Cooper Project, 1938–1942" (PhD Dissertation, University of Georgia, 2007).

that clustered in informal settlements and sold their produce for a lit-tle money. These tracts suitable for planting, too, were slated for flood-ing, typically with inadequate compensation to the owners. Homes and other structures remaining on denuded or condemned land were usu-ally demolished or burned. The radical transformation of the landscape shook those who had known it as a verdant realm of forests and fields. One woman recalled that as a young girl, she "came home from school that afternoon and got off the bus and ran in just screaming, 'What in the world!' Because they had come in and started cutting the big old tree in the front. We had a lot of big pine trees and they were all down!" Another remembered, "I just felt *lost*, I guess is the only word I can think of, when I saw it. I just felt a sense of loss."[2]

The pace and scope of clearing forests and moving earth in the short period from 1939 to 1941 far exceeded the efforts generations before of African-descended people to create plantations and the system of water control that produced rice, Santee cotton, and the Santee Canal dur-ing the days of slavery. In the decades following emancipation, the old plantation landscape had largely been abandoned, or at least neglected, although the descendants of earlier plantation communities continued to live on small farms in the area. Government authorities displaced them to higher ground in nearby towns as the frenetic final stages of despoiling the land came to a close. Although the living had been moved, the graves of their ancestors remained untouched, to be submerged with the springs that held the simbi.

The stark conversion of the landscape and the pending fate of this place left behind were captured in a photograph labeled "Negro grave-yard on abandoned land in Santee-Cooper basin near Moncks Corner, South Carolina." (Figure 8) Taken in March of 1941, the image shows the remnants of dried vegetation from the winter and earlier clearing work strewn around the graves. The only features that identify this location as a sacred site are the few small headstones that barely rise to the height of the desiccated stubble; and there is the clock. It would be easy to take this object out of its cultural context and interpret its presence as a com-mentary on how time had run out on this place and its people. Those who placed the clock on this grave, however, were thinking of another transi-tion. When carrying the body of the deceased in a wagon to the church

---

[2] Greg Day and Jack Delano, "Folklife and Photography: Bringing the FSA Home," *Southern Exposure* 5, nos. 2–3 (1977): 122–33 [127]; and Lovern, "Cultural Models," 254, 255.

FIGURE 8. "Negro graveyard on abandoned land in Santee-Cooper basin near Moncks Corner, South Carolina."
Source: LC-USF34–043572-D, Farm Security Administration/Office of War Information Black-and-White Negatives, Library of Congress.

graveyard, the living circled the church four times before burial. They also usually left the clock of the deceased person on the grave. The combination of the circling, clock, and leaving of the eating utensils and medicine bottles used just before death marked the movement of the deceased to the land of the dead.[3] This photo reveals another aspect of the meaning of the site for the living and dead – the burial had occurred not long before. The disturbed soil and lack of grass on the plot indicate that the person had been interred after the area had been condemned and cleared within the previous two years. Although all knew the fate of this grave, the living buried one of their people in the earth that would soon be covered with water. The nearby church had been dismantled in the previous two years, possibly even before the grave had been dug and filled. Yet this site was considered the proper place for the dead. Maybe the deceased had once made clear to family that he or she wanted to be buried with loved

[3] H.R. Dwight (Berkeley County, South Carolina), "Folk Customs and Folk Lore," Folder D-4–27A, WPA-SCL.

ones who remained in the doomed graveyard. Maybe the deceased once held this same land sacred, where generation after generation of African-descended people lived, made their homes, built their families, and died. Maybe the person in the grave had been unable to imagine entering the land of the dead through any other place in the land of the living.

In early November of 1941, the flooding of the basin began. Water filled the lowest portion by the middle of December.[4] The simbi springs and graves of ancestors now rested under the waters of Lake Moultrie.

The submersion of the stronghold of the Lowcountry simbi signaled the end of an old spiritual line that tethered African-descended people in South Carolina to an ancient cultural dialogue begun long ago with Niger-Congo ancestors. This dialogue engaged the most pressing matters of daily existence as well as the enduring concerns with the nature of the connections between the land of the living and the land of the dead. For Niger-Congo and Bantu ancestors (and everyone else for that matter), life was never without hardship, and the spiritual cultures they devised and revised reflected the continuation and innovation of ideas and practices that made sense of the continuing struggle to extend kin and community. Out of the countless generations of cultural discourse, the simbi emerged in one part of West-Central Africa as one expression of an older, broader understanding of the spiritual meanings of being in a harsh world that demanded people have a profound respect for and knowledge of the natural environments in which they lived. The already daunting array of ordeals that faced most people in West-Central Africa became more difficult as the growing Atlantic trade in captive Africans created a new threat and exacerbated familiar ones. The changing relationship between the simbi and the living involved in the Atlantic trade as captives, captors, and all others affected by its workings evinced the ways that people reconceptualized their connections to each other and to the land of the dead. For those unfortunate enough to experience captivity and the Middle Passage, this also entailed reconfiguring their understanding of their place in the land of the living. People carried across the kalunga to strange, new lands brought the simbi with them, and they did so for a reason.

Maybe we should say that they found the simbi on the shores of the great sea where the sun sets. After all, these new countries had forests, rivers, mountains, waterfalls, and springs just like the West-Central African homelands of the simbi. In any case, Africans who survived the terrible

---

[4] Lovern, "Cultural Models," 256.

crossing had to rely on something to cope with the death and dislocation engendered by Atlantic slavery. Those who knew the simbi back home and recognized them in the wilderness of the Americas did not have to invent anything new or suffer helplessly in the struggle to reorient themselves in their surroundings and reconnect to the land of the dead in a very different location in the land of the living. The simbi were with them.

From the legacy of Kongo captives taken to Saint-Domingue, people in what became Haiti continued to serve the simbi in various forms among the powerful spirits known as *loa*. They also regarded the simbi as the tutelary inhabitants of springs and marshes. The application of spiritual power through consecrated objects called upon the simbi as well because they provided access to the knowledge of both the benevolent and malevolent uses of that power and supported the manufacture of *paquettes*, calabashes filled with various powders and tightly wrapped in cloth bundles that functioned in healing practices as "guards" and instruments to stimulate the power of loa.[5] West-Central Africans who arrived in Cuba called upon a great water spirit known as Kisimbi Masa. As a "Father of the Water" and "master of the river," Kisimbi Masa inhabited certain waterways and lagoons, as did several other Kongo nature spirits including Mboma, Mamá Kalunga, Pungo Kasimba, Mbúmba Masa, Nkita Kiamasa, Nkita Kuna Mamba, and Baluande. Additionally, the Cuban simbi provided the spiritual force for the *Nkisi Masa*, caldrons assembled by spiritual experts that contained water plants, river mud, sea shells, and snakes and served to direct power from the land of the dead in the interests of the living.[6] African-descended people in Brazil who participated in the *candomblé* of the Angola nation revered the spirit Kisimbi as the equivalent of the African water spirits Dandalunda, Oxum, and Yemanjá. West-Central African water spirits known collectively as *Calungas* (*Kalungas*) coordinated with the West African water spirit Yemanjá to act as guardians of the sea, rivers, sailors, and women.[7]

[5] Herskovits, *Life In A Haitian Valley*, 151–2; Metraux, *Voodoo in Haiti*, 267, 310–12; Louis Maximilien, *Le Vodou Haitien: Rites Radas-Canzo* (Port-au-Prince, Haïti: Imprimerie de l'État, 1945), 185–8; Thompson, *Flash of the Spirit*, 125–7; and Heusch, *Roi de Kongo*, 371–5.

[6] Cabrera, *Reglas de Congo*, 128; and Castellanos and Castellanos, *Cultura Afrocubana*, 137.

[7] Cacciatore, *Dicionário de Cultos*, 77, 125, 164; Janzen, *Lemba*, 273–7; Nei Lopes, *Enciclopédia Brasileira da Diáspora Africana* (São Paulo: Selo Negro, 2004), 505, 553; Nei Lopes, "African Religions in Brazil, Negotiation, and Resistance: A Look from

Kongo captives carried to the Carolina Lowcountry remained loyal to the simbi, and the simbi rewarded them with many descendants, abundant harvests, generous hunting and fishing, and good health. The life-sustaining support of the simbi, however, did not mean that every birth, planting season, outing in the woods and on the waters, or epidemic turned out well for African-descended people. It never worked so favorably in West-Central Africa, and it certainly did not in the Lowcountry or anywhere else in the diaspora. Nonetheless, the Kongo newcomers who brought their knowledge of the simbi persevered and passed their knowledge on to the children of the communities they helped found. That knowledge remained vital for many generations and informed the profound transitions that reshaped the lives of Africans and their Lowcountry-born families from the late seventeenth century through the nineteenth century. In this way, they fashioned local elaborations of a Bantu-Atlantic dialogue about nature spirits and people that also continued to engage their distant kin – not only those spread throughout the Americas but also those who remained in West-Central Africa.

The simbi were a fundamental part of the process through which African-descended people made a claim to the place where they buried their dead and raised their children, a place that transcended assertions of "ownership" according to the legal instruments of property rights. The springs that the simbi inhabited predated the plantations, and this fact certainly registered in the developing knowledge of the Lowcountry simbi. Those people who claimed to own the land and the people on it could not own the simbi. The African-Native elder at Pooshee plantation confirmed this, and others knew already that the simbi could leave if they chose to. The presence of the simbi reminded the living that enslavers could never really own either the children of the simbi or the place that they made their home, at least not forever. Although Ravenel enclosed the spring against the warnings of the African-Native elder, the simbi ignored the insult and stayed. We may imagine that the Pooshee simbi stayed to continue to guard its children and see them through to emancipation in the 1860s and becoming titleholders of the land on which they and their ancestors had lived and worked for generations. Long after the plantations as noble estates and economic enterprises ceased to be, the simbi and the people of the simbi remained. They remained until a new force, fueled by a certain vision of Progress and Modernity, rapidly dislodged their accommodation of place, culture, and power forged over the course of two and a half centuries. Once the people were gone, forests removed, and graves abandoned, the simbi time – the *long* simbi time – had come to an end.

Index